Dusk to Dawn

Dusk to Dawn

Paul J. Quinn

Fantail

Hollis, New Hampshire

Library of Congress Catalog Card Number: 98-74247
ISBN 0-9655209-9-4

All paintings and diagrams were created by Paul Quinn.

To Grace

Published by:

Fantail
P.O. Box 462
Hollis, New Hampshire 03049
http://www.fantail.com

Contents

Foreword

On Tuesday, April 16, 1912, the early morning peace was shattered by the newspaper headlines, "TITANIC SINKS FOUR HOURS AFTER HITTING ICEBERG."

Around the world people endeavored to learn every detail about the terrible tragedy. They wanted to know of the heroism of the *Titanic*'s passengers and crew, the fate of those not listed in the "lives saved" columns and how the supposedly unsinkable ship did the unimaginable. The United States and British Inquiries revealed many insights into the causes of the tragedy and readers literally hung on every word printed on the subject. Because interest was so great, publishers were quick to capitalize on this new marketplace, publishing thousands of Titanic books, sold door to door on five cents commission, demand soon outstripping publication.

A handful of survivors were able to pen personal experiences of the tragedy, describing in intricate detail every aspect of their morbid "adventure." Some decided to improve or otherwise enhance their accounts with tidbits gleaned from the newspapers that left much to be desired, one survivor "remembering" a "herd of cows on board to give fresh milk for the children."

As time passed, interest waned until 1955 when Walter Lord published *A Night To Remember* which became a best-seller. Television and film producers insured the immortality of this work when the story was dramatized for the screen. Some considered the film version of the book the "greatest Titanic movie ever made, told as it really happened," and to nit-pick at errors was considered a kind of blasphemy! Once again, interest in the subject quickly died.

In July, 1963, following the death of a *Titanic* survivor, the Titanic Historical Society was founded with the goal "that the memory and history of the *Titanic* and the White Star Line be preserved for future generations." However, the turbulent 1960s discouraged remembering the past let alone chronicling its events and the Society's gallant efforts were almost forgotten. In 1968, a decision had to be made whether or not to continue. This year we celebrated our 35th Anniversary.

The *Titanic* made headlines again on September 1, 1985 when the lost White Star liner was found by a joint American and French team headed by Dr. Robert Ballard from the Massachusetts-based Woods Hole Oceanographic Institution and the French National Institute of Oceanography. Excitement and curiosity on an unparalleled scale emerged once again all over the world. So mesmerized were the public of this find, special press conferences were held at Woods Hole and in Washington, D.C. at the National Geographic Society's headquarters. Such a momentous discovery was a two-edged sword; the United States Senate sought to protect the gravesite by passing the Titanic Memorial Act in 1986, signed by

President Reagan. However, the *Titanic* lies in international waters, so the idealism of the Act's intentions was destroyed when commercial salvagers began retrieving objects. Assorted experts surfaced and a whole new era of printed works burst on to the bookshelves with theories ranging from the serious to the farcical, including changing the ship's name plates for insurance purposes, inferior or brittle steel and substandard rivets being the real culprits in the death of the *Titanic*. The iceberg's point of view had already been written by a marine biologist and now took second place as the cause of the tragedy.

It was inevitable that Hollywood would try once again to tell the story and thus 20th Century Fox and Paramount's *Titanic*, the greatest of all Titanic movies made its mark in the history of cinema with its harrowing realism; the agony of the ship breaking in two, people scrambling to live one minute longer while the great stern lifted then descended to the freezing sea below;

the horrific sight of hundreds of frozen corpses drifting, all of which made a tremendous impact on 1990s audiences. This movie, that Time Magazine pronounced, "would be a greater bomb than Waterworld," turned out to be the biggest blockbuster in motion picture history, breaking attendance records, studio income and earning eleven Academy Awards. Although the film left much to be desired in the characterization of historical figures, the depiction of the ship, in all her majesty, was outstanding and caused a tremendous amount of interest, especially with the younger generation, anxious to learn more about the tragedy.

One wonders what it was really like for those on board the *Titanic* experiencing the daily routine of shipboard life? What if we could sort through the reams of individual testimonies and comments of 1912 and literally piece together the jigsaw puzzle of this simple maiden voyage with an extraordinary ending? What if we could go back in

time and walk amongst the passengers and crew observing events through every moment-by-moment account?

In the golden age of television, there was a popular program which used a similar format narrated by news presenter Walter Cronkite. Important events were presented first hand to the viewer as if he or she had traveled back in time; the fall of the Alamo; Benjamin Franklin flying his kite; the sighting of Halley's Comet. At the end of the introduction a deep voice announced with emphasis, "You Are There." The same words apply to this work by Paul Quinn. We are about to enter another time, to travel on board the largest ship in the world, to meet and visit with her passengers and crew . . . and now, You Are There.

Edward S. Kamuda
President and Founder
The Titanic Historical Society, Inc.

Introduction

There was relative peace between the nations of the world, and it was a time when industry and science joined together to dazzle men and women with new opportunities and conveniences. Fortunes, both large and small, had recently been established and new ones were in the making. People were on the move, leaving their homesteads behind in search of better circumstances elsewhere. Governments were being reshaped in significant ways as their citizens forced them to become more democratic and representative. The automobile, which had previously been viewed as a quirky transportation novelty, was suddenly considered a serious alternative to the horse as a means of getting around locally, thanks to the introduction of the electric starter. Man had learned to fly less than ten years earlier, and some were already dreaming of an airplane with an enclosed passenger compartment. Einstein's theory of relativity was only seven years old and Rutherford's theory of an atom containing a nucleus with surrounding electrons had just been born. Amundsen and his team were first to reach the South Pole only four months earlier and Wegener was in the process of introducing his theory on continental drift. Funk was releasing a paper identifying "vitamines" as substances required by the body to prevent certain diseases. The year was 1912.

Huge business conglomerates known as trusts reached their peak during the turn of the century, some with enormous amounts of capital at their disposal. One of the most influential and powerful men that emerged from this arena was J.P. Morgan, who orchestrated the formation of the world's largest trust at the time, U.S. Steel. Morgan believed that competition created an instability and inefficiency in the marketplace. He and his partners would select an industry that held potential and then practice a methodology of buying a company, or series of companies within that field to gain a dominant position, then systematically work to eliminate the remaining competition through a strategy of capital investment, logistics, and aggressive pricing. In 1893 he set his attention to the lucrative North Atlantic shipping trade and formed a company called the International Navigation Company, based in New Jersey. For ten years it operated under a relatively normal profile. Then, in 1902 the company changed its name to the International Mercantile Marine Company and sprang to life with classic Morgan-like action. Taking advantage of a series of devastating price wars that left many shipping lines weakened, the International Mercantile Marine Company, otherwise known as the IMM, initiated several key acquisitions. Their primary target was the reputable White Star Line and it was formally purchased on December 31, 1902. Bruce Ismay, previously the president of the White Star Line, accepted a position as Chairman of the International Mercantile Marine.

Technology continued to push things forward, including the extremely competitive shipping trade. Germany, to the angst of Europe, was in the midst of a noticeable naval buildup, and they were applying the latest shipping technology to their vessels. Several of their liners captured the Blue Riband award for the fastest crossing between Europe and America. This emerging naval dominance spurred Great Britain, through the Cunard Line, to build two ocean greyhounds which, on top of their speed, would be the largest liners afloat. They were named the *Lusitania* and *Mauretania*. Although primarily aimed at countering the emerging German naval threat, these technologically dazzling twins inadvertently

The *Titanic* (right) poses with her sister ship during the *Olympic*'s return to Belfast for a new propeller.

The *Titanic* setting off on her maiden voyage.

the *Titanic*'s maiden voyage from March to April 1912.

As the spring of 1912 rolled around, Europe was in a relatively stable state. Libya was the only dangerous place to travel due to Italy's attempt to seize control of parts of the country. Many wealthy Americans, primarily from Canada and Northeastern United States, went to Europe and Africa to escape the dreary winter months. As warm weather returned in the Spring, so too did these wealthy tourists to their homes. They kept their itineraries open and booked their return passage from Europe. Scanning the schedules, the *Titanic*'s maiden voyage stood out as a treat. What better way was there to end a European vacation than to return to America on the largest ship in the world on her maiden voyage? Other people were on business and ready to return from their overseas meetings. First and second class bookings began to roll in.

Immigration to the United States was still running at a brisk pace. It peaked in 1907 at 1.2 million people, but was still just less than a million in 1911, and would repeat that rate in 1912. This type of passenger traffic created extraordinary opportunities for the passenger lines, including White Star. In fact, the *Titanic* was aimed directly at this market. As the *Titanic*'s sail-

triggered a competitive response from the White Star Line. Ismay succeeded in lining up funding from J.P. Morgan for the construction of three giant sister ships intended to be the largest in the world with the names *Olympic, Titanic,* and *Britannic*. They would not be the fastest, but their speed would be respectable and would be more than compensated with luxury and spaciousness. Work began on the *Olympic* and the *Titanic* at Harland and Wolff in Belfast, Ireland in 1908 with the *Olympic* finished first in 1911. During her first year of service, the *Olympic* experienced a collision from the British naval cruiser *Hawke*, then dropped a propeller at sea during a subsequent passage. Each repair drew resources away from completion of the second sister ship and the result was a postponement of

ing date approached, a coal strike erupted, choking off the supply of fuel to many vessels intending to depart on their scheduled voyages. In a sound decision, White Star canceled most of the sailings and transferred the residual coal and passengers to the *Titanic*. Even with these transferred tickets, the *Titanic*'s second and third class bookings were only just over 50% of its capacity. Summer would be better.

As sailing day neared, employees of Harland & Wolff and the White Star Line were frantically trying to finish the interior of the *Titanic* while she was berthed at her departing dock in Southampton. Carpet was still being laid in many of the cabins and doors and fixtures were still being installed. Right up to sailing day, a number of visitors took note of a bee hive type of activity within the ship. One thing was certain. The White Star Line was not going to postpone the maiden voyage of their premier liner for a second time, particularly so close to the sailing date. With some details unfinished, the second of the trio of giant sister ships was made ready for her big day.

The *Titanic* set sail on Wednesday, April 10, 1912 at 12:15 with a cross section of European and American life planning for a scheduled arrival in America on Wednesday morning of the following week. Due to a near collision with the liner *New York* shortly after departure from the Southampton dock, the *Titanic* was delayed in her scheduled arrival in Cherbourg, France later that afternoon. However, the connection was maintained and additional passengers boarded. The *Titanic* made one more stop the following day at Queenstown, Ireland. Large numbers of Irish emigrants, mainly steerage, boarded the *Titanic*. Some passengers who boarded in Southampton now disembarked along with the unloading of mail. At a little after 2:00 p.m., the *Titanic* was set into motion again. It was an exciting time that Thursday afternoon as the greatest ship in the world set off for New York City across the broad expanse of the Atlantic Ocean.

Friday was the first full uninterrupted day at sea and while the crew sorted out

The *Titanic* near the Isle of Wight, heading out to the open sea.

their responsibilities and acclimated to their work schedules, the passengers settled into their accommodations and explored the ship. The weather was good and the seas were calm. For those who did not suffer from sea sickness, the following days were filled with pleasure and relaxation. There was breakfast, a stroll on the deck while tak-

ing in the fresh ocean air, writing letters in the lounges, reading, lunch, relaxing in a deck chair, another stroll perhaps, conversation with friends and newly made acquaintances, dinner, music, more casual conversation, perhaps one more stroll on deck, and then off to bed with the gentle motion of the *Titanic* lulling one to sleep. First class passengers had the added benefits of a squash (racquet) court, swimming pool, sauna, and gymnasium to help them pass the time. They also had an A la Carte Restaurant, separate from the dining room, and a Café Parisien where they could dine for an additional price. Friday turned into Saturday, and by the time Sunday came around the passengers and crew had pretty well settled into their shipboard routines.

Behind the scenes the *Titanic*'s management was systematically breaking in the new machinery by incrementally firing additional boilers to boost power to the steam engines. With each passing day the *Titanic* gradually increased her speed and there was talk of doing an all out run on Monday to see what she was capable of achieving.

But all was not well during the voyage. A coal fire with an unknown origin started before the *Titanic* left Southampton and continued to smolder in one of the bunkers in boiler room number 5. It was not until Saturday afternoon that it was finally extinguished. On that same day the wireless office began to receive warnings of ice from ships passing in the opposite direction and the number of messages increased by the time Sunday arrived. In addition, there were complaints from various locations throughout the ship that the heat was not working

About the Survivor Accounts

To assist with understanding who was behind a particular account italicized in this book, passengers are identified with a "Mr.," "Mrs." or "Miss" before their names. Employees of the Titanic and other ships are identified by their last names only. The U.S. senators are also identified by their last name only, and can be recognized as those asking questions.

In a number of cases, survivors provided details about an event, moved onto a different subject either on their own initiative or other questioning from a senator, and then returned to the original topic later. In some instances, their accounts have been edited and pieced together to provide a single, coherent account of a particular incident.

Finally, a brief biography is provided at the back of this book, including the source of the quotations for each person whose accounts appear within these pages.

properly. Other passengers took note of unfinished work, such as crates still lying in a second class bathroom with uninstalled fixtures and some wall railings that were not yet mounted. Harland & Wolff's representative Thomas Andrews, and his staff of almost 20 assistants, were busy throughout the voyage attempting to fix as many of these finishing type issues as possible, given that they were now at sea amongst White Star Line customers.

But the passengers, for the most part, were oblivious to these matters and as Sunday evening came upon them they were content. Some were beginning to think about their arrival in New York in a couple of days. Dinner had been announced and passengers in all three classes were sitting down to what was later remarked to have been the best meal of the voyage. Because it was mid-April and because the ship was in the northern hemisphere, it was sometime around 8:00 p.m. when dusk began to wrap her arms around the liner.

As her crew and passengers steamed into the sunset with their world of new conveniences and luxuries, ushered in by a dazzling array of industry, technology and science, they were completely unaware of the horror that lay just ahead in their path.

This is the story of the last night aboard the *Titanic*.

the age of confidence and there was plenty of it on board. As the fifth day was winding down, most were completely relaxed with their surroundings and in good spirits. Many casual acquaintances grew into shipboard friendships, and conversation that Sunday evening flowed more easily than ever. The rhythm of the engines, the gentle sway of the ship, and the orchestra's music created a magical evening.

Mrs. Douglas: "The boat was so luxurious, so steady, so immense, and such a marvel of mechanism that one could not believe he was on a boat—and there the danger lay. We had smooth seas, clear, starlit nights, fresh favoring winds. Nothing to mar our pleasure."

Eight O'Clock

The *Titanic* dazzled in the glow of her final twilight when the deck lights came to life along the length of the ship. Most passengers were enjoying their dinner as she steamed toward the brilliant sunset, but for those out on deck, the view was something remarkable to behold.

Mr. Beesley: "And each night the sun sank right in our eyes along the sea, making an undulating glittering pathway, a golden track charted on the surface of the ocean which our ship followed unswervingly until the sun dipped below the edge of the horizon and the pathway ran ahead of us faster than we could steam and slipped over the edge of the skyline - as if the sun had been a golden ball and had wound up its thread of gold too quickly for us to follow."

Most passengers hit their stride with shipboard life and felt perfectly comfortable with the routine of the evening. This was

Mrs. Futrelle: "In the elegantly furnished drawing room, no premonitory shadow of death was present to cast a cold fear over the gaiety of the evening. It was a brilliant scene, women beautifully gowned, laughing and talking—the odor of flowers—ridiculous to think of danger. Why it was just like being at some beautiful summer resort. There was not one chance in a million of an accident happening, they said. But someone took that chance. There was no slacking of the speed as we went through the ice fields, for it was felt that no obstacle could stand in the path of this mighty Leviathan of the Seas."

While the passengers conversed over Sunday dinner in comfortable bliss, up on the bridge the crew stood watch as the ship plowed forward through the Atlantic. The *Titanic* operated under a very defined organizational structure in which the senior officers were given command of the bridge in rotation, with one or two junior officers providing support. In turn, the officers of the bridge were supported during their commands with a quartermaster on the bridge and aft bridge, and the lookouts in the crow's nest. Typically, the captain would only take direct command of the bridge during special circumstances such as port departures and arrivals, or navigation through bad weather such as fog or heavy seas. Of course, as captain of the ship, his mere appearance on the bridge would put him in command if he deemed it necessary to issue instructions. At 8:00 p.m. Second Officer Lightoller stood in command of the *Titanic*. As the quartermaster struck the bell for the top of the hour, there was a flurry of activity as the junior officers, the quartermaster and the lookouts in the crow's nest all underwent a change in watch.

Lowe: "I was on duty on Sunday evening from 6:00 p.m. to 8:00 p.m., and at 8:00 p.m. I went below. From 6 to 8, I was busy working out this slip table . . . and working a dead reckoning position for 8 o'clock p.m. to hand into the captain, or commander of the ship. We simply put the slip on the table, put a paperweight or something on it, and he comes in and sees it. It is nothing of any great importance."

Hichens: "I went on watch at eight o'clock. The officers on the watch were the second officer, Mr. Lightoller, senior in command; the fourth officer, Mr. Boxhall; and the sixth officer, Mr. Moody."

Boxhall: "Mr. Lightoller was on watch on the bridge when I went on watch at 8 o'clock with sixth officer Moody."

Pitman: ". . . I started working out the observations. In the chart room. In the chart house. I was there alone until 8 o'clock. I did not finish them. Mr. Boxhall took on then and finished them. I simply said, 'Here is a bunch of sights for you, old man. Go ahead.' And I went out."

To keep the lookouts fresh, they were rotated every two hours.

Smith: "Who was on watch from 8 to 10 that night in the crow's nest or lookout?"
Fleet: "Symons and Jewell."
Smith: "Who was on watch from 6 to 8?"
Fleet: "Hogg and Evans."

Without a doubt, the most significant topic on the bridge Sunday evening was the potential for coming upon ice sometime during the night. Captain Smith had already altered the course of the *Titanic* in an attempt to reduce the risk of meeting up with it by steering a slightly more southerly course.

Fletcher: "Where was the last change of direction made?"
Pitman: "5:50 on Sunday night."
Fletcher: "Do you know any such designation as the 'corner'?"
Pitman: "Yes. We were supposed to be at the corner at 5:50."
Fletcher: "What do you mean by that?"
Pitman: "That is 47 west and 42 north."
Fletcher: "At 5:50 p.m. you turned what you call the 'corner?'"
Pitman: "The corner, yes."

Lightoller was advised earlier of the ice conditions that lay to the west of the *Titanic*. As the watch changed over, his priorities were focused on the increasingly cold temperature and the potential for meeting up with that ice somewhere ahead. With disciplined efficiency he set the new watch in motion.

The *Titanic* was the premier vessel of the White Star Line and the officers selected to take her across the Atlantic on her maiden voyage were men who had proven themselves to be reliable, with seasoned track records at sea. White Star officers would have jumped at the chance to be assigned to the company's state-of-the-art liner, and these officers were considered very lucky to get the chance to serve on the *Titanic*.

Captain Edward Smith. 62 years old. He transferred from the *Titanic*'s sister ship, the *Olympic*. Smith had been working at sea for 43 years by the time he took command of the *Titanic*, 32 of them with the White Star Line. He was approaching retirement with speculation this voyage was to be his last, but it is possible that he may have stayed on with White Star until the *Britannic* was brought out in 1914. His wife and daughter lived in Southampton.

Chief Officer Henry Wilde. 38 years old. Transferred from the *Olympic* where he had served in the same capacity. He had been working at sea for almost 25 years, 6 of them with the White Star Line. He was transferred to the *Titanic* only a week or two before the voyage, triggering a reshuffling of the senior officers. Henry Wilde was a widower, his wife having died 16 months

The Officers of the *Titanic*

The *Titanic's* officers on the starboard boat deck.
Standing: McElroy, Lightoller, Pitman, Boxhall, Lowe.
Seated: Moody, Wilde, Smith, Murdoch.

earlier and leaving him to arrange care for his 4 children while away at sea.

First Officer William Murdoch. 38 years old. Transferred from the *Olympic*. Murdoch had been working at sea for 25 years, 12 of which were with the White Star Line. Murdoch was originally in line for a promotion to Chief Officer, but Wilde's last minute transfer to the *Titanic* placed Murdoch in the same position he held on the *Olympic*. Murdoch was married, with no children.

Second Officer Charles Lightoller. 38 years old. Transferred from the *Oceanic* where he had been First Officer. He had been working at sea for 24 years, 12 of them

with the White Star Line. The last minute assignment of Wilde to the *Titanic* resulted in a demotion from First Officer for Lightoller. He was married, with three sons yet to come. Lightoller's reassignment to Second Officer resulted in David Blair being bumped from the *Titanic*'s officer roster all together.

Third Officer Herbert Pitman. 34 years old. Transferred from the *Oceanic* along with Lightoller. He had been at sea for 17 years, the last 3 as an officer for the White Star Line. He was married, with no children.

Fourth Officer Joseph Boxhall. 28 years old. Transferred from the *Arabic* where he had been Third Officer. He had worked at sea for 13 years, 5 with the White Star Line. He was married, with no children.

Fifth Officer Harold Lowe. 28 years old. Transferred from the *Belgic* where he had been third officer. He had been working at sea for 14 years, 9 with the White Star Line. He was single at the time.

Sixth Officer James Moody. 24 years old. Transferred from the *Oceanic*. Moody had the fewest years of experience and had only joined the White Star Line a couple of years earlier. He was not married.

Hichens: " My first orders when I got on the bridge was to take the second officer's compliments down to the ship's carpenter and inform him to look to his fresh water, that it was about to freeze. I did so. On the return to the bridge–I had been on the bridge about a couple of minutes–when the carpenter came back and reported the duty carried out."

Lightoller: "I told the sixth officer, Mr. Moody, to ring up the crow's nest and tell them to keep a sharp lookout for ice, particularly small ice and growlers. That was received and replied to–and also to pass the word along."

Hichens: ". . . I heard the second officer repeat to Mr. Moody, the sixth officer, to speak through the telephone, warning the lookout men in the crow's nest to keep a sharp lookout for small ice until daylight and pass the word along to the other lookout men."

Up in the crow's nest, Symons and Jewell were greeted with a stiff breeze in their face, created by the forward motion of the ship. Their binoculars, or glasses as they called them, were still missing. Since these glasses were typically used to get a better look at something only after it had been sighted by regular eyesight, too much has sometime been made of their absence from the nest. All the same, the lookouts were probably smarting a little after receiving word from Lightoller's command to keep a sharp eye out for ice.

Smith: "Did you make any request for glasses on the Titanic?"
Fleet: "We asked them in Southampton and they said there was none for us."
Smith: "Whom did you ask?"
Fleet: "We asked Mr. Lightoller, the second officer."
Smith: "You expected glasses?"
Fleet: "We had a pair from Belfast to Southampton."
Smith: "Where did those go that you had from Belfast to Southampton?"
Fleet: "We do not know that. We only know we never got a pair."

As the crew settled into their watch, not only were the lookouts scanning the horizon for signs of ice, but Lightoller himself was searching as well.

Bourne: "The principal reliance is placed upon the man in the crow's nest, or the men in the crow's nest?"
Lightoller: "We place no reliance on them."
Bourne: "What are they there for?"
Lightoller: "They are there to keep a lookout, to assist us."
Bourne: "Then why is no reliance placed upon them?"
Lightoller: "Because, speaking personally, I never rely on any lookout. I keep a lookout myself, and so does every other officer."

The most noticeable recent event was the rapid drop in temperature.

Senator Smith: "What was the weather at that time?"
Boxhall: "Very fine and clear."
Smith: "Cold?"
Boxhall: "Yes; very cold."

Hichens: "I know the thermometer was down at 31 at 8 o'clock on Sunday evening –31½. It began to get very, very cold. Exceedingly cold. So cold, we could hardly suffer the cold. I thought there was ice about somewhere."

Mr. Peuchen: "All I know is that there was a big change in the temperature between the afternoon and the time I went on deck later on in the evening."

With knowledge of ice somewhere ahead, the noticeable drop in temperature over the previous hours surely put Lightoller on heightened alert. Although there has been speculation about what the captain and senior officers collectively knew about the danger ahead from the various ice warnings that trickled in on Sunday, evidence indicates that Lightoller knew exactly what lay ahead–and when they could expect to come upon it.

Bride: "There was a message delivered to the captain in the afternoon, sir, late in the afternoon regarding the ice field. From the Californian, sir. I received that message myself and delivered it to the captain. It stated that there were three large icebergs that the ship had just passed, and it gave their position. Late in the afternoon, but I cannot say the hour of the day. It was an unofficial message. In the first place the Californian had called me, sir with an ice report. I was rather busy just for the minute, and I did not take it. She did not call again. She transmitted the ice report to the Baltic, and as she was transmitting it to the Baltic I took it down. I took it to the captain."
Smith: "You took that message to the captain?"
Bride: "The officer on the bridge."
Smith: "Who was the officer on the bridge?"
Bride: "I could not say, sir. I do not know the officers, sir."

Smith: "Did you communicate this message to the captain?"
Bride: "No, sir. I gave it to the officer on watch, sir."

Smith: "No one called your attention to any telegram or wireless from any ship warning you of ice?"
Lightoller: "Yes."
Smith: "Who?"
Lightoller: "I do not know what the telegram was. The commander came out when I was relieved for lunch, I think it was. It may have been earlier. I do not remember what time it was. I remember the commander coming out to me sometime that day and showing me a telegram, and this had reference to the position of ice."
Smith: "What did you do about it?"
Lightoller: "Worked approximately the time we should be up to this position."
Smith: "What did you find?"
Lightoller: "Somewhere around 11 o'clock."

Smith: "If there had been any order given to keep a sharp lookout for ice, would it have been entered on an order book or the log?"
Pitman: "That is usually put on the commander's night order book."
Smith: "Did you see anything of that kind?"
Pitman: "I did not see the night order book that night, because it is not issued, as a rule until between 6 and 8."
Smith: "Did you see it the night before?"
Pitman: "Yes sir. I saw it the night before, because we had to sign it every night."

Even though Lightoller thought they would not be upon the ice until Murdoch's watch, he still had Moody tell the lookouts on his own watch to keep a sharp eye out for it as early as 8 p.m.

Captain Smith knew of the ice and charted a more southerly route as a precaution. Bruce Ismay knew of the ice and casually joked to a passenger that they would speed up so as to get through it faster. Lightoller knew of the ice and mentioned to Pitman that they would come upon it during Murdoch's watch.

Pitman: "We were just remarking that we should be in the vicinity of ice in Mr. Murdoch's watch. I had nothing to say in the matter. I was not interested in it. I just heard the remark passed, that was all."

It seems safe to conclude that the captain and the senior officers responsible for the navigation of the ship knew what they were coming up against. They likely felt that all the proper precautions were in place; they would keep a sharp eye out for

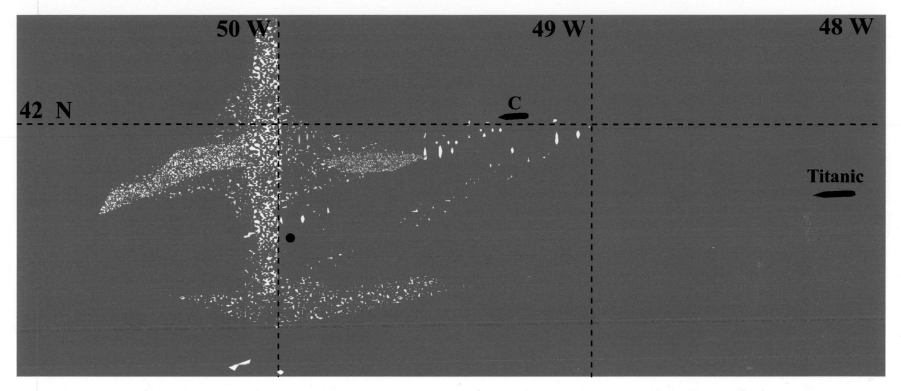

The position of the *Titanic* at 8:00 p.m. The ice field, as documented by reports from other ships that passed through the area on April 14, lies in waiting. The *Californian* can be seen to the north, approximately 30 miles ahead of the *Titanic*.

the ice, and if and when they came across any, the officer in charge would steer around it.

Newlands: "During your experience at sea has notice been given frequently by marconigram of the location of icebergs?"
Pitman: "Yes. We always pass it along from one to another."
Newlands: "What is the custom of the ships when they receive word of that kind? Is it the custom to slow down or to maintain their speed?"
Pitman: "To maintain speed, sir."
Newlands: "What do they rely upon for avoiding accidents?"
Pitman: "Picking up these bergs. As a rule, they are seen."

If there was anything out of the ordinary that night while the *Titanic* approached the ice field, it was the behavior of the junior officers. Among other duties, they assisted with the navigation of the ship by periodically charting the latest location of the *Titanic*. During questioning after the disaster, it is difficult to comprehend that, with a responsibility to the bridge, they could be so uninformed–and so disinterested–on the matter of approaching ice. Perhaps it was a window into the sense of general apathy that all the officers showed toward the mere possibility of ice somewhere ahead.

Smith: "Did not the second or first officer apprise you of the fact that they had information that you were in the vicinity of icebergs?"

Boxhall: "I knew we had had information. They did not apprise me that evening of it."

Smith: "When did they apprise you?"

Boxhall: "As a matter of fact they did not mention it to me."

Smith: "Had it never been mentioned to you?"

Boxhall: "Oh, yes. The captain mentioned it."

Smith: "When?"

Boxhall: "I do not know whether it was the day before or two days before. He gave me some positions of icebergs, which I put on the chart."

Smith: "Did the captain tell you that the Californian had wired the Titanic that they were in the vicinity of icebergs?"

Boxhall: "No. The captain gave me some wireless messages from Southampton, I think, that we had had before we had sailed and asked me to put these positions on the chart."

Smith: "Do you know whether a wireless had been received from the Amerika that the Titanic was in the vicinity of icebergs?"

Boxhall: "No, I could not say."

Smith: "So you want us to understand that you had no knowledge of the proximity of this ship to icebergs immediately proceeding -"

Boxhall: "I had no knowledge."

Smith: "One moment - immediately preceding the collision, or during the hours of your watch from 8 o'clock until the collision occurred?"

Boxhall: "I did not realize the ship was so near the ice field."

Fletcher: "What became of that telegram?"

Ismay: "I handed it back to Captain Smith, I should think about 10 minutes past 7 on Sunday evening. I was sitting in the smoking room when Captain Smith happened to come in the room for some reason–what it was I do not know–and on his way back he happened to see me sitting there and came up and said, 'By the way, sir, have you got that telegram which I gave you this afternoon?' I said, 'Yes.' I put my hand in my pocket and said, 'Here it is.' He said, 'I want it to put up in the officers' chart room.'"

Lowe: "I know there was something on about ice, but I do not know anything about it."

Smith: "Did you hear anything about it?"

Lowe: "I remember there was a position there, on the chart, something about ice, but I do not remember what it was."

Smith: "Do you mean there was something indicated on the chart?"

Lowe: "There was a slip that showed the position of the ice, the latitude and longitude, but who reported it, or anything else, I do not know anything about it."

Smith: "And you did not examine it carefully yourself?"

Lowe: "No, sir."

Smith: "Were you working on a table?"

Lowe: "Yes. I was working at the slip table."

Smith: "And as you were working at the slip table, you could look up and see this report?"

Lowe: "But I did not take any notice of it. It was only just the position, the latitude and longitude. And the word ice was above it."

Smith: "You are unable to say whether that was a wireless communication or whether that information was written down by some officer on that ship."

Lowe: "When you come to think of it, it could not have been anything else but wireless."

Smith: "Then, according to your impression, there was a wireless warning of that kind in the chart room, indicating the position in which ice might be expected at that hour or at that time?"

Lowe: "That is my conclusion. Yes."

Smith: "And you did not examine it carefully?"

Lowe: "No. I just looked at it casually."

Smith: "Did the course show that she was approaching ice?"

Pitman: "No sir. There was no ice reported exactly on the track."

Smith: "I want to know if this course showed that she was approaching ice."

Pitman: "We should pass the ice northward."

Smith: "In order to complete the record, the ice reported by the *Amerika* by a wireless message, was in latitude 41° 27' longitude 50° 08'?"

Pitman: "Yes."

Smith: "If the ship was properly located when she struck as being in latitude 41° 46', must not the course have been steered to the northward, in the direction of the reported iceberg?"

Pitman: "No. The position of that iceberg given by the *Amerika* is to the southward of us."

Smith: "The course was laid to the southward of ice reported by the *Amerika*, was it not?"

Pitman: "No. That position is 20 miles to the south of the position we were."

Smith: "Would you have allowed any time for the ice to drift?"

Pitman: "I do not know anything about getting its position from the *Amerika*."

Smith: "You never heard anything at all about their wireless warning and know nothing about the longitude or latitude which they reported icebergs?"

Pitman: "The only one was the one that was put on the chart, and I don't know whom that came from."

Smith: "Did you learn from him [Lightoller] that the *Californian* had warned the *Titanic* that she was in the vicinity of icebergs?"

Pitman: "I did not, sir. We had no conversation whatever."

Smith: "Did you hear anything about the wireless from the *Californian* on the direction of icebergs?"

Pitman: "I did not, sir."

Fletcher: "Was there only one iceberg indicated, or did the cross with the word, 'Ice' indicate the presence of ice generally?"

Pitman: "I think there was only one."

Fletcher: "Do you know how he came to note that one on the chart?"

Pitman: "Yes. We got it by marconigram from some ship."

Fletcher: "You do not remember seeing the marconigram?"

Pitman: "No. I do not. I remember Captain Smith showed the position to the officer of

the watch, or at least one of the junior officers, and he says, 'Take this position,' and he took it down and put it on the chart and stuck the leaf up in a rack. He wrote it on a sort of paper and stuck it on the frame."

Fletcher: "You do not recall exactly when that was done?"

Pitman: "No. It was some time Sunday."

Fletcher: "Did you hear any more about icebergs discussed among the officers, or in any other way?"

Pitman: "No."

Pitman notes that the iceberg in the *Amerika* report indicates ice 20 miles to the *south* of the *Titanic*. Captain Smith knew longitudes and latitudes backwards and forwards and clearly was aware that even by turning the corner later than normal, thereby taking a more southerly route, that this evasive action would *still* not clear them of the drifting ice ahead.

It is possible that Smith and the senior officers felt they had the situation under control and that the junior officers did not need to be kept informed of details such as wireless messages identifying specific locations. And more important, it may not have ever mattered. It seems likely that no matter what collective information was presented to the captain and his senior officers, that the resulting plan of action would always be the same. And that is, when they came upon the ice they would steer out of its way and only then possibly slow down.

Meanwhile, traveling ahead over the horizon in the same westerly direction as the *Titanic* was the *Californian*, under the command of Captain Stanley Lord. Aware of the ice as well, Captain Lord began to take additional precautions.

Lord: "We doubled the lookout from the crew, put a man on the forecastle head - that is, right at the bow of the ship - and I was on the bridge myself with an officer, which I would not have been under ordinary conditions. I went on the bridge at 8 o'clock."

Back behind the *Titanic*'s bridge the wireless office was just making out faint signals from Cape Race, Newfoundland. There was a flood of private messages that needed to be transmitted to America and Cape Race would be the recipient. Harold Bride, the *Titanic*'s junior wireless operator handed his headset off to Jack Phillips and went to bed.

It was about this time that the last three double ended boilers were fired up and put on line to furnish more steam to the engines. This was consistent with earlier plans and in preparation for an all out sprint by the *Titanic* on Monday. Up to this point, the *Titanic* had been backed off of her full

potential in order to break in the new machinery. But after five days at sea it was decided the *Titanic*'s engines were ready to show what they were capable of doing. In addition, the added speed would support the goal of possibly bringing the *Titanic* into New York early, on Tuesday night, with a better showing than the *Olympic*'s maiden voyage the prior year.

Ismay: "My recollection is that between Southampton and Cherbourg we ran at 60 revolutions, from Cherbourg to Queenstown at 70 revolutions, and when we left Queenstown we were running at 72 revolutions, and I believe that the ship was worked up to 75 revolutions, but I really have no accurate knowledge of that . . . assuming all the conditions were absolutely favorable, the intention was to have a run out of the ship on either Monday or Tuesday, at full speed, assuming that everything was satisfactory."

The last calculation of her speed, based upon actual traveled distance, was performed around 6:00 p.m. as the *Titanic* was turning what is known as "the corner." At that time, the *Titanic* was still running at a reduced speed.

Lowe: "Her speed from noon until we turned the corner was just a fraction under 21 knots."

Smith: "Can you tell what speed the ship was making at the time of these observations?"
Pitman: "About 21 ½."
Smith: "Did you regard that as pretty good speed?"
Pitman: "No. Nothing to what we expected her to do."
Smith: "Did you expect her to do pretty well?"
Pitman:"We thought it quite possible that she could reach 24."

The *Titanic*'s speed had been held in reserve during most of the voyage due to constraints imposed by the breaking in of her engines – and the shortage of coal.

Smith: "Were you trying to reach 24 knots?"
Pitman: "No. We had to study the coal. We had not the coal to do it."
Smith: "Tell me, if you can, upon what ground you base your report of 21½ knots speed."
Pitman: "By the log and the revolutions."
Fletcher: "And you say you had to study the question of coal? What do you mean by that? Did you take account of the amount of coal you had?"

Pitman: "Yes. I understood we had not quite sufficient. There was not sufficient there on board to drive her on at full speed."
Fletcher: "How do you know that?"
Pitman: "I had that from one of the engineers."
Fletcher: "Did you ask him whether he had enough coal to drive her at full speed?"
Pitman: "I knew we had not. He told me that we had not quite sufficient . . . He remarked we had not sufficient coal on board to drive her full speed all the way across."

Ironically, just as the *Titanic* was reaching the most dangerous part of her voyage, more of her boilers were lit and the speed of the ship was increased. This action speaks pointedly to just how unconcerned Bruce Ismay and Captain Smith were about the dangers of the ice that lay ahead.

Along with the increasingly crisp weather came crystal clear skies. There was no moon at all on Sunday night and the stars were visible in a brilliance not often seen.

Newlands: "That was a clear night was it?"
Boxhall: "Perfectly clear; starlight. You could almost see the stars set."

Symons: "It was a very clear night."

As dusk faded to darkness, the *Titanic* plowed forward through the Atlantic. The officers were not oblivious to the danger ahead, but were on full guard for any sign of ice on the horizon. The captain was maintaining the ship's speed in the face of ice warnings based upon two important command assumptions. The first assumption was that any ice they came upon would be sighted on the horizon with enough time to take evasive action. The second assumption was that the officer on watch would be capable of maneuvering the mammoth *Titanic* around any obstacle in its path. Both of these assumptions relied heavily upon the skill of his officers and crew. Both of these assumptions discounted the need to slow down the ship or warrant his own presence on the bridge. And so the *Titanic* steamed into that fateful Sunday night, accepting the challenge that lay ahead in her path not with indifference, but rather with complete confidence.

Down on B deck in the A la Carte Restaurant, the two men who had the most influence on the fate of the ship unknowingly enjoyed their last meal on the *Titanic*. Captain Smith was attending a dinner party thrown in his honor by George and Eleanor Widener. The Wideners must have been aglow from the social coup they achieved with this gathering. In addition to the prestige of dining with the captain of the *Titanic*, Major Archibald Butt, a close aide to the President of the United States, was seated at the table. Also in attendance were John and Marian Thayer, William and Lucille Carter, and the Widener's son, Harry, among others. The guests at this table collectively represented an enormous amount of wealth, influence, and prestige in 1912.

Miss Minahan: "My brother, his wife, and myself went to the café for dinner at about 7:15 p.m. ship's time. When we entered there was a dinner party already dining, consisting of perhaps a dozen men and three women. Captain Smith was a guest, as also were Mr. and Mrs. Widener, Mr. and Mrs. Blair, and Major Butt. Sitting within a few feet of this party were also Sir Cosmo and Lady Duff-Gordon, a Mrs. Meyers of New York, and Mrs. Smith of Virginia. Mr. and Mrs. Harris also were dining in the café at the same time."

It must have been quite a treat to sit at a table full of such interesting people. Archie Butt, for instance, may have offered some stories of life in Washington, D.C. Although a military aide by career at the time, Butt's ultimate legacy was to serve as a crucial witness to the Roosevelt and Taft presidencies, which he recorded in a series of letters and notes. These written observa-

As the *Titanic* approaches the ice field, two men who hold the most influence over the fate of the ship dine in the A La Carte Restaurant. Bruce Ismay is in the foreground. Captain Smith is to the left in the distance.

tions later proved to be invaluable historical records, referenced and quoted in many accounts about that period in the White House. He was a natural for poignant observations, like the one he made of Teddy Roosevelt, after joining a delegation that met the ex-president in New York upon his return from a year-long safari.

Mr. Butt: *"He was just the same in manner, in appearance, in expression, yet there was something different. We, all of us who had been closely associated with him in the past, felt it. I spoke of it. Senator Lodge spoke of it. Secretary Meyer, who is not keen to see much, he even spoke of it, and so did Nick. Loeb and I, for we rode together in the procession, talked almost entirely of him and each of us felt there was a change in him. Mr. Meyer thought he had grown older, but it wasn't that. Loeb, Senator Lodge, and I figured it out to be simply an enlarged personality. To me he had ceased to be an American, but had become a world citizen. His horizon seemed to be greater, his mental scope more encompassing. But it is there. He is bigger, broader, capable of greater good or greater evil, I don't know which, than when he left."*

Butt's observation of the effect that an overseas trip had on Roosevelt may have

Archibald Butt

led him to take one himself in the spring of 1912 to escape the friction between his two friends, who happened to be back-to-back presidents battling it out for the Republican nomination. He chose the *Titanic* to return to the lion's den of presidential politics.

Bruce Ismay was also in the restaurant, seated at a table for two with the ship's Doctor, William O'Loughlin. Ismay was facing the side of the room that had been

expanded in comparison to the same dining room on the *Olympic*.

Smith: *"Mr. Ismay, what time did you dine on Sunday evening?"*
Ismay: *"At 7:30."*
Smith: *"With whom?"*
Ismay: *"With the doctor."*
Smith: *"Did the captain dine with you?"*
Ismay: *"He did not, sir."*
Smith: *"Do you know where the captain dined on Sunday evening?"*
Ismay: *"He dined in the restaurant."*
Smith: *"The same place that you dined?"*
Ismay: *"In the same room; yes. I do not know what time he dined. I saw him in the dining room. I believe he dined with Mr. and Mrs. Widener. I think Mr. and Mrs. [Carter] were there, and Mr. and Mrs. Thayer."*
Smith: *"Was Major Butt there?"*
Ismay: *"I did not see him. I could not see the whole of the table. I could see only part of it. They were dining at the forward end of the restaurant. The starboard side. I was dining in the middle of the room on the same side of the ship. They were dining in an alcove. Part of their table was in an alcove. I could not see the whole of their table. In fact, I was sitting with my back toward them."*
Smith: *"You dined at half past 7?"*

Ismay: *"Yes, sir."*

Smith: *"How long did you remain at the table?"*

Ismay: *"I should think half or three quarters of an hour."*

Smith: *"During all that time, was the captain at his table?"*

Ismay: *"They were sitting at the table when I went out of the room, sir."*

It is natural that the mere presence of Captain Smith at a table with so many other influential people drew the attention of the surrounding diners, who very likely could only shoot a quick glance from time to time so as not to be impolite. It is interesting that Ismay chose to dine in the A la Carte Restaurant for the first time during this voyage on the same night that Captain Smith was attending a dinner party in his honor. One has to wonder if there was an element here of an employer keeping an eye on his employee. By all accounts from others at the surrounding tables, the dinner party seemed a bit stiff and formal—in contrast to the overall atmosphere of the whole restaurant.

Mrs. Douglas: *"On Sunday we had a delightful day; everyone in the best of spirits. The time the boat was making was considered very good, and all were interested in getting into New York early. We dined in the restaurant, going in about 8 o'clock. All stories of excessive gaiety are, to my mind, absolutely unfounded."*

Mr. Stengel: *"I have a distinct recollection of a Mrs. Thorne stating, while talking about the captain being to dinner, that she was in that party and she said, 'I was in that party, and the captain did not drink a drop. He smoked two cigars, that was all, and left the dining room about 10 o'clock.'"*

Seated at yet another table in the restaurant were Jacques and Lily May Futrelle, and Henry and Rene Harris. Jacques Futrelle was a well-known writer and Henry Harris was a famous Broadway producer. The four were having a wonderful time.

Mrs. Futrelle: *"The night was beautiful. The sea was placid and wonderful to look upon. Countless stars were reflected in all their glory in watery depths, which gave no hint of the treachery lurking in them. Phosphorescence gleamed upon the surface of the sea and reflected back its radiance from giant icebergs which were scattered over the face of the waters. There was not the slightest thought of danger in the minds of those who sat around the tables on the luxurious dining saloon of the Titanic. It was a brilliant crowd. Jewels flashed from the gowns of the women. And, oh, the dear women, how fondly they wore their latest Parisian gowns! It was the first time that most of them had an opportunity to display their newly acquired finery. The soft, sweet odor of rare flowers pervaded the atmosphere. I remember at our table there was a great bunch of American beauty roses. The orchestra played popular music. It was a buoyant, oh, such a jolly crowd. It was a rare gathering of beautiful women and splendid men. There was the atmosphere of fellowship and delightful sociability which makes dinner on the Sabbath on board ship a delightful occasion. I thought as I glanced over the saloon, was that it would be hard to find gathered in one place a crowd which would better typify the highest type of American manhood and womanhood. I remember Jacques and Mrs. Harris discussing at our table the latest plays on the American stage. Everybody was so merry. We were all filled with the joy of living. We sat over dinner late that night."*

Two decks below on D deck, the majority of first class passengers enjoyed another delicious dinner in what was then the largest room afloat, the first class dining saloon. This room was enormous and could seat all of the first class passengers in one sitting. There were alcoves along both sides of the room that allowed for some intimacy, but they remained open on one side to the larger, overall room. The walls and ceiling were painted white, creating an airy and upbeat atmosphere. By 8:00 p.m. passengers were several courses into their meal.

Mr. Dodge: "It was hard to realize when dining in the spacious dining saloon that one was not in some large and sumptuous hotel."

Shipbuilder Magazine: "The first class dining saloon is situated upon the saloon deck amidships and is an immense room, by far the largest afloat, extending for the full 92 feet of the ship's width and 114 feet in length. The style adopted is Jacobean English of the early seventeenth century, for details of the splendid decorations at Hatfield, Haddon Hall, and other great houses of that period having been carefully studied. But instead of the somber oak, which the sixteenth and seventeenth century builders would have adopted, the walls and ceilings have been painted white. The ceiling in particular is richly molded in a manner characteristic of the plasterer's art of Jacobean times. The superb effect achieved is well conveyed to the mind . . . but a complete perception of its magnificence can only

be obtained by actual presence on the ship when dinner is in progress. The side lights in the shell of the vessel are in groups of six and four lights alternately, each light being of large diameter. In front of these lights inside the saloon large leaded glass windows have been arranged, giving the effect of the windows in a large mansion. Dining accommodation is provided for 532 passengers at the same time."

Mr. Thayer: "My Father and Mother were invited out to dinner that night, so I dined alone at our regular table."

Burke: "Mr. and Mrs. Straus. They had a table to themselves."

The dining room stewards busied themselves by attending to their assigned tables. Within one of the starboard alcoves sat Frank Millet and Clarence Moore. They were the only two at their table on Sunday night, their usual companions having abandoned them that evening. Their friend, Archie Butt was upstairs at the restaurant. Walter and Virginia Clark were also missing and may have been dining in the A la Carte Restaurant as well.

Ray: "I was first class steward on the Titanic; to wait at the tables and see to the

saloon generally. I was waiting on the starboard side . . . I waited on Major Butt, Mr. Moore, Mr. Millet, Mr. Clark, and Mrs. Clark. Mr. Moore and Mr. Millet dined together about 7:30, and finished dinner about 8:15. Major Butt was not down because he was dining in the restaurant. I heard since that he was dining with the Wideners."

Frank Millet was in the twilight years of a relatively successful artistic career. He had made his name primarily as a portrait artist in the late 1800's and had ties to many prominent people of the time. One of the classic artists, John Singer Sargent had even done a painting called "Millet's Garden" in 1886 while staying at his house in western England. Nowadays, Millet found himself working in a Washington, D.C. post at the Commission of Fine Arts. Millet had exercised some influence on Archie Butt to accompany him on his business trip to Rome.

It was at dinner that passengers were afforded the opportunity to practice the art of casual conversation. And there was much to talk about. In the spirit of politeness and good social grace, one would not typically discuss something too controversial at dinner, saving such topics for later and perhaps with a smaller, more familiar group. The majority of the tables in the first class dining saloon seated five, six, and eight people. This frequently resulted in a mix of new acquaintances with fresh topics to discuss.

Since everyone was on travel, one of the easiest and most pleasant conversations to engage in would consist of recent adventures. Passengers could recount where they had been in Europe while on vacation or business. This could easily lead into a discussion of what one did for a living.

The landscape of 1912 Europe was very different from today. France had the distinction of being the only true republic, lead by the conservative republican Raymond Poincare, who was to become president in May. In many countries, royalty still retained real power over their citizens. Even in democratic countries such as Great Britain, King George still exercised significant influence over the House of Lords and international politics (King Edward died in May 1910). King Victor Emmanuel III of Italy was primarily a figurehead but would be left in a few years with the task of asking Mussolini to take over the reigns of the country. A vacation in Europe might have taken any one of the first class passengers to such places as the Austro-Hungarian Empire where Emperor Franz Joseph had been on the throne since 1848, the Russian Empire under the rule of

Czar Nicholas II, and the German Empire under the control of Kaiser Wilhelm II. If anyone had traveled through the Ottoman Empire where Sultan Muhammad V presided over a recently much weakened throne, they would have unknowingly been one of the last visitors before a huge portion of it broke away to form the Balkan League, setting the stage for World War I two years later. Vacationers returning from Europe on the *Titanic* had figuratively traveled across thin ice on the continent. As conversation flowed, so too did the first rate food and drink.

Mr. Peuchen: "Sunday evening I dined with my friends, Markleham Molson, Mr. Allison, and Mrs. Allison, and their daughter was there for a short time. The dinner was an exceptionally good dinner. It seemed to be a better bill of fare than usual, although they are all good."

The second class dining saloon shared the same kitchen as first, and as the cooks hit their stride on Sunday evening, the second class passengers equally benefitted. The dining room in second class was just as impressive in size, but certainly not as luxurious in appearance. Whereas first class enjoyed free moving leather chairs, in second class the wooden swivel seats were

bolted to the floor. Still, the room was attractive and upbeat.

Mrs. Cook: ". . . we had a Christmas dinner this night, everything was beautiful."

Mrs. Collyer: "I don't remember very much about the first few days of the voyage. I was a bit seasick and kept to my cabin most of the time. But on Sunday, April 14th I was up and about. At dinner time I was at my place in the saloon and enjoyed the meal, though I thought it was too heavy and rich. No effort had been spared to give even the second cabin passengers on that Sunday the best dinner that money could buy."

Whereas first class passengers consisted of a mix of wealthy vacationers and businessmen, second class was made up of vacationers, businessmen, and more upscale immigrants. Some, like Emilio Portalupi, were returning to the United States after visiting family in their homeland. The Browns were on their way from Cape Town to Seattle in the western part of the United States, where they were considering moving their hotel business. The Del Carlos had just been married in Italy a few months earlier and Argenia was bringing his wife to America, where he had already lived for some ten years. Still others, like Annie

Funk, were returning from missionary work in India.

Lawrence Beesley's table was a good example of how people from all walks of life were randomly seated together. Surrounding him were Reverend Carter and his wife, Charles Chapman of New York, Charles Davies of Portsmouth, England, Reginald Butler of Sunderland, England, Robert Norman of Glasgow, and the second class purser.

Third class passengers were also at dinner down on F deck, where meals were prepared from a separate galley. Although modest in comparison to the first and second class meals, they were a welcome closing to a wonderful day at sea. There were a number of different languages spoken in third class in the dining saloon, including Italian, French, Lebanese, Polish, Gaelic, and German. There were so many Lebanese passengers on this passage that they had their own seating in one of the four third class dining rooms.

Steerage passengers banded together at tables by language, and conversation wandered to many topics. Some spoke of where they were from and the circumstances that brought them to the *Titanic*. Others spoke of opportunities they had heard of in America, and their plans once they arrived.

Tariffs were numerous and steep in

A third class dining room. Four adjacent rooms on F deck were located amidship. (*Olympic*)

1912 between the European countries and the United States. Because this made imports expensive, most of what America consumed was manufactured in America. While these protective tariffs created a booming economy for the Northeast and Midwest industries in the United States, they also created a strong demand for workers. American industry welcomed immigrants with open arms since they were a source of cheap labor. As immigrants quickly found jobs and a better life compared to what they had in their homesteads, many wrote to their families telling of their relative success. As a result, numerous second wave immigrants had specific plans when they boarded the *Titanic*.

As the hour wore on, passengers finished their meals and began to trickle out of the dining rooms a few at a time. In first class, most walked only a few feet into the Reception Room and took a seat in one of

The lounge outside of the A la Carte Restaurant was arranged around the first class staircase aft.

Mrs. Smith: "The dinner did not seem to be particularly gay. While they had various wines to drink, I am positive none were intoxicated at a quarter of 9 o'clock when we left the dining room."

Miss Minahan: "I had read testimony before your committee stating that Captain Smith had talked to an officer on the bridge from 8:45 to 9:25. This is positively untrue, as he was having coffee with these people during this time. I was seated so close to them I could hear bits of their conversation."

Mrs. Douglas: "We did not leave the tables until most of the others had left, including Mr. Ismay, Mr. and Mrs. Widener, and their guests, and the evening was passed very quietly."

the numerous, casually arranged wicker chairs. If they were lucky, they found a seat in one of the sofas or cushioned arm chairs.

Mr. Peuchen: "After dinner my friends and I went to the sitting-out room and had some coffee."

Others in first class took elevators to A deck to settle into the quieter lounge or take a stroll along the promenade deck.

On B deck, passengers trickled out of the A la Carte Restaurant with several options. Some went into the Café Parisien adjacent to the restaurant for dessert or a drink. Others stepped just outside the restaurant doors into the B deck reception room surrounding the staircase aft and enjoyed a drink as another, smaller band of musicians played favorite musical pieces there. Bruce Ismay stopped here and took in the atmosphere. As diners left the restaurant, they could not help but take note of the captain and his party right near the door.

While the passengers sat in the B deck reception area outside the restaurant, Ismay included, they overheard occasional traffic one deck above as men came up from the first class dining saloon on D deck to have a smoke in the A deck smoking room.

In second class, passengers wandered to their rooms or up to the library or smoking lounge. Word passed around that there would by a hymn singing after dinner back in the dining saloon, so some bided their time until then. Others settled into a comfortable chair and returned to the book they had been reading on the voyage.

A slightly different set of rooms awaited third class passengers. Considering that their quarters were often cramped and shared with strangers, most would not go to their rooms unless they were ready for bed. Third class passengers could go to the D deck general space in the forward area of the ship surrounding the cargo hatches, or climb the stairs at the stern to the D deck general room and separate smoking room.

Miss Turja: "The third class accommodations were beautiful. The atmosphere was quite lively with a lot of talking, singing, and fellowship. It has been said that third class on the Titanic was as good as first class on many other ships of the day."

Mr. Dorking: "During the first days out of Southampton we had a delightful voyage. Everything worked smoothly and we were covering the miles at a record pace. The weather was fair and a great deal of the time was spent on deck by the passengers. Some found pleasure in the music room, playing cards and various indoor sports."

While most passengers were enjoying dinner, a few were in their cabins for reasons of illness or exhaustion.

The third class general room. This lounge was at the stern on C deck, next to the smoking room.

Mr. Harper: "I had been kept in my stateroom by tonsilitis ever since coming aboard the ship."

Mrs. Dyer-Edwards: "I went to bed at half past seven and my cousin, Miss Gladys Cherry who shared my room—number 77 on deck B—also retired. It was bitterly cold."

The kitchen that served both first and second class passengers. The third class kitchen was on F deck.

In an extreme case, Ella White was confined to her cabin the entire voyage. One of her feet was bound up after twisting it while entering the ship from at Cherbourg.

Mrs. White: "I remained in my room until I came out that night. I never took a step from my bed until that night."

As the hour came to an end, the first, second, and third class dining rooms were closing and stewards were cleaning off the tables and carrying the dirty dishes into the kitchen. The day was a long one for the cooks and they were just finishing up.

Collins: "[I was] Assistant cook, first class galley. I stopped work at 9 o'clock on Sunday night."

One exception was the A la Carte Restaurant. It did not close until 11:00 p.m.

It was a content moment throughout the ship as nourished passengers settled back to let the remainder of Sunday evening come to a peaceful and comfortable end. Most of the crew on duty were even relaxing because of the day of the week.

Bourne: "What time did you go on watch on the day the accident occurred?"
Brice: "Eight o'clock."

Bourne: *"What was your duty during that watch?"*
Brice: *"We were doing nothing, sir as it was Sunday night. They excuse us from washing the deck Sunday night."*

Captain Smith expressed his thanks for a wonderful dinner to his hosts and table companions and excused himself from the restaurant. His departure was probably noted by Ismay, still sitting in the reception area just outside the restaurant doors. Smith and Ismay apparently did not speak to each other during their respective meals, nor outside in the lounge. Both were engaged in conversations with their own guests.

One conflicting piece of information regarding the captain's departure from the restaurant comes from Daisy Minahan.

Miss Minahan: "Captain Smith was continuously with his party from the time we entered until between 9:25 and 9:45, when he bid the women good night and left. I know this time positively, for at 9:25 my brother suggested my going to bed. We waited for one more piece of the orchestra, and it was between 9:25 and 9:45 (the time we departed) that Captain Smith left."

It is unknown how Smith returned to the bridge, but the likely path would have been up the rear staircase, across the foyer outside the smoking room, out onto the promenade deck, forward to the crew's staircase, and up one flight to the bridge. It was just before 9:00 p.m. when he arrived.

Smith: "From 6 until 10 o'clock was the captain on the bridge at all?"
Lightoller: "Yes, sir."
Smith: "When did he arrive?"
Lightoller: "Five minutes to nine."
Smith: "When he came to the bridge at five minutes of nine what did he say to you or what did you say to him? Who spoke first?"
Lightoller: "I could not say sir. Probably one of us said, 'Good evening.'"

Unlike Chief Officer Wilde and First Officer Murdoch, Lightoller was the only senior officer who did not transfer from the *Olympic*—the last ship Smith commanded. Lightoller had instead come from the *Oceanic*. The second officer did, however, work under Smith in the past, including the prestigious *Majestic*. Having been years since then, conversation might have been a little slow and on the stiff side. Not that it mattered much. These men were hardened to such matters, having spent years at sea with routine transfers from one ship to another. In a voyage or two they would be accustomed to one another all over again.

Lightoller: "Captain Smith, or 'E.J.' as he was familiarly and affectionately known, was quite a character in the shipping world. Tall, full whiskered, and broad. At first sight you would think to yourself, 'Here's a typical Western Ocean Captain. Bluff, hearty, and I'll bet he's got a voice like a foghorn.' As a matter of fact, he had a pleasant, quiet voice and invariable smile. A voice he rarely raised above a conversational tone—not to say he couldn't. In fact, I have often heard him bark an order that made a man come to himself with a bump. He was a great favorite, and a man any officer would give his ears to sail under."

With a full meal in him and orchestra music still lingering in his thoughts, Captain Smith stood on the bridge of the *Titanic* as it sailed onward to New York. The ship was behaving remarkably well on her maiden voyage—as expected. The remainder of the passage looked to be a good one. The weather was fine, the seas calm, and reports from passing ships indicated clear skies ahead. All they needed to do was get by some ice that might be in their path during the night. It looked like the following day, Monday, would be perfect for the full speed sprint he and Ismay were planning for the *Titanic*.

Nine O'Clock

As the *Titanic* increased her speed, passengers and crew went about the remainder of their Sunday evening in good spirits. The lounges in all three classes filled to capacity as people settled in for an after dinner refreshment, conversation and music.

In the first class Reception Room on D deck, passengers were entertained by the musical talents of the orchestra, located by the grand piano on the forward starboard corner of the lounge. A person could sit close by and enjoy the concert, or farther away on the other side of the room, where the music would simply serve as a backdrop to conversation. While women in spectacular gowns and jewels wandered through the lounge with well dressed men at their sides, the band played on, taking requests along the way. People were generally impressed with the wide array of songs they knew.

The Reception Room was a perfect setting for such a gathering of wealth.

Shipbuilder Magazine: "The style adopted is Jacobean English similar to the dining room, but the furniture is, of course, different. The dignity and simplicity of the beautifully proportioned white paneling, delicately carved in low relief, will indeed form a fitting background to the brilliant scene when the passengers foregather before dining. The main staircase rises directly from this apartment, thus greatly increasing the palatial effect produced. Facing the staircase is a large and very beautiful panel of French tapestry adapted from one of a series . . . at the National Garde Meuble, and specially woven on the looms at Aubusson. The floor is covered with a dark richly coloured Axminster carpet."

Mr. Gracie: "That night after dinner, with my table companions, Messrs. James Clinch Smith and Edward A. Kent, according to usual custom, we adjourned to the palm room, with many others for the usual coffee at individual tables where we listened to the always delightful music of the Titanic's band. On these occasions, full dress was always en regle; and it was a subject both of observation and admiration that there were so many beautiful women—then especially in evidence—aboard the ship. I invariably circulated around during these delightful evenings chatting with those I knew, and with those whose acquaintance I had made during the voyage."

Passengers in first class relax in a corner of the Reception Room after dinner.

Sunday evening was the pinnacle of the voyage. It seemed as though everything was coming together to make the maiden voyage a memorable one. The dinner just finished was by far the best. The weather had been good throughout the passage, and now the flat surface outside made it seem as though the passengers were in an expensive hotel on land. The world in which they lived was hundreds of miles away, and for the time being they were free to enjoy this carefree existence in the middle of nowhere.

The *Titanic* was a brief witness to the final years of the gilded age where extravagance was admired and proudly displayed. It was a wonderful time to be wealthy, traveling about on holiday and bumping into other acquaintances doing the same. There seemed to be an endless flow of new innovations in the midst of an explosion of art, music, and other finer aspects of life. Many first class passengers owned several houses and spent their time traveling from one to another throughout the year, breaking up the routine by periodic holidays in Europe and elsewhere. In many ways it was like a continuous party for the wealthy of 1912, propelled by a strong growing economy in the United States and Europe, few taxes, and years of accumulated fortunes. But where the lives of these first class passengers flowed along a surface of glitter, excitement, and fun, there was an undercurrent to all of the merriment that foreshadowed the end of a remarkable period. World War I would mark the formal end of the Gilded Age, but in reality it was only a catalyst for a sentiment that had been already smoldering for several years.

For all the benefits society was receiving from advances in technology and many strong economies, there was a troubled tone lurking about the people. President Roosevelt observed it a few years earlier as "an unhealthy condition of excitement and irritation in the popular mind." As the industrial age ushered in a period of growth, the wealth it produced had been consolidating in the pockets of a limited number of people. Over the years, it produced a way of life that created a polarization between the working class and those in positions of wealth and power. Racism was running high throughout the world. Many European countries viewed each other with suspicion, and in some cases, contempt. In the United States, many citizens viewed the inflow of immigrants as a threat to their established way of life. Although plenty of opportunities existed for jobs consisting of hard labor paying low wages, boundless opportunities to make a fortune did not really exist. In the United States, and more so in Europe, people were conspicuously categorized by their race, sex, and religion. This culture of informally classifying everyone, practiced not only by the wealthy but by the middle and lower classes as well, effectively established a caste system. Many people began to tire of the stagnancy that came with such a system, triggering a reaction from voters that put Liberals in positions of power in Britain and France, and fueling President Roosevelt's earlier progressive movement in the United States. Socialism was making considerable headway in every country.

Although 1912 was a relatively peaceful time in the way of international conflicts, the social fabric of Europe and America was being pulled hard, and in different directions as people began to throw off the suffocation and influences of the Victorian age and insist on additional rights.

Women, particularly the wealthy and the educated, were demanding equal rights under the suffrage movement and this effort was proving to be a long and difficult road. First class passengers Ella White, Helen Candee, Margaret Brown and Marie Young, among others, were suffragists. In Great Britain and in the United States, one of the higher profile suffrage issues was the demand for the right to vote. In America, women were meeting with limited success by working the campaign at the state level,

The second class library also functioned as a general lounge. *(Olympic)*

ing herself in front of horses at the Derby in Great Britain. Men, for the most part were ambivalent about the movement and those sitting nearby such a discussion may have offered an opinion on either side of the issue. Some went up to the male enclave – the smoking room.

Mr. Peuchen: "I left the friends I had dined with about 9 o'clock, I think, or a little later. I then went up to the smoking room and joined Mr. Beattie, Mr. McCaffery, and another English gentleman who was going to Canada. We sat chatting and smoking there . . ."

In the second class lounge, also known as the library, passengers gained seats on a first come, first serve basis. Settling into a comfortable chair, the remainder of the night looked to be a relaxing one, filled with the sound of music from yet another orchestra available on the *Titanic.*

Mrs. Collyer: "After I had eaten, I listened to the orchestra for a little while . . .'

Shipbuilder: "The second class library is another beautiful apartment, the style in this case being Colonial Adams. The paneling is in sycamore, handsomely relieved with carv-

winning in Washington in 1910 and California in 1911. Suffragists were succeeding at getting referendums on the ballot for November in Arizona, Kansas, Oregon, Ohio, Michigan, and Wisconsin. Women in the Reception Room may have discussed the controversy raging within the suffragist's camp. There was a division of opinion as to whether the movement should be targeted at

the national level, similar to the approach women in Great Britain were taking, or at a state-by-state level. Some women may have reservedly pointed out their opposition to the movement altogether. The topic could have drifted to characters within the movement, such as Jane Addams and her national efforts in the United States, or Emily Davison's recent death as a result of throw-

ings, and the dado is in mahogany. The furniture, which is of special design, is also of mahogany, and is covered with tapestry. A large bookcase is provided at the forward end. The side windows are of large size, draped with silk curtains and arranged in pairs, which also well illustrates the beautiful paneling. A handsome Wilton carpet completes the fine effect produced."

Conversation by the fifth night at sea in the second class lounge may have drifted to more substantial topics of the time such as recent prohibition movements and whether one was for or against the consumption of alcohol. It was typical for a member of the suffrage movement to also be a prohibitionist, but it was not always the case that a prohibitionist was a suffragist, or sympathizer of the movement.

The Liberal Party in Great Britain had just made enormous changes by enacting the National Insurance Act of 1911. It provided mandatory health insurance for the poorest third of the country, totaling 14 million in all, and was to be funded by a combination of taxes and employer and employee contributions. The same act established a system of unemployment insurance that would last for fifteen weeks a year for those out of work. Such a program was far reaching and very controversial. A comparison of this national insurance to what other countries offered could have been a topic of discussion.

Mrs. Cook: " We then sat on a sofa together and Mr. Beauchamp and Mr. Ashby joined us and the former telling us some good jokes but the latter and I argued with one another for he praised America and ran down England which I didn't at all like but I will say no more of him for he is not among the survivors."

Miss Lehmann: "Sunday night I went to the library to write some letters to mail after I got to New York. When I had finished my letters I went below. Almost all of the people were English and as I could not speak English I did not want to stay up there and listen to something I could not understand. I had brought along lots of Swiss and French reading material so I went to bed."

Others in second class settled into the smoking room, where the atmosphere may have been slightly more unrestrained than the library. This room was larger than the library and did not carry the burden of doubling as a reading and writing room, like its counterpart.

Shipbuilder Magazine: "The second class smoking room is situated on the promenade deck B, immediately above the library, and is 36 feet long by 62 feet wide. In this case the decoration is a variation of the Louis Seize [XVI] period. The paneling and dado are of oak, relieved with carving. The furniture is of oak, upholstered with plain dark green morocco leather. The floor is laid with linoleum tiles of special design."

The wooden furniture in the lounges of third class did not encourage one to stay put for long, but many were engaged in the art of conversation anyway. In the United Kingdom, the Home Rule Bill was introduced into the British Parliament on the same day the *Titanic* departed from Southampton, and it is likely there was discussion about it among the Irish on this voyage. This bill attempted once again to provide an element of self-government to the Irish. Although some in Ireland may have pinned an element of hope to this bill, cynicism ran high on both sides of the Irish Sea when it came to Irish and British politics. In the opinion of most Irish, and almost certainly those on the *Titanic* leaving their country, Britain was at the very root of the economic and social problems plaguing their island, and the cause of their emigration. Things had actually improved considerably in Ireland over the last several

The third class smoking room. *(Olympic)*

Irish as a backward lot, incapable of ruling themselves and disloyal to the British Empire. England was in the midst of some soul searching regarding the relevancy of its empire to the average citizen, and the reappearance of the Home Rule Bill in Parliament was perceived as a symptom of a weakening national will. In 1912, English and Irish racism was running extremely high on both ends–just another burning ember in the smoldering European landscape.

In Italy, Prime Minister Giovanni Giolitti was in his fourth ministry and had just implemented in June 1911 the right to vote for all men who were literate or had served in the military. Since the political landscape within Italy was stable in comparison to Ireland, the typical Italian emigrants on board the *Titanic* that night were driven toward America for economic reasons as they tried to find better jobs.

As many Irish, Italians, Lebanese, Finns, and others reached adulthood, they took stock in their future. They were living on small family farms worked by their parents, frequently rented from a landlord. They realized there was not much opportunity in their current existence and that a better life could perhaps be found in America. As they sat on the *Titanic* that Sunday night, halfway between a new beginning and an abandoned homeland, many immigrants

decades, but that only raised the quality of life on the island to barely tolerable. A system of oppression and persecution over several hundred years had bred a poor and backward economy dependent on a system of small farms and fishing. There was very little industry in Ireland in 1912 and it was under the ownership or control of the British interests. Over the course of time a hatred developed between the Celtic and Anglo Saxon races, handed down from generation to generation. Many British viewed the

were filled with bittersweet emotions.

Conversations flourished in all the lounges and new acquaintances continued to bloom on this fifth night at sea.

Mr. Thayer: "After dinner I was enjoying a cup of coffee, when a man about twenty-eight or thirty years of age drew up and introduced himself as Milton C. Long, son of Judge Charles M. Long, of Springfield, Massachusetts. He was traveling alone. We talked together for an hour or so."

These two men in 1912 could have discussed a number of interests. Tennis was very popular, with sellout crowds at matches, and the two might have talked about who had a chance at the U.S. Title that year. Jack may have pointed out that he was acquainted with Dick Williams, one of the two tennis celebrities on board. They may have made note of yet another tennis celebrity, Karl Behr, on the *Titanic*. The summer *Olympics* were going to be held in Stockholm that year, and they may have discussed the potential of one of the athletes, Jim Thorpe. Thayer may have mentioned to Long how he was due to graduate from the Haverford School in a couple of months and how he was going to the College at Princeton in the Fall.

Some of the passengers were tired

A Survivor Match

Two years after the Titanic disaster, Dick Williams and Karl Behr would face each other in the 1914 U.S. Tennis Championship Quarterfinals. In front of a sold out crowd, 4,000 spectators applauded the two men as they stood on the tennis lawn at the Newport Casino in Rhode Island. Williams would win the match, 6-2, 6-2, and 7-5. The two were ultimately honored with places in the International Tennis Hall of Fame.

early on and decided to catch up on their sleep this particular evening. While the Reception Room still buzzed with conversation and orchestra music, Archibald Gracie made an exit.

Mr. Gracie: "From the palm room, the men of my coterie would always go to the smoking room, and almost every evening join in conversation with some of the well known men whom we met there, including within my own recollections Major Archie Butt, President Taft's Military Aide, discussing politics; Clarence Moore, of Washington D.C., relating his venturesome trip some years ago through the West Virginia woods and mountains, helping a newspaper reporter in obtaining an interview with the outlaw, Captain Anse Hatfield; Frank D. Millet, the well known artist, planning a journey west; Arthur Ryerson and others. My stay in the smoking room on this particular evening for the first time was short, and I retired early with my cabin steward, Cullen's promise to awaken me betimes next morning to get ready for the engagements I had made before breakfast for the game of racquets, work in the gymnasium and the swim that was to follow."

Avenues for entertainment in second and third class were limited in comparison to first, and as the hour moved along, a number of passengers decided to call it an early evening and also catch up on some sleep.

Mrs. Brown: "We went to our berths several hours before the accident Sunday night. We had been unable to get a stateroom together so my daughter and I were in a stateroom with another lady and my husband was in a room with several other men. My daughter and I were early asleep Sunday night and my husband was asleep too."

A passage on an ocean liner could be somewhat disruptive to a person who was a

A first class deluxe cabin.

Back on the bridge, the captain and the second officer continued their conversation, speaking generally of things.

Smith: *"How soon after you took watch did you see him?"*
Boxhall: *"As near as I can tell, I saw him about 9 o'clock."*

Smith: *"Was anything else said?"*
Lightoller: *"Yes. We spoke about the weather, calmness of the sea, the clearness, about the time we should be getting up toward the vicinity of the ice and how we should recognize it if we should see it—freshening up our minds as to the indications that ice gives of its proximity. We just conferred together, generally, for 25 minutes."*
Smith: *"Was any reference made at that time to the wireless message from the Amerika?"*
Lightoller: *"Captain Smith made a remark that if it was in a slight degree hazy there would be no doubt we should have to go very slowly."*

light sleeper—and even to someone who was not. Everyone on board had to overcome the typical sounds at sea like a muffled discussion in the next cabin, opening and closing doors, and the sound of voices passing in the hallway outside. Since most passengers in 1912 shared their bathrooms, there was a lot of traffic in the passageways to and from these rooms while people prepared for bed over the course of several hours. By Sunday night, many were a bit sleep deprived but gradually getting acclimated to these various noises. A good night sleep was high on the wish list of many passengers.

Mrs. Crosby: "My husband retired at about 9 o'clock that evening and I retired about 10:30."

Captain Smith and Second Officer Lightoller were waiting to come across the ice at this point. It would not be a surprise to them when they encountered it; rather, it was expected. The captain thought there was no need for someone of his position to stand around for hours on the bridge keep-

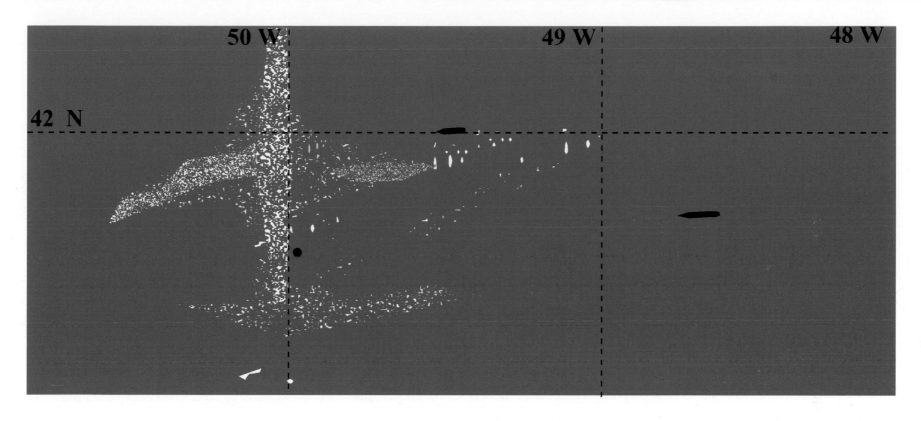

The *Titanic* at 9:00 p.m. The *Californian* continues her course to the north.

ing a lookout for ice when he had a capable crew on watch.

Smith: *"How long did he remain on the bridge after coming there at 5 minutes of 9?"*
Lightoller: *"He remained there until about 20 minutes past 9, or something like that."*

Smith: *"Then did he leave the bridge?"*
Lightoller: *"He left the bridge."*
Smith: *"With any special injunction upon you?"*
Lightoller: *"Yes sir."*
Smith: *"What did he say?"*
Lightoller: *"'If in the slightest degree doubtful, let me know."*

Smith: *"What did you say to him?"*
Lightoller: *"'All right, sir."*

Although that was the last time Lightoller saw the captain before the accident, there is evidence that he was always in the area. From the bridge, he went into the chart room to casually review the latest positions. Since he was cognizant of a number of wireless messages and the location of sighted ice, he probably had a good mental picture of the seascape ahead as he glanced at the chart.

Meanwhile, various other staff on the ship were up and about, some finishing their work for the day. Those in the service of passengers were very likely keeping their eyes on the time and quietly wishing they would go to bed. With their shifts soon coming to an end, their bunks called loudly to them.

Collins: "I stopped work at 9 o'clock on Sunday night, and I came up again and walked up and down the alleyway. I went into my bunk and fell asleep. That was about a quarter to 10. I fell asleep and was sound asleep . . ."

After retiring to the lounges for a while, some passengers were ready to walk off the extensive meal they had just enjoyed. In first class, Jacques and May Futrelle stepped up on deck for a walk.

Mrs. Futrelle: "It was suggested that we take a breath of fresh air after dinner and before retiring many passengers ventured out on the deck. I stepped out in the open to get one bit of fresh air, as I told Jacques, and

to look upon the night before I retired. There was a death chill in the air which sent a shudder through me and caused me to hurry back into the cheer and warmth of the cabin. No one had the slightest fear, however, for Mr. Andrews, who had some part in the construction of the vessel (he called it his baby), had laughingly assured us that at last man had constructed an unsinkable craft."

Some found the evening air too cold and instead took their last stroll of the day inside the ship, walking the passageways and public rooms in a comfortably controlled climate.

Miss Gibson: "On the night of the disaster there had been a great deal of merriment on board, the prospect of reaching the American shore having the effect of making everyone happy. After a stroll about the ship in company with my mother, I was invited by several friends to take part in a game of bridge, and I joined them after my mother had retired to her room on Deck E. The salon in which I joined my friends was on Deck A and we played until 10 p.m."

The increasingly frigid temperature was getting to Lightoller as well, who took note of the ship's lack of heat on the bridge.

Hichens: "The next order I received from the second officer was to go and find the deck engineer and bring him up with a key to open the heaters up in the corridor of the officers' quarters, also the wheelhouse and the chart room, on account of the intense cold."

Others were continuing to call it an evening, trickling down to their staterooms.

Mrs. Collyer: ". . . then at nine o'clock or half past nine I went to my cabin."

As 9:30 rolled around, passengers who remained up were simply biding their time in a pleasant manner. With a few exceptions, like Gracie's early Monday reservation for the squash court, there was no rush to get to bed in anticipation of some pressing business the following day. At sea, there were no such pressures, and the time passed in a pleasant and leisurely way in all classes.

Mrs. Cook: "Then Mr. Beauchamp asked me if I would take a walk on deck with him which I did the first with anyone besides Milley and the last. We did not stay long for it was bitterly cold and as we came in I saw Milley just coming down to the dining room for they had hymn singing and prayers . . ."

The second class dining saloon had been cleared of its dinner activities and the passengers were advised that they could return for the scheduled hymn singing. Some of the second class passengers had looked forward to this event all day and exited from the lounges.

Mr. Beesley: "After dinner, Mr. Carter invited all who wished to the saloon and with the assistance at the piano of a gentleman who sat at the purser's table opposite me, he started some hundred passengers singing hymns. They were asked to choose whichever hymn they wished, and with so many to choose, it was impossible for him to do more than have the greatest favorites sung. I think all were impressed with his knowledge of hymns and with his eagerness to tell us all he knew of them. It was curious to see how many chose hymns dealing with dangers at sea. I noticed the hushed tone with which all sang the hymn, 'For Those In Peril On the Sea.'"

Once the captain left Lightoller, the prior discussion about approaching ice induced the second officer to repeat his instructions to the lookouts.

Symons: "We had the order at 9:30 from Mr. Lightoller to keep a sharp lookout for

The second class dining room. The piano can be seen at the center in the distance. (*Olympic*)

ice, and we passed it on at 10 o'clock."

As half past the hour arrived, steam from the recently lit boilers was making its mark on the engines as the *Titanic* raced forward. Passengers in some areas took notice of the change in the ship's personality.

Mrs. Douglas: "As we went to our state-

room, C86, we both remarked that the boat was going faster than she ever had. The vibration as one passed the stairway in the center was very noticeable."

In the meantime, not only were the passengers trickling off to their cabins, but a steady procession of crew went below to their quarters as well.

Smith: "What time did you retire that night?"
Etches: "At half past 9, sir. I was due again at 12 o'clock."

While many headed off to sleep, the remaining passengers paid little heed, as they remained immersed in conversation, drink, and chamber music. The magic of *Titanic* was fully upon those still in her lounges, as old friends and new acquaintances continued to socialize.

Mrs. Warren: "After dinner in the evening and until about 10 p.m. we were seated in the lounge on the dining saloon deck, listening to the music."

Down on B Deck, a group of people were still enjoying themselves in the lounge outside the A la Carte Restaurant, including Ismay. Ismay always considered his primary role on these types of voyages to be an observer, from the perspective of a first class passenger. His thoughts, like Andrews', were frequently focused toward shipboard concepts that were popular, as well as things that were not. The White Star Line wanted to apply the experience and wisdom gained from the *Olympic* and *Titanic* to the upcoming construction of the third sister ship—the *Britannic*.

Ismay: "I had no business to bring me to New York at all. I simply came in the natural course of events, as one is apt to, in the case of a new ship to see how she works, and with the idea of seeing how we could improve on her for the next ship which we are building."

Leaning back in one of the comfortably cushioned wicker chairs of this stylish and cozy arrangement that surrounded the rear staircase, sipping a scotch whiskey, Ismay probably had no complaints about the *Titanic* at that moment. The vibration of the engines coming up through the first class staircase was as pure as the music from the nearby orchestra.

Mrs. Smith: "There was a coffee room directly outside of the café, in which people sat and listened to the music and drank coffee and cordials after dinner."

In second class, Charlotte Collyer was settling in for the night. She was tired and looking forward to turning out the lights and warming under the blankets. Indicative of the excellent service aboard the ship, a knock came on the door, probably in response to Collyer's request.

Mrs. Collyer: "I had just climbed into my

berth when a stewardess came in. She was a sweet woman who had been very kind to me. I take this opportunity to thank her for I shall never see her again. She went down with the Titanic. 'Do you know where we are?' she said pleasantly. 'We are in what is called the Devil's Hole.' 'What does that mean?' I asked. 'That is a dangerous part of the ocean,' she answered. 'Many accidents have happened near there. They say that icebergs drift down as far as this. It's getting to be very cold on deck so perhaps there is ice around us now.' She left the cabin and I soon dropped off to sleep, her talk about icebergs had not frightened me, but it shows that the crew were awake to the danger. As far as I can tell we had not slackened our speed in the least."

Speed was the new development on board. The *Titanic* was undoubtedly going faster, according to plan, and it was something the crew recognized–the increased energy pulsing from the ship–as the hours otherwise passed by uneventfully.

This staircase was a part of Ismay's view as he relaxed in the B deck reception room Sunday night. *(Olympic)*

Hichens: "At 9:45 o'clock p.m. Sunday, the ship was traveling at that rate and going full speed when the log was taken at 10 o'clock."
Smith: "You mean by full speed, 22 ½ miles per hour."

Hichens: "Yes, sir."

Lightoller glanced at the clock and saw that his watch was coming to an end in about fifteen minutes. He looked forward to the warmth of his cabin–and getting off his

feet. As a matter of routine during a change of watch, Hichens left the bridge and walked a few feet down a small corridor to check on the second officer's relief.

Hichens: "At a quarter to ten I called the

his bunk on the port side of the officers' quarters located on the forward boat deck. His cabin, as well as Wilde's was slightly larger than the other officers' as a perk to their position. Lying there in the dark, in a far away unconscious place, a sudden knocking sound came out of nowhere and penetrated his sleep, followed by the voice of Hichens respectfully telling him that he would be needed on the bridge in fifteen minutes. Murdoch pulled himself out of his dreams—to unknowingly prepare for the worst nightmare of his life.

As many passengers drifted off to sleep, the *Titanic*'s debutante hour had arrived. After years of construction and five days at sea, she was finally sailing at her intended service speed. Dancing through the dark waters at over 22 knots, 2,223 passengers and crew from all walks of life went about their Sunday evening in peace and contentment within her well appointed rooms and passageways. Although admired by many, there were only a handful of men on board who were intimate with her ways and aware of the significance of the evening. In the eyes of Chief Engineering Officer Joseph Bell, Harland and Wolff representative Thomas Andrews, Captain Edward Smith, and President and Managing Director Bruce Ismay, the *Titanic* had just come of age.

first officer, Mr. Murdoch to let him know it was one bell, which is part of our duty. Also took the thermometer and barometer, the temperature of the water, and the log."

Murdoch was sleeping soundly in

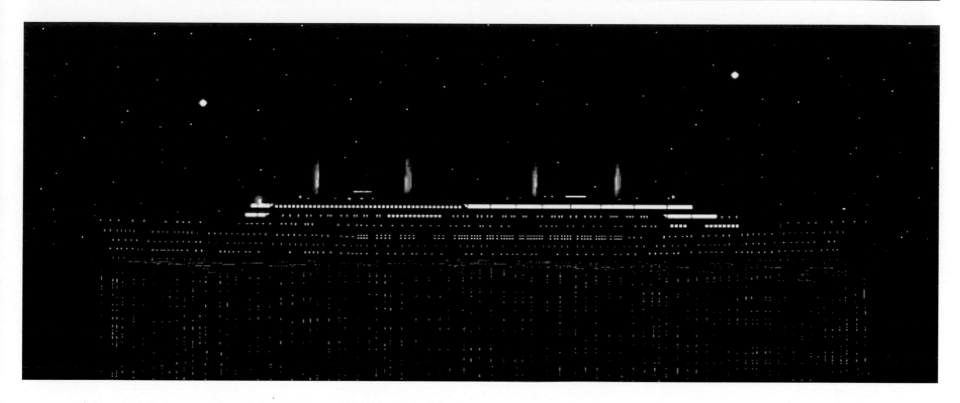

Ten O'Clock

At 10:00 p.m., many of the ship's stations changed hands. First Officer William Murdoch came onto the bridge to relieve Second Officer Charles Lightoller. Quartermaster Robert Hichens took the wheel from Alfred Olliver. Lookouts Frederick Fleet and Reginald Lee climbed to the crow's nest to relieve George Symons and Archie Jewell. Quartermaster George Rowe took over at the docking bridge on the poop deck. Fourth Officer Joseph Boxhall was in the middle of his and remained on the bridge during the 10:00 p.m. transition. So was Sixth Officer James Moody.

Boxhall: "Mr. Lightoller was on watch on the bridge when I went on watch at 8 o'clock with sixth officer Moody. Mr. Lightoller was relieved at 10 o'clock by Mr. Murdoch. Mr. Murdoch was on watch until the accident happened."

Olliver: "I had been relieved from the wheel at 10 o'clock and I was stand-by after 10 o'clock. I was running messages and doing various other duties."

There did not seem to be much familiarity between the officers and crew on the bridge. This may have stemmed from the fact that this was the first voyage on the *Titanic* and they were still getting to know each other, having all been transferred from other liners. The senior officers kept an emotional distance from the crew to maintain a level of discipline. In the case of the quartermaster, it did not help that he was physically secluded in the wheelhouse behind the bridge. A passenger later made an interesting observation about this.

Mr. Peuchen: "But he [Hichens] *was the man at the wheel, and he was calling out to the other boats wanting to know what officer was on duty at that time. He did not seem to know which officer at the time of the sighting of the iceberg was on duty.*"

Meanwhile, as the lookouts changed watch, the alert for ice was passed on.

Smith: "*You went to the lookout at 10 o'clock?*"
Fleet: "*Yes, sir.*"
Smith: "*Whom did you relieve?*"
Fleet: "*Symons and Jewell.*"
Smith: "*Did they tell you they had seen icebergs?*"
Fleet: "*No, sir. They only gave us the orders to look out for them.*"

Again, there was no doubt about what the officers of the bridge and the lookouts were coming up against.

Mr. Peuchen: "*I heard on the Carpathia that they* [*Titanic*'s officers] *were expecting icebergs or ice. I heard the third officer* [Pitman] *just mention it, casually, to two or three of them, that they knew that there was ice; that they were approaching ice.*"

Since it was dark, Lightoller stayed on the bridge for several minutes until Murdoch's eyes adjusted. The ship was traveling along at nearly top speed now—22½ knots. While the vessel hummed from the distant engines, the two discussed navigational conditions. Oddly enough, they did not seem to discuss the ice situation in much detail, even though Lightoller had calculated that the *Titanic* would be upon the ice region sometime around 11:00 p.m., which was less than an hour away. Perhaps there was no point in discussing the obvious.

Smith: "*I say, did you talk with Mr. Murdoch about the iceberg situation when you left the watch?*"
Lightoller: "*No, sir.*"
Smith: "*Did he ask you anything about it?*"
Lightoller: "*No, sir. I remarked on the general condition of the weather, and so on, etc., and then I just mentioned as I had done*

previously, '*We will be up around the ice somewhere about 11 o'clock, I suppose.*'"

Rather than discuss the ice itself, it seemed the normal course of exchange between the officers in command to instead focus on the conditions affecting visibility.

Lightoller: "*We remarked on the weather, about its being calm, clear. We remarked the distance we could see. We seemed to be able to see a long distance. Everything was very clear. We could see the stars setting down to the horizon. We were then making an easy 22 knots. It was pitch dark and dead cold. Not a cloud in the sky and the sea like glass.*"

Passengers stepping out on deck noticed the same conditions.

Mrs. Warren: "*The sea was like glass, so smooth that the stars were clearly reflected.*"

The temperature was 31 degrees. The wheelhouse and the officers' quarters were just beginning to warm up a little now that the heat had been turned on. But the bridge remained cold since it was open at both ends and exposed to the constant wind created by the ship's movement.

The two made small talk while

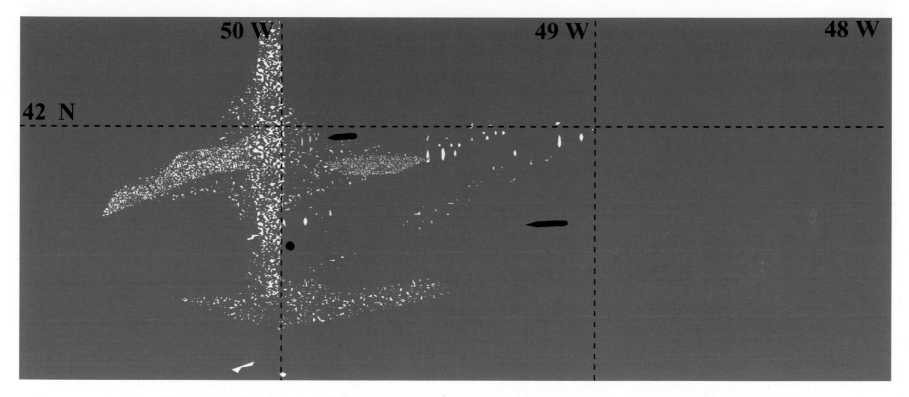

The position of the *Titanic* at 10:00 p.m. The liner may have already been in dangerous waters by this time.

standing there, looking forward into the night. Lightoller would have been in better spirits since his shift was just ending with his bunk waiting. Murdoch, by comparison, just woke up and was still getting his wits about him.

Lowe: "You must remember that we do not have any too much sleep and therefore when we sleep we die."

Boxhall went back to the chart room to work on calculating the *Titanic*'s position. Olliver passed the time on and off the bridge doing miscellaneous support tasks. As the shift settled in, Murdoch and Moody were left staring out into the cold Atlantic from the shadows of the bridge while Fleet and Lee gazed out from the crow's nest. This business of looking into the blackness of night for hours must have been tedious. But

it was a familiar role, not only to the look-outs, but the officers on duty as well. Eventually Lightoller departed, leaving Murdoch, Moody, Hichens, Boxhall, Fleet, and Lee to deal with the *Titanic*'s destiny.

Lightoller had some business to take care of before he could go to bed. He head-ed aft from the bridge.

Lightoller: "But first of all I had to do the

rounds, and in a ship of that size it meant a mile or more of deck, not including a few hundred feet of ladders, staircases, etc. Being a new ship it was all the more necessary to see that everyone was on the top line. I had been right fore and aft several decks, along a passage known as Park Lane, leading through the bowels of the ship on one side and bringing me out by a short cut to the after deck. Here I had to look round to see that the Quartermaster and others were on their stations, and then back to my warm cabin."

It was customary for the retiring officer from the bridge to walk the ship to make sure that everything was in order and that the crew were at their stations. This was a particularly important task on a ship the size of the *Titanic*. During Lightoller's tour he would have walked through the first, second, and third class passenger areas as well as the crew's.

Sometime after 10:00 p.m. the band in the first class Reception Room finished with their concert. Gradually, the majority of the passengers got up from their seats and said their good-nights to friends and acquaintances. Some headed for the Grand Staircase in the center of the room and climbed the steps to their cabins above on C, B, and A decks. Others descended the stairs for their staterooms on the starboard side of E deck. Additional passengers went by the staircase to the elevators behind them. Some had their staterooms on the same deck as the Reception Room, and passed through a door to the forward area of D deck. There were, of course some passengers who were not ready to go to bed yet, and they remained in their seats as the majority of people trickled out. While continuing with their conversations, they watched the band put their instruments away into their cases.

At the A la Carte Restaurant, passengers were parting.

Mrs. Futrelle: "Before retiring, my husband complained of a slight headache. We had both gone to our stateroom. Nearly everyone on board had retired except men who chatted over their cigars in the magnificent lounging room. There was a stillness which only comes with the sea. A faint tremor of the boat was the only thing which served to remind one that he was on the sea. Apart from this, one might well have imagined himself to be in one of the magnificent hotels of New York City."

As Lightoller reached the bottom of the Grand Staircase and crossed through the crew-only door into the long hallway on E deck known as Park Lane, he may have passed several third class passengers heading forward to their cabins.

Miss Jensen: "I shared the cabin with three young girls, two English and a Swede and we had turned in early because the passengers in 3rd class had instructions to be below deck before 22 hours."

Mr. Abelseth: "I was in compartment G on the ship. I went to bed about 10 o'clock Sunday night . . ."

As Lightoller passed the main staircase aft in second class, he may have heard the faint sound of singing, originating from the dining saloon one flight above.

Mr. Beesley: "The singing must have gone on until after ten o'clock, when seeing the stewards standing about waiting to serve biscuits and coffee before going off duty, Mr. Carter brought the evening to a close by a few words of thanks to the purser for the use of the saloon, a short sketch of the happiness and safety of the voyage hitherto, the great confidence all felt on board this great liner with her steadiness and her size, and the happy outlook of landing in a few hours in New York at the close of a delightful voyage. And all the time he spoke, a few miles ahead of us lay the 'peril on the sea' that was to sink this same great liner with many of those on board who listened with gratitude to his simple, heartfelt words."

As passengers settled into their cabins for the night, the quiet of the staterooms allowed them to hear a background noise that some found of particular interest.

Mr. Stengel: ". . . I called my wife's attention to the fact that the engines were running very fast. That was when I retired at 10 o'clock. I could hear the engines running when I retired, and I noticed that the engines were running fast. I said I noticed that they were running faster than at any other time during the trip."

The passengers dispersed into every direction of the ship as they left the lounges. Most went directly to their staterooms to retire, but others decided to go up for one last stroll before bed.

Mr. Thayer: "We talked together for an hour or so. Afterwards I put on an overcoat and took a few turns around the deck. It had become very much colder. It was a brilliant, starry night. There was no moon and I have never seen the stars shine brighter. They appeared to stand right out of the sky, sparkling like cut diamonds. A very light haze, hardly noticeable, hung low over the water. I have spent much time on the ocean, yet I have never seen the sea smoother than it was that night. It was like a mill pond, and just as innocent looking as the great ship quietly rippled through it."

Passengers who had become accustomed to taking a walk on deck before their bedtimes during the voyage were surprised on Sunday night when they stepped out through the door.

Mrs. Warren: "About the time stated we went to one of the upper decks where Mr. Warren wanted to take a walk, as was his custom before retiring. He did not, however, as the temperature had fallen very considerably and the air was almost frosty, although the night was perfect, clear and star light. We retired about 10:30 ship's time, and went to sleep immediately."

As passengers from all classes retired, they walked along the hallways, occasionally speaking in a hushed tone, before stepping into their staterooms and closing the doors with the final sound of a muffled click.

Mrs. Collyer: "It must have been a little after ten o'clock when my husband came in and woke me up. He sat and talked to me for how long I do not know, before he began to make ready to go to bed."

Miss Lehmann: "I had been in many beautiful hotels in Europe and in America but I have never seen anything quite as beautiful as this boat. I had a cabin by myself on the right side of the boat and it was on the outside so I had a port hole. I traveled second class but it was nicer than I had expected. The stewards were extremely courteous. I read until I got sleepy and then I turned the light off."

Mrs. Cook: "Well I must tell you that we had three nice men next to our cabin and they had a pillow fight and were having quite a jolly time when we went to sleep . . ."

Along with the lower fares that a third class passenger paid came additional roommates, frequently crowded into cabins equal in size to the smallest in first class.

Mr. Buckley: "This night of the wreck I was sleeping in my room on the Titanic, in the steerage. There were three other boys from the same place sleeping in the same room with me."

Miss Turja: "There were six of us in the one room . . ."

The first class smoking room. (*Olympic*)

The topics available for discussion in a 1912 smoking room were numerous. In matters of the United States, those with business interests might have discussed the ramifications of the recent breakup of two enormous trusts. The Supreme Court had ruled in 1911 in two separate cases that The Standard Oil Company and the American Tobacco Company had conspired to restrict competition. These trusts were being broken up by the government into smaller, individual companies. In October, Taft had approved plans by the Justice Department to bring an antitrust suit against U.S. Steel, which embroiled John D. Rockefeller and his ranks of lawyers in a highly publicized case. Clearly, these were warning shots across the bow of the International Mercantile Marine trust, owners of the *Titanic*.

The presidential election was warming up as well. The political landscape in 1912 would have dictated almost unanimously that the men from the United States, traveling in first class, were Republicans. The party was in the midst of what was shaping up to be a turbulent election in the fall. The primaries were a novelty in many of the states whereby voters were getting an opportunity for the first time to cast a vote on whom they thought should be the Fall candidate. Most missed their chance to par-

The heat was not working properly in some parts of the ship and now that the *Titanic* was sailing through a much colder climate influenced by the Grand Banks of Newfoundland, their rooms were getting a little uncomfortable.

Mrs. White: "Everybody knew we were in the vicinity of icebergs. Even in our staterooms it was so cold that we could not leave the porthole open. It was terribly cold."

Several dozen men were by now assembled in the first and second class smoking rooms, engaged in conversation or just passing the time quietly with a book.

ticipate in this new experience since they had been out of the country for March and most of April. In the Republican struggle for the nomination, President Taft was being challenged by the return of "Teddy" Roosevelt, who had just thrown his hat in the ring in February. Roosevelt was a very popular and strong challenger to the incumbent president, and Republicans were worried about the situation. Big business and the power establishment viewed him skeptically, and actually considered him a borderline radical because of the numerous reforms he ushered into law during his presidency from 1901 to 1909. Although they were not particularly worried about the Democratic Party, with the relatively unknown New Jersey Governor Woodrow Wilson emerging as the likely nominee, the Republican Party leaders did not look favorably upon Roosevelt's disruptive challenge to Taft. Voters watched developments with great interest.

Now that the passengers were retiring, many in the crew did the same.

Widgery: "In second class; I had charge of the bath on the forward deck; on the forward section of F deck. I went to bed right after inspection. I went to bed at 10 o'clock."

Lightoller finished making his rounds, and sometime around 10:30 came strolling along the port side of the boat deck. The area outside the officers' quarters was quiet, lit up with a glarish kind of light mounted on the wall of the deck house. As the ship moved forward a cold breeze blew gently across Lightoller's face from the Atlantic currents, whispering a warning of danger into his ears. Lightoller ducked into the door of the officers' quarters.

Lightoller: "The temperature on deck felt somewhere around the zero of Canada, although actually, it wasn't much below freezing, and I quickly rolled into my blankets. There I lay, turning over my past sins and future punishments, waiting until I could thaw and get to sleep."

As he lay in his bunk, he heard the electrical tapping of the wireless equipment. At this late hour on Sunday, there was a fraternity of radio operators communicating by morse code across the Atlantic airwaves. They shared a common bond through their exclusive code of radio buzzes, clicks and pauses. A good operator did not need to decipher the code back into words. Just as a written page is not examined letter by letter but instead comprehended in entire words, so too were these series of transmissions. Most of the operators in the Atlantic neighborhood that night were so fluent at the code that the individual transmissions came to them in words or entire thoughts.

On the *Carpathia*, the wireless operator, Harold Cottam was winding down his watch. In 1912, it was common on most vessels to have only one operator, and when he got tired, he would go to bed and the ship would be out of radio communication.

Smith: "What were you doing last Sunday evening about 10 o'clock?"
Cottam: "Receiving the news from Cape Cod, the long-distance station."
Smith: "What kind of news?"
Cottam: "General news."

Murdoch gazed out from the bridge at the darkness ahead. Many people today are under the impression that the captain was last seen on the bridge sometime around 9:30 p.m. as he left Lightoller, but Smith joined Murdoch during his watch as well, although there is no record of what they spoke about. Most likely, the talk was very similar to the one Smith had with Lightoller regarding visibility and the ice.

Smith: "Did you see the captain frequently Sunday night?"
Boxhall: "I saw him frequently during the watch, sir."

Smith: "From 8 o'clock on?"
Boxhall: "Up to the time of the accident."
Smith: "Up to the time the Titanic sank?"
Boxhall: "Yes, sir."
Smith: "How frequently?"
Boxhall: "On and off, most of the watch."

It is clear from Boxhall's observation that the captain did not retire from the bridge at 9:30 p.m. during Lightoller's watch, but instead kept a fairly regular presence most of the night. With his knowledge of the ice sightings from other liners and the locations they reported, it seems that Captain Smith was interested in Boxhall's calculations on their latest position.

Smith: "Where was he when you saw him at these times?"
Boxhall: "Sometimes out on the outer bridge. I would go out and report. I was working observations out, if you understand, most of that watch; working out different calculations and reporting to him. And that is how it was I came in contact with him so much."
Smith: "Where was he at other times when you saw him?"
Boxhall: "Sometimes in his chart room and sometimes on the bridge, and sometimes he would come to the wheelhouse, inside of the wheelhouse."

Smith: "How do you know he would go to the wheelhouse?"
Boxhall: "I would see him pass through."

With Lightoller's earlier comment that the Titanic should be upon the ice sometime around 11:00 p.m., Smith likely remained on the bridge throughout most of Murdoch's watch waiting for the encounter.

Just over the horizon lay the Californian. Captain Lord was just preparing to leave the bridge.

Lord: "At half past 10 it was 27–the water at night. The air was 30. When I came off the bridge at half past 10, I pointed out to the officer that I thought I saw a light coming along and it was a most peculiar light and we had been making mistakes all along with the stars, thinking they were signals. We could not distinguish where the sky ended and where the water commenced. You understand, it was a flat calm. He said he thought it was a star and I did not say anything more. I went down below. I was talking with the engineer about keeping the steam ready, and we saw these signals coming along and I said, 'There is a steamer coming. Let us go to the wireless and see what the news is.' But on our way down I met the operator coming and I said, 'Do you know anything?' He said, 'The Titanic.'"

Back on the Titanic, the hymn singing in the second class dining saloon finished and was followed with refreshments and more socializing. The group enjoyed the warm conversation that followed over tea. Some sat in the swivel dining chairs near the piano in the center of the room, while others stood.

Mrs. Cook: ". . . and Miss Wright sang two solos, the last hymn we had 'Eternal Father Strong to Save' chosen by Mr. Beauchamp. We then had a cup of tea and went to bed."

Mr. Beesley: "After the meeting had broken up, I talked with the Carters over a cup of coffee, said good night to them, and retired to my cabin at about quarter to eleven. They were good people and this world is much poorer by their loss. I had been fortunate enough to secure a two-berth cabin to myself–D56–quite close to the saloon and most convenient in every way for getting about the ship."

As the last of the passengers continued to retire, so too did the crew, particularly the stewards.

Crowe: "I was steward on the Titanic. I was on duty up until 10:30 on the night of the disaster, and I turned in about 11 o'clock. It *might have been a little later."*

Andrews: "I have been a steward now—this is my fourth year. I came off watch about a quarter to 11 and went down and turned in."

Meanwhile, many of society's elite were still relaxing in the small lounge surrounding the rear first class staircase on B deck, outside of the A la Carte Restaurant. Ismay had joined up with others coming out from dining and they were engaged in conversation.

Mrs. Smith: "My husband was with some friends just outside of what is known as the Parisian Café. I stayed up until 10:30 and then went to bed. I passed through the coffee room, and Mr. Ismay and his party were still there. The reason I am positive about the different time is because I asked my husband at the three intervals what time it was. I went to bed, and my husband joined his friends."

Eloise Smith left the reception area of the restaurant at approximately the same time Helen Candee, Hugh Woolner, Edward Kent, Clinch Smith, Bjorn Steffansson, and Edward Colley were walking in the opposite direction. The group abandoned the Reception Room and were heading for the

The Café Parisien. Among other purposes, it served as a haven for after-dinner dessert and drinks.

Café Parisien for drinks. As they traveled through the room before disappearing behind the double doors leading out to the café, Ismay probably glanced up from his conversation to see if he recognized them.

It is not clear who Ismay socialized with, but his small party could have discussed any number of current events. They may have been talking about the scheduled appearance in New York City of the London Symphony Orchestra for the first time in the United States, or perhaps the rapid growth of art museums—150 openings in 1912 alone. For the first time ever, international art exhibitions were planned for museums in Buffalo, Newark, and New York. Someone may have mentioned that J.P. Morgan was transporting his collection of international

art valued at $60 million over from London to the United States that year. Another person might have expressed their opinions on an exhibit of Picasso and Braque recently seen in Paris, where a daring style known as Cubism was displayed. This art form would surely have evoked opinions from anyone familiar with it. Someone may have mentioned their preference for Far Eastern art, such as Japanese paintings, which in turn lead to a discussion of the Japanese royal family's presentation of cherry trees to the United States. They were to be planted all along the river in Washington, D.C. that year. And on and on the discussion would have gone regarding the cultural items of interest to the wealthy and influential.

As the hour approached 11:00, the restaurant closed for the night and the small band in the reception area stopped playing. Ismay and others said their goodnights and departed. Ismay's cabin was just down the hall from the restaurant.

Smith: "What is the number of that room?"
Ismay: "B–52 is the room I had."
Smith: "You had the suite?"
Ismay: "I had the suite. I was sleeping in that room as a matter of fact."

Throughout the ship, the stewards began to shut down the rooms for the night.

Hardy: *"As second class steward, my duties were to be around the ship until 11 o'clock at night, when I would see to the closing up of the rooms and the turning out of the lights."*

With the *Titanic* now visible on the horizon, Captain Lord of the *Californian* issued an instruction to his wireless operator, Cyril Evans. To his ultimate misfortune, it was his last proactive attempt at preventing the unfolding tragedy.

Evans: *"The captain told me he was going to stop because of the ice, and the captain asked me if I had any boats, and I said the Titanic. He said, 'Better advise him we are surrounded by ice and stopped.' So I went to my cabin, and at 9:05 New York time I called him up. I said, 'MGY,' three times, and gave him my own call signal once, which is 'MWH.' I said, 'Say, old man, we are stopped and surrounded by ice.' He turned around and said, 'Shut up, shut up, I am busy. I am working Cape Race,' and at that I jammed him. By jamming we meant when somebody is sending a message to somebody else and you start to send at the same time, you jam him. He does not get his message. I was stronger than Cape Race. Therefore my signals came in with a bang, and he could read me and he could not read Cape Race."*

The private promenade attached to Bruce Ismay's suite. Unaware that the *Californian* at the moment was attempting to warn the *Titanic* of the danger just ahead, he may have taken some fresh air here for a few minutes prior to going to bed.

Lord: *"We told them we were stopped and surrounded by ice."*
Smith: *"Did the Titanic acknowledge that message?"*
Lord: *"Yes, sir. I believe he told the operator he had read it, and told him to shut up, or stand by, or something; that he was busy."*

To the distant observer, such as the *Carpathia*'s wireless operator, there was no sign that anything unusual was in the making. Harold Cottam listened in on routine message trafficking across the airwaves.

Smith: *"After you finished the Cape Cod business, what did you do then?"*
Cottam: *"At the latter end of the news from Cape Cod, he was sending a lot of messages for the Titanic."*
Smith: *"What time was that?"*
Cottam: *"About 11 o'clock."*

It was much quieter now on the *Titanic*. The few remaining stewards on duty were waiting to close the public rooms. Only the smoking rooms, one in each class, would remain open to the passengers after 11:00 p.m. Those in the other lounges either headed to one of these rooms, or headed to bed.

Almost 2,000 people were asleep on the *Titanic*. Some dreamed of people and places they left behind. Some dreamed of conversations and events that never were, and never would be. They dreamed about their destinations. They dreamed about their parents, about their brothers and sisters, or about their friends. Some dreamed of pleasant places while others dreamed of dark and ominous things. These dreams swirled around the darkened quarters and state-rooms of the ship much the same way smoke from the funnels drifted off into the starry sky behind the *Titanic*. They were the dreams of two thousand innocent souls who were about to be cast into a compelling and horrifying turn of events.

Eleven O'Clock

The dark icy waters waited patiently for the *Titanic* in the final hour of April 14, 1912. There was a calm about them, a smooth surface prepared for the largest ship in the world. First, the lights appeared far away on the horizon, drew closer, then passed by like some gigantic locomotive on a darkened plane. The water splashed around both sides of the bow as it parted to make way for the *Titanic*, casting a spray into the air in a false show of subservience to the huge liner. But the peacefulness of the glass-like surface and brilliant starry sky betrayed the *Titanic* from knowing what Fate had arranged for her ahead.

The *Titanic* defiantly steamed through the dangerous waters certain of her invincibility. The peril ahead was no match for the confidence on the bridge, and the ship sliced through the black night with a determination that would not be shaken by mere warnings of ice. The *Titanic* had her first date with New York City in a few days and nothing was going to delay her from that appointment.

Murdoch, no doubt, was attentive to the dark course ahead of him. As he stared into the starlit night from the wing of the bridge, Smith came by one last time. Boxhall's account is repeated for emphasis.

Smith: "Did you see the captain frequently Sunday night?"
Boxhall: "I saw him frequently during the watch, sir."
Smith: "From 8 o'clock on?"
Boxhall: "Up to the time of the accident."

The *Titanic*'s officers expected to be upon the ice around 11:00 p.m. and Smith and Murdoch searched the darkness for it. Even though the lack of a swell and absence of a moon would make it difficult to spot an iceberg, the starlit night with clear visibility, combined with such a smooth sea, probably had a calming effect on the captain. At 11:00 p.m., there was still no sign of ice.

Down below, all six boiler rooms were in service and the stokers were periodically feeding each boiler with coal. An indicator in the rooms kept them informed when each one needed to be fed and the process was moving along smoothly. In boiler room number 6, Frederick Barrett and George Beauchamp were feeding the fires and looking forward to the end of their shift in an hour. There was always time to talk with others and this night was no different. The engineers on duty, Jonathan Shepherd and John Hesketh, circulated about the forward boiler rooms.

In contrast to the heat in the boiler rooms, the predominant observation by most passengers that night was of the low temperature. Many of the staterooms and public lounges were cold, hinting at an ongoing problem that Thomas Andrews and his staff had still not resolved.

Mrs. Shelley: ". . . this room was just as cold as the cell from which we had been removed, and on asking the steward to have heat turned on, he answered that it was impossible as the heating system for the second class cabins refused to work. That of all the second class cabins, only three—the three first cabins to be reached by the heat—had any heat at all, and that the heat was so intense there that the occupants had complained to the purser, who had ordered the heat shut off entirely. Consequently, the rooms were like ice houses all of the voyage."

Mrs. Shelley made a point of asking steerage passengers after the accident about whether they had heat in their area and was told of the same conditions. So, as the temperature continued to drop during the afternoon and into Sunday night, the cold crept through many areas of the ship. The icy hand of death seemed to be wrapping its fingers around the vessel.

Mrs. Bishop: "We noticed the intense cold. In fact, we had noticed that about eleven o'clock that night. It was uncomfortable cold in the lounge."

Jack Thayer was finishing his walk. Rather than a premonition of trouble in the air, there was the satisfaction of an excellent voyage to think over in the breeze of the moving vessel.

Mr. Thayer: "I went onto the boat deck. It was deserted and lonely. The wind whistled through the stays, and blackish smoke poured out of the three forward funnels. The fourth funnel was a dummy for ventilation purposes. It was the kind of a night that made one feel glad to be alive. About eleven o'clock I went below to my stateroom."

With the lounges closing up and the general lateness of the day, the public areas of the ship were just about empty, except for the smoking room in each class.

Hardy: "The way we work on board ship, all unnecessary lights are out at 11, and then there are four bedroom stewards kept on from 11 until 12. Then two bedroom stewards come along for the middle watch from 12 until 4 in the morning. Then they are relieved at half past 5 by all hands for the day, until the following night."

A dozen or so men congregated for a drink, card playing, and conversation in the first class smoking room. These men were the night owls of 1912. Among them were Peuchen and three other acquaintances.

Mr. Peuchen: "We sat chatting and smoking there until probably 20 minutes after 11, or it may have been a little later than that. I then bid them good night and went to my room. I was located on C deck, stateroom 104. Mr. Hugo Ross, who was my friend, I think was in A–12"

Nearby, another party of mutual acquaintances sat at a table. Lucien Smith had just come up from the Café Parisien to join them.

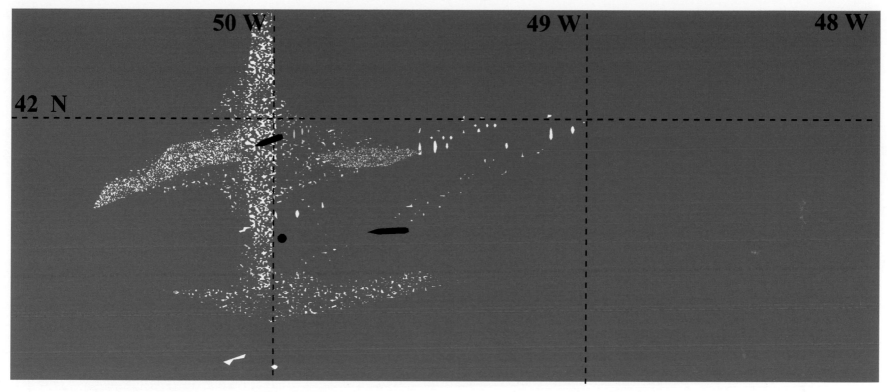

The position of the *Titanic* at 11:00 p.m. The *Californian* has come to a stop and is now surrounded by ice on the edge of the field.

Mr. Woolner: *"I was in the smoking room."*
Smith: *"Who was in there with you, if any-one, that you now know or could name?"*
Mr. Woolner: *"Mr. Steffanson, a Swedish gentleman whose acquaintance I made on board, sat at my table."*
Smith: *"Anyone else?"*
Mr. Woolner: *"Yes; a Mr. Kennett. I think, but I am not quite certain, a Mr. Smith. He had been with us quite a short time before."*

While Peuchen left the first class smoking room, Beesley lay in his second class cabin bunk, reading.

Mr. Beesley: *"After undressing and climb-ing into the top berth, I read from about quarter past eleven to the time we struck. During this time I noticed particularly the increased vibration of the ship and I assumed that we were going at a higher speed than at any other time since we sailed from Queenstown. Two things led me to this conclusion. First, that as I sat on the sofa undressing, with bare feet on the floor, the jar of the vibration came up from the engines below very noticeably. And second, that as I sat up in the berth reading, the spring mattress supporting me was vibrating more rapidly than usual. This cradle-like motion was always noticeable as one lay in bed, but that night there was certainly a marked increase in the motion."*

As the earlier part of the hour ticked away without incident, Captain Smith must have concluded that things were under control, and stepped into his quarters. Murdoch would certainly let him know if there were any significant changes in the situation. Without realizing that they were just then entering the worst part of the ice region, the captain walked off the bridge and back to his room.

No one will ever know what Captain Smith was thinking as he laid in his bed that Sunday night. He may have thought about his dinner conversations at the Widener party. He may have thought about passing within view of the *Olympic* the next day, traveling in the opposite direction to Southampton. It was a proud time for him. Contentedly, he drifted off to sleep.

Murdoch continued his watch, unaware of the magnitude of the ice field they had entered. It is statistically likely that the *Titanic* was steaming through the ice region for some time, as documented the following morning.

Bisset: "I have never since seen, and never wished to see, so much ice as I had seen that day, so far south in the Atlantic."

Mr. Gracie: "Away off in the distance we saw these icebergs in the direction from which we had come during the night."

Moore: "There were lots of bergs around and there was a great field of ice, I should say between 20 and 30 miles long."
Newlands: "Solid ice?"
Moore: "Yes. The stretch of ice was very low, but there were also big bergs."
Newlands: "Would it have been possible for a ship to make its way among that ice?"
Moore: "No, sir."

Etches: "Well, there were three at different points, but the field extended such a long distance and they were in the field apparently. But the separate bergs that we saw were a long way from the field of ice, the floating ones. They were separated from the field of ice."

Hichens: "In the morning when it turned daybreak, we could see icebergs everywhere. The icebergs was up on every point of the compass, almost."

Mr. Peuchen: "There were several icebergs. There were at least three icebergs that you could see plainly. There was one toward the front, the way our boat was facing, and one on the west. I should think there was one

toward the north and one toward the south. We seemed to be in a nest of icebergs, with some smaller ones, of course. I think you could see—at least to count, I think—five. They were at least 100 feet high, two of them, and of a width I should think of 300 feet and 400 feet long. Somewhat like an island. Another was sort of smaller in size. Some were jagged, but very high, and a number of them not so high."

Mrs. White: "After we got aboard the Carpathia we could see 13 icebergs and 45 miles of floating ice, distinctly, right around us in every direction."

Rostron: "I also saw icebergs all around me. There were about 20 icebergs that would be anywhere from about 150 to 200 feet high and numerous smaller bergs; also numerous what we call growlers. You would not call them bergs. They were anywhere from 10 to 12 feet high and 10 to 15 feet long above the water."

Lowe: "I did not count them, but I should say anywhere up to 20. I should say 4 to 5 miles. All around."
Smith: "Were they all within a range of 4 or 5 miles?"
Lowe: "Yes. All within a radius—at the outside—of 6 miles."

Pitman: "There were numerous bergs around me, maybe half a dozen. Some may have been 100 feet or 150 feet. That high above the water."

Captain Moore: "In consulting my officers as to the breadth of this, one said it was 5 miles and another said it was 6 miles. That was the width of it. Of course, it extended as far as the eye could reach, north and south. I should say 20 miles, perhaps more than that. It was field ice and bergs; bergs interspersed in the pack, and bowlders. I should say altogether, there must have been between 40 and 50 I counted that morning."

Although the crew on watch were keeping a sharp eye out for ice, it was too dark to realize what they were then entering. If lights could have been suddenly turned on for the whole area, it would have been a shock to see the extent of ice through which the giant steamship was racing. But there were no lights. They could see nothing.

Newlands: "It is always difficult to see them at night?"
Boxhall: "No, not always. On such a night as that, even if there is no moon, you can very, very often see an iceberg by the water on the sides of it–that is, if there is a little breeze. But when the water is in one of those oily calms . . . it was like an oily calm when the Titanic struck, and for a long, long time after we were in the boats, and you could not see anything at all then."

Ironically, the design of the bridge placed the man at the wheel, Quartermaster Hichens, in a secluded room. Any change in direction would be issued to him as a command from an officer.

Hichens: "I am in the wheelhouse and of course, I couldn't see nothing. I might as well be locked in a cell. The only thing I could see was my compass."

In the meantime, the *Californian* remained stopped in the ice. A lethargic atmosphere settled over the ship while she waited for daylight to proceed on to Boston through these dangerous conditions. Ernest Gill was a seaman on the *Californian*.

Gill: "The stars were shining brightly. It was very clear and I could see for a long distance. The ship's engines had been stopped since 10:30 and she was drifting amid floe ice. I looked over the rail on the starboard side and saw lights of a very large steamer about 10 miles away. I could see her broadside lights. I could see her over there, a big ship, and a couple of rows of lights. I watched her for fully a minute. They could not have helped but see her from the bridge and lookout. It was now 12 o'clock and I went to my cabin. I woke my mate, William Thomas. He heard the ice crunching alongside the ship and asked, 'Are we in the ice?'" I replied, 'Yes, but it must be clear off to the starboard, for I saw a big vessel going along full speed.'"

The *Californian's* wireless operator continued to listen to the *Titanic's* outgoing messages even after trying to warn the liner of ice and being told to shut up. Perhaps he was curious about the communications of such a wealthy clientele. Soon, however the outgoing messages stopped, and Evans called it a night.

Bride: "As far as I can recollect, Phillips had finished working with Cape Race 10 minutes before the collision with the iceberg. He made mention of the fact when I turned out."

Evans: "The last time I exchanged signals with them? At 11:25 I still had the phones on my ears and heard him still working Cape Race about two or three minutes before the half hour ship's time, that was, and at 11:35 I put the phones down and took off my clothes and turned in."

Lord: *"I went past his room at about a quarter to 12, and there was no light in there. That would indicate he was asleep."*

As the *Titanic* steamed into the cold heart of the ice field, the participants in one of the greatest disasters began to position themselves for the history books. The *Californian*'s wireless operator turned off his set and went to bed as Captain Lord was proceeding to the chart room to lie down. No one on either the *Titanic* or the *Californian* had even an inkling of the impending disaster.

The last of the day stewards on the *Titanic* were also heading into their bunks.

Hardy: *"I did not retire until 25 minutes after 11. I went down to my room after going around the ship and seeing that all the unnecessary lights were out."*
Fletcher: *"Where was your berth located?"*
Hardy: *"E deck. Right amidships, as near amidships as possible."*

The crewmen who were on duty were having a fairly easy time of it on Sunday night and passed away the minutes peacefully, most of them in their own area just under the deck of the bow. Sitting around at tables, some joked with each other and talked about anything to keep boredom at bay. Others read in out of the way places, like a corner of the mess room. Some stood just outside of the well deck door, having a smoke. It was a relaxing time.

Haines: *"I was standing under the forecastle, waiting for any orders so that I would be available if they wanted me. It being Sunday night, the men did not work Sunday night, and the men were in the mess room, and I was outside, sir. If it had been any other night, we would have been washing the decks."*

Buley: *"I was in the watch on deck, the starboard watch. If it was Sunday night, we never had anything to do. Ordinary nights we should have been scrubbing the decks. I was sitting in the mess, reading at the time."*

Evans: *"On Sunday we do not do anything in regard to scrubbing and the like of that. Sunday night was my watch on deck, and I was sitting at the table reading a book . . ."*

Bourne: *"Where were you at the time of the accident?"*
Brice: *"Outside of the seamen's mess room."*

The ship's barber, long off duty, was taking it easy as well.

Weikman: *"I was sitting in my barber shop on Sunday night, April 14, 1912 at 11:40 p.m. . . ."*

Since midnight would mark yet another change of watch throughout the ship, the quiet found on board at 11:30 p.m. on a Sunday night at sea was savored by the crew.

Jack Thayer left the deserted deck to turn in. He descended the Grand Staircase from the boat deck to A, then A to B, and then one more flight of stairs to C deck, passing an empty foyer on each level. There must have been some pleasure in walking the ship without hundreds of passengers about, like having the *Titanic* all to oneself for just a while. The only sound was the hum and vibration of the engines off in the distance. Reaching C deck, Jack headed to the hallway on the right, and walked along the intricately carved paneling until he reached his cabin number.

Mr. Thayer: *"I occupied a stateroom adjoining that of my father and mother on the port side of C deck. After a short conversation with my father and mother, and saying good night to them, I stepped into my room to put on pajamas expecting to have another delightful night's rest like the four preceding. I had called 'Good Night' to my father and mother in the next room. In order to get plenty of air I had half opened the port, and the breeze was coming through with a quiet humming whistle. There was a steady rhythmic pulsation of the engines and screws, the feel and hearing of which becomes second nature to one, after a few hours at sea. It was a fine night for sleeping and with the day's air and exercise, I was sleepy."*

Cunningham: "I was stateroom steward on the Titanic. I was stationed on D deck forward that night; to answer bells–the wants of any passenger. I had just been called to go on watch. I was lying on my bunk with my clothes on. One of the other stateroom stewards; he said, 'It is time to turn out.'"

While the lookouts continued their watch, they assumed the horizon was open to their view and did not realize there were hidden masses of ice lurking in the darkness, obscuring parts of the skyline. One of the objects being obscured was the *Californian* to the north, stopped on the other side of an iceberg floating between the two ships.

Burton: "You saw some light on the horizon that night?"
Fleet: "Not on the lookout sir."
Burton: "Not on the lookout?"
Fleet: "The only thing we saw was the iceberg. We had no lights on that watch."
Burton: "You did not see this light of which mention has been made until you got into the lifeboat?"
Fleet: "No, sir."

The minutes passed quietly. It was 11:35. Boxhall was off on an errand leaving Murdoch, Moody, Hichens and Olliver on the bridge. Murdoch was out on the starboard wing. Moody was inside the bridge. Olliver was attending to the miscellaneous maintenance tasks of 1912 bridge equipment. Hichens was inside the wheelhouse.

Meanwhile, Captain Smith, Chief Officer Wilde, Second Officer Lightoller, Third Officer Pitman, and Fifth Officer Lowe all rested in the peace of their cabins in various stages of sleep.

It was now 11:38. Murdoch, Moody, Fleet and Lee all kept watch, thoughts drifting as they will to various things, such as prior conversations, plans for the future, wishes for the present, and ideas of idle entertainment. Boxhall completed his errand and was walking along the boat deck.

Boxhall: "I was just approaching the bridge. Starboard side."

Olliver moved on to examine a compass just behind the bridge.

Olliver: "I happened to be looking at the lights in the standing compass at the time. That was my duty, to look at the lights in the standing compass, and I was trimming them so that they would burn properly."

Passengers were in their beds. There must have been something cozy about being under the blankets on such a cold night, being transported by the world's largest liner to New York. Many could not stay awake for long. A view of the *Titanic* from a distance showed cabin lights over the last couple of hours blinking off one by one as tired passengers settled in for sleep.

Mrs. White: "I was just sitting on the bed, just ready to turn the lights out."

Henry Stengel and his wife had turned their lights off some time earlier and were asleep. As if subconsciously aware of the impending danger, he did not sleep soundly. In the darkness of their cabin, his sudden restlessness woke up his wife.

Mr. Stengel: "I had retired. My wife called me. I was moaning in my sleep. My wife called me and says, 'Wake up, you are dreaming.'"

Then it happened. Fleet took notice

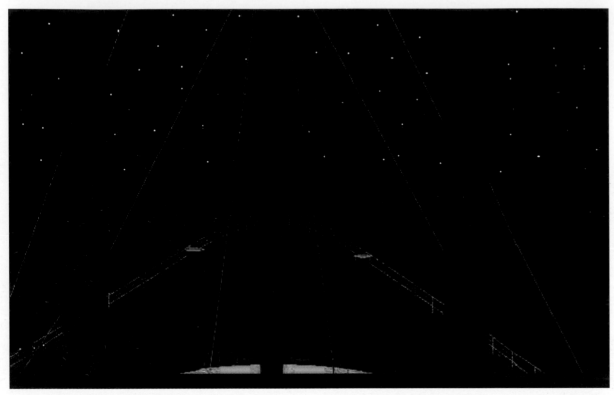

The iceberg emerges from the dark, directly in the path of the *Titanic*.

Each second from this moment was critical. There was a twelve story high, 882 foot long, 46,000 ton object racing at 22½ knots directly toward a mountain of ice. As to what happened in the seconds following the sighting is open for discussion, due to some inconsistency in Fleet's comments in the wake of the tragedy. A reconstruction of events based on the following selected observations seems to be the most plausible.

Smith: "What did you report when you saw this black mass Sunday night?"
Fleet: "I reported an iceberg right ahead."
Smith: "To whom did you report that?"
Fleet: "I struck three bells first."

Boxhall: "At the time of the impact I was just coming along the deck and almost abreast of the captain's quarters, and I heard the report of three bells. That signifies something has been seen ahead."

Three bells are a warning to the bridge that there is something in the ship's path. Although not on the bridge at the time, Lightoller's own feelings about sightings are repeated.

Lightoller: "Speaking personally, I never rely on any lookout. I keep a lookout myself, and so does every other officer."

of something in the blackness that seemed like it had a shape. The shape took form and emerged as a definite object, a "black mass" as he later described it, directly in front of the *Titanic*.

Fleet: "Before I reported, I said, 'There is ice ahead,' and then I put my hand over to the bell and rang it three times, and then I went to the phone."

The bell was audible within the forecastle where the crew on duty was relaxing.

Osman: ". . . outside the seamen's dining room. I was waiting for one bell, which they strike one bell just before the quarter of the hour, before the four hours when you get a call to relieve. And I heard three bells strike, and I thought there was a ship ahead."

After hearing three bells, Murdoch needed time to see the object for himself and identify what it was. It was so dark that the task was not easy.

Olliver: "When I heard the report, I looked, but could not see anything . . ."

Once Murdoch was able to distinguish what the object was, the fact that it was dead in the *Titanic*'s path required him to assess whether one side looked easier to get around than the other. The iceberg and the best path around it had to be studied for a moment. Since it was so dark, it was impossible to make an instantaneous decision as it might have been under better lighting conditions. All of this only took seconds, but they were critical seconds which seemed excruciatingly long to Fleet and Lee.

Burton: "Did you notice that the boat was bearing out to the left from the berg, or was it going right ahead toward it?"
Fleet: "It was going right ahead, as far as we knew."

Murdoch made the decision to go around the left side of the iceberg. Rushing onto the bridge, he yelled out his order to the quartermaster. Moody ran to the wheelhouse to see that the order was carried out. Boxhall was still on the starboard side of the boat deck, with only the sounds of the bridge available for his observation.

Boxhall: "Almost at the same time I heard the first officer give the order 'Hard astarboard,' and the engine telegraph rang."

With Moody in the wheelhouse, and Boxhall out on the starboard boat deck, Murdoch ran to the telemotors and moved them himself to full astern. By now the iceberg was much closer and adrenaline began flowing through all on watch.

Hichens: "The chief officer [Murdoch] rushed from the wing to the bridge, or I imagine so, sir. He rushed to the engines. I heard the telegraph bell ring; also give the order 'Hard astarboard', with the sixth officer standing by my left side, repeated the order, 'Hard astarboard. The helm is over, sir'."
Smith: "Is that the only order you received before the collision or impact?"
Hichens: "That is all, sir."

Fleet and Lee watched for a few seconds as the *Titanic* continued gliding straight toward the iceberg. They did not have a view of the bridge from their location because of the canvas backdrop to the nest, so they were uncertain as to what was going on there.

Smith: "Was that a cold night, Sunday?"
Fleet: "Yes, sir."
Smith: "What protection against the weather have you in the crow's nest?"
Fleet: "We have nothing ahead, and there are just two bits of screen behind us."
Smith: "Canvas?"
Fleet: "Yes, sir."

Worried about how close the iceberg was getting, Fleet reached for the phone and rang up the bridge.

Burton: "Did you notice how quickly they turned the course of the boat after you sounded the gongs?"
Fleet: "No, sir. They did not do it until I went to the telephone."

There is an implication in the way Fleet makes this observation that he did not go straight for the telephone, but instead waited some short period of time. After all, three bells were the official warning to the bridge that there was an object straight ahead of the ship. When the *Titanic* continued heading right at it, he chose to call the bridge, not knowing that the officers were

First Officer Murdoch

After Moody saw the first officer's command of "hard astarboard" carried out at the wheel by Hichens, he probably stepped into the doorway between the wheelhouse and the bridge to watch the result, and await any further commands from Murdoch. The two officers now watched with increasing alarm as the ship continued to bear down on the ice. Right about this time the phone from the crow's nest began to ring. At such a critical moment, with Murdoch taking evasive maneuvers and Moody awaiting his next command, the telephone call from the look-out nest was ignored.

Sixth Officer Moody

already acting on the warning.

Fleet: "That is all we have to do up in the nest; to ring the bell, and if there is any danger ring them up on the telephone."
Smith: "The fact that you did ring them up on the telephone indicated that you thought there was danger?"
Fleet: "Well, it was so close to us. That is why I rang them up."

Mr. Peuchen: "I spoke to him [Fleet] about it . . . In the conversation he said he rang three bells, and then he signaled the bridge."

Mr. Peuchen: "The only thing he [Fleet] said was that he did not get any reply from the bridge."
Smith: "From the telephone?"
Mr. Peuchen: "I heard afterwards that really the officers were not required to reply. I spoke to the second officer on the boat regarding the conversation, and he told me it is simply a matter of whether the officer wishes to reply or not. He gets the information, probably, and acts right on it without attempting to reply to the crow's nest."

Just about the time the telephone rang, the engine room disengaged the forward propulsion in preparation for throwing

the ship into reverse. This, in the period of thirty seconds or less, had virtually no effect on the 22 ½ knot forward speed of the ship. But the telemotor's communication sent the crew below into action.

Barrett: "There is a clock face in the stoke-hole and a red light goes up for 'Stop.' I was talking to Mr. Hesketh when the red light came up, and I shouted, 'Shut all the dampers.'"

Fleet stood at the phone waiting for a response. The combination of still seeing no change in the direction of the *Titanic* and the lack of response from the bridge on the phone left a bad impression with Fleet that he would later recount to a number of people. While standing there with the phone in his hand, waiting in vain for someone from the bridge to answer his call, the *Titanic* finally seemed to react.

Fleet: "But when I was at the phone, it was going to port."
Fletcher: "How long were you at the telephone?"
Fleet: "I suppose half a minute."
Fletcher: "When you turned from the telephone and observed the course of the ship, you saw she had turned to port?"
Fleet: "Yes, sir."
Fletcher: "Did she turn immediately and suddenly, or gradually to port."
Fleet: "Just started to go as I looked up."

There was just not enough time to steer out of the way of the iceberg. There was the warning from the crow's nest, Murdoch's assessment of the situation, his commands for evasive action, the implementation of those commands at the wheel and in the engine room, and finally the handling response of an 882 foot long liner. To Murdoch's credit, he came very close to pulling it off, for the bow of the *Titanic* was turning when they met the iceberg. Had he

11:40 p.m. – The moment of impact.

been given just a few more seconds, the enormous ship would have cleared the iceberg all together. But the window for evasive action was too small, and just as the hopes of Murdoch, Moody, Fleet and Lee were rising, the ship began to shudder, as the ice moved along the starboard side. Impact.

Smith: "How large did it get to be, finally when it struck the ship?"
Fleet: "When we were alongside, it was a little bit higher than the forecastle head."

Olliver: "When I heard the report, I looked, but could not see anything, and I left that and came and was just entering on the bridge just as the shock came. I knew we had touched something."

Smith: "Was the blow felt immediately?"
Boxhall: "A slight impact."
Smith: "How slight?"
Boxhall: "It did not seem to me to be very serious. I did not take it seriously."

Smith: "When she struck this obstacle, or this black mass, was there much of a jar to the ship?"
Fleet: "No sir."
Smith: "Was there any?"

The exact location where the ship first came into contact with the iceberg.

Fleet: "Just a slight grinding noise."
Smith: "Did it alarm you seriously when it struck?"
Fleet: "No sir. I thought it was a narrow shave."
Smith: "Did any of the ice break onto the decks?"
Fleet: "Yes. Some on the forecastle light and some on the weather deck."

The passengers who were still awake were unaware of the drama taking place over the last minute, but most of them soon felt a strange sensation travel through the *Titanic.*

Mr. Beesley: "And then, as I read in the quietness of the night, broken only by the muffled sounds that came to me through the ventilators of stewards talking and moving along the corridors, when nearly all the passengers were in their cabins, some asleep in beds, others undressing, and others only just down from the smoking room and still discussing many things, there came what seemed to me nothing more than an extra heave of the engines and a more than usually obvious dancing motion of the mattress on which I sat. Nothing more than that—no sound of a crash or of anything else. No sense of shock, no jar that felt like one heavy body meeting another. And presently the

Pieces of ice broke off and crumbled down onto both decks shown in this picture.

same thing repeated with about the same intensity. The thought came to me that they must have still further increased the speed. And all this time the Titanic was being cut open by the iceberg and water was pouring in her side, and yet no evidence that would indicate such a disaster had been presented to us. It fills me with astonishment now to think of it."

Mr. Thayer: "I wound my watch—it was 11:45 p.m. and was just about to step into bed when I seemed to sway slightly. I immediately realized that the ship had veered to port as though she had been gently pushed. If I had had a brimful glass of water in my hand not a drop would have been spilled, the shock was so slight."

Those on duty watched the iceberg move menacingly along the right side of the ship. It must have been a fascinating break in the monotony of their watch to see this enormous chunk of ice glide by from the edge of darkness. The spectacle likely left everyone in a momentary state of inaction.

Olliver: "The iceberg was about the height of the boat deck; if anything, just a little higher. It was almost alongside of the boat. The top did not touch the side of the boat, but it was almost alongside of the boat. The sound was like she touched something, a long grinding sound, like. The shape was pointed. I only saw the tip of the iceberg. It was not white, as I expected to see an iceberg. It was a kind of dark blue hue. It was not white."

Of course, it was not the visible part of the iceberg that was of concern. Beneath the water was a larger portion which opened up the *Titanic* by separating plates and rivets. Captain Moore of the *Mount Temple* had seen enough icebergs to comment.

Captain Moore: "In some cases you may get close to them. In others they have long spurs running underneath the water. In daytime in clear water you can see the spurs, because they show quite green under the water."

With the stop order appearing on the indicator, firemen in all boiler rooms were shutting the dampers that fed air to the fires. Barrett and others in room 6 were busy with the same when the incredible happened.

Barrett: "That order was obeyed, but the crash came before we had them all shut. There was a rush of water into my stokehole. We were standing on plates about six feet above the tank tops, and the water came in about two feet above the plates."

Steward Crawford ran out of the B deck door that faced the bow in time to document how high the iceberg was.

Crawford: "I was on watch until 12 o'clock, and I was waiting for my relief to come up. I was to be relieved at 12 o'clock. I heard the crash, and I went out on the outer deck and saw the iceberg floating alongside. It looked like a large, black object going alongside the ship. I could not see the top because there was a deck above us."

Another crewman under the forecastle did not run out to see the passing iceberg, but described the sound of it.

Brice: "It was like a heavy vibration."
Bourne: "But it made a noise?"
Brice: "A rumbling noise, sir."
Bourne: "That continued how long?"
Brice: "About 10 seconds; somewhere about that."

A number of passengers took notice of the sound created by the iceberg as it rubbed along just outside their portholes.

White: "It was just as though we went over about a thousand marbles."

Mr. Chambers: ". . . I noticed no very great shock, the loudest noise by far being that of jangling chains whipping along the side of the ship."

Chambers' observation is an interesting one. Did he actually hear chains? If so, that would imply that the iceberg grabbed the anchor on the starboard side and yanked it alongside the ship. More likely, he probably heard the sound of ice resonating along the rivets above his deck, with chunks of it falling off. The *Titanic* continued forward, presenting the illusion that the iceberg itself was moving toward the stern.

Mr. Harder: "We had (cabin) E-50; that is on E deck. At twenty minutes to twelve we were not asleep yet, and I heard this thump. It was not a loud thump; just a dull thump. Then I could feel the boat quiver and could feel a sort of rumbling, scraping noise along the side of the boat. When I went to the porthole, I saw this iceberg go by. The porthole was closed. The iceberg was, I should say, about fifty to one hundred feet away. I should say it was about as high as the top deck of the boat. I just got a glimpse of it, and it is hard to tell how high it was."

Mr. Peuchen: ". . . I know a great many of the passengers were made afraid by this ice-berg passing their portholes. The ship shoved past this ice, and a great many of them told me afterwards they could not understand this thing moving past them—those that were awakened at the time. In fact, it left ice on some of the portholes, they told me."

Mr. Stengel: "Another passenger said that the ice came into his porthole. His porthole was open."

Mr. Harper: "Our stateroom was pretty well forward on the starboard side and was perhaps thirty feet or more above the water. My first knowledge about it was that of being awakened by a grinding sound that seemed to come from far below our deck. It was not a loud crash; it was felt almost as much as heard. So the moment I was awakened by the noise . . . I sat up in bed and looked out of the nearest port. I saw an iceberg only a few feet away, apparently racing aft at high speed and crumbling as it went."

Murdoch watched in disbelief as this floating mass of ice passed along the bridge, still rubbing along the side of the *Titanic* as though the two were magnetized to each other. While the slight tremor from the impact rattled the ship—and Murdoch's nerves—the first officer attempted to salvage an already bad situation by getting the stern of the ship away from the iceberg.

Olliver: "I know the orders I heard when I was on the bridge was after we had struck the iceberg. I heard hard aport, and there was the man at the wheel and the officer. The officer was seeing it was carried out right. Mr. Moody, the sixth officer, was stationed in the wheelhouse."
Burton: "Where was the iceberg, do you think, when the helm was shifted?"
Olliver: "The iceberg was away up stern."

By this time, the iceberg was passing along the second class area back near the fourth smokestack. Someone in the second class smoking lounge happened to see it come along outside the outer promenade windows and yelled out to everyone to look.

Beesley: ". . . one of them had seen through the windows an iceberg go by towering above the decks. He had called their attention to it and they all watched it disappear, but had then at once resumed the game."

About 30 seconds after the iceberg struck the bow, it passed along the poop deck—the last deck at the very stern of the ship. There, Quartermaster Rowe stood on duty, where his watch was suddenly visited by a large wall of ice.

Burton: "Just where were you when you saw the iceberg?"

Rowe: "On the poop sir. Underneath the after bridge. I felt a slight jar and I looked at my watch. It was a fine night and it was then 20 minutes to 12. I looked toward the starboard side of the ship and saw a mass of ice."

Burton: "About how high was that iceberg?"

Rowe: "Roughly, 100 feet, sir."

Burton: "Was there anything distinctive about the color of that iceberg?"

Rowe: "Not a bit, sir. Just like ordinary ice."

Burton: "But you saw it brushing by?"

Rowe: "Yes, sir. It was very close to the ship, almost touching it."

Burton: "How far would you say?"

Rowe: "It was so near that I thought it was going to strike the bridge."

Burton: "Did it strike the bridge?"

Rowe: "No, sir. Never."

Burton: "Only 10 or 20 feet away?"

Rowe: "Not that far, sir."

Burton: "Could you hear the ice scraping along on the boat where you were?"

Rowe: "No, sir."

Burton: "So you do not know whether it was rubbing against the hull there or not?"

Rowe: "No, sir."

Burton: "What is your best judgement about that?"

Rowe: "I do not think it was."

Burton: "How near were you to the starboard side of the boat when you first noticed it rubbing."

Rowe: "About 8 or 10 feet. I went to the side."

Murdoch knew from the shudder that the ship may have been damaged. After issuing his command to "hard aport," he rushed to the panel for the watertight doors.

Burton: "Do you know whether the watertight doors were closed or not?"

Olliver: "The first officer closed the watertight doors, sir."

Burton: "When?"

Olliver: "On the bridge, just after she struck."

Burton: "How did you know they were closed?"

Olliver: "Because Mr. Murdoch reported, and as I entered the bridge I saw him about the lever."

Burton: "Did he have any way of telling whether they were closed or not?"

Olliver: "There is a lever on the bridge to close the watertight doors, and he turned the lever over and closed them."

Burton: "Was there an instrument there to show the doors as they closed? Did you ever see one of those instruments?"

Olliver: "No. I never saw one."

Burton: "With little lights that burn up as each door closes, and then go out?"

Olliver: "No, sir."

Burton: "There was no instrument like that on the Titanic?"

Olliver: "I did not see any."

Newlands: "How do you close them?"

Pitman: "There is a lever 7 or 8 inches long."

Newlands: "Where is that?"

Pitman: "On the bridge, close to the man at the wheel. All you have to do is to just pull it over like that [indicating by describing half a circle]."

Newlands: "What is the effect of that?"

Pitman: "That closes the doors electrically."

Fletcher: "They just come right down, and they do not open and shut, out and in?"

Pitman: "Oh no. Straight down that way [indicating]. There is an electrical bell beside them. You ring that a few minutes before closing so as to give anyone a chance to get out of the way who might be standing underneath."

Taylor: "I was asleep when the accident

A Picture Tells A Thousand Words

This photograph was taken by Father Browne on Thursday morning as the *Titanic* steamed from Cherbourg, France to Queenstown, Ireland. Captain Smith was apparently putting the ship through a trial; some speculate that he was testing the compasses on the bridge. The picture is striking in that it reveals the Titanic's turning abilities. In the distance and in the foreground, the wake from the propellers shows that the ship could turn sharply. It is important to note too, that on the morning of this photograph the *Titanic* was traveling at a reduced speed compared to that fateful Sunday night.

Lightoller: "When a vessel is running at a lower rate of speed, she is slower on the helm...which means that she would take longer to swing on her helm in proportion to her reduced speed."

Why was the *Titanic* unable to steer out of the iceberg's path? Two notable theories suggest an undersized rudder and/or a mistaken command by Murdoch. But an undersized rudder would not produce a crisp turn as shown in the photograph, so it seems safe to conclude that the *Titanic* did not suffer from such a shortcoming. But what was the effect of Murdoch's decision to reverse the engines? This is less certain.

There was nothing out of the ordinary in Murdoch's decision to reverse the engines when he saw ice. The *Californian* did the same thing an hour earlier.

Lord: "But on seeing the ice, we were so close we had to reverse the engine and put her full speed astern ..."

The center propeller ran only in the forward direction. It could not be reversed. Once the command for full astern was issued, this propeller slowed to a stop, gradually reducing flow across the rudder. The other two propellers were driven by the steam reciprocating engines and could be reversed. But like any mechanical drive system, immediate reversal was impossible. The forward speed had to be reduced first. Whereas Hichens promptly put the helm over, it took time for Murdoch to reach the telemotors and signal the engine room. It took time for the engine room staff to react. It took time to reverse the engines. And it took time for the propellers to regain an effective revolution. It is intriguing to consider the effect reversed propellers had on the *Titanic*'s turning response, pulling water back along the forward moving rudder. But it is questionable how much influence "full astern" would have had within the 30 to 60 critical seconds following the sighting.

Senator Bourne: "Taking a ship of the Titanic's tonnage, going at a speed of 21 knots, in what distance could you stop if you reversed the engine?
Lightoller: "Reversed the engine full speed astern?"
Bourne: "Yes."
Lightoller: "I forgot what the stopping time was. We tried it in Belfast. I suppose about a minute and a half, maximum."
Bourne: "And within what distance; what part of a mile?"
Lightoller: "A quarter of a mile; about a quarter of a mile."

The *Titanic* was traveling at 22½ knots at the time ice was sighted, and struck it hard enough to puncture the hull. Observations indicate the iceberg continued to the stern and quickly faded far into the darkness, suggesting that engine reversal

The propellers and the rudder. (*Olympic*)

was lagging - if not outright absent - during the critical seconds prior to the collision.

The lookouts stated they were almost on top of the ice by the time the ship finally began to turn. Based on the photograph, the *Titanic* should have shown some kind of response to the helm well before the reversed propellers were able to meddle with the rudder's effectiveness.

In Father Brown's photograph, the distance between the first and second sharp turns likely represents the distance between the *Titanic* and the iceberg at the time it was sighted. Unfortunately, it is not clear how far the turning point is on the horizon. But still, a study of the surf nearby and how it recedes offers some perspective on the distance. It does not seem all that great.

Fleet: "Well, it was so close to us. That is why I rang them up."

Fleet mentioned being at the telephone about a half a minute. Boxhall did not reach the bridge until after the collision, by which time the captain already came out of his cabin with Murdoch explaining . . .

Boxhall: "Mr. Murdoch followed on to say, "I put her hard astarboard and run the engines full astern, but it was too close. She hit it.'"

Olliver only had time to walk from a back room onto the bridge from the time he heard the warning until the collision. Hichens implies that the ship was up against the ice as he was turning the wheel.

Hichens: "The sixth officer repeated the order, 'The helm is hard astarboard, sir.' But during the time, she was crushing the ice, or we could hear the grinding noise along the ship's bottom."

When the iceberg came out of the darkness to meet the speeding liner, Murdoch only had seconds to steer the *Titanic* out of the way. An undersized rudder or a decision to reverse the engines does not seem to be the true cause of the Titanic's inability to steer out of the way of the iceberg. In the end, when all has been said and done, there was simply too little time.

occurred. *The alarm bell for accidents rang outside of our door."*

As Barrett tried to comprehend the sight of water pouring into the side of the ship, the alarm went off and the watertight doors between number 6 and the next boiler room aft, number 5 began to close. With a survivalist instinct in full gear, Barrett raced for the door to escape the torrent.

Barrett: "Together with Mr. Hesketh I jumped through the doorway into number 5 section. The watertight door between the section was then open, but it shut just as we jumped through. This door is worked from the bridge. I do not know whether any more men in my stokehole were saved. The water was coming in fast enough through the side of the ship to flood the place."

As Barrett and Hesketh looked around them in boiler room number 5, they saw that the water was coming into this compartment as well, but not nearly as bad as the one from which they just escaped.

As the ice disappeared into the darkness behind the *Titanic*, numerous passengers and crew went through the "what was that?" reaction.

Osman: "Just after that I heard the collision and I went out in the fore square, that is, the fore well deck, just against the seamen's mess room. Looking in the fore well square I saw ice was there. It looked as if there was a piece broken off after she struck and the ice fell on board. I went and picked up a piece of ice and took it down in my sleeping room."

Mr. Woolner: "We felt it in the smoking room. We felt a sort of stopping, a sort of, not exactly shock, but a sort of slowing down. And then we sort of felt a rip that gave a sort of a slight twist to the whole room. Everybody, so far as I could see, stood up and a number of men walked out rapidly through the swinging doors on the port side and ran along to the rail that was behind the mast—I think there was a mast standing out there—and the rail just beyond. I stood hearing what the conjectures were. People were guessing what it might be, and one man called out, 'An iceberg has passed astern,' but who it was I do not know. I never have seen the man since."

Mr. Peuchen: ". . . I had only reached my room and was starting to undress when I felt as though a heavy wave had struck our ship. She quivered under it somewhat. If there had been a sea running I would simply have thought it was an unusual wave which had struck the boat, but knowing that it was a calm night and that it was an unusual thing to occur on a calm night, I immediately put my overcoat on and went up on deck."

Miss Gibson: "We remained in the salon. About half an hour later we felt a slight jar. No one in the party thought anything of it and we continued to laugh and converse for fully fifteen minutes."

Back on the bridge, the incident passed just as quickly as it came upon them. The iceberg was gone and the full reverse of the engines was pulling the ship to a stop. Murdoch, who must have been very distressed by what happened, exercised an appearance of control and issued what ultimately proved to be his last command while in charge of the bridge.

Hichens: "Then the first officer told the other quartermaster standing by to take the time, and told one of the junior officers to make a note of that in the log book. That was at 20 minutes of twelve."

As Moody approached the log to

Opposite page: A stoker in boiler room 6 momentarily pauses to grasp what he is seeing as Barrett and Hesketh rush for the passage to boiler room 5.

record the collision, the captain came out of the navigation room and onto the bridge.

Hichens: "The skipper came rushing out of his room—Captain Smith—and asked, 'What is that?' Mr. Murdoch said, 'An iceberg.' He said, 'Close the emergency doors.' Mr. Murdoch replied, 'The doors are already closed.'"

Boxhall saw very little of the event from the starboard side of the boat deck and proceeded directly to the bridge.

Boxhall: "I found the sixth officer and the first officer, and the captain. The captain said, 'What have we struck?' Mr. Murdoch, the first officer, said, 'We have struck an iceberg.' Mr. Murdoch followed on to say, 'I put her hard a starboard and run the engines full astern, but it was too close. She hit it.' Mr. Murdoch also said, 'I intended to port around it but she hit before I could do any more.' Mr. Murdoch continued to say, 'The watertight doors are closed, sir.'"

Olliver: "When he first came on the bridge he asked the first officer what was the matter, and Mr. Murdoch reported, sir that we had struck an iceberg, and the captain ordered him to have the watertight doors closed, and Mr. Murdoch reported that the watertight doors were closed."

Boxhall: "The captain asked him if he had rung the warning bell. He said, 'Yes, sir.' It is a small electric bell which rings at every watertight door. We all walked out to the corner of the bridge then to look at the iceberg. The captain, first officer, and myself. I was not very sure of seeing it. It seemed to me to be just a small black mass not rising very high out of the water, just a little on the starboard quarter. I could not judge the size of it, but it seemed to me to be very, very low lying."

The iceberg quickly became invisible again. Even knowing it was out there, they could not find it. Boxhall thought he saw a low-lying iceberg, but the one that collided with the Titanic was not low lying.

The crewmen who were taking it easy under the forecastle were the first to see indications of trouble.

Buley: "You could hear it immediately. Down where we were, there was a hatchway, right down below, and there was a tarpaulin across it, with an iron batten. You could hear the water rushing in, and the pressure of air underneath it was such that you could see this bending. In the finish, I was told it blew off."

Jones: "I was sitting in the forecastle. I heard something, just the same as a ship going through a lot of loose ice, and everybody ran on deck right away. When we went on deck we could see some ice on the deck."

Evans: ". . . and I was sitting at the table reading a book and all of a sudden I felt a slight jar. I did not take any notice of it for a few minutes, until one of the other able seamen came down with a big lump of ice in his hands, and he said, 'Look what I found on the fore well deck,' and he chucked it down on the deck . . ."

Hardy: "I had not been in more than five minutes before I heard this slight shock. I got up and slipped on my pants and coat over my pajamas and went on deck to see what the trouble was."

Captain Smith ordered the ship stopped. The ensuing quiet was the single largest contributor to alarming the passengers. The hum of the engines was the life sign of the voyage and the sudden stop did not go without notice.

Mr. Stengel: ". . . and as I woke up I heard a slight crash. I paid no attention to it until I heard the engines stop. When the engines stopped I said, 'There is something serious.

There is something wrong. We had better go up on deck. I just put on what clothes I could grab, and my wife put on her kimono and we went up to the top deck and walked around there."

Mr. Beesley: "And so, with no thought of anything serious having happened to the ship, I continued my reading. And still the murmur from the stewards and the adjoining cabins, and no other sound. No cry in the night. No alarm given. No one afraid— there was then nothing which could cause fear to the most timid person. But in a few moments I felt the engines slow and stop. The dancing motion and the vibration ceased suddenly after being part of our very existence for four days, and that was the first hint that anything out of the ordinary had happened. We have all heard a loud ticking clock stop suddenly in a quiet room, and then have noticed the clock and the ticking noise, of which we seemed until then quite unconscious. So in the same way the fact was suddenly brought home to all in the ship that the engines—that part of the ship that drove us through the sea—had stopped dead."

Mrs. Ryerson: "At the time of collision I was awake and heard the engines stop, but felt no jar."

Mr. Thayer: "Almost instantaneously the engines stopped. The sudden quiet was startling and disturbing. Like the subdued quiet in a sleeping car at a stop after a continuous run. Not a sound except the breeze whistling through the half open port."

Mrs. Douglas: "The shock of the collision was not great to us. The engines stopped."

Mr. Dodge: "The shock to the steamer was so slight that many of the passengers who had already retired were not awakened thereby. My wife and I, however, were both awakened by the shock to the vessel. Listening for a moment, I became aware of the fact that the engines had been stopped."

Mrs. Brown: "I was awakened by a shock. It seemed quite violent to me. The engines were stopped and the ship seemed very quiet at first. I feared at once that there had been an accident."

Lying in their beds, the awakened passengers listened in the darkness of their cabins as an eerie quiet atmosphere settled into the ship. Many were not sure what they felt since they had been asleep, but whatever it was, it woke them up. They may have laid there, staring at the faint light coming from the passageway through the vent at the

The forecastle. Third class passengers and crew came out of the doors near the stairs to find out what happened. (*Olympic*)

bottom of the door, waiting for the engines to resume. Some listened to the muffled sound of voices coming from the next cabin. In time, they heard a cabin door open and close and the sound of footsteps going down the hallway. As they lay under the warmth of their blankets, two questions remained in their thoughts. What *was* that shudder? And why were the engines stopped?

Mr. Beesley: "Acting on it, I jumped out of bed, slipped on a dressing gown over pajamas, put on shoes, and went out of my cabin into the hall near the saloon. Here was a steward leaning against the staircase, probably waiting until those in the smoke room above had gone to bed and he could put out the lights. I said, 'Why have we stopped?' 'I don't know, sir,' he replied, 'but I don't suppose it is anything much.' 'Well,' I said, 'I am going on deck to see what it is,' and started towards the stairs. He smiled indulgently at me as I passed him and said, 'All right, sir, but it is mighty cold up there.' I am sure at that time he thought I was rather foolish to go up with so little reason, and I must confess I felt rather absurd for not remaining in the cabin."

Mr. Thayer: "Then there was the distant noise of running feet and muffled voices, as several people hurried through the passageway."

Mrs. Warren: "Our room was on the starboard side of deck D, about 30 feet above the water and in line with the point of impact. About 11:45 ship's time we were awakened by a terrible crash, followed by a grinding noise and the stoppage of the vessel. I arose immediately, turned the lights on and asked Mr. Warren what terrible thing had happened. He said, 'Nothing at all,' but just at that moment I heard a man across the corridor say, 'We have certainly struck an iceberg.'"

Miss Lehmann: "I went to a very light sleep

and it seemed all at once that I was on a train and it was grinding to a very sudden stop. The first thing that entered into my mind was that we were in New York. I sat up first and then got out of bed and walked over to the lounge that was right under the porthole and looked out. It seemed that there were lights outside. I think now it must have been either the stars or else the reflection of the lights of the Titanic on the iceberg we had just hit."

One by one passengers ventured out of their rooms to find out what was going on, many of them in a foggy state of mind, squinting and bleary eyed from the light.

Crawford: " I went back, and there were a lot of passengers coming out."
Smith: "Where were you when this collision occurred?"
Crawford: "I was right forward in B deck."

Mrs. Dyer-Edwards: "I was awakened by a slight jar and then a grating noise. I turned on the light and saw that it was 11:46 and I wondered at the sudden quiet. Gladys had not been awakened and I called her and asked did she not think it strange that the engines had stopped. As I opened our cabin door I saw a steward. He said we had struck some ice."

Mr. Chambers: "At the request of my wife I prepared to investigate what had happened, leaving her dressing. I threw on sufficient clothes, including my overcoat. I went up, in a leisurely manner, as far as the A deck on the starboard side. There I noted only an unusual coldness of the air. Looking over the side I was unable to see anything in any direction."

Ismay: "I presume the impact awakened me. I lay in bed for a moment or two afterwards, not realizing, probably, what had happened. Eventually I got up and walked along the passageway and met one of the stewards, and said, 'What has happened?' He said, 'I do not know, sir.'"

Mrs. Crosby: "Our staterooms were located on the B deck. I had not retired long when I was suddenly awakened by the thumping of the boat. The engines stopped suddenly. Captain Crosby got up, dressed, and went out . . ."

Mr. Pickard: "I was one of the third class passengers on the Titanic. My cabin was number 10 in the steerage at the stern. We had all been asleep and all of a sudden we perceived a shock. We did not hear such a very terrible shock, but we knew something was wrong, and we jumped out of bed and we dressed ourselves . . ."

Mr. Portalupi: "After the collision I ran up on deck in my bath robe."

Selena Cook had drifted off to sleep earlier to the sound of the men in the next cabin having a pillow fight. Disoriented, she awoke with a start.

Mrs. Cook: "I at first jumped up in bed and said, 'Oh don't those boys make a noise.' Then I heard a horrid grating as though we had run into a lot of gravel and then there was a terrible flush of water and the engines stopped. Milley at once got out of bed and put on some shoes and her big coat and said she was going up to see what was the matter but us other three only sat looking at one another and Miss Brown laid down and said she was going to sleep."

Mr. Beesley: "I climbed the three flights of stairs, opened the vestibule door leading to the top deck, and stepped out into an atmosphere that cut me, clad as I was, like a knife. Walking to the starboard side, I peered over and saw the sea many feet below, calm and black; forward, the deserted deck stretching away to the first class quarters and the captain's bridge; and behind, the steerage quarters and the stern bridge. Nothing more; no iceberg on either side or astern as far as we could see in the darkness. There were two

The second class smoking room. Beesely entered the door to the left and asked some men who were playing cards if they knew what had happened. (*Olympic*)

or three men on deck and with one–the Scotch engineer who played hymns in the saloon–I compared notes of our experiences. None of us could see anything, and all being quiet and still, the Scotchman and I went down to the next deck. Through the windows of the smoking room we saw a game of cards going on, with several onlookers, and went in to enquire if they knew more than we did. The general impression was that we had just scraped the iceberg with a glancing blow on the starboard side, and they had stopped as a wise precaution to examine her thoroughly all over. 'I expect the iceberg has scratched off some of her new paint,' said one, 'and the captain doesn't like to go on until she is painted up again.' We laughed at his estimate of the captain's care for the ship. One of the players, pointing to his glass of whiskey standing at his elbow, and turning to an onlooker said, 'Just run along the deck and see if any ice has come aboard. I would like some for this.'"

Mr. Abelseth: "I think it was about 15 minutes to 12 when I woke up. And there was another man in the same room—two of us in the same room—and he said to me, 'What is that?' I said, 'I don't know, but we had better get up.' So we did get up and put our clothes on, and we two went up on deck in the forward part of the ship."

Miss Sjoblom: "The shock when the boat struck the iceberg woke me up. Everyone became excited at once. I got up and put on some clothes so that I could go outside."

Miss Turja: "I thought some thing must be wrong with the engines. I got up and slowly dressed myself . . . The other ladies did the same thing. There was one real old lady, and another who had only been married a short time. Her husband was making the trip over with her."

Mrs. Futrelle: "About 11:30 we felt a slight concussion. For the moment neither of us experienced any feeling of alarm. I asked Jacques what he thought of it. 'Oh I guess it's nothing.' he said, 'We have simply bumped into a baby iceberg. If that's what it is, it's of no more importance than if the ship had struck a match.' I couldn't help but feel alarmed despite Jacques' confidence. A moment later there was the sound of scurrying feet in the halls which divided the staterooms. There was a babel of inquiring and anxious voices."

Hundreds of crewman were asleep at the time, most of them along "Scotland Road" on the port side of E deck. Some of the crew's quarters were cramped, to say the least, with several dozen men arranged in rows of bunks. Sleep was hard to come by in the service of a vessel and in such a communal housing arrangement. For many, the slight jar was no reason to get out of bed.

Burke: "When I first felt the impact I did not know exactly what to make of it. I thought probably she had dropped her propeller, or something. I did not get up right away. I waited for probably a quarter of an hour."

Widgery: "I went to bed and was asleep when the accident happened. It woke me up, and I wondered what it was, and it seemed to me like a grating. One of the men got up and opened the port, and it was blowing very cold and we told him to shut it. We were talking amongst ourselves for a little while and I did not think it was much and turned over and started to go to sleep again."

Ward: "I was just turning in when she struck. When I felt the shock, I got up. I went to the port and opened it. It was very bitterly cold. I looked out and saw nothing. It was very dark. I thought at first it was the propeller gone, the way she went. I got back into my bunk again."

Etches: "I was awakened by something but I did not know what it was and I called to my mate and I said, 'What time is it that they are going to call us next?' It was then between 25 minutes and 20 minutes to 12. He said, 'I don't know.' I turned over to go to sleep again."

But for many of the crew, the disturbance set their curiosity in motion which would not allow them to go back to sleep. They reacted in much the same way as the passengers.

Ray: "A kind of a movement that went backward and forward. I thought something had gone wrong with the engine room. I did not think of any iceberg. Twenty-eight slept in the room. They were all awakened by the impact."

Archer: "I was in my bunk, asleep. I heard a kind of a crush, something similar to when you let go the anchor; it sounded like the cable running through the hawse pipe. No shock and no jar; just a grating sensation. I jumped out of my bed, put on a pair of trousers, and ran up on deck to find out what was the matter. I saw some small pieces of ice on the starboard side, on the forward deck."
Bourne: "How much ice was there?"
Archer: "Not an extraordinary lot, sir."
Bourne: "No heavy pieces?"
Archer: "No, sir."
Bourne: "Not any 50 or 100 ton chunks?"
Archer: "No, nothing like that. Just small pieces."
Bourne: "No pieces any larger than your head?"
Archer: "No. I never saw any larger than that."

Buley: "It seemed as though something was rubbing alongside of her at the time. I had on my overcoat and went up on deck, and they said she had struck an iceberg."

Crowe: "I was just dozing. About 11:40

there was a kind of shaking of the ship and a little impact, from which I thought one of the propellers had been broken off. Well, had I been asleep I do not think it would have awakened me, that is, had I been in a heavy sleep."

Hemming: "I was awakened by the impact. I went out and put my head through the port-hole to see what we hit. I made the remark to the storekeeper, 'It must have been ice.' I said, 'I do not see anything.'"

Clench: "I was asleep in my bunk when the accident occurred, and I was awakened by the crunching and jarring, as if it was hitting up against something. I am a light sleeper. If anybody touches me, I will jump quick. Of course, I put on my trousers and I went on deck on the starboard side of the well deck and I saw a lot of ice."

Andrews: "I was wakened by a movement of the ship. I thought something might have gone wrong with the engines. Several of the boys woke up with the shock also. So with that I got out of my bunk and went into the working alleyway, seeing lots of stewards out. I walked up and down the alleyway several times with another steward. After that I went back to the quarters. I went back and laid down for a few minutes and then got up again."

Collins: "I put on my trousers, got out of my bed and they were letting off steam in the stoke hole. I asked what was the matter, and it seemed she struck an iceberg. I . . . went up onto the deck, up forward, and I saw the deck almost packed with ice on the starboard side. The word came down the alleyway that there was no harm, and everyone returned to their bunks. I went back into the bedroom and was told to lie down . . ."

With the exception of Fifth Officer Lowe, the Titanic's officers were awakened by the commotion.

Smith: "Where were you when the impact occurred?"
Lightoller: "In my berth."
Smith: "Asleep?"
Lightoller: "No sir. I was just getting off asleep."
Smith: "What was the force of the impact?"
Lightoller: "A slight jar and a grinding sound."
Smith: "Was there a noise?"
Lightoller: "Very little."

Pitman: ". . . the collision woke me up. There was a sound that I thought seemed like the ship coming to an anchor–the chain running out over the windlass. It gave just a little vibration. I was about half awake *and about half asleep. It did not quite awaken me. I got up and walked on deck without dressing. I had a look around, and I could not see anything and could not hear any noise, so I went back to the room and sat down and lit my pipe. I thought that nothing had really happened, that perhaps it might have been a dream, or something like that."*

Captain Smith ordered the fourth officer to go down and investigate.

Boxhall: "I went right down below in the lowest steerage as far as I could possibly get without going into the cargo portion of the ship, and inspected all the decks as I came up, in the vicinity of where I thought she had struck. I found no damage. I found no indications to show that the ship had damaged herself."

After Captain Smith sent Boxhall down to investigate, he decided to set the liner in motion again. The motive for this command is intriguing, but undocumented. Smith may have been aware on his own, or advised by the engine room that there was a tremendous amount of steam backing up under pressure while the ship sat idle in the water and may have decided to set the *Titanic* in motion to vent it off. Or was there another reason? Is it possible that Captain Smith was concerned about delaying the voyage any further due to this embarrassing little rub with ice in the middle of the night, and decided to get under way? As an indication of the confidence Smith held in his ship, he walked to the telemotor and set the *Titanic* to slow ahead. On the heels of that brush with ice, he was not about to resume a full ahead speed—at least not until daylight.

Olliver: ". . . whilst I was on the bridge she went ahead, after she struck. She went half speed ahead. The captain telegraphed half speed ahead."
Burton: "Did she have much way on?"
Olliver: "No, sir. I reckon the ship was almost stopped."

Smith: "How long after the impact was it before the engines were stopped?"
Mr. Stengel: "A very few minutes. I should say two or three minutes, and then they started again, just slightly. Just started to move again. I do not know why."

Mr. Thayer: "Very shortly the engines started up again—slowly—not with the bright vibration to which we were accustomed, but as though they were tired."

Mr. Beesley: ". . . I left the smoking room and went down to my cabin, where I sat for some time reading again. Presently, hearing people walking about the corridors, I looked out and saw several standing in the hall talking to a steward—most of them ladies in dressing gowns. Other people were going upstairs and I decided to go on deck again, but as it was too cold to do so in a dressing gown, I dressed in a Norfolk jacket and trousers and walked up. There were now more people looking over the side and walking about, questioning each other as to why we had stopped, but without obtaining any definite information. The ship had now resumed her course, moving very slowly through the water with a little white line of foam on each side. I think we were all glad to see this. It seemed better than standing still."

While many recognized the sound of the engines resuming, a few did not realize what it was. When the *Titanic*'s engines vibrated back to life, pushing the vessel forward again, May Futrelle mistook the sensation as yet another jar.

Mrs. Futrelle: "I felt the ship quiver from bow to stern. It seemed to me that the ship lurched sidewise from the force of a new impact. There was a grating noise. Neither of the blows to the ship had been sufficient to impress my husband with the belief that anything serious had happened. He was not inclined to investigate or even to make inquiries as to the nature of the disturbance. It was only when I had urged him to see what the trouble was that he dressed himself and went out to investigate."

As the *Titanic* got underway, Captain Smith sent Olliver down with instructions for the carpenter. Boxhall had not yet returned.

Olliver: "The captain gave me orders to tell the carpenter to go and take the draft of the water."
Burton: "Where did you find the carpenter?"
Olliver: "Down below, already doing it. In the working alleyway. It is like forward. It is a forward part of the ship—not right forward. It is on E deck."
Burton: "Did you see any water down there?"
Olliver: "No, I did not, sir."
Burton: "Did he say he had found any water?"
Olliver: "He did not tell me."

It was about this time that Chief Officer Wilde made his appearance on the bridge, when Boxhall and Olliver were down below. After receiving a status, he quickly headed for the area below the fore-castle to make an assessment of his own.

For just a few minutes on the bridge, things seemed like they were returning to normal. Discipline dictated that officers off duty not bother the bridge with their curiosity, but Lightoller came around the corner of the hallway into the wheelhouse and stole a glance.

Smith: "You could see the bridge distinctly, and the captain was on the bridge?"
Lightoller: "The captain and first officer."
Smith: "Did you see any other officers at that time?"
Lightoller: "I did not notice them."

With Boxhall and Olliver sent below, Lightoller's view was hardly one of a bridge under siege of panic. In fact, it was almost like the whole event had been reset and tried all over again—this time the right way. The *Titanic* was going slow ahead. Smith was on the bridge and everyone knew they were in dangerous waters.

Smith: "Did you see Mr. Murdoch after that?"
Lightoller: "Yes, sir. I saw him when I came out of the quarters after the impact."
Smith: "Where was he?"
Lightoller: "On the bridge."

Smith: "With the captain?"
Lightoller: "One on one side, and one of the other side of the bridge. One on each side."
Smith: "Did you speak to him after that?"
Lightoller: "No, sir."

With the *Titanic* underway once more, Smith and Murdoch were on the wings of the bridge keeping an eye out for more icebergs. The scene is a fascinating one. The *Titanic* had just been dealt a death blow a few minutes earlier, and yet there was Captain Smith and First Officer Murdoch keeping watch while the *Titanic* resumed her way. To Lightoller, this brief scene left him with the impression that everything was fine. Something unusual may have happened, but whatever it was, everything was okay now.

Fletcher: "Was she not actually stopped entirely from going forward?"
Lightoller: "No, she was not. That is why I said, in my previous testimony, that the ship was apparently going slowly, and I saw the first officer and the captain on the bridge, and I judged that there was nothing further to do."
Smith: Had no alarm been given at that time?
Lightoller: "None."
Smith: "Then you returned? How long did

Visions of prior damage to the *Olympic* may have entered Smith's mind as he sent for the carpenter.

you remain on deck?"
Lightoller: "About two or three minutes."
Smith: "At that time who else was on deck at that point?"
Lightoller: "Excluding the bridge, I saw no one except the third officer, who left his berth shortly after I did."
Smith: Did he join you?"
Lightoller: "Yes"
Smith: "Did you confer about what had happened?"
Lightoller: "Yes sir."
Smith: "What did you conclude had hap-

pened?"
Lightoller: "Nothing much."

Just about this time, Captain Smith received the last piece of good news for the remainder of the night.

Boxhall: " Then I went to the bridge and reported to the captain that I could not see any damage. He said, 'Go down and find the carpenter and get him to sound the ship.'"

With Boxhall's good news, the captain's subsequent orders may have stemmed not from a concern of water entering the ship, but perhaps of other types of damage caused by the ice, such as broken portholes or plates. After all, he could see the ice on the well deck and knew that there had been a good bump to the iceberg. After the collision between the *Olympic* and the *Hawke* under his command the prior year, he could have envisioned similar damage to the *Titanic* above the waterline. In reacting to the captain's orders, Boxhall knew what a labyrinth the *Titanic* could be and wasted no time in enlisting assistance.

Evans: ". . . and I went up the ladder there and I met one officer. He told me to go down and find the carpenter and sound all the

wells forward, and report to the bridge."

It is unknown what Smith was thinking at this time, but Boxhall's report had to have raised his hopes. At this point, he may even have been mentally calculating how much of an impact traveling slow ahead until sunrise would have on their arrival time in New York.

Meanwhile, more and more passengers were on the move within the ship and more were waking up from their slumbers with each passing minute.

Mr. Woolner: "I then went to look for Mrs. Candee, because she was the lady in whom I was most interested, and I met her outside her stateroom. I said, 'Some accident has happened, but I do not think it is anything serious. Let us go for a walk."

Mrs. Brown: "The passengers had seen reports about icebergs on the ship's bulletins and of course there was more or less talk about them among us, just as we discussed the speed that the ship was making and speculated as to when we should reach New York. My first thought was, 'We have struck an iceberg.' I put on some clothes and told my daughter to dress. I went at once to my husband's stateroom and found him still sleeping. 'We've struck an iceberg,' I said,

'Get dressed at once.' He did not think the situation was dangerous but I urged him to go on deck and find out what happened."

The crew and steerage passengers in the bow did not have to guess much as to the danger. Their neighborhood of the ship was in the center of activity.

Haines: "When I first heard the blow, I heard some air escaping right forward, and I ran forward to the exhaust from the fore peak tank. I saw the fore peak tank was filling and the air was coming out and the water was coming in. It was an overflow pipe. Just as I got there the chief officer, Mr. Wilde had gotten there, and the lamp trimmer was there, Mr. Hemming. He asked if there was any water in the forepeak and the storekeeper went into the forepeak and there was no water there. That is the forepeak, not the forepeak tank. The forepeak tank was full. The chief officer then went on the bridge to report."

Hemming: "I went up under the forecastle head to see where the hissing noise came from. I did not see anything. I opened the forepeak storeroom, me and the storekeeper went down as far as the top of the tank, and found everything dry. I came up to ascertain where the hissing noise was still coming

from. I found it was the air escaping out of the exhaust of the tank. At that time the chief officer, Mr. Wilde, put his head around the hawse pipe and says, 'What is that Hemming?' I said, 'The air is escaping from the forepeak tank. She is making water in the forepeak tank, but the storeroom is quite dry.' He said, 'Alright,' and went away. I went back and turned in. Me and the storekeeper went back and turned into our bunks."

Hardy: "I had gone up then to B deck to look over the ship's side to see if I could see anything. I could not see anything and I went below and retired again and was reading a few minutes . . ."

Etches: "I partly dressed and looked out of the door, and I saw the third class passengers coming along from forward with their portmanteaus. I had gotten about 30 yards, probably, when I met a passenger with a piece of ice that size [indicating], and he said, 'Will you believe it now?' and threw it down on the deck. With that I went back and finished dressing and went up on deck."

Olaus Abelseth and his relatives were some of those third class passengers that Henry Etches saw coming along Park Lane.

Mr. Abelseth: "Then there was quite a lot of ice on the starboard part of the ship. They wanted us to go down again, and I saw one of the officers and I said to him, 'Is there any danger?' He said, 'No.' I was not satisfied with that, however, so I went down and told my brother-in-law and my cousin who were in the same compartment there. They were not in the same room, but they were just a little ways from where I was. I told them about what was happened and I said they had better get up."

Back up in first class, some of the wives sent their husbands out for news, while others went out together.

Mrs. Warren: "I then asked Mr. Warren to go and see what was the matter. He first started out partly dressed, but decided to dress fully before going out. After doing which, he went to one of the corridors and returned in a very few minutes with a piece of ice saying it had been handed him as a souvenir."

Mrs. Ryerson: "My husband was asleep, so I rang and asked the steward, Bishop, what was the matter. He said, 'There is talk of an iceberg, ma'am, and they have stopped, not to run into it.' I told him to keep me informed if there were any orders. It was bitterly cold so I put on a warm wrapper and looked out the window (we were in the large cabin on B deck, very far aft) and saw the stars shining and a calm sea, but heard no noise."

Mr. Harder: "I thought we would go up on deck to see what had happened, what damage had been done. So we dressed fully and went up on deck and there we saw quite a number of people talking and nobody seemed to think anything serious had happened. There were such remarks as, 'Oh, it will only be a few hours before we will be on the way again.'"

Mr. Peuchen: " As I started to go through the grand stairway I met a friend who said, 'Why, we have struck an iceberg.' I cannot remember his name. He was simply a casual acquaintance I had met. He said, 'If you will go up on the upper deck,' or 'If you will go up on A deck, you will see the ice on the fore part of the ship.' So I did so. I went up there. I suppose the ice had fallen inside the rail, probably 4 to 4 ½ feet. It looked like shell ice, soft ice. But you could see it quite plainly along the bow of the boat. I stood on deck for a few minutes, talking to other friends, and then I went to see my friend, Mr. Hugo Ross, to tell him that it was not serious, that we had only struck an iceberg."

Crawford: ". . . as I was going around Mr. and Mrs. Bishop came out and asked me what was the matter. I said we had run into a piece of ice."

Mrs. Bishop: "My husband awakened me at about a quarter of 12 and told me that the boat had struck something. We both dressed and went up on deck, looked around, and could find nothing."

Mrs. Futrelle: "He was not inclined to investigate or even make inquiries as to the nature of the disturbance. It was only when I urged him to see what the trouble was that he dressed himself and went out to investigate. Upon leaving our stateroom he encountered Mr. Henry Harris, the theatrical magnate. Both told me to go across the hall into the stateroom occupied by Mrs. Harris and to stay with her until they had returned. Mrs. Harris was pale and frightened.

Just as Jacques Futrelle and Henry Harris went off to investigate, the crew began to lower the watertight doors in the higher deck areas. The doors down below lowered automatically when Murdoch pulled the lever on the bridge, but those on the higher decks had to be operated manually and passengers took note of the activity.

Mrs. Futrelle: "Our fear was increased twofold when we heard the harsh clanging of the great gong forward. I was afraid. The explanation of the reason for ringing the gong came to us in a flash. That very afternoon one of the officers had explained to us that this gong was only used as a signal for the closing of the watertight compartments in case of emergency."

Smith: "Let us go a little higher, and tell me about the doors, and the construction there."
Lightoller: "They are operated by hand, closed by lever. They can be closed from the deck above, or from the deck you are on. There is a specially constructed key that fits into the deck above. When you turn it around, the door closes. One man can close or open it."
Smith: "You must first have a key?"
Lightoller: "Yes. Keys are kept alongside of the doors. When the door is closed it so engages a system or series of wedges that is watertight."

On E deck, some of the crew were trying to get back to sleep when the commotion surrounding the closing of the doors interrupted their attempts.

Wheelton: "I was awakened between 10

minutes to 12 and a quarter to 12 by a shock. It felt as if it was the dropping of a propeller or something like that. I got out of bed. I lifted the port and I looked out of the port. Everything was calm. It was very cold. I went to the door of my room and spoke to some of the men, and then I got back into bed again. I was roused next by someone shouting, 'Watertight doors!'"

Etches: "At that minute I heard a loud shout, 'Close the watertight bulkheads.' I recognized it as our boatswain's voice. It was extra loud. I looked out and he was running fore to aft. That would be under 10 minutes. Seven minutes, I would say, as near as possible."

On the other side of E deck in first class, the commotion drew the attention of some passengers who took note that all was not well with the mechanics of the watertight system.

Mr. Bishop: "There is one thing, in regard to the watertight compartments on E deck. It has to do with the mechanical closing of them. Some way or other it had a brass plate in the deck, and from what I know—I do not know from my own observation, but only from what I have heard from some other people I knew on the boat—immediately after the accident they saw the members of the crew trying to do something to these holes in the deck with a key such as they use in the shut-offs to the water system in cities, and placing the key down there, they failed to turn the one on that side, and they immediately went to the other side and could not close that. They said, 'There is no use. We will try the other side.' What it was or how serious it was I do not know."

While the crew worked to close the upper watertight doors, only the first few passengers noted a list in the ship.

Mr. Chambers: "I returned below, where I was joined by my wife and we came up again to investigate, still finding nothing. However, there was then a noticeable list to starboard with probably a few degrees of pitch. And as the ship had had a list to port nearly all afternoon, I decided to remain up, in spite of a feeling of perfect safety."

On the bridge, Captain Smith detected the list in the ship as well and walked to the commutator to confirm his suspicions.

Hichens: "The captain sent then for the carpenter to sound the ship. He also came back to the wheelhouse and looked at the commutator in front of the compass, which is a little instrument like a clock to tell you how the ship is listing. The ship had a list of five degrees to the starboard."

Smith: "How long after the impact, or collision?"

Hichens: "I could hardly tell you, sir. Judging roughly, about five minutes. About five to ten minutes."

This list was a very bad revelation for Captain Smith. The *Titanic* was taking on water on her maiden voyage. This not only eliminated the idea of arriving in New York City early and making great press, but now the new *Titanic* might have to hobble into port with some of her compartments flooded. Thank God, he probably thought, for the watertight compartments. Ismay and the White Star Line would certainly not be happy about all this. Smith may have dwelled for a dark moment on Ismay's influence over the speed of the ship. As he was mulling over this worsening situation, a stream of visitors began to arrive.

Ismay: "I then went back into my room, put my coat on, and went up on the bridge, where I found Captain Smith. I asked him what had happened, and he said, 'We have struck ice.' I said, 'Do you think the ship is seriously damaged?' He said, 'I am afraid she is.'"

Although Ismay portrayed himself as minimally involved on the bridge after the accident, it would have been entirely out of his character—and his role as President of the White Star Line—to have then left the bridge and the unfolding matter in the sole hands of Captain Smith. Unfortunately, no further conversations are documented between Smith and Ismay. Just about the time of Ismay's arrival on the bridge, Smith received another visitor.

Boxhall: " I was proceeding down, but I met the carpenter. I said, 'The captain wants you to sound the ship.' He said, 'The ship is making water', and he went on the bridge to the captain, and I thought I would go down forward again and investigate."

The carpenter filled Smith, Ismay, Wilde, and possibly Purser McElroy in on the disturbing details of how their new ship was filling with water in numerous forward compartments. And this was not a trickle of water. The water was coming in rapidly in some areas. No sooner had the carpenter finished than a mail clerk arrived with additional news.

Boxhall: "And then I met a mail clerk, a man named Smith, and he asked where the captain was. I said, 'He is on the bridge.'

He said, 'The mail hold is full' or 'filling rapidly.' I said, 'Well, you go and report it to the captain and I will go down and see,' and I proceeded right down into the mail room."

While bad news flowed into the bridge, water flowed into third class accommodations on G deck. Unlike other passengers who gradually learned of the *Titanic's* problems, steerage passengers in the bow were informed firsthand, and in an abrupt way.

Mr. Buckley: "This night of the wreck I was sleeping in my room on the Titanic in the steerage. There were three other boys from the same place sleeping in the same room with me. I heard some terrible noise and I jumped out on the floor, and the first thing I know my feet were getting wet. The water was just coming in slightly. I told the other fellows to get up, that there was something wrong and that there was water coming in. They only laughed at me. I got on my clothes as quick as I could, and the three other fellows got out. The room was very small, so I got out, to give them room to dress themselves."

Thomas Andrews arrived on the bridge about now as well as Boxhall return-ing from his second trip down below.

Boxhall: ". . . I proceeded right down into the mail room. I went down as far as the sorting room deck and found mail clerks down there working. Taking letters out of the racks, they seemed to me to be doing. I could not see what they were putting them in. I looked through an open door and saw these men working at the racks, and directly beneath me was the mail hold, and the water seemed to be then within 2 feet of the deck we were standing on and bags of mail floating about. I went right on the bridge again and reported to the captain what I had seen. He said alright."

With bad news pouring in, Smith decided have a look for himself. Sometime around 11:50 p.m. he left the bridge with Murdoch, Moody, Andrews, McElroy, and Ismay. First he ordered the ship stopped and wrote some instructions for Chief Officer Bell. Wilde and Boxhall were on the bridge to see the ship safely brought to a halt.

Robinson: "The mail man passed along first and he returned with Mr. McElroy and the

Opposite Page: Cargo Hold 3, looking aft.

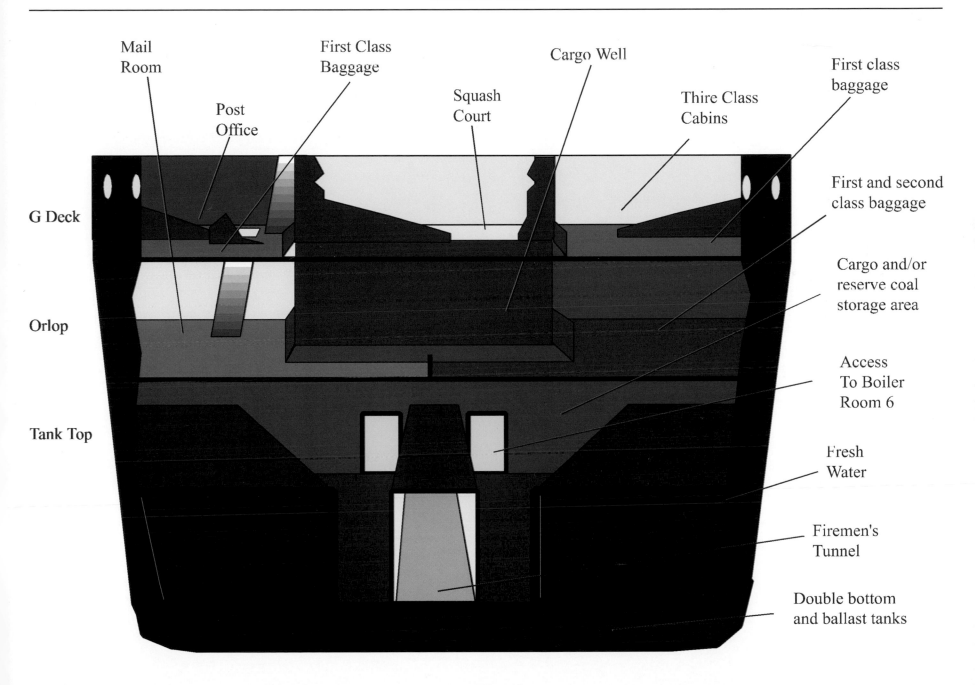

Mail Room

First Class Baggage

Cargo Well

Post Office

Squash Court

Thire Class Cabins

First class baggage

First and second class baggage

Cargo and/or reserve coal storage area

Access To Boiler Room 6

Fresh Water

Firemen's Tunnel

Double bottom and ballast tanks

G Deck

Orlop

Tank Top

Captain and they went in the direction of the mail room . . ."

Mrs. Douglas: "The engines stopped, then went on for a few moments, then stopped again."

Olliver: "As soon as I got on the bridge, I had another message. A message to take to the chief engineer. I cannot say the message. It was on a piece of paper and the paper was closed."

Ward: "I would not like to say exactly when she stopped, but I suppose about 10 minutes or so after the shock she was slowing down then, and almost stopping then, I suppose."

Mrs. Collyer: "They tried to start the engines a few minutes later but after some coughing and rumbling there was silence once more."

It was about this time that Boxhall must have taken note that Lightoller, Pitman, and Lowe should be informed.

Lightoller: ". . . Fourth Officer Boxhall opened my door and, seeing me awake quietly said, 'We've hit an iceberg.' I replied, 'I know you've hit something.' He then said, 'The water is up to F deck in the mail room.' That was quite sufficient. Not another word passed."

Lowe: " Mr. Boxhall, the fourth officer told me that we had struck an iceberg, but I do not remember it. It must have been while I was asleep. You must remember that we do not have any too much sleep and therefore when we sleep we die."

Pitman: "A few minutes afterwards I thought I had better start dressing, as it was near my watch, so I started dressing, and when I was partly dressed Mr. Boxhall came in and said the mail room—there was water in the mail room. I said, 'What happened?' He said, 'We struck an iceberg.'"

When the engines were disengaged, the steam no longer had an outlet and the pressure backed up through the exhausts.

Lightoller: "The ship had been running under a big head of steam, therefore the instant the engines were stopped the steam started roaring off at all eight exhausts, kicking up a row that would have dwarfed the row of a thousand railway engines thundering through a culvert."

As the entourage from the bridge headed off to investigate, there was already a swirl of activity below the forecastle in the bow of the ship. Third class passengers and crew who were berthed in the area were forced into sudden, unexpected action.

Mr. Buckley: "Two sailors came along, and they were shouting: 'All up on deck unless you want to get drowned!' When I heard this I went for the deck as quick as I could."

Weikman: "I went forward to the steerage on G deck and saw one of the baggage masters, and he told me that water was coming in the baggage room on the deck below. I think the baggage man's name was Bessant."

Evans: " I went down the engineer's alleyway to find him, and I met the boatswain there and he said, 'Who are you looking for, Evans?' I said, 'The carpenter.' He said, 'He has gone up.' He said, 'What is the matter?' I said, 'I do not know. I think we have struck an iceberg.' The boatswain went up, then."

Mr. Abelseth: " Both of them got up and dressed and we took our overcoats and put them on. We did not take any life belts with us. There was no water on the deck at that time. We walked to the hind part of the ship."

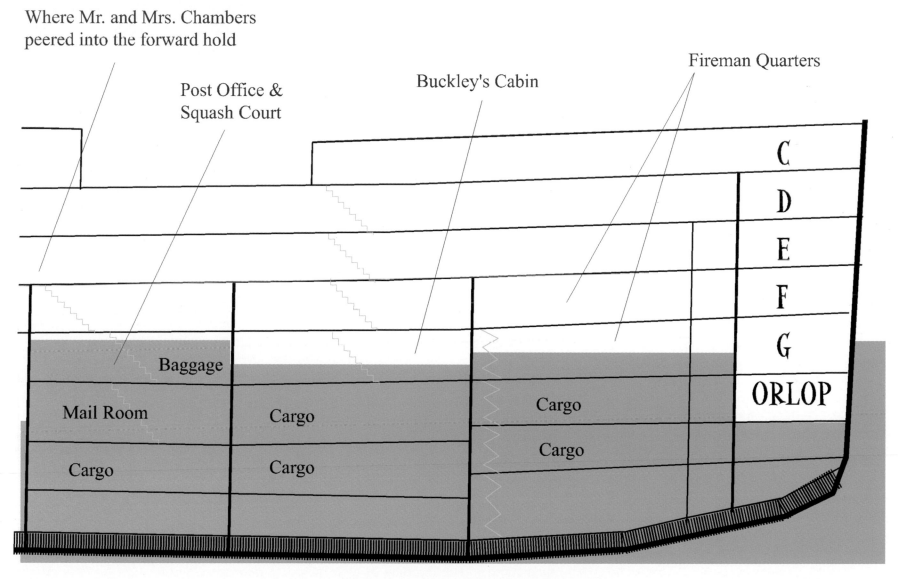

Where Mr. and Mrs. Chambers peered into the forward hold

Post Office & Squash Court

Buckley's Cabin

Fireman Quarters

C
D
E
F
G
ORLOP

Baggage

Mail Room

Cargo

Cargo

Cargo

Cargo

Cargo

Cargo

The forward watertight compartments flooded at different rates.

Perkis: "I turned out after being called by the joiner of the ship. He came to the room and told us we had better turn out. He told us then, that we had struck something. I took no notice of it. I stayed there until I thought it was time to turn out to relieve the deck at 12 o'clock."

Etches: "As I was going through the door I met a bedroom steward named Stone. He was the man my mate was supposed to relieve. He was bedroom steward on E deck. I said, 'What is the time?' He said, 'Never mind about that. There is something else for you to do. I saw them pull up bags of mail, and the water was running out of the bottom of them.'"

Clench: "With that I went in the alleyway again under the forecastle head to come down and put on my shoes. Someone said to me, 'Did you hear the rush of water?' I said, 'No.' They said, 'Look down under the hatchway.' I looked down under the hatchway and I saw the tarpaulin belly out as if there was a lot of wind under it, and I heard the rush of water coming through."
Bourne: "How soon after you struck?"
Clench: "I should say about 10 minutes, sir."

Archer: "After I saw the ice I went back in the door and put on a pair of shoes, a Guernsey, and a cap."

Taylor: "I went down in our room again [on F deck]. I stayed in the room about 10 minutes and somebody reported that there was water in number 1 hatch . . . we saw it come bursting up through the hatches. Then we packed our bags, took them in the mess room, in the alleyway, to wait for orders."

Jones: "Then I went forward, and I could see a lot of the firemen coming up out of the forecastle and I looked down below, and I heard a rush of water. I went down below, in number 1 and I could see the tarpaulin of the hatch lifting up the same as if there was air coming up there, and I went on deck then and I could see all the firemen coming up from there. The firemen brought up their bundles not because they thought the boat was going to sink, but because they wanted to take them out of the water, as the water was coming in. The last I saw of them they thought so—that it would not sink."

Whereas the captain had set off to determine the condition of the ship, the stokers who were off duty had already made up their minds. The flooding of their quarters created a mass movement and scores of them came up to the boat deck. Wilde was on the bridge while the captain went below. He saw the commotion just outside of the bridge and took control of the situation.

Mr. Peuchen: "When I came on deck first, on this upper deck, there were, it seems to me, about 100 stokers came up with their dunnage bags, and they seemed to crowd this whole deck in front of the boats. One of the officers—I do not know which one, but a very powerful one—came along and drove these men right off that deck. It was a splendid act. He drove them, every man, like a lot of sheep, right off the deck. He drove them right ahead of him, and they disappeared. I do not know where they went, but it was a splendid act. They did not put up any resistance. I admired him for it."

At some point below deck, the captain's entourage split up just before, or after meeting up with Chief Officer Bell on E deck. His assessment may have given the group some hope.

Ismay: "I then went down below, I think it was, where I met Mr. Bell, the chief engineer, who was in the main companionway. I asked if he thought the ship was seriously damaged, and he said he thought she was, but was quite satisfied the pumps would keep her afloat."

The view from E deck, looking down into the flooded G deck post office and baggage room.

But all was not well with the *Titanic* by 11:55 p.m. The pumps were not even coming close to keeping up with the inflow of water in the fourth compartment. The cargo hold, mail room and second and third class baggage rooms on Orlop deck were submerged. In the fourth compartment from the bow, G deck was submerged. In the third compartment, the water was a few feet above the floor. Because the fourth compartment flooded the fastest, it reached an equilibrium with the water outside for a brief period while the other punctured compartments caught up. This created the impression for anyone observing the water in the fourth compartment that the water was no longer rising.

Mr. Chambers: "Upon returning to the stateroom for the purpose of completing dressing, I looked at the starboard end of our passageway where there was the companion leading to the quarters of the mail clerks and farther on to the baggage room and, I believe, the mail sorting room. And at the top of these stairs I found a couple of mail clerks wet to their knees, who had just come up from below, bringing their registered mail bags. As the door in the bulkhead in the next deck was open I was able to look directly into the trunk room which was then filled with water and within 18 inches or 2

Captain Smith

feet of the deck above. We were standing there joking about our baggage being completely soaked and about the correspondence which was seen floating about on the top of the water. I personally felt no sense of danger as this water was forward of the bulkhead. While we were standing there three of the ship's officers—I did not notice their rank or department—descended the first companion and looked into the baggage room, coming back up immediately saying that we were not making any more water. This was not an announcement, but

merely a remark passed from one to the other."

Meanwhile, in the third compartment there was understandably quite a stir as water swirled about the third class cabins. It is interesting to see in the following observation that Buckley notes the presence of women in the bow section of third class. It is generally believed that only single men were berthed there, but his observation implies differently.

Mr. Buckley: "When I got up on the deck I saw everyone having those life belts on [except] only myself. So I got sorry and said I would go back again where I was sleeping and get one of those life preservers because there was one there for each person. I went back again, and just as I was going down the last flight of stairs the water was up four steps, and dashing up. I did not go back into the room because I could not."

Smith: "Did you find any people down in the steerage when you went back the second time?"

Buckley: "There were a number but I cannot say how many. All the boys and girls were coming up against me. They were all going for the deck."

Smith: "Were they excited?"

Buckley: "Yes, they were. The girls were

very excited and they were crying and all the boys were trying to console them and saying that it was nothing serious."

At some point just before midnight, down in the bowels of the ship, Andrews and Smith were able to diagnose the condition of the *Titanic*. It was there, in the forward part of E or F deck, surrounded with the commotion of a flooding ship, that they concluded it was terminal. The first six compartments had been damaged by the collision and all six were taking in water. The first five were hopelessly flooding. The *Titanic* was going to sink. Stunned, the two parted ways. The captain headed for the Grand Staircase, possibly with the intent of taking the elevator up past the five flights of decks to the boat deck.

Weikman: "When I was on E deck I met the captain returning from G deck, who had been there with Mr. Andrews . . ."

Upon his arrival at the foot of the stairs, he must have realized that it would be safer to walk up the steps, and began his ascent. Andrews did not bother to return to the bridge with Captain Smith. With an immediate sense of urgency, he started passing the word that the bow areas needed to be evacuated right away.

Thomas Andrews

Weikman: "I then went upstairs and met Mr. Andrews, the builder, and he was giving instructions to get the steerage passengers on deck."

The exodus began. But while passengers were being evacuated from their flooded cabins, many of the off-duty stewards, whose quarters lined E deck, completely failed to grasp the seriousness of the situation.

Ward: "I lay there for about 20 minutes and in the meantime the steerage passengers were coming from forward, coming aft, carrying life belts with them. Some of them got their grips and packages and had them with them, and some were wet. Still, I didn't think it was anything serious, and I lay there for some time, a little while longer. . ."

Collins: ". . . I got up again. I did not take off any of my clothes, and I came out again and saw the stewards in their white jackets in the passageway. The passengers were running forward, the stewards were steering them, and they made a joke of it, and we all turned in then . . ."

Crowe: "I got out of my bed. On E deck. I came out into the alleyway and saw quite a number of stewards and steerage passengers carrying their baggage from forward to aft. I inquired of the trouble and was told it was nothing and to turn in again. The stewards were making quite a joke of it. They did not think of the seriousness of it at the time. I heard there were several hundred tons of ice found. Another man brought a piece along from the forward part of the ship. I went back to my bunk again . . ."

Third class passengers began to trickle to the stern, full of news and observations of what was going on in the bow.

Mr. Abelseth: "We walked to the hind part of the ship and got two Norwegian girls up. One was in my charge and one was in charge of the man who was in the same room with me. He was from the same town that I came from. The other one was just 16 years old, and her father told me to take care of her until we got to Minneapolis. The two girls were in a room in the hind part of the ship, in the steerage."

First and second class passengers continued to search for signs of anything that would indicate there was a problem.

Mr. Woolner: "We walked the after deck for quite a considerable time. I should think for 10 minutes or more."

Mr. Dodge: ". . . and shortly afterwards, hearing hurried footsteps on the boat deck, which was directly over our stateroom, I concluded that I would go out and inquire what had occurred. Partially dressing, I slipped out of our room into the forward companionway, there to find possibly half a dozen men, all speculating as to what had happened. While we stood there an officer passed by somewhat hurriedly and I asked him what was the trouble. He replied that he thought something had gone wrong with the propeller, but that it was nothing serious.

Leaving the few passengers that I had observed, still laughing and chatting, I returned to my stateroom. My wife being somewhat uneasy, desired to arise and dress. I assured her that nothing had occurred which would harm the ship, and persuaded her to remain in bed."

Mrs. Cook: "When Milley came back she said she was going to get dressed and I said I would do the same. As the three of us were dressing one of the men next to us said, 'I advise you girls to get dressed as soon as you can,' for he thought there was danger ahead. We all looked like marble and a thousand and one thoughts ran into my mind. So as I dressed I pinned my broaches into my underclothes and put my watch and chain on my ticket and also my rings. I did not put a blouse on for I couldn't fasten it so I threw it off again. All this time I was pleading with Miss Brown to get up, for I told her I was sure she was the only one in bed. She then got up at once. I put on my big black coat and hat and tied it with the veil that Mable gave to me which I still have. I put my dear father's watch into my pocket that I had under my pillow and picked up my little black hand bag that had a few treasures in it and some money."

Miss Lehmann: "I heard the two ladies come into their room that was next to me. Their voices sounded as though they were very excited. Although I couldn't understand a word they were saying I knew something had happened. They left their cabin and then I thought that I really should get dressed and find out the reason for stopping in the middle of the night, because I knew then that we were no longer moving."

Olliver arrived in the engine room to deliver the captain's message to Bell. The chief engineering officer had just returned from the forward part of the ship where he had already spoken with Ismay, and possibly the captain. Very likely, the instructions from the captain advised Bell to shut down the boilers and engines, but leave enough power on tap to keep the ship operational.

Burton: "Where did you find the chief engineer?"
Olliver: "Down in the engine room. He was at work down there. The engines were not running. They were stopped. I delivered the message, and I waited for an answer. I waited for two or three minutes. Then he saw me standing and he asked me what I wanted. I said I was waiting for an answer to the message I took him. He told me to take back—to tell the captain that he would get it done as soon as possible."
Burton: "The lights were all going?"

Olliver: "Yes, sir. The lights were going in the engine room, but I believe they opened the watertight door leading to the stokehold, and it looked very black inside there. I cannot say the number of the stokehole, but it is the stokehole next to the engine room. There was a man went through whilst I was down. An engineer went in."
Burton: "Had you ever been in this stokehold before?"
Olliver: "Yes, sir."
Burton: "Was there a light there then?"
Olliver: "A faint light, sir."
Burton: "But there was no faint light there at this time?"
Olliver: "No, sir. It was black."

All ladders leading up from the boiler rooms exited onto E and A decks. Olliver used E deck as his route to return to the bridge from the engine room, just about the time the stokers came through the doors.

Burton: "Did you see any stokers come out of the stoke room?"
Olliver: "They were coming out of the stoke rooms along the alleyway."

And still an air of casualness pervaded the ship even down in the bow.

Clench: "I went down below and put my Guernsey on, my round hat on, and after that I sat down on a stool having a smoke."
Bourne: "Although you had seen this water coming in?"
Clench: "I had seen this water coming in, and I thought it was alright."

In the wireless room, everything was normal still, even though Phillips was aware that the ship was stopped because of trouble. No one had issued any directions so far. It was as if nothing significant had occurred.

Bride: "It was about five minutes to twelve. I had promised to relieve Mr. Phillips earlier than usual, you see. I went out to speak to him before I dressed. I only had pajamas on. I asked him how he was getting on. He had a big batch of telegrams from Cape Race that he had just finished."

Some of the passengers had been up and about during the collision and decided to resume their earlier activity. Dorothy Gibson was playing cards with friends in a cabin on A deck as the danger ever so slowly unfolded.

Miss Gibson: "Then it was that I noticed considerable nervousness on the part of the stewards and such of the officers as came within range of my vision, but nothing was said by them to give the passengers an inkling of what had happened. Good nights having been said, I stepped out upon deck with the intention of taking a short stroll before retiring, when I noticed that the great ship was leaning heavily on one side. I am not enough of a sailor to know whether it was port or starboard, but the fact remains she was lopsided. In the meantime the big steamship kept sagging down and when I asked one of the officers what significance the water on one of the stairways carried he replied with a smile that there was no cause for alarm. 'One of the compartments has been punctured,' he said with a faint smile, 'but the ship is sturdy enough to weather a little thing like that.'"

Gibson must have looked down one of the forward staircases leading from E deck to a hold. A number of first class passengers assembled around the foyers on each deck of the Grand Staircase. Henry Stengel came in from finding nothing of interest on the boat deck and descended the stairs.

Mr. Stengel: "There were not many people around there. That was where the lifeboats were. We came down to the next deck, and the captain came up. I supposed he had come up from investigating the damage. He had a very serious and a very grave face. I then said to my wife, 'This is a very serious matter, I believe.' I think Mr. Widener and his wife–I think it was Mr. Widener–followed the captain up the stairs, and they returned, and I presume they went to their staterooms."

Solid information was hard to come by, and many knew little more than they did twenty minutes earlier. This strange stopping of the ship in the middle of the Atlantic required an explanation and a continuous procession of passengers emerged from their rooms with the same set of questions for the stewards.

Crawford: ". . . as I was going around Mr. and Mrs. Bishop came out and asked me what was the matter. I said we had run into a piece of ice."

Others were beginning to return to their cabins, having found nothing particularly alarming to keep them standing around in the hallways. The mystery as to why the ship had stopped was solved; they had simply bumped into an iceberg. The excitement was fading.

Mr. Harper: "We walked very slowly up the steps of the big stairways, for I was pretty weak, and when we got to the next deck above, I sat down on a lounge and rested five or six minutes. Then we climbed up to the next deck, and so on. At last we got up to the gymnasium, which was on the top deck, and I sat down beside my wife. Men and women were standing about in groups talking. Everybody seemed confident that the ship was all right. She certainly seemed all right. The engines had been stopped soon after we struck and by this time she had slowly lost headway and was standing still. The sea was quiet, a flat calm, but all the ship's lights were lit and there was not a suggestion of excitement anywhere. A few people were talking about the lifeboats, but they were laughed at. 'Lifeboats!' said a woman near me. 'What do they need of lifeboats? This ship could smash a hundred icebergs and not feel it. Ridiculous!' After a little time, word was passed among the passengers that we better go back to bed. 'The ship will be delayed two hours,' the stewards said, 'and then go on to New York.' At this a great many people went away from our neighborhood. Whether they went back to bed or not, I don't know; but I can't remember seeing their faces again. They dropped away a few at a time–casually drifted off."

Mrs. Futrelle: "Mrs. Harris was suffering from a broken arm, which she carried in a sling. I clasped her free hand and together we waited, fear-struck and silent for the return of our husbands. We had both dressed hurriedly. I had aided her in wrapping a heavy coat about her. It seemed but a few moments before our husbands returned and told us there was nothing to fear. I was faint with fright, but endeavored to control myself."

Mrs. Douglas: "We waited some little time, Mr. Douglas reassuring me that there was no danger before going out of the cabin. But later Mr. Douglas went out to see what had happened, and I put on my heavy boots and fur coat to go up on deck later. I waited in the corridor to see or hear what I could. We received no orders. No one knocked at our door. We saw no officers nor stewards–no one to give an order or answer our questions."

As the midnight hour descended upon *Titanic*, most of her crew and passengers were just waiting. It was, after all, almost midnight and most of them wanted to go back to bed. All of this commotion was somewhat entertaining for a voyage, but it was late, and if nothing new developed soon, then it would be best to get some sleep.

Twelve O'Clock

It is well documented that while a large number of people were awakened by the collision and went out to explore, others slept right through it and into the midnight hour. There were so many noises on a ship at sea that eventually one learned to just screen them out in order to get a good night sleep. Throughout the ship, some passengers were still in a peaceful state of bliss. But they would wake up soon enough.

Mr. Gracie: "I was awakened in my stateroom at 12 o'clock. The time, 12 o'clock, was noted on my watch, which was on my dresser which I looked at promptly when I got up. At the same time, almost instantly, I heard the blowing off of steam and the ship's machinery seemed to stop. It was so slight I could not be positive of it. All through the voyage the machinery did not manifest itself at all from my position in my stateroom, so perfect was the boat. I looked out of the door of my stateroom, glanced up and down the passageway to see if there was any commotion, and I did not see anybody nor hear anybody moving at all. But I did not like the sound of it, so I thought I would partially dress myself, which I did, and went on deck. I went on what they call A deck. Presently some passengers gathered around. We looked over the sides of the ship to see whether there was any indication of what had caused this noise. I soon learned from friends around that an iceberg had struck us. Presently along came a gentleman, described by Mr. Stengel here, who had ice in his hands. Some of this ice was handed to us with the statement that we had better take this home for souvenirs. Nobody had any fear at that time at all. I looked on deck outside to see if there was any indication of a list. I could not distinguish any."

Midnight marked the start of a new watch for many of the crew, and if the calamity at the bow and in the hallway outside had not been enough to get them out of their bunks, the scheduled start of their work shift was. Hogg was one of the lookouts scheduled to start his watch.

Hogg: "I dressed myself and we relieved the lookout at 12 o'clock, me and my mate Evans."

Even though the ship was stopped in the water, the lookouts had not been informed of any changes. Fleet and Lee resumed their watch after the collision. Remaining in the nest, they had watched the collision, saw the ship stop, watched it go forward again, and then observed the *Titanic* come to a stop again. Now, as the ship was starting to list to starboard, they were being relieved.

Smith: "How long did you stay there?"
Fleet: "About a quarter of an hour to 20 minutes after."
Smith: "After what?"
Fleet: "After the accident."
Smith: "And then did you leave this place?"
Fleet: "We got relieved by the other two men."

Information was starting to leak its way through various channels of conversation. Most of it was premature speculation.

Miss Lehmann: "I dressed and went up on deck. I saw a French musician that I had met talking to another lady. She went away and then I asked him what was wrong. He just told me that we would have to go on another boat to get to New York and that I should go down and get my coat."

Mrs. Cook: "We then started to go up on deck. When we got outside the steward put our life jackets on us that we were carrying in our hands. But he said, 'Go back to bed. There's no danger.' but I said to Milley, 'Let's go up and have a look around now that we are dressed.'"

Second class passengers saw nothing out of the ordinary up on deck except for other people sprinkled about here and there. It was too cold to stay on deck very long with nothing to keep them up there, so many only lingered for a few minutes. The same went for third class passengers at the stern of the ship.

In first class the situation was pretty much the same unless a passenger went all the way forward on the promenade deck and through the door to an open space. From there, one could see a scattering of broken ice down on the third class well deck along with a few steerage passengers and a growing number of crew.

Mr. Peuchen: " I also called on Mr. Molson at his room, but he was out. I afterwards saw Mr. Molson on deck and we chatted over the matter, and I suppose 15 minutes after that I met Mr. Hays, his son-in-law, and I said to him, 'Mr. Hays, have you seen the ice?' He said, 'No.' I said, 'If you care to see it I will take you up on the deck and show it to you.' So we proceeded from probably C deck to A deck and along forward, and I showed Mr. Hays the ice forward."
Smith: "When you and Mr. Hays went forward to look at the ice, how much of it could you see?"
Peuchen: "I should think about 4½ feet of ice, probably 1½ to 2 inches thick. That is, it would be thicker on the rail than it would be on the bow. I heard the men walking over it, and it would crunch under their feet."

When the engines had stopped earlier, passengers received the first indication that something was not right. Shortly after midnight, people noticed a second sign that something was wrong. The ship was definitely listing now.

Mr. Peuchen: "I happened to look and noticed the boat was listing, probably half

Opposite page: Steam roars from the smokestacks as the *Titanic* glides to a stop.

an hour after my first visit to the upper deck. I said to Mr. Hays, 'Why she is listing. She should not do that, the water is perfectly calm, and the boat has stopped.' I felt that looked rather serious. He said, 'Oh, I don't know. You cannot sink this boat.' He had a good deal of confidence."

Mr. Harder: " I walked around the deck two or three times when I noticed that the boat was listing quite a good deal on the starboard side. So Mrs. Harder and myself thought we would go inside and see if there was any news. We went in there and talked to a few people and all of them seemed of the opinion that it was nothing serious. I saw Mr. and Mrs. Bishop, and I saw Colonel and Mrs. Astor, and they all seemed to be of the opinion that there was no danger."

Smith: "How soon after that did the boat begin to list?"
Mr. Peuchen: "I should think about 25 minutes afterwards."

Even with ice on the bow and a developing lean to starboard, an air of calmness and confidence prevailed. While many passengers chose to remain up, others decided they had seen all there was to see.

Mrs. Bishop: "We looked all over the deck,

walked up and down a couple of times, and one of the stewards met us and laughed at us. He said, 'You go back downstairs. There is nothing to be afraid of. We have only struck a little piece of ice and passed it.' So we returned to our stateroom and retired."

The fourth watertight compartment from the bow had incurred the greatest damage of all the compartments. It flooded the fastest. As a result, while the other compartments continued to take in water, the fourth compartment already reached equilibrium with the outside sea level. The mail room was in this compartment and when the water stopped rising just a few feet from reaching the floor of F deck, the Chambers decided to return to their cabin nearby. Their steward was in a calming mode.

Mr. Chambers: "Then my wife and myself returned in the direction of our stateroom, a matter of a few yards only, and as we were going down our own alleyway to the stateroom door our room steward came by and told us that we could go on back to bed again, that there was no danger. In this I agreed with him, personally."

Others on E deck in first class were more skeptical and were not about to go

back to bed based upon the opinion of a passing steward.

Mr. McGough: "My stateroom was on the starboard side, deck E, and was shared with me by Mr. Flynn, a buyer for Gimbel Brothers, New York at 33rd and Broadway. Soon after leaving our stateroom we came in contact with the second dining room steward, Mr. Dodd in the companionway, of whom we asked the question, 'Is there any danger?' and he answered, 'Not in the least,' and suggested that we go back to bed, which we did not, however, do. It was the intention to go up on the promenade deck, but before doing so I rapped on the door of the stateroom opposite mine, which was occupied by a lady, and suggested to her that she had better get up at once and dress, as there was apparently something wrong."

People like James McGough and Captain Edward Crosby listened to their early instincts. During the first half hour after the collision, passengers, one by one or in couples set out to investigate, and McGough and Crosby added to the small stream of inquisitors.

Mrs. Crosby: "Captain Crosby got up, dressed, and went out and came back again and said to me, 'You will lie there and drown,' and went out again. He said to my daughter, 'The boat is badly damaged, but I think the watertight compartments will hold her up.' My husband did not come back again after he left me, and I don't know what became of him, except that his body was found and brought to Milwaukee and buried."

The water was pouring into the ship for 25 minutes by the time Captain Smith returned to the bridge with his dark secret. Wilde was there with Murdoch and Moody. Boxhall was probably in the chart room. Lightoller, Pitman, and Lowe were not present. With the *Titanic* stopped in the middle of the Atlantic, her head slightly down by the bow with a list to starboard, the officers waited in suspense as Smith opened his mouth. He issued a command to prepare the lifeboats for lowering and assemble the passengers on deck. The *Titanic*'s maiden voyage had just been canceled.

Wilde was instrumental in putting the command into effect. He sent the word down for "all hands on deck," meaning that all seamen were to report, regardless of whether it was their watch. The most effective way to have this done was through a disciplined chain of command.

Haines: "I went down to look at number 1 hole. The tarpaulin was bellying up, raising, showing that the water was coming in. I went on the bridge and reported to the chief officer. I told him number 1 hole was filling. He gave me an order then to get the men up and get the boats out."

Olliver: "As soon as I came on the bridge I delivered back the message I was told to deliver to the captain. As soon as I delivered that message, the chief officer sent me to the boatswain of the ship and told me to tell the boatswain to get the oar lines and to uncover the boats and get them ready for lowering, and I done so, and came back on the bridge. "

Clench: "Then, after I lighted the pipe, I heard the boatswain's pipe call all hands out on deck. We went up to where he stood under the forecastle, and he ordered all hands to the boat deck."

Within minutes the ship awoke into action as the word spread among seamen that they were wanted on deck. Murdoch also took part in getting the orders out.

Buley: "The next order from the chief officer, Murdoch, was to tell the seamen to get together and uncover the boats and turn them out as quietly as though nothing had happened."

Hemming: "We went back in our bunks a few minutes. Then the joiner came in and he said, 'If I were you I would turn out, you fellows. She is making water one-two-three, and the racket court is getting filled up.' Just as he went, the boatswain came and he says, 'Turn out, you fellows,' he says, 'you haven't half an hour to live.' He said, 'That is from Mr. Andrews.' He said, 'Keep it to yourselves and let no one know.'"

Hardy: ". . . the chief first-class steward came to my room and asked me to get up, as he thought it was pretty serious, that she was making water forward. I went with him forward to see what water she was making . . . then I did not see it, in fact. I could only hear it. It was making too much noise to come in in any great volume. The fall of the water was not like a volume. It was coming in fast, but you could hear it falling . . . We could see it coming up the stairs gradually."

The pursers, whose functions were similar to hotel managers, were given the order to awaken the passengers and get them up on deck. From the very start, the tone set was one of routine, that this was all a matter of precaution.

Hardy: ". . . and on my return to my end of the ship I met Purser Barker. He advised

me or told me to get the people on deck with their life belts on as a precaution. Immediately I sent down for all hands to come up. They all came along, and I went among the people and told those people to go on deck with their life belts . . . "
Fletcher: "How did the order come?"
Hardy: "From Purser Barker. That is, Purser Barker brought it himself personally to me. There is a first class purser and a second class purser. They would get it direct from the bridge, I presume. They are our superiors aboard the ship, and we take our orders through them."

Because the majority of the crew, particularly the stewards were berthed on the port side of E deck, first class passengers on the starboard side of the same deck were first to hear of the new orders. Within minutes of the decision to get the passengers up on deck, they were in the know.

Mr. Chambers: ". . . I finished dressing, my wife being already fully and warmly clothed, and she in the meanwhile having gone out into the passage to note any later developments, came rushing back to me saying that she had seen another passenger who had informed her that the call had been given for life belts and on the boat deck. I went out myself, and found my room steward passing down the alleyway and had the order verified."

The seamen and the stewards were set into motion with amazing efficiency considering that there was no speaker system on board. There was a defined chain of command in place and it proved itself very instrumental in coordinating hundreds of men and women who were in the service of the *Titanic*.

Ward: ". . . the head waiter came down, Moss, his name was, and said we were all to go on deck and to put on some warm clothing before we went up, as we were liable to be there some time. With that I think most everybody in the 'glory hole' as we call it, got dressed and went on deck. I just put on things to keep me warm because I did not think it was anything serious."

Ray: "I was going off to sleep again when they came in and told us to get to the lifeboats."
Smith: "Who told you that?"
Ray: "First the saloon steward and then Mr. Dodd, the second steward."
Smith: "How long was that after the impact?"
Ray: "As near as I could make out, it was about 20 minutes. It was around 12 o'clock."

Burke: "About a quarter of an hour or 20 minutes later the order came for life belts. The order came to get our life belts and get up on deck and take our overcoats. Mention was made of the fact that it was very cold. I immediately got up with everybody else."

Collins: ". . . and the word came in that we were to get out of our beds and get the life belts on and get up to the upper deck."
Bourne: "At what time was it that this word came? How long after the ship struck?"
Collins: "Well, it was exactly—I am sure—half an hour, sir. Quite half an hour, it was."

The seamen—not to be confused with the firemen or stewards—filed up to the boat deck to begin preparations. The image of the deserted boat deck, quiet on a lonely Sunday night was forever gone.

Archer: "We went on deck to the top of the forecastle ladder, to the boatswain, and we waited for the watch, and he gave us orders and we proceeded to the boat deck and proceeded to uncover and clear away the boats."

Evans: "We went up and we looked down the forward hatch, where the tarpaulin was raising up with the wind, and I seen the boatswain again, and he told me to go down *and tell the seamen to come up and uncover the boats, and make them ready for going out."*

Jones: "As soon as I went on deck somebody gave the order, 'All hands on the bridge.'"

Taylor: "The officer was coming along the alleyway and ordered us to put on life belts. A majority of them did not realize that she would sink. Because they were all skylarking and joking about it."

Newlands: "What did that mean, that the entire crew was to go up on the boat deck?"
Moore: "All the able seamen."
Newlands: "Would that include firemen?"
Moore: "It had nothing to do with firemen. So far as I can say, all the seamen from the forecastle were ordered up to clear away the boats and to take off the boat covers."

Crowe: ". . . a saloon steward came down shortly afterwards and told me to come up on the upper deck with as much warm clothes on as I could get. I went up on the boat deck."

Some third class passengers were standing in the forward well space, watching with great interest as seamen headed up to the boat deck. Their cabins toward the bow on G deck were flooding. Most of the third class passengers, to their ultimate demise, were shepherded by the stewards and crew up the long E deck corridor to the stern where the remainder of steerage were located—high and dry. But a few were lucky enough to instead climb the stairs to this third class area on the forward well deck. Once the seamen went up to the boat deck, these third class passengers decided they would go up too.

Mr. Buckley: "They tried to keep us down at first on our steerage deck. They did not want us to go up to the first class place at all. I cannot say who they were. I think they were sailors. There was one steerage passenger there, and he was getting up the steps and just as he was going in a little gate a fellow came along and chucked him down. Threw him down into the steerage place. This fellow got excited and he ran after him and he could not find him. He got up over the little gate; a little gate just at the top of the stairs going up into the first class deck. He did not find him. The first class deck was higher up than the steerage deck, and there were some steps leading up to it, 9 or 10 steps, and a gate just at the top of the steps. It was not locked at the time we made the attempt to get up there, but the sailor, or whoever he was, locked it. So that this fellow that went up after him broke the lock on it, and he went after the fellow that threw him down. He said if he could get hold of him he would throw him into the ocean."

The scene described above is single handedly the biggest contributor to the legendary illusion of hundreds of steerage passengers being locked behind gates below deck, clamoring and pleading to be let up to the boat deck. In fact, the staircase Daniel Buckley and other steerage passengers encountered was only about three to four feet high along a forward B deck railing in an open area outside. The discrimination that Buckley observed a few minutes after midnight was real, however, and it would rear itself again at the stern – and more effectively. With apparently no direct order from the captain or officers to do so, the crew of the *Titanic* were going to follow a concerted and conscious course of action to keep the steerage passengers away from the boat deck.

With the arrival of third class passengers from the flooded bow, word quickly spread in steerage of trouble. Some decided to get dressed right away.

Miss Mulvihill: "I lay still for several minutes, not knowing what was the matter.

Then I slipped on a heavy coat over my nightgown, pulled on my shoes and went out into the passage. The people were rushing up the stairways, and way down in the steerage I could hear the women and men shrieking and screaming. The women called for their children. The men cursed."

Anna Turja stopped by to see another Finnish woman with whom she had made an earlier acquaintance. The woman was busy with a handful of her own small children and the whole thing seemed a bit overwhelming to her.

Miss Turja: ""We will never get away from here alive,' she said to herself in despair."

The *Titanic*'s crew were moving into action with impressive speed. By the time Fleet went down to his quarters, they were already putting the captain's recent orders into effect.

Fleet: "I went down below and I found there was nobody down there, and the quartermaster come down and said we were all wanted on the bridge. I did not see anyone there. I seen them all at the boats, getting them ready and putting them out."

As the boat deck came alive, the off-duty officers were left to decide on their own whether they were needed or not. Wilde had quickly risen after the collision and investigated the area under the forecastle. Boxhall had advised the remaining three officers that the ship was taking in water, but he never told them to report to the bridge. Instead, they were left to their own judgement as to what they should do next.

Lightoller: "He went out, closing the door, whilst I slipped into some clothes as quickly as possible and went out on deck."

Pitman: "So I put a coat on and went on deck, and saw the men uncovering the boats and clearing them away. I walked along to the after end of the boat deck, and met Mr. Moody, the sixth officer. I asked him if he had seen the iceberg. He said no, but he said, 'There is some ice on the forward well deck.' So, to satisfy my curiosity, I went down there myself. So I saw a little ice there. I went further, to the forecastle head to see if there was any damage there. I could not see any at all. On my return, before emerging from under the forecastle head, I saw a crowd of firemen coming out with their bags, bags of clothing. I said, 'What is the matter?' They said, 'The water is coming in our place.' I said, 'That is funny.' I looked down Number 1 hatch then,
and saw the water flowing over the hatch. I then immediately went to the boat deck . . ."

Lowe, by comparison, never fully woke up when told of the news and he continued to sleep in his quarters.

Captain Smith focused on two objectives just after midnight. First, he wanted passengers off the ship without a panic, and second, help had to be summoned immediately from other vessels. Once Smith issued the command to begin preparations for evacuation, he walked back to the wireless room. Bride and Phillips were alone, speculating about the commotion. Sleep was a premium under almost any circumstance, and regardless of the activity outside, Phillips prepared to go to his bunk. The captain suddenly appeared in the doorway.

Bride: He [Phillips] told me that he thought she had got damaged in some way and that he expected that we should have to go back to Harland & Wolff's. I took over the watch from him. He was going to retire, sir. He got inside of the other room when the captain came in, then. He told us that we had better get assistance. That is exactly what he said. He said, 'You had better get assistance.' When Mr. Phillips heard him he came out and asked him if he wanted him to use a distress call. He said, 'Yes, at once.'"

For Phillips and Bride, the captain's instructions brought an immediate level of excitement to the otherwise routine wireless traffic. But Captain Smith must have recoiled at his own words as he almost yelled his instructions above the roar of the escaping steam to Phillips. Smith might have asked the two what ships were nearby. Could Phillips have told him about the *Californian* then, and the warning the *Titanic* had received only an hour ago? The noise of the steam outside did not make it conducive for discussion. On his way out of the cabin, Smith probably advised them that the *Titanic*'s location would follow shortly.

Smith: *"Who sent this call?"*
Bride: *"Mr. Phillips."*
Smith: *"Was the message sent immediately?"*
Bride: *"Immediately."*
Smith: *"Do you know what the message was?"*
Bride: *"CQD about half a dozen times. MGY half a dozen times."*
Smith: *"Will you kindly explain the meaning of these letters or that code?"*
Bride: *"CQD is a recognized distress call. MGY is the code call of the Titanic."*

Marconi: *"CQ is the call for all stations. If you call CQ on a ship it means, 'All other stations stand at attention and reply.' I did not make the signal originally. I presume the object was to indicate in a certain way to all stations the danger or peril that existed. I should add that the international danger signal, introduced or decided on by the Berlin convention is SOS. I do not know what it means. It denotes danger or distress. I believe that was sent too, from the Titanic, but of course, Mr. Bride will tell you it is the fact."*

The distress signal went out into the night air. Because one morse code message is just like another in terms of the sound it produces, no heightened tone or exclamation in the manner of delivery was possible. The call for help arrived at the headsets of distant operators on other ships with the same routine buzzing as any other message. The content, of course, should have relayed the urgency.

The *Frankfurt* responded within minutes prematurely raising the hopes of Phillips, Bride, and Smith. Phillips sent Bride to tell Smith of the news. He found him standing alongside the port side boats 2 through 8, watching the crew at work.

Bride: *"He told me to go to the captain and report the Frankfurt. He was in communication with the Frankfurt, sir. He had sent the Frankfurt our position."*

Smith: *"And you delivered that message to the captain?"*
Bride: *"Yes, sir."*
Smith: *"Where was he at the time?"*
Bride: *"He was on the boat deck, sir."*
Smith: *"Not on the bridge?"*
Bride: *"No, sir."*
Smith: *"What did he say in reply when you handed him this message?"*
Bride: *"He wanted to know where she was."*
Smith: *"What did you do then?"*
Bride: *"I went back to the cabin with Mr. Phillips. Mr. Phillips was waiting for the position of the boat then, sir."*

One has to wonder if Bride kicked himself for not realizing that he should have had the *Frankfurt's* location before rushing off to the captain. Meanwhile, Boxhall was working out the ship's location so that it could be sent out along with the distress call.

Boxhall: *"Then I went into the chart room and worked out the ship's position. I submitted her position to the captain. He said, 'Take it to the Marconi room.' I found the two operators there, Phillips and Bride. There was too much noise of the steam escaping, so I wrote the position down for them and left it. Left it on his table there. He saw it. He made a call and he was listening, and I did not interrupt him."*

For Captain Smith and Bruce Ismay in particular, the first few minutes after midnight must have been too horrible for words. The news before them was as bad as a human spirit could tolerate. They had just run the *Titanic*, with 2,223 people on board, into an iceberg and now the ship was going to sink with too few lifeboats. All the chance circumstances and ignored warnings that have since held generations captivated by this tragedy must have crashed into the two with the impact of a wrecking ball, leaving them almost physically sick from the realization that the *Titanic* would soon be at the bottom of the ocean. Captain Smith at least had his own command responsibilities to distract him. Ismay, on the other hand, had time to reflect.

Smith: *"Did you see Mr. Ismay at that time?"*
Lightoller: *"On the boat deck."*
Smith: *"How long before she sank?"*
Lightoller: *"At first, before we started the boats, when we started to uncover the boats."*
Smith: *"How long was that after the collision?"*
Lightoller: *"About 20 minutes."*
Smith: *"What was he doing?"*
Lightoller: *"Standing still."*
Smith: *"Was he talking with anyone?"*

Bruce Ismay

Lightoller: *"No, sir."*
Smith: *"He was alone?"*
Lightoller: *"Yes sir."*

Smith: *"Did you see Mr. Ismay that night?"*
Mr. Peuchen: *"I think I saw him standing for a moment without his hat on, just a moment, on the port side. On the boat deck."*

As the first dramatic wireless calls for help went out across the Atlantic, the boat deck sprang to life with a flurry of activity. Crewmen started preparing the lifeboats. The scene must have been an ominous one to any passengers up on deck.

Boxhall: *". . . and then the order came out for the boats. I went around the decks and was clearing the lifeboats, helping take the covers off . . . and assisting generally around the decks."*

Scarrott: *"We had no sooner got below when the boatswain called all hands on deck to uncover and turn all the boats out ready for lowering. We did not think then there was anything serious. The general idea of the crew was that we were going to get the boats ready in case of emergency, and the sooner we got the job done the quicker we should get below again. The port side boats were got ready first and then the starboard ones."*

Buley: *"I was over on the starboard side at first. We lowered all the starboard boats, and went over and done the same to the port boats. They are on deck and the davits are turned inboard. You have to unscrew these davits and swing the boat out over the ship's side. The next order was to lower them down to a line with the gunwale of the boat deck . . . "*

Because there had not been a boat drill, it appears the discipline for launching the boats began to break down early when crewmen were discouraged from standing by and working their own boats.

Bourne: *"Had you been assigned to a boat?"*
Archer: *"Yes, sir. Number 7."*
Bourne: *"Did you go right to your own boat, number 7?"*
Archer: *"No. We did not have orders to go to number 7. We had orders to uncover all boats."*

Although most of the crew had been informed to get on deck, the news had not yet passed to the passengers. Even as signs of a pending evacuation became present, passengers were in another state of mind.

Mr. Beesley: *"I soon decided to go down again and as I crossed from the starboard side to the port side to go down by the vestibule door, I saw an officer climb on the last lifeboat on the port side–number 16– and begin to throw off the cover, but I do not remember that anyone paid any particular attention to him."*

Beesley had likely seen Frederick Clench climbing up onto the lifeboat.

Clench: *"We proceeded up on the boat deck, and when we got up there he told us to go to the starboard side and uncover the boats. I went down to number 11 boat, unlacing the cover, and just as I started to unlace, along come an officer."*
Bourne: *"Were you assigned to number 11?"*
Clench: *"No. Number 4 was my boat. We were sent there to uncover the boat, and an officer came along and drafted me on the other side, the port side. I went to number 16 on the port side–the after boat, and started getting out the boat falls to let them down. I got out the two falls and coiled them down on the deck. When I was putting the plug in the boat in readiness to be lowered, they were swinging the boat out. I was in the boat at the time she was swinging out; fixing the plug. I jumped out of that boat and got her all ready for lowering, and helped get the other falls out of the other boats. Number 14 boat we went to next."*

With orders working their way through the ship to report to the boat deck, the passengers were to learn momentarily that this latest commotion was not just a brief interruption. They would not be getting underway again in just a few minutes.

During this time the steam continued to roar out of the exhaust pipes along the smokestack with a deafening intensity. It was so loud that Senator Fletcher later wondered if the sound had traveled across the surface within an earshot of the *Californian*. As the *Titanic* prepared her lifeboats under the roar of the steam, Ernest Gill was smoking a cigarette on the *Californian*, idly watching the distant lights.

Fletcher: *"If there had been a vessel that night within 5 miles of the Titanic, could not her whistle have been heard that distance?"*
Pitman: *"No. But you could have heard her blowing off steam at a far greater distance than you could hear the steam whistle. She was blowing off steam for three quarters of an hour, I think, and you could hear that much farther than you could hear any steam whistle."*

Fletcher: *"Did you hear any noise, escaping steam or anything of that sort?"*
Gill: *"No, sir."*

First class steward Alfred Crawford remained on duty on B deck. To him, things were beginning to settle down some. He had just seen Bruce Ismay return to his cabin. A number of others also reported seeing nothing serious up on deck.

Smith: *"Do you know any of the passengers in your part of this ship?"*
Crawford: *"I know three ladies, Mrs. Rogers, Miss Rogers, and her niece. Also Mr. Steward, that I had in my section, and there was a Mr. and Mrs. Bishop."*

For Crawford, things changed the moment Albert Stewart came down the Grand Staircase and appeared in the passageway.

Crawford: *". . . a gentleman—a Mr. Stewart - came down and asked me to help dress him and to tie his shoes and I did so. He went on deck and came back again and told me that it was serious, that they had told passengers to put on life belts. I got the life belts down and tied one on him and also one on others. I gave them to other ladies and gentlemen on the deck. After that, during that time, I saw Mr. Ismay come out of his room, and a bedroom steward named Clark, and they went on deck."*

Ismay had returned to his suite with the distinct purpose of dressing more suitably for the boat deck. Unlike Andrews, and in line with Ismay's aloof manner, he did not advise the stewards to get the passengers up on deck as soon as possible. He was focused on his own agenda. Traveling up the Grand Staircase, he sought out Captain Smith again.

Ismay: *"I think I went back onto the bridge."*

Ismay likely asked the captain for his assessment of things. A call for help was being made on the wireless, and the *Frankfurt* had already responded. The lifeboats, as Ismay could already see, were being readied for lowering. The two may have talked about the ability of the ship to maintain its power and keep the pumps going. They may have mentally calculated exactly how many passengers the lifeboats could hold and decided at that time on the "women and children first" strategy.

While Ismay and Smith spoke, first class passengers were ever so slowly finding out that they were supposed to go on deck. Some were informed by the stewards; most actually heard about it through word of mouth from other passengers. A sense of urgency was clearly lacking in first class.

Mrs. Bishop: *"About 15 minutes later we were awakened by a man who had a stateroom near us. We were on B deck, number 47. He told us to come upstairs. So we dressed again thoroughly and looked all over our belongings in our room and went upstairs."*

Mr. Bishop: *"I did not hear any alarm. The alarm we had was from another passenger, a friend of ours on the ship. Mr. Stewart. He was lost."*

Steward Andrew Cunningham was attending the cabins in the forward area of D deck. It seems passengers were better informed than he was, as they knew to put on their life belts before he had even heard the order. There was a staircase near his station that led to E deck just a few feet from where the Chambers couple had peered down several minutes earlier.

Cunningham: *"I answered one or two of the bells. The ladies wanted to know how to put on life belts. There had been no order passed then. They asked me how to put them on, and I showed several of them; six or seven probably. I looked down on E deck to see how things were there. There was a stairway that led from the E deck to the post office, and the water was down there then. That was level with F deck. From my own knowledge, when I saw the water in the post office deck, I thought it was pretty bad then. There was another bell rung, and I came up and answered it."*

The barrage of questions thrown at the stewards left some of them with short tempers, particularly when they believed nothing serious was wrong. In their minds, they probably just wished their passengers would go back to sleep to make their watch easier.

Miss Gibson: "On my way below to Deck E, I encountered a steward and asked him if there was anything wrong. He tried to push me aside, but I stood resolutely and then he snapped out, 'Nothing wrong!' and disappeared to the deck above. It was at this stage of the proceedings that I became somewhat uneasy and made haste to arouse my mother."

Mrs. Warren: "By that time I had dressed and had laid out the life belts but Mr. Warren said there was absolutely no danger and that with her watertight compartments the vessel could not possibly sink and that in all probability the only effect the accident would have would be the delaying of our arrival in New York three or four days. We felt, however, too restless to remain in our room, so went out in the corridor again and talked with both the employees of the vessel and passengers. The general opinion prevailing was that there was no danger except for the expression on the part of one man who stated that the water was coming in below forward."

The casual attitude was no different in second class. By now, the ship had surely stopped, but Lawrence Beesley mistook the vibration from shutting down the boilers, releasing the residual steam, and the operation of the generators as signs that the engines were still running.

Mr. Beesley: "As I passed to the door to go down, I looked forward again and saw to my surprise an undoubted tilt downwards from the stern to the bows. As I went downstairs a confirmation of this tilting forward came in something unusual about the stairs, a curious sense of something out of balance and of not being able to put one's feet down in the right place. It was perceptible only by the sense of balance at this time. On D deck were three ladies standing in the passage near the cabin. 'Oh! Why have we stopped?' they said. 'We did stop,' I replied, 'but we are now going on again.' 'Oh, no,' one replied, 'I cannot feel the engines as I usually do, or hear them. Listen!' We listened and there was no throb audible. Having noticed that the vibration of the engines is most noticeable lying in a bath, where the throb comes straight from the floor through its metal sides, I took them along the corridor to a bathroom and made them put their hands on the side of the bath. They were much reassured to feel the engines throbbing down below and to know we were making some headway. I left them and on the way to my cabin passed some stewards standing unconcernedly against the walls of the saloon. One of them, the library steward again, was leaning over a table, writing. It is no exaggeration to say that they had neither any knowledge of the accident nor any feeling of alarm that we had stopped and had not yet gone on again full speed. Their whole attitude expressed perfect confidence in the ship and officers."

Confidence ruled the early part of the night. Even the pessimistic ones were unknowingly optimistic.

Mr. Gracie: "At that time I joined my friend, Mr. Clint Smith, and he and I in the cabin did notice a list, but thought it best not to say anything about it for fear of creating some commotion. Then we agreed to stick by each other through thick and thin if anything occurred, and to meet later on. He went to his cabin and I went to mine. In my cabin I packed my three bags very hurriedly. I thought if we were going to be removed to some other ship it would be easy for the steward to get my luggage out."

From time to time a passenger would pick up on a clue from one of the ship's staff and act upon it. But this was generally difficult to do, because most of the ship's staff simply had no idea how serious the entire situation was. Finally, around 12:15, the news that passengers were to put on their life belts and go up on deck began to spread in earnest.

Mrs. Warren: *"Following this, we then went to our rooms, put on all our heavy wraps and went to the foot of the grand staircase on deck D, again interviewing passengers and crew as to the danger. While standing there a Mr. Perry, I think his name was, one of the designers of the vessel, rushed by going up the stairs. He was asked if there was any danger but made no reply. But a passenger who was afterwards saved told me that his face had on it a look of terror. Immediately after this, the report became general that water was in the squash courts, which were on the deck below where we were standing, and that the baggage had already been submerged. Just at this point a steward passed, ordering all to don life belts and warm clothing and go up to the boat deck at once, saying that this move was simply a precautionary measure. According to my impression, the time was now about 45 minutes after the accident. We went back to our room for a third time, seized the life belts and hastened to a point two decks*

Passengers assembled in the Reception Room shortly after midnight awaiting news. (*Olympic*)

above where an officer assisted in adjusting our life belts."

Mrs. Futrelle: *"At about the same time that our husbands came back to us an officer passed by. He spoke to Mr. Harris in a low tone. I did not catch what he said, but there was something in his tone which frightened me, I don't know why. As the officer went on his way Mr. Harris turned to us and said, 'I don't like the looks of things.' Then we looked out into the cabin and saw people putting on life belts. None of them seemed greatly alarmed, but we thought it wise to follow their examples. Both Jacques and Mr. Harris tried to quiet our fears by joking with us about it. Their efforts were not successful, however. Jacques and I returned to our stateroom. I asked him if he had his*

money with him, and he passed some laughing remark about not needing it. It's queer to think of the things one will do in a moment of great stress. I remember that I took a drink of water. I didn't think to take my valuables with me, not even the pearl necklace which I treasured so much and which was Jacques' last gift to me. With our life jackets strapped in place we went into the saloon. Never shall I forget the picture of white faced women clinging to their husbands. There was no panic and very little noise. The men were calm and possessed, with women frightened but sustained by the examples set by their husbands."

Mr. Peuchen: *"I hardly got back in the grand staircase–I probably waited around there ten minutes or more–when I saw the ladies and gentlemen all coming in off of the deck looking very serious, and I caught up to Mr. Beattie, and I said, 'What is the matter?' He said, 'Why, the order is for life belts and boats.' I could not believe it at first, it seemed so sudden."*

Mr. Chambers: *"As I was at the time fully dressed and wore my heavy overcoat, in the pockets of which I had already placed certain necessities, we started up. My wife had presence of mind enough to take a life belt. I opened my steamer trunk and took out a small pocket compass, and sending my wife on ahead, opened my bag and removed an automatic pistol. We then proceeded immediately upward, my wife being rather alarmed, as she had also been at the time of the collision. But for her I should have remained in bed reading."*

The stewards found themselves busy now with passengers requesting help with life belts. A bell could be pushed from inside the passengers' cabins, and now they must have swamped the board.

Crawford: "I went to all the ladies' cabins. They were all rushing out, and I told them I didn't think there was any immediate danger, and after the order was passed for the life belts, I tied the life belts on the ladies and an old gentleman by the name of Stewart, and tied his shoes on for him."
Smith: "You say after the order was passed for the life belts?"
Crawford: "Yes."
Smith: "Who gave that order?"
Crawford: "The captain, I believe."
Smith: "How long after the collision?"
Crawford: "I should say about 30 minutes."
Smith: "Were there any children on that deck?"
Crawford: "No, sir. There was none on the deck where I was."

There was no systematic notification of first class passengers. The stewards were unprepared for the news and apparently did not approach the process with anything resembling an orderly cabin-to-cabin sweep. Whereas some passengers were notified, numerous others were never contacted at all by their stewards and only learned of the trouble by hearing the commotion outside their cabins.

Miss Minahan: "I was asleep in C-78. I was awakened by the crying of a woman in the passageway."

Miss Gibson: "By this time the officers had aroused the passengers and they were besieging the bulwarks and asking more questions than any one man could answer in a week."

Although second class seemed to get a slightly later start than first class in going up on deck, the procedure was more orderly, more direct, and more effective.

Mr. Beesley: "Turning into my gangway, I saw a man standing at the other end of it fastening his tie. 'Anything fresh?' he said. 'Not much,' I replied. 'We are going ahead slowly and she is down a little at the bows, but I don't think it is anything serious.'

'Come in and look at this man,' he laughed; 'he won't get up.' I looked in and in the top bunk lay a man with his back to me, closely wrapped in his bedclothes and only the back of his head visible. 'Why won't he get up? Is he asleep?' I said. 'No,' laughed the man dressing, 'he says . . .,' but before he could finish the sentence the man above grunted, 'You don't catch me leaving a warm bed to go up on that cold deck at midnight. I know better than that.' We both told him laughingly why he had better get up, but he was certain he was just as safe there and all this dressing was quite unnecessary. So I left them and went again to my cabin. I put on some underclothing, sat on the sofa and read for some ten minutes, when I heard through the open door, above, the noise of people passing up and down, and a loud shout from above, 'All passengers on deck with life belts on.'"

With an efficiency unseen in first class, the second class stewards diligently worked their cabins one by one with the resemblance of a squadron.

Hardy: ". . . we assisted the ladies with the belts, those that hadn't their husbands with them, and we assisted in getting the children out of bed. I also aroused the stewardesses to assist them. The whole of the men came,

and they assisted me in going around calling the different passengers. On all the decks—D, E, and F. I had 12 [rooms]. *The whole class numbered 70. We are entrusted with the passengers and that keeps us fully employed. The method I used was to just open the doors and throw them back and go right on down through the rooms myself."*
Fletcher: "What did you say?"
Hardy: "Just, 'Everybody on deck with life belts on at once.'"
Fletcher: "How many doors do you think you opened?"
Hardy: "I should think 20 or 24. Before I got there the men were along doing the same thing, the bedroom stewards. They all went into their own sets of rooms."

The hallways were abuzz. Stewards were passing the news. Passengers were at their doors asking questions. A number of people were heading up on deck, while others were coming back down.

Mr. Portalupi: ". . . having meantime returned to my stateroom and dressed."

Mrs. Cook: "And as we got up to boat deck they were calling out, 'All hands on deck' and immediately afterwards was calling 'Women and children in the boats.' Milley and I looked at one another but neither

spoke a word. Then I started to cry and I noticed that Milley was shaking me as we stood arm in arm."

In all the confusion of being roused, many passengers were not furnished with much detail from the crew. As a result, a lot of passengers did not know to dress warmly, probably thinking they were only going up on deck as a precaution before returning to their cabins. Others may have been so alarmed by the stewards' news, that they overreacted and assumed there was not a second to lose.

Mrs. Brown: "I did not think to dress very warmly but put on my best clothes which I had been wearing Sunday. I had low slippers on. Presently my husband came back to me. He looked very serious. 'Get on these cork jackets,' he said and helped Edith and me into life jackets. Then he put on one himself. He linked his arm into mine and led me up to the boat deck. He said the women and children were being put into lifeboats and that we had struck a berg."

While Ismay was on the bridge with Smith, he may have passed along his observation about the relaxed atmosphere he witnessed on B deck when leaving his suite. The two may have agreed it would be good

for Captain Smith to make a formal announcement to the cream of their repeat business—the first class passengers. Smith was known as the millionaire's captain because of his casual relationship with many of the wealthy. By informing them directly, he could set the proper cautionary tone and prevent a panic or rush for the boats.

Mrs. Bishop: "After being there [A Deck] *about five or ten minutes one of the men we were with ran up and spoke to the captain, who was just then coming down the stairs."*
Smith: "Who was the man?"
Bishop: "Mr. Astor. The captain told him something in an undertone. He came back and told six of us, who were standing with his wife, that we had better put on our life belts. I had gotten down two flights of stairs to tell my husband, who had returned to the stateroom for a moment, before I heard the captain announce that the life belts should be put on. That was about three or four minutes later that the captain announced the life belts should be put on. We came back upstairs and found very few people up."

Mrs. Dyer-Edwards: "As we hurried along Lambert Williams came up and explained that the watertight compartments must surely hold. Just then an officer hurried by. 'Will you all get life belts on! Dress warm-

ly and come up to A deck!' Quite stunned by the order, we all went. As I was going in to our stateroom my maid said water was pouring into the racquet court."

Mr. McGough: "Mr. Flynn and I then ascended to promenade deck A, and after being up there about 10 minutes were notified to put on life preservers as a matter of precaution. We then had to go all the way from promenade deck back to our stateroom, which was on E deck."

Mrs. White: "Nothing had been said about the lifeboats in any way, when suddenly Captain Smith came down the stairway and ordered us all to put on our life preservers, which we did."

Mr. Harder: "A little while after that an officer appeared at the foot of the stairs, and he announced that everybody should go to their staterooms and put on their life belts. That, I think was a little after 12, about 12 o'clock, that is roughly."

Mrs. Crosby: "I then got up and dressed, and my daughter dressed, and followed my husband on deck, and she got up on deck and the officer told her to go back and get on her life preserver and come back on deck as soon as possible."

Mr. Stengel: "Shortly after that the orders were given to have the passengers all put on life preservers. I went back to my stateroom and put a life preserver on my wife, and then she tied mine on. We went back up to the top deck."

First and second class passengers were now on the move. The evacuation had begun. To most of the passengers though, this was mainly an exercise in precaution. They all knew now that the *Titanic* had collided with an iceberg, and they all knew from the lean to starboard that she had been damaged. But what most of them did not know was that the unsinkable *Titanic* was going to sink. To them, all of this activity was an inconvenience, an oddity. Only the passengers prone to worrying were showing any sign of panic. The good natured among them decided to make the best of things and enjoy the excitement.

Mrs. Bishop: "We were on B deck, and we came back up to A deck. There was very little confusion, only the older women were a little frightened. They were up, partially dressed. So I sent a number of them back and saw that they were thoroughly dressed before they came up again."

Mr. Chambers: "We kept on upward, pass-ing at the various landings people who did not appear to be particularly frightened until we arrived on the A deck, going out on the port side where I shortly found the deck steward, joked with him about opening his little office room, and obtained our two steamer rugs."

Mrs. Dyer-Edwards: "We dressed as warmly as we could and went up to A deck. Mr. Brown, the purser, touched his hat as we passed, saying, 'It is quite all right. Don't hurry!'"

Adding to the perception that this was all a matter of precaution, the first ones to reach the upper decks waited a considerable amount of time with no direction.

Mrs. White: "We stood around another 20 minutes, then, I should think."

Jack Thayer arrived on deck with his parents and their maid. Thayer considered the boat deck to be called "A" deck, and the real A deck to be called "B" deck.

Mr. Thayer: "We all went out onto A deck, trying to find where we were supposed to go. They were then uncovering the boats and making preparations to swing them out. Everything was fairly orderly and the crew at least seemed to know what they were doing."

Many first class passenger were simply not going to be rushed. They were used to being in control of things, and they were determined to take this whole exercise of precaution at their own pace. The stewards and the crew did not help matters.

Mrs. Warren: "From the time of the accident until I left the ship there was nothing which in any way resembled a panic, and I believe that a panic would have been impossible owing to the immense size of the vessel, but there seemed to be a sort of aimless confusion and an utter lack of organized effort."

Etches: "My mate called down to E deck and I went to the other ladder to A deck, where I was to relieve the man. When I got on A deck, the bedroom steward was assisting passengers then and most of the doors were open. That was the forward end of A deck. I said, 'Have you called all of your people?' He said, 'Yes, but I can't get them to dress.' They were standing in the corridors partly dressed. I said, 'I will go down on my deck,' and with that I went down to B deck, arousing my passengers. That is when I met Mr. Harrison and Mr. Andrews the builder."

Ward: "We went up the midship companionway, up to the top deck, and meeting Mr. Dodd on D deck, he told us to go forward to the saloon and see if there was anyone about, and if there was, to order them up on deck and to collect the life belts and to bring them up to the deck cloakroom. I went forward and did not see anyone around there and came back and I got seven life belts on my way up. When I got on deck, I adjusted preservers on people that hadn't got one."

Mr. Stengel: "I heard the order given to the stewards to arouse the passengers, and afterwards I heard somebody remark, 'Did you ever see such actions?' or something like that, or some remark like, 'Did you ever see such actions as the stewards are showing?' It seems they were not arousing the people."

Miss Minahan: "I roused my brother and his wife, and we began at once to dress. No one came to give us warning. We spent five minutes in dressing and went on deck to the port side. The frightful slant of the deck toward the bow of the boat gave us our first thought of danger."

Mr. Peuchen: "There was no alarm sounded whatever. In fact, I talked with two young ladies who claimed to have had a very narrow escape. They said their stateroom was right near the Astor's, I think almost next to it, and they were not awakened. They slept through this crash, and they were awakened by Mrs. Astor. She was in rather an excited state, and their door being open—and I think the Astor door was open—they think that was the means of their being saved."

Mrs. Ryerson: "It was 12 o'clock. After about 10 minutes I went out in the corridor and saw far off people hurrying on deck. A passenger ran by and called out, 'Put on your life belts and come up on the boat deck.' I said, 'Where did you get those orders?' He said, 'From the captain.' I went back then and told Miss Bowen and my daughter who were in the next room to dress immediately, roused my husband and the two younger children, who were in a room on the other side, and then remembered my maid, who had a room near us. Her door was locked and I had some difficulty in waking her."

Mrs. Douglas: "As I waited for Mr. Douglas to return I went back to speak to my maid, who was in the same cabin as Mrs. Carter's maid. Now people commenced to appear with life preservers and I heard from someone that the order had been given to put them on. I took three from our cabin, gave one to the maid, telling her to get off in the small boat when her turn came. Mr. Douglas met me as I was going up to find him and asked, jestingly, what I was doing with those life preservers. He did not think even then that the accident was serious. We both put them on, however, and went up on the boat deck."

Hugh Woolner and Helen Candee were continuing their stroll on the promenade deck, unaware that events were taking a dramatic turn. They seemed quite absorbed in their conversation until they passed by a doorway.

Mr. Woolner: "As we passed one of the entrances to the corridor, I saw people coming up with life belts. So I went inside and asked the steward, 'Is this orders?' I shouted to someone going by; standing at the entrance, and he said, 'Orders.' I went back to Mrs. Candee and took her to her stateroom and we got her life belt down from the top of the wardrobe and tied hers onto her and then she chose one or two things out of her baggage, little things she could put into her pocket, or something of that sort, and I said, 'We will now go up on deck and see what has really happened.'"

Mrs. Smith: "I was asleep when the crash came. It did not awaken me enough to frighten me. In fact, I went back to sleep again. Then I awakened again, because it seemed that the boat had stopped. About that time my husband came into the room. Still, I was not frightened, but thought he had come in to go to bed. I asked him why the boat had stopped and in a leisurely manner he said, 'We are in the north and have struck an iceberg. It does not amount to anything, but probably delay us a day getting into New York. However, as a matter of form, the captain has ordered all ladies on deck.' That frightened me a little, but after being reassured there was no danger, I took plenty of time in dressing—putting on all my heavy clothing, high shoes, and two coats, as well as a warm knit hood."

The rising water had almost finished with F deck in the first four compartments. All of the cargo and mail were now submerged. The two story squash court was flooded up to the ceiling. Eighty third class cabins were under water along with all of the stokers' quarters. While the majority of people were turning their attention to the boats, the water crept up onto E deck right above the third and fourth compartments. E deck was significant with respect to the fate of the *Titanic*. Most of the watertight doors, in the damaged area and aft, only went as high as the ceiling of F deck. E deck held access to the aft watertight compartments and it would be E deck by which the water would ultimately sink the *Titanic*.

Robinson: "I saw two mail-bags and a man's Gladstone bag, and on looking down the staircase I saw water within six steps of coming on to E deck . . . after the collision about half an hour."

Someone noted that the watertight doors between the sixth and seventh compartments on F deck were still not closed. These doors separated the swimming pool from the Turkish Baths and it was important they be closed. That way, if and when water overflowed into the sixth compartment, it would not have access to the seventh.

Hardy: "We commenced to close the watertight doors on F deck. I assisted the bedroom stewards also in sending the people up through the companionways to the upper decks."
Fletcher: "Who told you to close the watertight doors?"
Hardy: "We had this order also from Mr. Barker, when he told me to rouse the people as a precaution."

Mr. Harder: "So we immediately went down

to our stateroom and took our life belts and coats and started up the stairs and went to the top deck. We had E-50. That is on E deck. I forgot to say that when I went down into my stateroom in order to get the life belts, when we came out of the stateroom with the life belts I noticed about four or five men on this E deck, and one of them had one of those T-handled wrenches, used to turn some kind of a nut or bolt, and two or three of the other men had wrenches with them— Stilson wrenches, or something like that. I did not take any particular notice, but I did notice this one man trying to turn this thing in the floor. There was a brass plate or something there. It was marked 'W.T.,' and I do not know whether it was a 'D' after that or something else. A few days before that, however, I noticed that brass plate, and naturally, seeing the initials 'W.T.,' I thought it meant watertight doors, or compartments. It was on the starboard side of the boat in the hallway. I think this brass plate was situated between the stairs and the elevators. The stairs were right in front of the elevators and right in between there, I think, was this brass plate. We heard one of these men with the wrenches say, 'Well, it's no use. This one won't work. Let's try another one.' They did not seem to be nervous at all. So I thought at the time there was no danger; that they were just doing that for the sake of precaution."

Second class passengers climbed their main staircase to the boat deck. (*Olympic*)

Mr. Chambers: "I remember being somewhat surprised that these doors were not nowadays operated by electricity, this being only a landsman's point of view. As a matter of fact, they were operated from the deck above, the E deck, by first removing a small boiler plate which fitted flush with the deck and was unscrewed by means of the two-forked end of a pin-spanner; that apparently giving access to the square or hexagon end of a shaft which, being rotated by another box wrench some 2 feet 6 inches in length, with a T-handle, operated a double series of bevel gears, the last shaft having on it a pinion meshing in a door rack and closing the door. The cover plates to the mechanism of the watertight doors, as far as I am able to state, were not removed before our final departure for the upper decks."

Miss Minahan: "A stewardess who had been saved told me that after the Titanic left Southampton that there were a number of carpenters working to put the doors of the air tight compartments in working order. They had great difficulty in making them respond, and one of them remarked that they would be of little use in case of accident, because it took so long to make them work."

Further back in second class, the procession to the boat deck was in full swing. The main staircase became crowded with passengers in various states of dress climbing the steps with bewildered looks.

Mr. Beesley: "Going upstairs with other passengers—no one ran a step or seemed alarmed—we met two ladies coming down. One seized me by the arm and said, 'Oh! I have no life belt. Will you come down to my cabin and help me to find it?' I returned with them to F deck—the lady who had addressed me holding my arm all the time in a vise-like grip, much to my amusement— and we found a steward in her gangway who took them in and found their life belts. Coming upstairs again, I passed the purs-

er's window on F deck, and noticed a light inside. When halfway up to E deck, I heard the heavy metallic clang of the safe door, followed by a hasty step retreating along the corridor towards the first class quarters. I have little doubt it was the purser who had taken all the valuables from his safe and was transferring them to the charge of the first class purser in the hope they might all be saved in one package. That is why I said that perhaps the envelope containing my money was not in the safe at the bottom of the sea. It is probably in a bundle with many others like it, waterlogged at the bottom."

The covers had been removed from the lifeboats and the crew were busy swinging them out. All of this took some time and kept the crew busy for the first half hour on deck. Some of them knew exactly where they were stationed, while others just moved around from one boat to the next as they were needed.

Widgery: "An order came up that all men had to take their life belts and go up on deck. I went down to F deck, and when I got down there, there was nobody there but our bedroom steward. All the passengers had gone. I went up on deck to my boat, number 7."

Scarrott: "The port side boats were got ready first and then the starboard ones. As the work proceeded, passengers were coming on deck with life belts on. Then we realized the situation. Every man went to his station."

Hemming: "My station was boat number 16 on the boat list. I went and helped turn out; started with the foremost boat, and then worked aft. As I went to the deck, I went there where there were the least men, and helped to turn out the boats. Then I went to the boats on the port side to do the same, until Mr. Lightoller called me and said, 'Come with me,' and he said, 'Get another good man.' I says, 'Foley is here somewhere.' He says, "I have no time to stop for Foley.' So he called a man himself, and he said, 'Follow me.' So we followed him and he said, 'Stand by to lower this boat.' It was number 4 boat. We lowered the boat in line with the A deck when I had an order come from the captain to see that the boats were properly provided with lights. I called Mr. Lightoller and told him that I would have to leave the boat's fall, so he put another man in my place."

Although passengers were told to get up on deck with their life belts on, several of the earlier ones stopped at A deck. It was very cold outside and with a group standing about in the A deck foyer, with others back in the first class lounge, the gathering seemed to feed on itself until the deck was a complete crowd scene. Those first class passengers who took the unusual step of going all the way up to the boat deck and then outside were in the minority.

Mrs. Bishop: " Then we went up onto the boat deck on the starboard side. We looked around, and there were so very few people up there that my husband and I went to the port side to see if there was anyone there. There were only two people, a young French bride and groom, on that side of the boat, and they followed us immediately to the starboard side. By that time an old man had come upstairs and found Mr. and Mrs. Harder of New York. He brought us all together and told us to be sure and stay together, that he would be back in a moment. We never saw him again."

Mr. Chambers: "We then proceeded up the port outside companion onto the boat deck. There did not at any time seem to be any particular group of passengers around the boats on the port side, although there were seamen there unlimbering the gear. Owing to the list being to the starboard, I assumed that the boats which were lowered on the starboard side would be sure to clear the ship, while those on the port side might have some difficulty. This was only an assumption as I have not heard of any such difficulty since. We than proceeded over the raised deck caused by the unusual height of the ceiling in the lounge and came down again onto the boat deck proper on the starboard side. There I gave my wife a drink from my flask, filled my pipe, put on my life belt at her urgent request, she having hers already on, and we stood at the rail for a few moments."

Many times there were equal numbers of passengers returning to their cabins as leaving. They either forgot something down below or were looking for someone.

Mr. Woolner: "I went back to my cabin and brought out and put one on myself, and I took the other one—there were two in the room—with me. I met someone in the passage who said, 'Do you want that?' and I said, 'No,' and gave it to him. I then took Mrs. Candee up onto the boat deck and there we saw preparations for lowering the boats going on."

After Andrews assisted in getting the steerage passengers out of the forward compartments, he proceeded into the first class area. He was concerned about whether each

A first class cabin on B deck.

and every cabin had been checked to confirm sleeping passengers were not left behind. Even though large numbers of people were up on A deck now, an equally large number of people were still lingering in their cabins.

Etches: "He [Andrews] stopped me. I was going along B deck, and he asked had I waked all my passengers. Mr. Harrison came up then and I said, 'No. I am going to see if the Carter family are up.' I went to open the door. Mr. Harrison said, 'I can tell you they are up. I have just come out of my cabin.' His cabin adjoined. Mr. Andrews then told me to come down on C deck with him and we went down the pantry staircase together. Going down he told me to be sure and make the passengers open their doors

and to tell them the life belts were on the top of the wardrobes and on top of the racks, and to assist them in every way I could to get them on, which I endeavored to do."

Smith: "Did you assist in putting life belts on them?"

Etches: "Yes, sir, but more on C deck. I threw the life belts down, and then threw some of them into the corridor. Mr. Andrews said to be sure there were no life belts left. The first cabin I went to was at the foot of the pantry stairs. I pulled the bottom drawer out there and stood on it and got out life belts, and as a gentleman was passing there, I gave him one of those. He was a stout gentleman; appeared to be an Englishman. He said, 'Show me how to put this on,' and I showed him how, and then he said, 'Tie it for me.' I said, 'Pull the strings around to the front and tie it,' and as he was doing it I ran outside and opened other doors, and then most of the doors were opened along C deck."

Smith: "Is that the last time you ever saw him?"

Etches: "No, sir. We walked along C deck together. The purser was standing outside of his office in a large group of ladies. The purser was asking them to do as he asked them and to go back in their rooms and not to frighten themselves, but as a preliminary caution, to put the life belts on and the stew-

ards would give them every attention. Mr. Andrews said, 'That is exactly what I have been trying to get them to do,' and with that he walked down the staircase to go on lower D deck. That is the last I saw of Mr. Andrews. It would be about 20 minutes past 12."

It was 12:20 and Andrews was distressed by how many people were still not on deck. By now water was flooding the forward part of E deck, and with that in mind, he went on to check the first class cabins in the forward part of D deck, just one deck above.

Mrs. Warren: "We saw in front of the purser's office ship's papers and valuables laid out and I asked if we could take anything with us, but was told not."

Crawford: "I went around to all the staterooms and told Mrs. Rogers and Miss Rogers to dress, and I helped tie life belts on them. After I saw all the passengers on the boat deck, I went on the boat deck myself, and I went to number 5 lifeboat."

Smith: "What about Mr. Guggenheim and his secretary, and the others?"
Etches: "They were in their room. I took the life belts out. The life belts in this cabin were in the wardrobe, in a small rack, and the cabin was only occupied by two. There were three life belts there, and I took the three out and put one on Mr. Guggenheim. He apparently had only gone to his room, for he answered the first knock. He said, 'This will hurt.' I said, 'You have plenty of time, put on some clothes and I will be back in a few minutes.'"
Smith: "Did you go back there?"
Etches: "Yes, sir."
Smith: "Was he there?"
Etches: "Yes. He followed me along. I then found number 78 cabin door shut and I banged with both hands on the door loudly, and a voice answered, 'What is it?' Then a lady's voice said, 'Tell me what the trouble is.' I said, 'It is necessary that you should open the door, and I will explain everything, but please put the life belts on or bring them in the corridor.' They said, 'I want to know what is the matter.' I said, 'Kindly open the door,' and I still kept banging. I passed along and I found one cabin was empty, and then I came to another cabin and a lady and a gentleman stood at the door. They were swinging a life belt in their hands."
Smith: "Did this woman open the door when you pounded so hard?"
Etches: "I did not see the door opened."
Smith: "Do you know who was in that room?"
Etches: "It was a shortish name, and I fancy it began with S. They were a stiff-built gentleman and a rather short, thin lady. They were undoubtedly Americans."

The crew were finishing preparations on most of the boats and swinging them over the side of the ship. As the actual evacuation approached, there were only a curious few on deck to witness the scene.

Boxhall: "First the boat has to be cleared. After the boats are cleared the chocks are knocked down, or dropped down by patent levers, and the boat is hanging free. Then the davits are screwed out and the boat is suspended over the ship's side all ready for lowering away."

Moore: "I went on the starboard side of the boat deck and helped clear the boats. Swung three of the boats out."

Mr. Bishop: "We had been on the boat deck in the neighborhood of 10 minutes, watching them prepare the boats for lowering. At the time there were very few people up on deck."

Just as scores of passengers began to assemble in first and second class public rooms, the third class passengers gathered on the well deck and poop deck outdoors, as

The main third class staircase. It exited to the open well deck at the stern. The entrances to the general room (left), and the smoking room (right) can be seen on opposite sides of the stairwell. (*Olympic*)

brother-in-law, 'I can see it plain, now. It must be a light. I could not say, but it did not seem to be so very far. I thought I could see this mast light, the front mast light.'*

Down in the crowded and confusing hallways of D, E, F, and G decks in steerage, a number of passengers were becoming agitated with the uncertainty of the situation. Keeping in mind that most of these passengers did not necessarily think their lives were in danger, the whole process of being forced from their rooms in the middle of the night and being made to stand around without having any clear answers was a great inconvenience.

Mr. Pickard: ". . . we dressed ourselves and went out, and we could not get back again. I wanted to go back to get my things but I could not. The stewards would not allow us to go back. They made us all go forward on the deck. There were no doors locked to prevent us from going back. I did not take much notice of it and I went to the deck. The other passengers started in arguing. One said that it was dangerous and the other said it was not. One said white and the other said black. Instead of arguing with those people, I instantly went to the highest spot. The steerage passengers, so far as I could see, were not prevented from getting

well as the general and smoking rooms on C deck aft.

Miss Turja: "I was not a bit scared, but most of the others seemed to be, and there were many who fainted. It was very cold. None of us hurried. We were not told what had happened, and had to do our own thinking. When we got dressed, we went out on deck."

On deck, Olaus Abelseth and others could see a distant boat on the horizon.

Mr. Abelseth: "We all went up on deck and stayed there. We walked over to the port side of the ship and there were five of us standing, looking, and we thought we saw a light. We were then on the port side there, and we looked out at this light. I said to my

up to the upper decks by anybody or by closed doors, or anything else. While I was on the ship no one realized the real danger, not even the stewards. If the stewards knew, they were calm. It was their duty to try to make us believe there was nothing serious. Nobody was prevented from going up. They tried to keep us quiet. They said, 'Nothing serious is the matter.' Perhaps they did not know themselves. I did not realize it the whole time, even to the last moment. Of course, I would never believe such a thing could happen."

Miss Mulvihill: "Then I hurried back into my room, stood up on the wash stand and took down a life belt. This I adjusted about me and then hurried out into the passage."

Just like Pickard, Anna Turja and her entourage made a key decision shortly after 12:00 a.m. that would ultimately save her life. Once they were outside on deck, the small group decided to promptly climb the outside stairs that led up to second class. As they did, they encountered a crewman who told them to go back down to their own area. Fortunately for her, they refused to obey the man and continued forward, but from that moment onward, the crew formed a new resolve to keep the steerage passengers in their own area. As Anna Turja passed

through, the crewman closed the deck gate and locked it. Easy access to the boats had just ended for steerage.

As third class passengers prepared to vacate their tiny rooms, many took items important to them. If they were to be separated from their baggage for a while, as it now appeared, they were not going to take chances with their life's savings or ground transportation in the United States.

Miss Sjoblom: "When outside I had not time to go back again. My railroad ticket to Tacoma and a small amount of money were sewed in a little bag and hung around my neck so that I could not lose it."

The crew completed the captain's orders by having all of the boats swung out. But the captain had not yet ordered the evacuation of the ship. With the boats ready, he was approached most likely by Wilde or Murdoch and informed of the status.

Smith: "Were you outside on the deck, or on any deck, when the order was given to lower the lifeboats?"
Ismay: "I heard Captain Smith give the order when I was on the bridge."
Smith: "Will you tell us what he said?"
Ismay: "It is very difficult for me to remember exactly what was said, sir."

The staircase from the well deck to B. There was a gate at the top of these stairs which was eventually locked and guarded by crewmen. (*Olympic*)

Smith: "As nearly as you can."
Ismay: "I know I heard him give the order to lower the boats. I think that is all he said. I think he simply turned around and gave the order."

Ismay always downplayed his influence over the captain on that voyage and as a result, he never volunteered details of what had taken place in the ten to twenty intermittent minutes he was on the bridge. The conversation was no doubt pointed and businesslike. Both were likely operating in a damage-control mode, trying not to get overwhelmed by it all. From Ismay's brief description, the captain was facing him when asked about the lifeboats, and had to turn around from Ismay to issue the fateful orders. This implies that Smith and Ismay were engaged in conversation.

Smith: "Was there anything else said, as to how they should be manned or occupied?"
Ismay: "No sir; not that I heard. As soon as I heard him give the order to lower the boats, I left the bridge."

The crew were impressive in their efficiency at preparing fourteen boats, but the subsequent system for manning each one with a proper number of seamen began to reflect a growing confusion on deck. Some of the crew knew their boat assignments while others did not. Some went to their assigned boat, while others obeyed a conflicting order, or decided on their own to work at another boat as circumstances dictated.

Mr. Peuchen: ". . . they were not at their stations, ready to man the boats. I imagine this crew was what we would call in yachting terms a scratch crew, brought from different vessels. They might be the best, but they had not been accustomed to working together."

Crawford: "Number 8 was my station. I went to the starboard side to number 5 boat."

Hemming: "I went away into the lamp room, lighting the lamps . . . "

Collins: "We went up to the deck when the word came. Then I met a companion of mine, a steward, and I asked him what number my boat was, and he said number 16."

Sometime around 12:20, as the bow of the *Titanic* settled further into the water, the lookouts stood alone and forgotten in the crow's nest. Common sense eventually dictated that there was no point to their current watch, and the two climbed down the ladder inside the mast. As will be seen later, the next person with an interest in climbing into the crow's nest would be Lightoller—under very different circumstances.

Hogg: "We stopped about 20 minutes, and lifted up the back cover of the nest—the weather cover—and I saw people running about with life belts on. I went to the telephone then, to try to ring up on the bridge and ask whether I was wanted in the nest when I saw this. I could get no answer on the telephone. I went straight on the boat deck. Number 6 was my proper boat; what I signed for. I assisted in starting to uncover the boats. Then I was sent for a Jacob's ladder. I was told to drop it [on deck]."

What Hogg found on the boat deck was a strange scene. The lifeboats were all swung out, but there were very few people on deck and no one was being loaded into them.

Ward: "Everybody was moving around and in a most orderly manner. There did not seem to be any excitement. In fact, there was a lot of ladies and gentlemen that were just treating it as a kind of joke."

Buley: "I think that is what the majority thought, that the ship would float. They thought she would go down a certain distance and stop there."
Fletcher: "Did you hear any of them say that?"
Buley: "Yes, several of them. They said they were only getting the boats out for exercise and in case of accident."

Anna Turja arrived from third class with her roommates and one of their brothers onto the boat deck about this time. But there did not seem to be anything going on there, and it was so cold that she decided to go down the Grand Staircase to the next deck to get warm. In the foyer of the A deck staircase, she immediately heard the sound of music coming from the band, who were now playing in the lounge. Wandering back through the revolving doors, she was captivated by what she then considered a concert in progress. She sat down.

Ismay left the bridge and walked along the same stretch of the boat deck that Boxhall had traveled during the collision only forty-five minutes earlier. He stopped next to lifeboats number 5 and 7.

Ismay: "I heard the order given to get the boats out. I walked along to the starboard side of the ship, where I met one of the officers. I told him to get the boats out."

Pitman: "I stood by number 5 boat. They would not allow the sailors to get anything, as they thought we should get it again in the morning. In the act of clearing away this boat a man said to me, that was dressed in a dressing gown with slippers on, he said to me very quietly, 'There is no time to waste.' I thought he did not know anything about it at all. So we carried on our work in the usual way."

Smith: "Who was it?"

Pitman: "Mr. Ismay. I did not know who it was then. I had never seen the man in my life before. So I continued on getting this boat uncovered and swinging out. It struck me at the time the easy way the boat went out, the great improvement the modern davits were on the old-fashioned davits. I had about five or six men there, and the boat was out in about two minutes. Number 5 boat. Then this man in the dressing gown said we had better get her loaded with women and children. So I said, 'I await the commander's orders,' to which he replied, 'Very well,' or something like that. It then dawned on me that it might be Mr. Ismay, judging by the description I had had given me."

Smith: "How were you dressed?"

Ismay: "I had a suit of pajamas on, a pair of slippers, a suit of clothes, and an overcoat."

Mr. Gracie: "As I went up on deck the next time I saw Mr. Ismay with one of the officers. He looked very self contained, as though he was not fearful of anything and that gave encouragement to my thought that perhaps the disaster was not anything particularly serious."

Pitman: "So I went along to the bridge and saw Captain Smith, and I told him that I thought it was Mr. Ismay that wished me to get the boat away with women and children in it. So he said, 'Go ahead. Carry on.' I came along and brought in my boat."

Ward: " I went to my boat—I was stationed at number 7—and she was already lowered to the same level as the deck. They called for the ladies to get in. Some got in, and there were a few men got into it; quite a few of the crew up there, and they did not want them for that boat. They did not want me for that boat, although I was told off for that boat. They just took sufficient men to man the boat. Then I went aft to number 9 boat."

Etches: "I went along to the purser's place. He said, 'It is necessary to go up on the boat deck,' and he said, 'Tell all the other bedroom stewards to assemble their passengers on the boat deck and stand by.' I went on the boat deck, and they were just loading boat number 7. I said to the quartermaster, 'Is this boat number 5?' He said, 'No. It is the next boat.'"

As number 7 was prepared for loading, Purser McElroy arrived from his office on C deck. Either Wilde or Murdoch assigned him to supervise the preparation of boat number 9 and he began to round up a number of residual crew standing around 7.

Widgery: *"I went up on deck to my boat, number 7. The starboard side. When I got up there, it was just about to be lowered. The purser sent me along to number 9."*

Haines: *"I worked on the boats. Got all the boats swung out. Then I went and stood by my own boat, number 9."*
Smith: *"Did you help load the other boats?"*
Haines: *"No, sir. We were turning out the after boats while they were filling the forward ones."*

By now the water was flowing down the stairs from E deck into the third class cabins above boiler room number 6. Down below, the boiler room was almost submerged. It is a pity to think how close the *Titanic* came to remaining afloat. The water level early on inside the ship was always very close to the level outside of the ship, demonstrating how close she was to reaching equilibrium. The pumps were keeping ahead of the inflow of water in boiler room number 5, and its resistance to flooding offered a much needed buoyancy to the ship. But the valiant efforts to keep the compartment afloat came undone when the water reached the top of the bulkhead that divided 5 and 6.

The *Titanic* was designed in such a way that, even though the watertight bulkheads only went up as high as the ceiling of F deck, the flooring of E deck and F deck as well effectively capped off the boiler room below, slowing the flow of water into the next compartment. But there were three locations where this was not the case, and where the water had free access from one compartment into the next. Unfortunately for the *Titanic*, one of these locations was between boiler room 5 and 6. The smoke from burning coal in the boilers fed into a series of finger-like exhaust chambers. These individual steel exhaust fingers from the five boilers in number 5 and four in number 6 merged into a single chamber above the two rooms that in turn fed into the first smokestack. This large single exhaust chamber rested on the bulkhead in a free area above the two rooms. It was this free area that unfortunately allowed the rising water in boiler room 6 to simply overflow into number 5 just like the analogy of an ice cube tray. As the crew struggled to keep boiler room 5 dry, the water from number 6 eventually poured over the wall into it. This sudden influx of water was mistaken as a collapsing bulkhead.

Meanwhile, people still wandered about the ship as if there were nothing urgent to worry about.

Ray: *"I dressed myself and put on my life belt and went along the working alleyway to the back stairway, and waited to take my turn with about 20 others, and we went straight on up to C deck. I saw the second steward up there and he asked me to get a life belt. I went through five staterooms and saw nobody there in either of them. I found a life belt in the fifth stateroom and took it to him, and proceeded on up to the boat deck."*

Even though Steward Ray was somewhat late in his arrival on deck, it made little difference since there was not much happening at his assigned lifeboat anyway.

Ray: *"Mr. Moore I saw coming from the smoke room afterwards, with other people whom I did not notice, just before going to my station . . . to number 9 boat which was my boat allotted to me."*
Smith: *"Whom did you find there at the boat?"*
Ray: *"Sailors and about a dozen other men. The crew in general and one or two passengers."*

Lifeboat 7 was the first boat to be loaded. Murdoch indicated that passengers were to step forward and begin boarding.

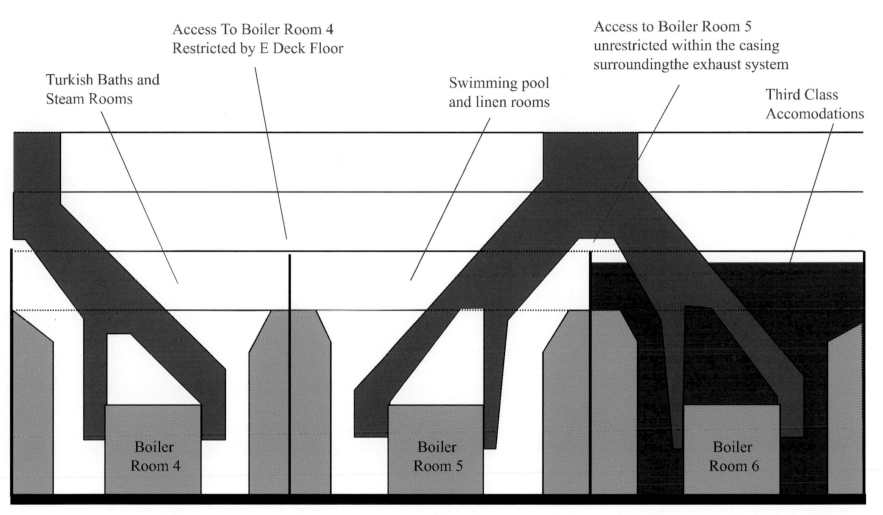

Turkish Baths and
Steam Rooms

Access To Boiler Room 4
Restricted by E Deck Floor

Swimming pool
and linen rooms

Access to Boiler Room 5
unrestricted within the casing
surroundingthe exhaust system

Third Class
Accomodations

Boiler
Room 4

Boiler
Room 5

Boiler
Room 6

Hogg: "As I got past the number 7 boat on the starboard side, Mr. Murdoch, chief officer, said, 'See that those plugs are in that boat.' I put the plugs in, and I said, 'The plugs are all correct, ' and I jumped out again. I jumped out to assist with the falls

and he said, 'You step in that boat.' I said, 'Very good, sir.' Mr. Murdoch lowered one end . . . Evans lowered the other end."

Etches: "I looked at number 5 and they were taking the covers off and preparing her and I assisted

to launch number 7 boat. There was Mr. Murdoch, Mr. Ismay, Mr. Pitman, and a quartermaster, Olliver, two stewards, and myself there."

Steam roared from the exhausts. The crew uncovered the boats and swung them out. Passengers assembled on deck. All the while, Fifth Officer Lowe slept in his quarters on the port side of the boat deck. Boxhall thought he had awakened him some thirty or so minutes before. Finally, the sobering world unfolding on the *Titanic* worked its way into his consciousness.

Lowe: "I was awakened by hearing voices, and I thought it was very strange, and somehow they woke me up and I realized there must be something the matter. So I looked out and I saw a lot of people around, and I jumped up and got dressed and went up on deck. I found that all the passengers were wearing belts. I also found that they were busy getting the boats ready to go overboard. I met somebody, and they said she had struck an iceberg, and I could feel by my feet that there was something wrong."

The fact that the Fifth Officer was left to sleep right up to the point where the first lifeboat was being lowered hints at the disorganization on deck as the senior officers grappled with the logistics of evacuating the world's largest liner.

The slow mobilization on deck by the first class passengers continued.

Mrs. White: "There was no panic. I insisted on Miss Young getting into something warm, and I got into something warm, and we locked our trunks and bags and went on deck."

Since the starboard side boat deck seemed more organized from the very beginning, it is possible that Lightoller or another officer had the door to the port side boat deck temporarily locked until they were ready to load passengers.

Mrs. Warren: "Continuing up to the boat deck, we tried to get out on the port side but were unable to open the door. Noticing the starboard door standing open we went out that way. This boat deck was the top deck of the vessel, uncovered and only a few houses on it, such as contained the gymnasium, a lounge, etc. At the time we reached this deck there were very few passengers there, apparently, but it was dark and we could not estimate the number. There was a deafening roar of escaping steam, of which we had not been conscious while inside. The only people we remembered seeing, except a young woman by the name of Miss Ostby, who had become separated from her father and was with us, were Mr. Astor, his wife and servants, who were standing near one of the boats which was being cleared preparatory to being lowered. The Astors did not get into this boat. They all went back inside and

I saw nothing of them again until Mrs. Astor was taken onto the Carpathia."

While passengers milled about aimlessly on the upper decks, the water continued its steady reach into the staterooms and quarters of E deck.

Newlands: "Were you in the water?"
Taylor: "No, sir."
Newlands: "Did it reach you?"
Taylor: "Yes, afterwards. It went into our room afterwards."
Newlands: "How long was it in getting in there?"
Taylor: "About three-quarters of an hour."

Fifth Officer Lowe stepped onto the deck to find out what was going on. Only a few minutes after waking up, he was in his uniform and standing by lifeboat number 7.

Lowe: "I met somebody, and they said she had struck an iceberg, and I could feel by my feet that there was something wrong. She was by the bow. She was very much by the bow. She had a grade downhill."

Murdoch and Ismay were already in the process of loading lifeboat 7.

Etches: "Mr. Ismay, in the first place, was

asking the gentlemen to kindly keep back, as it was ladies first in this boat and they wanted to get the boat clear first. The gentlemen were lined up, those that were trying to assist, and Mr. Ismay said, 'Kindly make a line here and allow the ladies to pass through,' and I think it was Mr. Murdoch's voice that was calling out, 'Ladies, this way. Is there any more ladies before this boat goes?' The boat was three parts full of ladies, to my knowledge. In number 7 boat I saw one child, a baby boy, with a small woolen cap over his head. I remember it well."

Mrs. Bishop (7): *"About five minutes later the boats were lowered, and we were pushed in. At the time our lifeboat was lowered I had no idea that it was time to get off. I think it was No. 7. Officer Lowe told us that. We had no idea that it was time to get off, but the officer took my arm and told me to be very quiet and get in immediately. They put the families in the first two boats. My husband was pushed in with me, and we were lowered away with 28 people in the boat. There were only about 12 women. [And the rest] were men. Among those there were several unmarried men in our boat, I noticed, and three or four foreigners in our boat."*

There was an advantage here for

The starboard side of the boat deck. A corner of the emergency boat cover can be seen in the foreground, followed by lifeboats 3, 5 and 7. The entrance to the Grand Staircase is in the distance, just behind the vertical ladder in the center of the picture. *(Olympic)*

men to save themselves. Murdoch and Ismay had already asked for women and children only, but they were still getting their wits about them during a process like this, and men whose instincts told them they could take advantage of the situation, did so. In addition, Murdoch throughout the evening would display an ambivalence about the women and children rule. This ambivalence in the long run actually made him the more efficient officer because he managed to get his boats loaded much faster.

Mr. McGough (7): *"After procuring our life preservers we went back again to the top deck, and after reaching there discovered that orders had been given to launch the lifeboats and that they were already being launched at that time. They called for the women and children to board the boats first. Both women and men, however, hesitated and did not feel inclined to get into the small boats, thinking the larger boat was the safer. I had my back turned, looking in the opposite direction at that time and was caught by the shoulder by one of the officers who gave me a push, saying 'Here, you are a big fellow. Get into the boat.'"*

Mr. Bishop (7): *"There was some confusion there at the time and I did not pay much attention. There was an officer stationed at the side of the lifeboat, and as my wife got in I followed immediately, and he helped me into the boat, or rather indicated, and I fell into the boat."*

Pitman: "I was clearing number 5 at the same time that number 7 was coming off. I had nothing whatever to do with that number 7 boat. I would say there were over 30, between 30 and 40 in there."

At a glance, 30 or so passengers looked sufficient to Murdoch. Setting the precedent for many lifeboats that night, he ordered number 7 away with empty seats. The lowering proved to be complicated.

Etches: "My part was that I was clearing the falls. They were catching in the falls, or at least the falls were catching in people's feet, as they were jumping around, and I cleared the falls as they were lowering them away."

And so lifeboat 7 was lowered without incident. It touched down on the water sometime around 12:25 a.m. In an age where information was transmitted not electronically but by person-to-person contact, the captain and his senior officers managed in just less than 45 minutes to begin evacuation of the largest ship in the world.

Mr. McGough (7): "When our lifeboats left the vessel, we were directed to row away a short distance from the large boat, feeling it would be but a short time until we would be taken back on the Titanic. We then rested on our oars."

Hogg (7): "I asked a lady if she could steer, and she said she could. I said, 'You may sit here and do this for me, and I will take the stroke oar.' I pulled a little way from the ship, about a quarter of a mile, I should think. The sea was very smooth."

As lifeboat 7 descended, Rowe watched from the aft bridge. This seemed odd to him, since no one told him anything about this. He no doubt had watched the third class passengers assemble on the decks around him after the ship stopped, but the sight of this lifeboat pulling away was an entirely different matter.

Rowe: "I then remained on the after bridge to await orders through the telephone. No orders came down, and I remained until 25 minutes past 12, when I saw a boat on the starboard beam. You could not tell the number. I telephoned to the fore bridge to know if they knew there was a boat lowered. They replied, asking me if I was the third officer. I replied, 'No, I am the quartermaster.'

They told me to bring over detonators which are used in firing distress signals."

Boxhall: "I was around the bridge, but the first boat that was lowered was lowered away from aft. On the starboard side. I received the communication through the telephone in the wheelhouse that the first boat had been lowered. I did not notice the time. I do not know who it was that told me through the telephone."

It is somewhat amusing to piece these two observations together. There, on the after bridge, is Quartermaster Rowe calling to inquire about the fact that a lifeboat is being lowered along the starboard side. On the bridge, Boxhall takes the call and thinks he is being officially advised of this event. Boxhall uses the call to get Rowe to bring detonators, otherwise known as the distress rockets, to the bridge.

Hichens: "I left the wheel at 23 minutes past 12, sir. I was relieved by Quartermaster Perkis. I think the first officer, or one of the officers said, 'That will do with the wheel. Get the boats out.'"

As the evacuation went into motion on a ship the size of the *Titanic*, the number of separate activities taking place began to multiply. It all required a good amount of coordination, communication, and continuous discipline. Considering they had only worked together for a few days on this new ship, it is impressive that the captain and his officers managed to pull off an evacuation with relatively few incidents in just under two hours.

Ward: *"I went to number 9 boat and assisted to take the canvas cover off of her. Then we lowered her down to level with the boat deck and a sailor came along with a bag and threw it in the boat. This man said he had been sent down to take charge of the boat by the captain. The boatswain's mate, Haynes, was there, and he ordered this man out of the boat and the man got out again."*

Added to the complexity of coordinating this activity was the ongoing roar of the steam.

Mr. Chambers: *"I would like to call particular attention to the fact that from the moment the engines were stopped, steam was of course blown out from the boilers. This, coming through one single steam pipe on the starboard side of the forward funnel, made a terrifically loud noise. So loud, indeed, that persons on the boat deck could only communicate by getting as close as*

The entranceway to the Grand Staircase. Toward 12:30, passengers filed out onto the boat deck and were herded aft, away from the forward lifeboats.

possible and speaking loudly. As a matter of fact, I shouted in my wife's ear. All this time I considered that the lifeboats were merely a precaution and upon my wife's suggestion, we moved up forward to the entry from the deck house."

Mr. Beesley: *". . . a harsh deafening boom that made conversation difficult and no doubt increased the apprehension of some people merely because of the volume of noise."*

Lifeboat number 5 was ready and the crew tried to round up as many passengers as they could find. For some unknown reason, a majority of the first class passengers still had not come up from A deck. And in an uncoordinated bit of timing, second class passengers who were on deck did not have easy access to the initial lifeboats being lowered in first class due to mid-rise gates positioned between the two areas. But as the loading began, people finally started to arrive on deck, although in small numbers.

Miss Minahan: *"The frightful slant of the deck toward the bow of the boat gave us our first thought of danger. An officer came and commanded all women to follow, and he led us to the boat deck on the starboard side."*

Mr. Chambers: *"There were still quite a number of passengers coming out, the stewards standing there directing them to the boats aft. Instead of going aft, we stepped behind the projection of this entry, which was of the vestibule type and waited until the people had apparently ceased coming and the steward was no longer there."*

Third Officer Pitman assisted with loading number 5.

Pitman: *"I stood on it and said, 'Come*

along, ladies.' There was a big crowd. Mr. Ismay helped to get them along; assisted in every way. We got the boat nearly full, and I shouted out for any more ladies. None were to be seen. So I allowed a few men to get into it."

Mrs. Warren (5): "We discovered that the boat next to the one the Astors had been near had been lowered to the level of the deck, so went towards it and were told by the officer in charge to get in. At this moment both men and women came crowding towards the spot. I was the second person assisted in. I suppose that Mr. Warren had followed, but saw when I turned that he was standing back assisting the women. People came in so rapidly in the darkness that it was impossible to distinguish them, and while I did not see him again, I thought that he also was in, as there seemed to be still room for more when the boat was lowered. There were, according to my recollection, either 35 or 36 people in the boat, and I was not aware that Mr. Warren was not with us until afloat and his name was called with no response."

Wheelton: "I went down to the deck. They were just getting away lifeboat number 5 then. I assisted in getting away lifeboat number 5."

Lowe arrived as boat 7 was lowered but did not help with it. He instead assisted Murdoch, Pitman, and Ismay with 5.

Lowe: "Let us see. I crossed over to the starboard side. I lowered away. The first boat I helped to lower was number 5, starboard boat. That is, under the orders of Mr. Murdoch."
Smith: "Did Mr. Murdoch assist you?"
Lowe: "No. He was the senior officer. I was the junior."
Smith: "Was he superintending?"
Lowe: "He was superintending that deck."

Crawford: "I saw him [Ismay] lowering a boat on the starboard side too, and Mr. Murdoch . . . it was just under the bridge. I saw him assisting the ladies into this one particular boat. He and Mr. Murdoch had lowered the boat into the water."

Ismay: "We simply picked the women out and put them in the boat as fast as we could."
Smith: "You picked them from among the throng?"
Ismay: "We took the first ones that were there and put them in the lifeboats. I was there myself and put a lot in."
Smith: "You helped put some of them in yourself?"

Ismay: "I put a great many in."
Smith: "Were children shown the same consideration as the women?"
Ismay: "Absolutely."

Lowe: "There were only little knots around the deck, little crowds."

Fletcher: "Were there lights about the deck where the boats were being loaded?"
Etches: "Yes, sir. The cabin doors and all were open, giving a good light there."

In contrast to the evacuation that had already begun, and oblivious to the fact that lifeboat 7 had just been lowered, first class passengers stood about in the lounges and Grand Staircase foyers biding their time. At the same time, stokers were evacuating boiler rooms 3 and 4 and climbing up the emergency escape ladder positioned within the second funnel casing. This ladder exited at two locations. The first exit was at the working hallway on E deck. The second exit was on A deck, near the foyer to the Grand Staircase. For some reason, the men climbed all the way up to A deck.

Mrs. Futrelle: "The first rush of men with the fear of death in their faces came when a group of stokers climbed up from the hold and burst through the saloon, their grimy faces appearing wild and distracted in the brilliant light. The appearance of these stokers was the signal that the great heart of the ship had stopped beating, that the water had reached the engines. In a moment we understood that the situation was desperate, that the compartments had refused to hold back the rush of water. The black-faced group of men who poured from the vitals of the ship clustered together for a moment in one corner of the cabin."

Although most of the crew had been mustered for boat duty, some of the stewards came on duty and reported to their cabin areas. With lifeboats already on their way down to the water, passengers still lingered.

Cunningham: "About half past 12 all the stateroom stewards came on duty again, to their respective stations. I went back to my own station on C deck, and my passengers had then been aroused. There were only three left, then."

Smith: "Did you hear any order of that kind given before half past 12?"

Cunningham: "No, sir."

Smith: "That was about 55 minutes after the ship had struck the iceberg?"

Cunningham: "Forty-five or fifty minutes."

Smith: "Do you know whether any of the passengers were given any warning by any order or by any person before that time, do you know that of your own knowledge?"

Cunningham: "Not that I know of. A sort of a general order was passed around."

With the ship in mortal danger and the order passed around to report on deck with life jackets, the passengers seemed to have a will of their own, milling about below deck.

Mrs. Futrelle: "At this moment the band was playing 'Alexander's Ragtime Band.' What a scene that was—the men of the first cabin, many of them still in evening clothes with drawn, set faces who but a few short minutes ago were in command of all the things of the world, now found themselves face to face with the specter of death. Did they flinch? Not one. They were not the kind of men who stampeded in the face of danger. Oh, their courage was superb! The stokers for the most part were fear-stricken. They looked across to the men of the first cabin and took courage from the example set them, however. As for the women, perhaps their hearts did beat a little faster, perhaps there was a horrible fear in them, but they did not show it. Outwardly they were as calm as if they had come to attend a tea, that is, the majority of them were. I noticed that in this moment of stress, however, every woman on board was close to her husband. Most of the women in the first cabin had dressed hurriedly, many of them had not removed their evening gowns, others were half undressed and had thrown heavy coats over their dressing gowns. I saw one woman barefooted, saw others in their stocking feet, some had on their hats, the latest creations from Paris, while others who had dressed at leisure and prepared for an emergency, wore knitted wool caps. It was incongruous to see a woman in beautiful evening dress in her stocking feet."

In the wireless room, Phillips was busy sending out the distress call over and over again. The captain may have entered and specifically asked him who he thought that ship on the horizon could be. Or, Phillips on his own might have realized that he still had not heard from the Californian, the ship so close that its signal boomed in on him an hour or so ago when he was sending private messages. For whatever motivation, 18 minutes after sending out the first distress call, Phillips took a break from repeating the code "CQD MGY" and addressed a wireless message specifically to the ship.

Cape Race Log: "12:30. Titanic calls Carpathia and says, 'We require immediate assistance.' 12:33. Titanic gives same information to *Californian*, giving *Titanic's* position."

But the *Californian* would not respond, much to the frustration of Captain Smith. Out on deck, lifeboat number 5 was still loading.

Pitman: " Then I jumped on the ship again. So Murdoch said, 'You go in charge of this boat.' He said, 'You go away in this boat, old man, and hang around the after gangway.' I did not like the idea of going away at all, because I thought I was better off on the ship. I filled my boat fairly easily. About 40. I should say about half a dozen men there. There would not have been so many men there had there been any women around, but there were none."

Etches: "After getting all the women that were there, they called out three times – Mr. Ismay called out twice, I know, in a loud voice – 'Are there any more women before this boat goes,' and there was no answer. Mr. Murdoch called out, and at that moment a female came up whom I did not recognize. Mr. Ismay said, 'Come along. Jump in.' She said, 'I am only a stewardess.' He said, 'Never mind, you are a woman. Take your place.' That was the last woman I saw get into number 5 boat."

Mr. Chambers (5): "Then we started forward again, and as nearly as I can remember, stopped at the last one of the forward starboard group of lifeboats. This was already swung out level with the deck, and to my eyes appeared sufficiently loaded. However, my wife said that she was going in that boat, and proceeded to jump in, calling me to come."

Olliver (5): "There was the officer, Mr. Pitman, myself, sailor, and two firemen and two stewards."

Fletcher: "When you took boat number 5 and lowered that boat, you say you saw some men standing around the deck, but no women or children. Were the men excited? Were they desirous of taking a boat, or was their attitude one of confidence that the Titanic was going to float, and that they were in about as safe a position on board the Titanic as they would be in the lifeboat?"
Pitman: "Well sir, there was no push to get into the boat. I said there was no room for any more, and they simply stood back."
Fletcher: "They wanted to get in?"
Pitman: "They would have gotten in if they had been told to get in."
Fletcher: "But they did want to get in? Or would they rather stay on the boat?"
Pitman: "They did not push themselves at all."

Mr. Harder (5): "There we saw the crew manning the lifeboats; getting them ready, swinging them out. So we waited around there and we were finally told, 'Go over this way. Go over this way.' So we followed and went over toward the first lifeboat, where Mr. and Mrs. Bishop were. That boat was filled, and so they told us to move onto the next one. Somebody told us to move down toward the second one. We got to the second one and we were told to go right in there. I have been told that Mr. Ismay took hold of my wife's arm – I do not know him, but I have been told that he did – and pushed her right in. Then I followed. I should say it was about a foot and a half. Anyway, you had to jump. When I jumped in there, one foot went in between the oars and I got in there and could not move until somebody pulled me over."

Mr. Stengel: "While they were loading the lifeboats, the officers or men who had charge of loading the lifeboats said, 'There is no danger. This is simply a matter of precaution.'"

Burton: "Was it crowded around there?"
Olliver: "No, not so overcrowded."

Mr. Stengel: "They did not come up very fast. There were not many people on deck when my wife's boat went off, and I think my wife's boat was about the second boat. There were not very many people on the top deck at that time."

Burton: "What do you think? Do you think they believed the ship would float?"
Osman: "I thought so, myself. I thought it was going down a certain depth, and would float after that."

Gradually, lifeboat 5 filled and then prepared for lowering.

Smith: " Now, when you filled lifeboat number 5, did the women hesitate or demur about going in, or were they anxious to go?"
Lowe: "Well, I do not remember about that particular boat, but during the course of the evening I distinctly remember saying 'One more woman', or 'Two more women,' or 'Three more women,' and they would step forward and I would pass them into the boat."

Etches (5): "Mr. Murdoch said to me, "Are you the steward appointed to this boat?' I said, 'Yes, sir. Number 5 boat is mine.' He said, 'Then jump in and assist those men with the forward fall.' I took my place. At the same moment, Mr. Pitman called out, 'Is there a sailor in the boat?' I looked around and I said, 'No, sir.' He said to this man

Olliver, who was standing on the deck, 'Are you a sailor?' He said, 'Yes, sir.' He said, 'Take your place in this boat,' and he jumped in. Mr. Murdoch then stepped up and said, 'Are you the officer going in this boat?' He said, 'Yes, sir.' Then he said, 'Take your place,' and held out his hand and shook hands and said, 'Good bye and good luck.'"

Pitman (5): " So Murdoch told me, he said 'You go ahead in this boat and hang around the after gangway.' He shook hands with me and said, 'Good bye. Good luck.' And I said, 'Lower away.'"

Just as the boat began to go down, several men saw the empty seats descending and seized on the opportunity.

Mr. Stengel: "After my wife was put in a lifeboat she wanted me to come with them, and they said, 'No. Nothing but ladies and children.'"

Etches (5): "There was a stout gentleman, stepped forward then. He had assisted to put his wife in the boat. He leaned forward and she stood up in the boat, put her arms around his neck and kissed him, and I heard her say, 'I can't leave you,' and with that I turned my head. The next moment I saw him

sitting beside her in the bottom of the boat, and some voice said, 'Throw that man out of the boat.' But at that moment they started lowering her away, and the man remained."

Mr. Chambers (5): "As I knew she would get out again had I not come, I finally jumped into the boat, although I did not consider it, from the looks of things, safe to put very many more people in that boat. As I remember it, there were two more men, both called by their wives, who jumped in after I did. One of them, a German, I believe, told me, as I recollect it later on the Carpathia, that he had looked around and had seen no one else and no one to ask whether he should go in or not, and had jumped in."

Mr. Stengel: "I saw two, a certain physician in New York and his brother jump into the same boat my wife was in. Then the officer or the man that was loading the boat, said, 'I will stop that. I will go down and get my gun.' He left the deck momentarily and came right back again. These two gentlemen had put their wives in, and were standing on the edge of the deck and when they started lowering they jumped in. My wife said there were five, but I saw only two."

Lowe: "I first of all went and got my revolver. You never know when you will need it. Then

I went and helped everybody all around."

Mr. Stengel: *"Then I heard the orders given to put all the women and children in the boats and have them go off about 200 yards from the vessel. It seemed to me an officer. Of course, I was a little bit agitated and I heard them and I did not look particularly to see who it was."*

Mr. Chambers (5): *"By the time we were settled and I began to take note of the things on the ship I noticed a tall young officer clad in a long overcoat, which may help identify him, giving orders to another officer to go into our boat and take charge of the boats on our side. Preliminary to this, and before lowering, all of which was done with absolute calm, I heard someone in authority say, 'That is enough before lowering. We can get a lot more in after she is in the water.' As a parting injunction he gave our officer, whom I later found to be a Mr. Pitman, instructions to hold onto his painter and pull up alongside the gangway after the boat had reached the water. I remember these conversations particularly, as at the time I was wondering at the source of the order, being morally certain myself that no doors in the ship's side had been opened."*

As lifeboat 5 descended, a famous scene unfolded in which Ismay has been portrayed as borderline hysterical, jeopardizing the safety of the lifeboat. What actually happened, however is somewhat different. The lifeboat was not lowered by each end at an even pace. One end started to go down faster than the other and it became apparent that the boat was on its way to dropping everyone into the water. Ismay, who was leaning over the side, naturally became excited and started urgently yelling instructions in order to correct the problem.

Mrs. Warren (5): *"The lowering of the craft was accomplished with great difficulty. First one end and then the other was dropped at apparently dangerous angles and we feared that we would swamp as soon as we struck the water."*

Lowe: *"He [Ismay] was at the ship's side like this (indicating). This is the ship. He was hanging on the davit like this (indicating). He said, 'Lower away, lower away, lower away,' and I was slacking away just here at his feet. I told him, 'If you will get to hell out of that I shall be able to do something'. He did not make any reply. I said, 'Do you want me to lower away quickly?' I said, 'You will have me drown the whole lot of them.' I was on the floor myself lowering away. He walked away. And then he went* to number 3 boat. The next boat forward of mine, that is, on the same side. And I think he went ahead there on his own hook, getting things ready there, to the best of his ability."

Crawford: *"Mr. Ismay stopped Mr. Murdoch from lowering the boat a bit because the after end was getting hung up. Mr. Murdoch called out to the aft man that was lowering the fall to lower away all the time, that he would beat him, and they lowered the boat to the water."*

Even as Pitman left the *Titanic* in a lifeboat, the seriousness of the situation still had not registered.

Smith: *"When you shook hands with Murdoch and bade him good bye, did you ever expect to see him again?"*
Pitman: *"Certainly I did."*
Smith: *"Do you think, from his manner, he ever expected to see you again?"*
Pitman: *"Apparently not. I expected to get back to the ship again, perhaps two or three hours afterwards."*

As if the drama of the lowering were not stressful enough, Olliver was frantically trying to get the plug into place before number 5 touched down on the surface.

Olliver (5): "There were so many people that when I got in the boat I went to put the plug in, and there were so many people around me I could not get near the plug to put the plug in. As he was lowering the boat I implored the passengers to move so that I could put the plug in, so that as soon as they put the boat in the water I let the tripper go and water came into the boat. When we were alongside, I could not see, because I was busy in the bottom of the boat, and I could not see what was about, because I was pretty near suffocated myself doing what I was doing. But I then forced my way to the plug and put it in. If it was not for that, the boat would have been swamped."

Mr. Chambers(5): "Shortly before we reached the water our officer called and finally blew his whistle for them to stop lowering, that he might find out whether the plug was in or not. The inquiry was called in a loud tone of voice to which one of the crew in our boat replied that it was; that he, himself had put it in. Meanwhile a voice from above called down, as nearly as I can recollect it, 'It is your own blooming business to see that the plug is in anyhow.'"

Although not documented, such a terse comment from up on the deck very likely came from the short-tempered Lowe, who had already yelled at Ismay only a few minutes earlier over the method of the lifeboat's lowering.

Mr. Harder (5): "As we were being lowered, they lowered one side quicker than the other, but we finally reached the water safely, after a few scares. That was on account of the crew up on the deck. They had two or three men on each side, letting out the rope and they let out the rope on one side faster than the other. That caused the boat to assume this position going down [indicating] and we thought for a time that we were all going to be dumped out. When we got down into the water, somebody said the plug was not in, so they fished around to see if that was in, and I guess it was in. Then they could not get the boat detached from the tackle, so they fussed around there for a while and finally they asked if anybody had a knife and nobody seemed to have a knife. Finally, one of the passengers had a knife in his possession and they cut some rope. What it was, I do not know. I understand there was some new patented lever on there, some device that you pull, and that would let loose the whole thing. Whether they did not know that was there or not, I do not know. I presume they did not, because they did not seem to get it to work, and they finally had to resort to this knife."

Mrs. Warren (5): "After the lifeboat was safely afloat great difficulty was experienced in finding a knife with which to cut the lashings of the trigger to relieve the boat from the falls. When we reached the water the ship had settled so that my impression was that I was looking through the portholes into staterooms on deck D, which we had formerly occupied, and as we pulled away we could see that the Titanic was settling by the head with a heavy list to starboard."

Olliver (5): "When we got away from the ship I should say 25 or 30 yards, I should say the water was about, I should say there (indicating). She had sunk between 15 and 20 feet right at the bows."

Pitman (5): "We then cast the boat off and pulled away some safe distance from the ship. It was not for an hour that I realized she would go—an hour after we got into the water. I quite thought we would have to return to the ship again, perhaps at daylight. My idea was that if any wind sprang up we should drift away from the ship and have a job to get back again."

Mr. Harder (5): "They seemed to be able to row as well as possible. Of course, those boats are very unwieldy sort of things, and have great big long oars. We rowed out there some distance from the ship. How far it was, I do not know. It may have been as far as a quarter of a mile, and it may have been one eighth of a mile."

The lowering of boats 5 and 7 freed up some of the crew. An officer noticed a lack of food in the two boats sent away, and ordered Wheelton on an errand.

Wheelton: "I assisted in getting away lifeboat number 5. I was ordered to the storeroom."

Newlands: "How about the steerage passengers. Did any of them come up on the upper deck?"

Wheelton: "Oh, yes. They could come up just as I did. When I went to get the bottle of biscuits, I had to go right down to their quarters for it. The storeroom lies below their quarters. There was nothing to prevent me from going down to the storeroom."

Wheelton assumed that the steerage passengers had the same knowledge as he did about the *Titanic's* labyrinth of corridors and staircases. He also did not realize that the steerage passengers had probably placed their trust in the crew to tell them when the time was right to go up to the boat deck.

Smith: "When you got to lifeboat number 9

and saw those eight or ten men standing around it and one or two passengers and no women, what took place?"

Ray: "I went to the rail and looked over and saw the first boat leaving the ship on the starboard side. By that time I was feeling rather cold, so I went down below again to my bedroom the same way that I came up."

When passengers stepped out onto the deck—many in a sleepy and disoriented state—some were caught off guard by just how cold it was. The lucky ones returned to their cabins and dressed more heavily. The remainder suffered with the cold for the rest of the night.

Mr. Peuchen: "I then went to my cabin and changed as quickly as I could from evening dress to heavy clothes. As soon as I got my overcoat on I got my life preserver and I came out of my cabin. In the hallway I met a great many people, ladies and gentlemen with their life belts on, and the ladies were crying, principally, most of them. It was a very serious sight, and I commenced to realize how serious matters were. I then proceeded upstairs to the boat deck, which is the deck above A. I saw the boats were all ready for action; that is, the covers had been taken off of them, and the ropes cleared, ready to lower. This was on the port side."

There was not much activity on the boat deck in second class for the better part of the midnight hour. The Brown family decided to cross the gates into first class and walk around to pass the time, most likely along the port side.

Mrs. Brown: "I saw what seemed to be tons of ice on the forward deck. The ship seemed to have crushed far into the berg. 'Now keep up the best you can and get saved,' said my husband. There was great excitement on the deck."

It was now getting on toward 12:35. The Ryerson family moved about their cabins at a leisurely pace as they prepared for their venture up on deck. Victorine, their maid, helped them along.

Mrs. Ryerson: "By this time my husband was fully dressed and we could hear the noise of feet tramping on the deck overhead. He was quite calm and cheerful and helped me put the life belts on the children and on my maid. I was paralyzed with fear of not all getting on deck together in time, as there were seven of us. I would not let my younger daughter dress, but she only put on a fur coat, as I did over her nightgown. My husband cautioned us all to keep together and we went up to A deck, where we found quite

The *Titanic* and the expanse of her boat deck. Lifeboats 9 through 15 can be seen to the left and 1 through 7 on the right.

a group of people we knew. Everyone had on a life belt and they all were very quiet and self-possessed."

Gracie finished packing his three suitcases and was ready to go up on deck.

Mr. Gracie: "Presently, I noticed that women and men had life preservers on, and under protest, as I thought it was rather previous, my steward put a life preserver around myself and I went up on deck, on the A deck. Here I saw a number of people, among others, some ladies whom I had told

when I first came on the ship at Southampton that I hoped they would let me do anything I could for them during the voyage. These ladies were Mrs. E.D. Appleton, Mrs. Cornell, and Mrs. Browne, the publisher's wife, of Boston, and Miss Evans. They were somewhat disturbed, of course. I reassured them and pointed out to them the lights of what I thought was a ship or steamer in the distance. Mr. Astor came up and he leaned over the side of the deck, which was an inclosed deck, and there were windows and the glass could be let down. I pointed toward the bow, and there were distinctly

seen these lights—or light, rather one single light. It did not seem to be a star, and that is what we all thought it was, the light of some steamer."

It was a strange scene then. The lowering of lifeboats was off to a slow start and passengers stood about, biding their time. It was all seemingly taken at a leisurely pace. It is small wonder the situation was not perceived to be as serious as it should have been.

Mr. Beesley: "Reaching the top deck, we

found many people assembled there, some fully dressed, with coats and wraps, well prepared for anything that might happen, others who had thrown wraps hastily round them when they were called or heard the summons to equip themselves with life belts, not in much condition to face the cold of that night. Fortunately there was no wind to beat the cold air through our clothing. Even the breeze caused by the ship's motion had died entirely away, for the engines had stopped again and the Titanic lay peacefully on the surface of the sea—motionless, quiet, not even rocking to the roll of the sea. Indeed, as we were to discover presently, the sea was as calm as an inland lake save for the gentle swell which could impart no motion to a ship the size of the Titanic. To stand on the deck many feet above the water lapping idly against her sides, and looking much farther off than it really was because of the darkness, gave one a sense of wonderful security; to feel her so steady and still was like standing on a large rock in the middle of the ocean."

Even in third class, the passengers simply waited on time and kept an eye out for anything that may have been of interest.

Mr. Abelseth: "A little while later there was one of the officers who came and said to be quiet, that there was a ship coming. That is all he said. So I said to them, we had better go and get the life belts as we had not brought them with us. So my cousin and I went down to get the life belts for all of us. When we came up again we carried the life belts on our arms for a while."

Of course, once in a while a note of danger would reach a person.

Mr. Abelseth: "There was a friend of mine who told me that he went back for something he wanted and then there was so much water there that he could not get to his room."

And on it went. Some passengers figured if they were going to just stand around for a while before the boats were ready, they might as well go back to their cabins and get something warmer to wear. This trickle of returns to the cabin continued for most of the night.

Cunningham: ". . . I went back to my own section—C deck, aft—and all my passengers were gone except three. They had gone up on the boat deck with life belts on, all except three."
Smith: "How do you know they had gone up there?"
Cunningham: "Because the stewardess had called the ladies and they were not in their rooms."
Smith: "And where were the other three?"
Cunningham: "Mr. Cummings was in his stateroom. He had come down for an overcoat. He had been on deck. Later, Mr. Clark came along and entered his stateroom and he then put on a life belt. Then Mr. Stead asked me how to fix on a life belt and I helped him put it on and that was the last man of my passengers."

And still, up on deck, the roar of steam continued. The effect was strange, as passengers in various states of dress stood on deck, virtually unable to speak with one another because of all the noise.

Buley: "You could not hear yourself speak then."

But people persisted in speaking anyway, yelling into each others ears. Most talk focused on speculation surrounding the Titanic's fate.

Smith: "Did you see Mr. Hays after he passed this word with you about the icebergs?"
Mr. Peuchen: "Yes, I saw him again on the upper deck, just before I started to help with the boats. I shook hands with him then and

he said, 'This boat is good for eight hours. I have just been getting this from one of the best old seamen, Mr. Crossley'–I think he mentioned his man–'of Milwaukee,' and some person else, and he said, 'Before that time, we will have assistance.'"

Thankfully, from a historical perspective, when Wheelton was sent to get biscuits for the boats, he chose B deck as part of his route to run the errand, and documented the noble character of Andrews along the way.

Wheelton: " I went down to the storeroom. The way I went to the storeroom was down B deck, along B deck. As I went along B deck, I met Mr. Andrews, the builder, who was opening the rooms and looking in to see if there was anyone in, and closing the doors again."

Although Steward Etches met Andrews on B deck almost a half an hour earlier, it appears Andrews was doing one last check to make sure none of the passengers–the first class ones at least–did not go to the bottom of the ocean asleep in their beds. While he searched the rooms, he no doubt came across the occasional passenger returning for something warmer. One of them was Victorine Chaudenson.

Mrs. Ryerson: "We stood about there for quite a long time–fully half an hour, I should say. I know my maid ran down to the cabin and got some of my clothes."

Mrs. Smith: "While I dressed, my husband and I talked of landing, not mentioning the iceberg. I started out, putting on my life preserver, when we met a steward who was on his way to tell us to put on life preservers and come on deck. However, I returned to the room with the intention of bringing my jewelry, but my husband said not to delay with such trifles. However, I picked up two rings and went on deck."

Although the Smith's arrival on deck after 12:30 was much later than the average, their relaxed pace made virtually no difference in the end. By the time they reached the port side of the deck, not a single lifeboat had been lowered yet. Part of the delay seemed due to a general fussing over the contents of the boat.

Lightoller: "We clear it away first, then heave it out over the side, then lower it down level with the rail and then commence to fill it with people. Previous to that we have to take the covers all off, haul out all the falls and coil them down clear."
Smith: "How long do you think it took you to uncover and lower that lifeboat?"
Lightoller: "It is difficult to say, sir. 15 or 20 minutes."

Mr. Peuchen: "I was standing there near the second officer, and the captain was standing there as well at that time. The captain said –I do not know whether it was the captain or the second officer said– 'We will have to get these masts out of these boats, and also the sail.' He said, 'You might give us a hand,' and I jumped in the boat, and we got a knife and cut the lashings of the mast, which is a very heavy mast, and also the sail, and moved it out of the boat, saying it would not be required."

Another cause for delay in launching the port side boats was due to a decision by Captain Smith to load the first boat from the promenade deck. When lowered to A deck, there was a problem with the windows.

Mr. Woolner: [speaking of earlier in the voyage] " . . . I took also particular note of the mechanism for raising and lowering the glass windows on the A deck, and I watched the sailors winding them up with these spanners that are used for that purpose. It struck me as being rather a slow job."

Either way, the captain was committed for the time being, and an announcement was made. The plan required passengers to assemble on A deck, so they were led from the lounges to the promenade area. Some who were already on the boat deck were led down the crew's staircase near the bridge.

Mrs. Futrelle: "We could not have been in the first cabin but a few moments when an officer came in and in quiet tones said, 'Ladies, you will please go to the promenade deck.' The first sign of hysteria on the part of women came at this moment. A little French woman, whose name I don't remember began to weep in a frightened sort of way. Every woman in the cabin clasped her husband more tightly. This was the first moment that we were convinced that there was awful danger. There was not a whimper from the men. They escorted their wives to the door leading out to the promenade deck with the same nonchalance which would have been displayed had they been escorting the women to a cloakroom. When we stepped out of the cabin the officers said, 'Women and children will go out to the promenade deck. The men will remain where they are.' No man was supposed to be on the boat deck. This was the obvious requirement of the discipline which the officers attempted to put into force. Oh, that was a terrible moment! It was awful, awful!"

Anna Turja remembered an officer locking the door to the first class lounge after passengers were ordered out onto deck. *(Olympic)*

In the lounge, some of the crew came in and stopped the band from playing. Everyone was ordered out on deck. The room was cleared and the doors locked.

Mrs. Smith: "After getting to the top deck, the ladies were ordered on deck A without our husbands. I refused to go, but after

being told by three or four officers, my husband insisted and, along with another lady, we went down."

Smith: "How long was this after the collision?"
Mr. Woolner: "I did not look at my watch, but I should think it was half an hour."
Smith: "Did you hear him say anything or did you say anything to him?"
Mr. Woolner: "Yes, I did." I made one remark to him. He said, 'I want all the passengers to go down on A deck because I intend they shall go into the boats from A deck.' I remembered noticing as I came up that all those glass windows were raised to the very top, and I went up to the captain and saluted him and said, 'Haven't you forgotten sir, that all those glass windows are closed?' He said, 'By God, you are right. Call those people back.' Very few people had moved, but the few that had gone down the companionway came up again, and everything went on all right."

Mrs. Ryerson: "Then we were ordered to the boat deck. I only remember the second steward at the head of the stairs, who told us where to go. My chief thought and that of everyone else was, I know, not to make a fuss and to do as we were told."

Mrs. Smith: "After staying there some time

with nothing seemingly going on, someone called upstairs saying they could not be lowered from that deck for the reason it was inclosed in glass. That seemed to be the first time the officers and captain had thought of that, and hastened to order us all on the top deck again. There was some delay in getting lifeboats down. In fact, we had plenty of time to sit in the gymnasium and chat with another gentleman and his wife. I kept asking my husband if I could remain with him rather than go in a lifeboat. He promised me I could. There was no commotion, no panic, and no one seemed to be particularly frightened. In fact, most of the people seemed interested in the unusual occurrence, many having crossed 50 or 60 times. However, I noticed my husband was busy talking to any officer whom he came in contact with. Still, I had not the least suspicion of the scarcity of lifeboats, or I never should have left my husband."

Mrs. Stephenson: "We were in the companionway of A deck when the order came for 'Women and children to Boat Deck and men to starboard side.' Miss Eustis and I took each other's hands, not to be separated in the crowd, and all went on deck, we following close to Mrs. Thayer and her maid and going up narrow iron stairs to the forward boat deck, which, on the Titanic was the

captain's bridge. At the top of the stairs, we found Captain Smith looking much worried and anxiously waiting to get down after we got up."

Smith probably wanted to assess the window situation for himself to determine if he should proceed with his plan to load passengers from the promenade deck, or take them off the ship directly from the boat deck. This confusion and general lack of progress toward loading the boats on the port side did not exactly instill a sense of urgency with the passengers.

Murdoch, Lowe, and Ismay meanwhile had their attentions on lifeboat 3. As they prepared to take on passengers, Rowe passed by on his way to the bridge, without speaking. His arms were full with distress rockets. More than an hour after the ship stopped, he noticed that the boilers were still letting off a roar of excess steam.

Rowe: ". . . there was an awful noise made by the escape of steam."

Murdoch and company may have taken brief note of Rowe's distress rockets as he passed before resuming their efforts to load number 3.

This was a classic period of disorganization with respect to maximizing the

capacity for each lifeboat. While officers were short of people to fill the boats, third class passengers were being kept back on their decks at the rear of the ship.

Smith: "Did you have any difficulty in filling number 3?"
Lowe: "Yes, sir. I had difficulty all along. I could not get enough people."
Smith: "Did any women attempt to get in either of these boats and not succeed in getting in?"
Lowe: "No, sir."
Smith: "Was the conduct of the people when you were loading these boats excited or otherwise?"
Lowe: "Everything was quite quiet and calm. The only thing—and of course you would expect that—was that the people were messing up the falls, getting foul of the falls, and I had to halloa a bit to get them off the falls. Everything else went nicely, very nicely. Quietly and orderly."
Smith: "Was there any weeping or lamentation?"
Lowe: "No, not that I heard."

With racism running high in 1912, there was very likely an element of it in the behavior of the crew toward the other nationalities of steerage. While first and second class passengers enjoyed general access to the boat decks, third class passengers were detained in their area down on the stern. While the crew stood guard at the gate at the top of the stairs that led from the well deck up to the second class B deck, some of the passengers refused to tolerate the existing situation and took matters into their own hands.

Mr. Abelseth: *"There were a lot of steerage people there that were getting on one of these cranes that they had on deck that they used to lift things with. These steerage passengers were crawling along on this, over the railing and away up to the boat deck. A lot of them were doing that. This gate was shut. I do not know whether it was locked, but it was shut so that they could not go that way."*

Miss Mulvihill: *"Some of the Italian men from way down in the steerage were screaming and fighting to get into the lifeboats. Captain Smith* [Bertha Mulvihill incorrectly assumed the officer she saw was the captain] *stood at the head of the passageway. He had a gun in his hand."*

Although the steerage passengers would clearly suffer the most from this kind of class discrimination, it was not directed exclusively at them. While Murdoch and

Lowe searched for women and children at lifeboat 3, and the same for Lightoller at number 6, the crew were preventing second class passengers from going forward on deck into the first class area.

Mr. Beesley: *"About this time, while walking the deck, I saw two ladies come over from the port side and walk towards the rail separating the second class from the first class deck. There stood an officer barring the way. 'May we pass to the boats?' they said. 'No madam,' he replied politely, 'your boats are down on your own deck,' pointing to where they swung below."*

Ironically, the boats to which the officer gestured were already lowered down to A deck–a first class area. Second class passengers did not have access to A deck from their stairwell, so it was impossible for the woman to comply with the officers suggestion. This kind of uncoordinated supervision of the decks by the crew ultimately decreased the number of people who would escape from the sinking ship.

While some passengers were trying to get to a lifeboat, others with easy access to them turned down their chance for survival. This random assembly of passengers resulted in a crowding of some areas while other places on deck were almost deserted.

While the stewards effectively got the second class passengers up on deck, they remained on the boat deck aft, while officers searched for more women and children at the forward end of the same deck.

Hardy: *"I got them all up on the outer decks and they were grouped about the ship in different parts . . ."*

Lowe: *"I know there must have been pretty nearly an equal percentage of men and women in number 3. Because there were not many women there. She was very heavily loaded. I should say 40 to 45 maybe. We will say 40."*
Smith: *"How did it happen that you did not put more people into lifeboat number 3 than 45?"*
Lowe: *"There did not seem to be any people there."*
Smith: *" You did not find anybody that wanted to go?"*
Lowe: *"Those that were there did not seem to want to go. I hollered out, 'Who's next for the boat?' and there was no response."*
Smith: *"Was the top deck crowded?"*
Lowe: *"No. There was a little knot of people on the forepart of the gymnasium door."*

Newlands: *"Did you not think at the time that it ought to have been more heavily loaded?"*

Moore (3): "It seemed pretty full, but I dare say we could have jammed more in. The passengers were not anxious to get in the boats. They were not anxious to get in the first lot of boats."

Newlands: "What was your feeling at the time?"

Moore: "I thought, myself, that there was nothing serious the matter until we got away from the ship and she started settling down."

Suddenly, a rocket went off from the bridge and shot high into the air. At the top of its climb, it exploded into a ball of descending stars, casting a brief flash of light onto the deck below.

Rowe: "I took them [the rockets] to the fore bridge and turned them over to the fourth officer. I assisted the officer to fire them."

Mr. Beesley: "But if there were anyone who had not by now realized that the ship was in danger, all doubt on this point was to be set at rest in a dramatic manner. Suddenly a rush of light from the forward deck, a hissing roar that made us all turn from watching the boats, and a rocket leapt upwards to where the stars blinked and twinkled above us. Up it went, higher and higher, with a sea of faces upturned to watch it, and then an explosion that seemed to split the silent night in two, and a shower of stars sank slowly down and went out one by one. And with a gasping sigh one word escaped the lips of the crowd: 'Rockets!' Anybody knows what rockets at sea mean."

Mrs. Cook: "As we made our way along the deck to try to get into the boats the first distress rocket went up and then I knew we were in great danger but everybody was perfectly calm and we stood there watching the boats fill up one after another."

Starboard on the *Titanic*. Lifeboats 7, 5, 3 and 1 can be seen on the boat deck.

As Murdoch continued to load lifeboat 3, Fourth Officer Boxhall proceeded to fire off rockets every five minutes from the rail of the bridge, only several feet away on the starboard side.

Lowe: *"They were incessantly going off. They were nearly deafening me."*

Smith: *"Did Officer Murdoch have charge of that boat?"*

Lowe: *"Yes. He was there up to the finishing of number 3."*

Smith: *"Did Mr. Ismay assist in filling that boat?"*

Lowe: *"Yes. He assisted there, too. He was there, and I distinctly remember seeing him alongside of me—that is, by my side—when the first detonator went off. I will tell you how I happen to remember it so distinctly. It was because the flash of the detonator lit up the whole deck. I did not know who Mr. Ismay was then, but I learned afterwards who he was, and he was standing alongside of me."*

Smith: *"Did you say anything to him?"*

Lowe: *"I did not."*

On the port side, it looked as though some progress was finally being made in the evacuation. At the same time, the *Titanic* was recovering from her list to starboard.

Mrs. Futrelle: *"I had no sooner reached the deck than she began to list to port. Even then there was no panic."*

Mr. Thayer: *"It was now about 12:45 a.m. The noise was terrific. The deep vibrating roar of the exhaust steam blowing off through the safety valves was deafening, in addition to which they had commenced to send up rockets. There was more and more action. After standing there for some minutes, talking above the din, trying to determine what we should do next, we finally decided to go back into the crowded hallway where it was warm. Shortly we heard stewards passing the word around, 'All women to the port side.' We then said good bye to my mother at the head of the stairs on [Boat] deck and she and the maid went out onto the port side of that deck, supposedly to get into a lifeboat. Father and I went out on the starboard side, watching what was going on about us. It seemed we were always waiting for orders and no orders ever came."*

Marian Thayer and her maid participated in the confusion surrounding lifeboat number 4. All the while, valuable time was being lost. With a lingering uncertainty about whether the boats were to be lowered from the boat deck or A deck, Lightoller took the bull by the horn with respect to lifeboats 6 and 8, which were still hanging level with the boat deck.

Lightoller: *"I asked him: 'Shall I put the women and children in the boats?' The captain replied, 'Yes, and lower away.'"*

At last, around 12:45 a.m. the lifeboats on the port side began to load. With the roar of steam in the background, Lightoller yelled into the night air for women and children to come forward. Smith supervised the loading and directly assisted with moving the passengers along.

Mr. Woolner: *"He [Smith] sort of ordered the people in. He said, 'Come along, madam,' and that sort of thing."*

Mr. Peuchen: *" Then there was a cry, as soon as that part was done, that they were ready to put women in. So the women came forward, one by one. A great many women came with their husbands."*

When the time came to get into the boat, many wanted nothing to do with the exercise, particularly since husbands could not go. There was a sense of security associated with the open deck of the liner that contrasted sharply with climbing into a small boat dangling seven decks above the water by ropes—all because the White Star Line wanted to take some precautions.

Lightoller: *"They were not at all eager to get into the boat, anyway, any of them. I had to sing out. Naturally, no one looked on it as serious and they were not in any hurry to go down to the sea in a boat."*

Mrs. Smith: "When the first boat was lowered from the left hand side I refused to get in and they did not urge me particularly."

Perhaps it was because Captain Smith was nearby that Lightoller was so unconscionably strict about who was to gain access to the boats. Or maybe it was an overt fear of a potential rush by hundreds of passengers and crew at one time. But whatever the reason, an overly disciplined, almost mean tone was set from the beginning during the loading of boats under Lightoller's control.

Smith: "How were these passengers selected in going to the lifeboats?"
Lightoller: "By their sex."
Smith: "Whenever you saw a woman?"
Lightoller: "Precisely."
Smith: "She was invited to go into one of these boats?"
Lightoller: "Excepting the stewardesses. We turned several of those away."

Mr. Peuchen: "They would only allow women in that boat, and the men had to stand back. That was the order. The second officer stood there and he carried out that to the limit. He allowed no men except the

Port side of the *Titanic*. Lifeboats 2, 4, 6 and 8 are visible on the forward deck, with 10, 12, 14, and 16 aft.

sailors, who were manning the boat, but there were no passengers that I saw got into that boat. I was busy helping and assisting to get the ladies in. After a reasonable complement of ladies had got aboard, she was lowered, but I did not see one single passenger get in that first boat."
Fletcher: "You mean male passenger."
Peuchen: "Yes; male passenger."

Each lifeboat, with the exception of the two emergency boats on each side of the bridge, could hold 65 people. The lifeboats had been tested prior to the *Titanic*'s departure with a full load of crewmen. Clearly, the officers should have been aware of this statistic. But such knowledge did not hold up against the reality of the night. Because of the arrangement of the seats, the lifeboat quickly presented an impression of being full enough when only 30 or so people were seated in it.

Smith: "From what you have said, you discriminated entirely in the interest of the passengers–first the women and children, in filling them?"
Lightoller: "Yes, sir."
Smith: "Why did you do that? Because of the captain's orders, or because of the rule of the sea?"
Lightoller: "The rule of human nature."
Smith: "The rule of human nature? And there was no studied purpose, as far as you know, to save the crew?"
Lightoller: "Absolutely not."
Smith: "Who determined the number of people who should go into the lifeboats?"
Lightoller: "I did."
Smith: "How did you reach a conclusion as to the number that should be permitted to go in?"
Lightoller: "My own judgment about the strength of the tackle."
Smith: "How many did you put in each boat?"
Lightoller: "In the first boat I put about 20 or 25. Twenty sir."

Mr. Peuchen: "Every woman on the port side was given an opportunity. In fact, we had not enough women to put into the boats. We were looking for them. I cannot under-stand why we did not take some men. The boats would have held more."

Even after the delay attributable to the confusion with lifeboat 4, the loading process proceeded at a much slower, and less efficient pace than on the starboard side, mainly due to this ongoing effort to fill the boats exclusively with women and children. If enough women and children could not be found to fill the boat, well then, the boat would be lowered rather than allow husbands, fathers, and other men into the boat. The system fed on itself in terms of its inefficiency. By not allowing husbands and fathers into the boats, Lightoller and Captain Smith inadvertently motivated many women to stay on deck.

Mr. Woolner: ". . . I did not count them, but it struck me as not being very full. But it was rather difficult to get it filled. There was a certain amount of reluctance on the part of the women to go in, and then some officer said, 'It is a matter of precaution,' and then they came forward rather more freely."

Isador and Ida Straus, founders of Macy's Department Store, loitered nearby boat 8, but the crew could not convince Mrs. Straus to enter without her husband.

Jones: "There was an old lady there and an old gentleman, and she would not come in the boat. If she said anything we could not hear it because the steam was blowing so and making such a noise."

Smith: "Did Mrs. Straus get into the boat?"
Crawford: "She attempted to get into the boat first and she got back again. Her maid got into the boat."
Smith: "What do you mean by 'she attempted' to get in?"
Crawford: "She went to get over from the deck to the boat, but then went back to her husband."
Smith: "Did she step on the boat?"
Crawford: "She stepped onto the boat, onto the gunwales, sir. Then she went back."
Smith: "What followed?"
Crawford: "She said, 'We have been living together for many years, and where you go I go.'"

Mr. Woolner: "The second time we went up to Mr. Straus, and I said to him, 'I am sure nobody would object to an old gentleman like you getting in. There seems to be room in this boat.' He said, 'I will not go before the other men.'"

The dilemma that confronted the Strauses was the same presented to numerous couples on deck that night. There seemed to be little motivation for a couple or family to separate. With so many lifeboats lining the deck, many families decided to wait on events and stay together rather than split up just for the purpose of this White Star Line midnight exercise.

Mrs. Douglas: "Mr. Douglas told me if I waited we might both go together, and we stood there waiting. We heard that the boat was in communication with three other boats by wireless. We watched the distress rockets sent off—they rose high in the air and burst. No one seemed excited."

Passengers really did not know what to think about all of this commotion while they stood on deck. The ship was damaged, but what about the watertight compartments? Were the lifeboats just going to sit out in the cold dark Atlantic for a couple of hours and then return to the *Titanic* once the crew decided it was safe to come back aboard? Was that ship on the horizon heading their way to assist? The perception of danger was a gradual one for most, slowly increasing as the night wore on, as various signs that all was not well revealed themselves in piecemeal fashion.

Mr. Portalupi: "There was no confusion. Officers told us everything was all right,

The boat deck. Lifeboat 8 is in the foreground, and number 2 is hanging at the ready in the distance.

that the vessel would remain afloat for many hours until help arrived in response to the wireless call for help. Everybody believed them. I chanced to see the boats being lowered from the upper deck. That gave me my first fright."

Lightoller apparently was never told by the captain that the *Titanic* was sinking. In a significant way, he had the same attitude as the passengers, believing that they were probably safer on deck.

Smith: "How did it happen you did not put more people into that boat?"
Lightoller: "Because I did not consider it safe."
Smith: "In a great emergency like that, where there were limited facilities, could you not have afforded to try to put more people into that boat?"

Lightoller: "I did not know it was urgent then. I had no idea it was urgent."
Smith: "You did not know it was urgent?"
Lightoller: "Nothing like it."

Regardless of the majority faith in the safety of the ship, some women exercised caution and came forward immediately when the call first went out. Ella White had a bound up foot, but still wanted one of the first available seats.

Mrs. White (8): "We got into it very easily. We got into the lifeboat without any inconvenience whatever. As I said, my condition was such that I had to be handled rather carefully, and there was no inconvenience at all."

Jones (8): "I got the collapsible boat on the port side ready. I got my own boat, number 8 ready. An officer sent me for a lamp and as I was going forward there was a man coming with two or three lamps in his hand. I went back again and this number 8 boat was there, all swung out and there were about 35 ladies in it. I jumped in the boat. The captain asked me, 'Was the plug in the boat?' and I answered, 'Yes, sir.' 'All right,' he said. 'Any more ladies?' There was one lady came there and left her husband. She wanted her husband to go with her, but he

Some of *Titanic*'s lifeboats. With seating for just a few on each plank, it is easy to see how a boat would appear full enough with 30 or so people loaded into it. In some of the boats, stowaways hid under the seats at each end.

backed away and the captain shouted again –in fact, twice again– 'Any more ladies?'

It was emotionally exhausting for some to witness husbands and wives separating by the side of the boat deck. After watching such scenes, it became a source of aggravation to several passengers to then observe the qualifications of the crew who were told to get into the boat by Lightoller. To some, it did not seem right that these employees were getting seats in the boats.

Mrs. White (8): "Another thing which I think is a disgraceful point. The men were

asked, when they got into our boat, if they could row. Imagine asking men that who are supposed to be at the head of lifeboats– imagine asking them if they can row."

Mrs. Futrelle: "People simply couldn't believe that the Titanic could sink. One by one the women were seated, no hurry, no rush. In fact, there were only fifteen who went into that first boat. I heard the captain order the crew to lower away. Every woman's eyes were turned towards the cabin where the men stood. I could not make up my mind to leave my husband when I saw the lifeboat about to go down. I was afraid

the water looked so treacherous. I ran back, threw my arms around his neck and said, 'Jack, I don't want to leave you.' Oh, do be calm, dear,' he said and allowed me to stay with him for a while. He said there was no great hurry and that I might remain with him for a few minutes. Oh, those few precious minutes were a lifetime. Jack just stood there with the men with his arm about me and I clung to him. We did not say much. There were other women who did not wish to leave their husbands. After Jack had kissed me again, and told me not to worry, that everything would be all right, he led me out to the main deck but he never stepped upon it–so conscientiously did he obey orders– so splendid was his bravery."

Mrs. White (8): "I do not think there was any particular bravery, because none of the men thought it was going down. If they had thought the ship was going down, they would not have frivoled as they did about it. Some of them said, 'When you come back you will need a pass,' and 'You cannot get on tomorrow morning without a pass.' They never would have said those things if anybody had had any idea that the ship was going to sink. There was no excitement whatever. Nobody seemed frightened. Nobody was panic-stricken. There was a lot of pathos when husbands and wives kissed each other good-bye, of course."

With only 28 passengers in a lifeboat that had a capacity for 65, the decision was made to lower lifeboat number 8—the first to go on the port side. Captain Smith, who had been generally standing away from the edge assisting the passengers forward, walked up to the edge of the boat.

Mrs. Dyer-Edwards (8): "Captain Smith stood shoulder to shoulder with me as I got into the life boat, and his last words were to the lone seaman—Tom Jones—'Row straight for those ship lights over there. Leave your passengers on board of her and return as soon as you can.' Captain Smith's attitude was one of great calmness and courage, and I am sure he thought the ship—whose lights we could plainly see—would pick us up and that our life boats would be able to do double duty in ferrying passengers to the help that gleamed so near."

Crawford (8): "After that Captain Smith came to the boat and asked how many men were in the boat. He gave me orders to ship the rowlocks and to pull for a light. He directed me to a light over there. Captain Smith could see the light quite plain, as he pointed in the direction that we were to make for."

The swimming pool. (*Olympic*)

Jones (8): "He [the captain] told me to row for the light, and land the passengers and return to the ship."

The command to lower away was issued and the first boat on the port side descended to the water. The passengers still on board watched all this with great interest, as the faces in the lifeboat gradually disappeared behind the edge of the deck.

Crawford (8): "We were on the port side; No. 8 boat on the port side."
Smith: "Who superintended the loading?"
Crawford: "The chief officer superintended it, and myself."
Smith: "And the lowering?"
Crawford: "And Captain Smith."
Smith: "All those lifeboats on the port side?"

Crawford: "Captain Smith and the chief officer; Captain Smith and the steward lowered the forward falls of the boat I was in."

In the interim, the pace on deck continued to increase.

Mr. Beesley: "All this time people were pouring up from the stairs and adding to the crowd. I remember at that moment thinking it would be well to return to my cabin and rescue some money and warmer clothing if we were to embark in boats, but looking through the vestibule windows and seeing people still coming upstairs, I decided it would only cause confusion passing them on the stairs and so remained on deck."

It was 12:50 a.m. Boiler room 5 had only a few feet of air left before it would be completely submerged. Water reached a side crew staircase on E deck that led down to the laundry and linen areas. It poured down the steps, slid under several doorways and made its appearance at the swimming pool and changing rooms. It crept across the floor and then poured into the pool, filling it to the brim. A minute or two later and the entire pool was under water.

The *Titanic* was down by the head. The G deck porthole lights at the bow were long gone and the string of lights along F and E decks pointed into the water at the forward end of the ship.

During the second half of the hour the decision was made on the starboard side to get the boats aft going concurrent to the forward ones. While Murdoch and Lowe worked on the odd numbered boats 1 through 7, the rear of the boat deck came alive as the evacuation was set into motion. Wilde and Murdoch were the brains to this strategy, and it proved to be very effective.

Mr. Beesley: "I was now on the starboard side of the top boat deck. We watched the crew at work on the lifeboats, numbers 9, 11, 13, 15, some inside arranging the oars, some coiling ropes on the deck—the ropes which ran through the pulleys to lower to sea—others with cranks fitted to the rocking arms of the davits. Just then an officer came along from the first class deck and shouted above the noise of escaping steam, 'All women and children get down to deck below and all men stand back from the boats. The men fell back and the women retired below to get into the boats from the next deck. Two women refused at first to leave their husbands, but partly by persuasion and partly by force they were separated from them and sent down to the next deck."

While the action continued on the boat deck, Wheelton walked through the heart of the ship on his errand for biscuits.

Wheelton: " I went along B deck and used what we call the accommodation staircase, which goes through the ship, and is used by the stewards. I went down to the storeroom and I got a bottle of biscuits and I carried them up to the main dining room, through the reception room, up the main staircase. I got onto the deck."

If Wheelton had glanced down the staircase to E deck, he would have seen that it was still dry—and been falsely reassured there was nothing serious to worry about.

On the boat deck, people wandered about with little or no direction from the officers and crew, who were busy themselves with lowering the boats. Some of the second and third class passengers were entertaining themselves by admiring the luxuriousness of the first class lounges and promenades.

Mr. Woolner: ". . . I said to Steffanson, 'Let us go down on the deck below and see if we can find any people waiting about there.' So we went down onto A deck and we found three women who did not seem to know their way, and we brought them up. They might have been, I should think, second or third class passengers, but I did not examine them very carefully. You see, it was not very light."

Lifeboat 8 was lowered without incident. When it reached the water, some of the passengers saw cracks in the facade presented by Smith and Lightoller's strict women and children only rule.

Mrs. White (8): ". . . before we cut loose from the ship two of the seamen with us—the men, I should say; I do not call them seamen; I think they were dining room stewards—before we were cut loose from the ship they took out cigarettes and lighted them; on an occasion like that! All of those men escaped under the pretense of being oarsmen. The man who rowed me took his oar and rowed all over the boat, in every direction. I said to him, 'Why don't you put the oar in the oarlock?' He said, 'Do you put it in that hole?' I said, 'Certainly.' He said, 'I never had an oar in my hand before.' I spoke to the other man and he said, 'I have never had an oar in my hand before, but I think I can row.' Those were the men that we were put to sea with at night—with all those magnificent fellows left on board who would have been such a protection to us. Those were the kind of men with whom we were put out to sea that night."

Number 8 set off naively for the light on the horizon with the mistaken belief they would soon be at its side with news about the *Titanic*. They did not realize the ship was approximately ten miles away and that they would never reach it in time.

Jones (8): "I thought they were only sending us away for an hour or so until they got squared up again. Until they get her pumped out. One lady; she had a lot to say, and I put her to steering my boat. She was a countess or something. I believe her husband was in New York."

Mrs. White (8): "We simply rowed away. We had the order on leaving the ship to do that. The officer who put us in the boat—I do not know who he was—gave strict orders to the seamen, or the men, to make for the light opposite and land the passengers and get back just as soon as possible. That was the light that everybody saw in the distance. I saw it distinctly. It was a boat of some kind."

Back on deck, Smith and Lightoller turned their attention to lifeboat number 6.

Smith: "Did you see any attempt to get in?"
Mr. Peuchen: "No. I never saw such order. It was perfect order. The discipline was splendid. The officers were carrying out

their duty and I think the passengers behaved splendidly. I did not see a cowardly act by any man. The boat was loaded, but I think they could have taken more in this boat. They took, however, all the ladies that offered to get in at that point. Then, as soon as the boat was lowered, we turned our attention to the next."

After lifeboat 8 was lowered on the port side, the captain momentarily returned to the bridge to oversee the firing of the rockets, and to focus on the mystery ship on the horizon. At one point it seemed to be approaching and the general feeling on the *Titanic* was one of curiousness.

Fletcher: "Did you see the captain that night?"
Hardy: "Yes, sir. I did; on the bridge before our boat left. He was superintending the rockets, calling out to the quartermaster about the rockets."

Boxhall: "I had been firing off rockets before I saw her side lights. I fired off the rockets and then she got so close I could see her side lights and starboard light."

The rockets were a fascinating addition to an already bizarre night, as they periodically shot up into the sky and exploded high above the passengers and crew.

Boxhall: "Just white stars. Bright. I do not know whether they were stars or bright balls. I think they were balls. They were the regulation distress signals. Not red."

At one point it looked like the ship was coming to their assistance as a result of the rockets. Boxhall and Smith watched the light intently.

Captain Smith knew the *Titanic* was going to sink, but he may have always believed that help would arrive before the awful moment. At 12:50, the wireless room did not yet offer positive news of a timely rescue by another vessel. Smith began to realize that the fate of more than 1,000 people rested on the distant light on the northern horizon. The rockets were becoming a critical tool in the captain's attempt to save the lives of his passengers.

Bright: "They told us to bring a box of detonators for them—signals. Each of us took a box to the bridge. When we got up there, we were told to fire them—distress signals."
Smith: "Who fired them?"
Bright: "Rowe and I, and Mr. Boxhall, the fourth officer."
Smith: "How long did you continue firing these rockets?"
Bright: "I could not say. After we would fire one we would go and help clear the boats

away, and then we would come back again."
Smith: *"This firing of rockets continued for some time, did it?"*
Bright: *"I should say probably half an hour."*

On the *Californian*, Gill smoked a cigarette on deck as the rockets went up.

Gill: *"I had been on deck about 10 minutes when I saw a white rocket about 10 miles away on the starboard side. I thought it must be a shooting star. In seven or eight minutes I saw distinctly a second rocket in the same place and I said to myself, 'That must be a vessel in distress.' It was not my business to notify the bridge or the lookouts, but they could not have helped but see them. I am quite sure that the Californian was less than 20 miles from the Titanic, which the officers report to have been our position. I could not have seen her if she had been more than 10 miles distant and I saw her very plainly."*

Buley: *"There was a ship of some description there when she struck, and she passed right by us. We thought she was coming to us and if she had come to us, everyone could have boarded her. You could see she was a steamer. She had her steamer lights burning. She was off our port bow when we struck ... I should judge she was about 3 miles."*

On the starboard side, lifeboat 3 loaded fairly quickly, due in part to the fact there were so few people at this location on the boat deck, and of those, some had no interest in climbing aboard. Charlotte Cardeza, her son Thomas, and their maid, Annie Ward happened to come up on the boat deck at this time and walk over to the activity. Charlotte and her son occupied one of the two most expensive accommodations on board, the B deck suite, complete with its own private promenade deck. Bruce Ismay had been occupying the other one. The Cardezas paid a small fortune to stay in that suite for the maiden voyage, and now they were abandoning the ship in the middle of the night. For a brief moment, the occupants of the millionaire's suites–Ismay and the Cardezas–stood together on the sinking liner until Ismay assisted them into the boat.

Moore (3): *"After all the ladies and children that were about there got in, I suppose anyone jumped in, then."*
Newlands: *"What officer was there?"*
Moore: *"The first officer, Mr. Murdoch."*
Newlands: *"Did he tell these men to go in?"*
Moore: *"No, sir. He never told them. He got all the women and children in and the men started to jump in. And when we thought we had a boat full there, we lowered away."*

Lowe: *"I was standing at the side of the ship watching the after end."*

Moore (3): *"When we swung number 3 out I was told to jump in the boat and pass the ladies in. I was told that by the first officer. After we got so many ladies in, and there were no more about, we took in men passengers. We had 32 in the boat, all told, and then we lowered away."*

Mrs. Crosby (3): *"I think it was the first or second boat that we got into. I do not recollect other boats being lowered at that time. I did not see them. We got into the lifeboat that was hanging over the rail alongside the deck. We got in and men and women, with their families, got in the boat with us. There was no discrimination between men and women. About 36 persons got in the boat with us. There were only two officers in the boat, and the rest were all first class passengers."*

Mr. Harper (3): *"We passengers still remaining on the deck gathered around and watched the men at work. Very slowly, and stumbling here and there, the people began to get in. It was like stepping down, say, from this table to the chair alongside. We took a look at both boats. My wife thought the one farther off [lifeboat 1] was better because there would be hardly a dozen peo-*

ple left to go in it after the big boat beside us was filled. I looked them both over, saw that the farther boat had no watertight compartments in it while the one near had, so I said, 'No, let's take this. It will float longest.' With that I handed my wife down into the nearer, bigger boat, and she comfortably seated herself on a thwart. Other women and other men climbed aboard. I stepped in and sat down among the stokers. There was no one in sight on the decks. I had on my arm a little brown Pekingese spaniel we had picked up in Paris and named Sun Yat Sen in honor of his country's first president. The little dog kept very quiet."

Newlands: "Were you given any instruction to pull in any particular direction?"
Moore (3): "No, sir. I think everyone pulled toward this white light."
Newlands: "What did you think that light was at the time?"
Moore: "I thought it was a fisherman. It was only just one single light."
Newlands: "It was a genuine light, you think?"
Moore: "Yes. One bright light."

It was a little after 12:50. As Murdoch leaned over the side to see lifeboat 3 safely in the water, he noticed that none of the four boats toward the stern had been lowered. They hung alongside the promenade deck, but nobody was in them yet. Murdoch turned to Lowe and instructed him to load lifeboat 1, and then headed to the Grand Staircase entrance.

During this same time when lifeboat 3 was loaded, Steward Ray waited at his assigned boat 9. After a while, he decided he could not take the cold any longer and would make better use of his time while his boat was waiting. He left the deck and descended to the steward's quarters.

Boiler room 5 was completely submerged and the swimming pool above it was flooded too. The water on E deck was on the move again, sliding in under the doors of the first class cabins and moving up the hallway toward the Grand Staircase.

Ray: "I got my overcoat on. There was nobody in number 3 when I left. Number 3 room, where I slept. I went along E deck and forward, and the forward part of E deck was under water. I could just manage to get through the doorway into the main stairway. I went across to the other side of the ship where the passengers' cabins were. Saw nobody there. I looked to see where the water was and it was corresponding on that side of the ship to the port side. I walked leisurely up to the main stairway, passed two or three people on the way, saw the two

pursers in the purser's office and the clerks busy at the safe taking things out and putting them in bags, and just then Mr. Rothschild left his stateroom and I waited for him. I had waited on him on the Olympic. I spoke to him and asked him where his wife was. He said she had gone off in a boat. I said, 'This seems rather serious.' He said, 'I do not think there is any occasion for it.' So we walked leisurely up the stairs until I got to A deck and went through the door. I went out there onto the open deck and along to number 9 boat. It was just being filled with women and children. I assisted."

Most third class passengers waited for instructions, but some took things into their own hands and located a way to the boat deck. Berk Pickard sought out the aft entrance to the second class staircase, which only went as high as B deck.

Mr. Pickard: "I said to myself that if the ship had to sink, I should be one of the last. That was my first idea, which was the best. I went and I found the door. There are always a few steps from this third class, with a moveable door, and it is marked there that second class passengers have no right to penetrate there. I found this door open so that I could go into the second class, where I did not find

Water creeps
along E deck
in first class.

many people, only a few that climbed on the ladder and went into the first class, which I did."

Wilde had his hands full at the moment, supervising some crew with getting the boats aft ready and into place. Ismay provided brief assistance with lifeboat 1, but soon headed up the deck to lifeboat 9. A strategy of loading boats from A deck, which failed a few minutes earlier with number 4, was put into place, aft on the starboard boats, with better results.

Brice: "Number 9 went out from A deck. I lowered the boat from the boat deck to A deck."

Murdoch descended the Grand Staircase to A deck where first class passengers were lingering around the foyer and herded them through the door onto the starboard promenade deck. There, Purser McElroy stood by and assisted Murdoch.

Haines (9): "As soon as we finished turning out the boats I went to my own station. I got to my own boat just in time, as they filled my boat. We had the boat crew there and Mr. Murdoch came along with a crowd of passengers and we filled the boat with ladies. I know of one incident there where a lady would not come into the boat. She would not come into the boat when they were fill-

The starboard entrance to the Grand Staircase. Murdoch stepped through this door with a crowd of passengers trailing behind him and headed aft to lifeboat 9. *(Olympic)*

ing it. The officers were trying to get her in. Mr. Murdoch, then was trying to get her in the boat, and she would not get into the boat. I think she was afraid to get into the boat."

Ward: " I think the purser—I am not sure on that point—said, 'Are you all ready?"

Haynes answered, 'Yes' and with that he said, 'Pass in the women and children that are here into that boat.' There were several men standing around and they fell back and there was quite a quantity of women and children helped into the boat. One old lady made a great fuss about it and absolutely refused to get into the boat. She went back to the companionway and forced her way in and would not get into the boat."

It was not easy for many women in their dresses and nightgowns to climb over the 3½ foot high rail into the lifeboat.

Ward: "One woman had already fallen and hurt herself a little–a French lady. The purser told two more men to get in and assist these women down into the boat. From the rail of the boat it is quite a step down to the bottom of the boat, and in the dark they could not see where they were stepping."

To the credit of Murdoch and McElroy, they allowed men into the boats after the available women and children were loaded. At this earlier hour, the number interested in getting into the boats was manageable. Most men still preferred to remain on the *Titanic* because of confidence in the ship and a concern for their own image; it was not the most chivalrous thing, in their minds, to climb aboard a lifeboat while they were calling for women and children. By allowing the men to top off the boats, Murdoch saved at least 100 more souls.

Widgery (9): They had taken the canvas off of number 9 and lowered it, and just then

The rail that passengers had to climb over.

some biscuits came up from the storekeeper. I helped him put one of the boxes into the bottom of the boat, and the purser took hold of my arm and said, 'Get in the boat.' He said, 'Get in the boat and help the boatswain mate pass the ladies in.' So I got in the boat and stepped on the side, and we passed the ladies in. We thought we had them all in, and the purser calls out, 'Are there any more women?' Just then someone said, 'Yes.' This woman came along, rather an oldish lady, and she was frightened, and she gave me her hand. I took one hand, and

gave it to the boatswain's mate, and he caught hold of the other hand, and she pulled her hand away, and went back to the door and would not get in. One of them went after her, but she had gone down the stairs. The chief officer was there and called out for any more women, and there seemed to be none, and he told the men to get in, four or five of them. We were filled right up then. Then they started to lower away."

Pickard was an extremely lucky third class male passenger. Whereas hundreds of third class men went down with the ship, he simply walked up to the promenade deck and obtained a seat in one of the boats in full view of the officers, and in the middle of a crowd.

Mr. Pickard (9): "I found there only a few men and about two ladies. They had been putting them into lifeboats and as no women were there, we men sprang in the boat. We had only one woman and another young girl. There were two women. They stood just in front of me."

Haines (9): "I counted them. I guess there were about 45 to 48. When there were no more women forthcoming, the boat was full. They were singing out for the women, and the men then jumped in the bows of her and filled the bow up. The two sailors, and then I could not exactly say how many men, but there were three or four stewards and three or four firemen. We had some firemen and two or three men passengers. I could not say within one or two, but around 60 I had."

Ward (9): "Then the purser told me to get into the boat and take an oar. I did so, and we still waited there and asked if there were any more women. There were none coming along. There were no women to be seen on the deck at that time. They took three of four men into the boat and the officers that were standing there thought there was quite sufficient in it to lower with safety and we lowered down to the water, everything running very smoothly."

Once boiler room 5 flooded and the bow sank deeper, the *Titanic* gained some stability back and rid herself of the lean to starboard. This may have been interpreted by some that the ship was beginning to stabilize due to her watertight compartments.

Fletcher: "Was she listing badly when you lowered boat number 9?"
Ward (9): "No, sir. She was not listing at all. She was down by the head but not listing."

Ismay had the option of helping

This demonstration on the *Olympic,* held after the disaster, shows lifeboat 9 hanging alongside the promenade deck. The lifeboat hung closer to the edge of the rail that night on the *Titanic.*

Lowe with boat number 1, but the two had not exactly bonded over the earlier incident at lifeboat 5. Ismay was free to choose where he wanted to help. The forward deck was virtually deserted so he left Lowe and proceeded to boat 9. Murdoch was still down on the promenade deck but McElroy had already returned on top in preparation of supervising the davits. While Brice and other crew let out the ropes, Ismay assisted.

Fletcher: *"Did you say you saw Mr. Ismay at boat number 9?"*
Ward (9): *"Yes, sir. He was on deck when our boat left. I heard him say, 'Steady, boys,' or something like that–it was some expression like that–when he was standing talking to Mr. McElroy."*

Smith: *"What officer stood with you at the boat you lowered, that is, at the boat, and helped load it and lower it?"*
Haines: *"Mr. Murdoch."*
Smith: *"Was there any other officer there?"*
Haines: *"No, sir. I never saw any of them. Only Mr. Murdoch. He was in charge. He filled our boat alone, sir. When she was full, two or three men jumped in the bow of her. He said, 'That is enough,' and he lowered her down."*

Fletcher: *"Were there any more men on the*

The *Olympic* lifeboat demonstration, showing the long descent of number 9 to the water.

deck?"
Widgery (9): *"Yes, sir, several men up on the deck, quite a lot. There were no more women there."*

Ward (9): *"We had a full boat. We got away from the ship's side before number 11 was in the water, and Haines gave orders to pull away, and we had some difficulty in unlashing the oars on account of them being lashed up. No one had a knife, for some time."*

Haines (9): *". . . we filled the boat with ladies and lowered the boat, and he [Murdoch] told me to lay off and keep clear of the ship. I got the boat clear and laid out near the ship. I did not think the ship would sink, of course. When I saw her going down by the head, I pulled further away, for the safety of the boat. About 100 yards away at first."*

Widgery (9): *"Then we were lowered down to the water, and just before we went away the chief officer called out to the boatswain to keep about 100 yards off. We got into the water and I cut loose the oars–I was the only one that had a knife amongst us–and we stood off a little ways."*

Ward (9): *" We had not room to pull the oars. They had to move their bodies with us when we were rowing, so she was pretty well*

160

packed. How many there were I could not say. We pulled off about, I should say, a couple of hundred yards, and Haines gave orders to lay on the oars, which we did."

The whole process of getting off the *Titanic* in a lifeboat was a stressful one and there were many whose nerves were a bit frayed by the time they were in the water. It all seemed too strange.

Mr. Pickard (9): "We were lowered down and when I was lowered down I saw the whole ship, as big as she was, the right side a little bit sinking and I was far from imagining that it was the beginning of the end. When I was going away from the ship, of course I was rather frightened. I was sorry at not being on the ship and I said to the seaman, 'I would rather be on the ship.' He was laughing at me, and he said, 'Do you not see we are sinking?' I was rather excited and I said, 'It is fortunate that now the sea is nice, but perhaps in five minutes we will be turned over.'"

While lifeboat 3 was loaded and lowered on the starboard side, number 6 was loaded on the port. After lifeboat 8 was sent away, Smith left for the bridge to supervise the rockets and assess the ship on the horizon, leaving Lightoller in charge of the evacuation. Whereas three boats had already been lowered on the starboard side, with two more in process, Lightoller was only as far as loading the second on the port side. Murdoch was proving early on to be more efficient at getting the lifeboats loaded and away from the ship. On the port side, Peuchen noted one of the root causes.

Mr. Peuchen: "I might say I was rather surprised that the sailors were not at their stations, as I have seen fire drills very often on steamers where they all stand at attention, so many men at the bow and stern of these lifeboats. They seemed to be short of sailors around the lifeboats that were being lowered at this particular point. I do not know what was taking place in other parts of the steamer."

Some of the ship's employees had a conflict with their responsibilities. Steward Cunningham was supposed to report to lifeboat 7, but also take care of his passengers by seeing that they went up on deck.

Smith: "Did you respond to your station when you first heard of the accident?"
Cunningham: "No, I did not. I waited down in my rooms, closed them all and shut off the lights, and went on deck. When I pulled up there that boat had gone, I think. Number 7 had gone."

The lifeboat drill, typically performed on Sundays at sea, was canceled for no apparent reason on this voyage and the result was a significant scrambling of resources to load, lower, and man the boats for rowing.

Lightoller: "As far as ever I could I put two seamen in a boat. If I didn't have a seaman there, I had to put a steward there. Sometimes there would be three seamen in a boat. As soon as the boats were lowered to the level of the rail, I would detail one man to jump in and ship the rudder, one man to cast adrift the oars, and one man would see that the plugs were in, and it would take three men."

Lightoller was working on loading lifeboat number 6 at 12:55 a.m. There is some indication that this lifeboat may have actually started loading before number 8, but regardless, it was actually lowered afterwards. Part of the confusion as to which boat was lowered first from the port side—number 6 or number 8—stems from Woolner's statement that Helen Candee got off on the first boat. Since Candee was in boat 6, it is assumed that number 6 was the first boat to leave.

Mr. Woolner: "My great desire was to get

her [Mrs. Candee] into the first boat, which I did, and we brought up a rug, which we threw in with her and we waited to see that boat filled. It was not filled, but a great many people got into it, and finally it was quietly and orderly lowered away."

But Peuchen also went away in number 6, and he clearly describes in detail seeing a boat lowered before his. In addition, Eloise Smith was also in boat number 6 and describes it as the second boat to leave from her position on the port side.

Mr. Peuchen: "After a reasonable complement of ladies had got aboard, she was lowered, but I did not see one single [male] passenger get in that first boat."

As Lightoller stood by number 6, he again called out for women and children, and even as the time was approaching 1:00 a.m., still could not convince many to get in.

Mr. Peuchen: "I had finished with the lowering of the first boat from the port side. We then went to the next boat and we did the same thing—got the mast and the sail out of that. There was a quartermaster in the boat, and one sailor, and we commenced to put the ladies in that boat. After that boat had got a full complement of ladies, there were

no more ladies to get in, or if there were any other ladies to get in they did not wish to do so, because we were calling out for them—that is speaking of the port side—but some would not leave their husbands. I saw one lady where they had to sort of pull her away from her husband, he insisting upon her going to the boat and she did not want to go."

Mr. Woolner: "It was a very distressing scene—the men parting from their wives."

Smith: "How many did the second boat contain?"
Lightoller: "About 30."
Smith: "Do you remember whether you counted off 30?"
Lightoller: "No, sir. I had no time."

After Smith watched a rocket sent up from the bridge, he studied the light on the horizon with Boxhall for a few minutes and then returned to the port side boat deck.

Mrs. Smith (6): "In the second boat they kept calling for one more lady to fill it, and my husband insisted that I get in it, my friend having gotten in. I refused unless he would go with me. In the meantime Captain Smith was standing with a megaphone on deck. I approached him and told him I was alone and asked if my husband might be

allowed to go in the boat with me. He ignored me personally, but shouted again through his megaphone, 'Women and children first.' My husband said, 'Never mind, captain, about that. I will see that she gets in the boat.' He then said, 'I never expected to ask you to obey, but this is one time you must. It is only a matter of form to have women and children first. The boat is thoroughly equipped, and everyone on her will be saved.' I asked him if that was absolutely honest and he said, 'Yes.' I felt some better then, because I had absolute confidence in what he said. He kissed me good-bye and placed me in the lifeboat with the assistance of an officer."

Fleet (6): "I was told by Mr. Lightoller to get in the boat and help the women in."
Fletcher: "Were there any women left on the deck who did not get in the boats?"
Fleet: "I did not see any. All what was there got in the boats. But they may have come up afterwards, when we were lowered. I could not say."
Fletcher: "Did the men ask to get into the boats?"
Fleet: "No."

The scene on deck was an odd one to be sure. With the roar of steam finally coming to an end, the band came up from A deck and began to play right next to the Grand Staircase entrance. With upbeat ragtime music filling the air, and the periodic burst of a rocket overhead, passengers stood in the shadowy light around number 6 with a stoic manner that underplayed the unfolding tragedy.

Smith: "Any jostling or pushing or crowding?"
Lightoller: "None whatever."
Smith: "The men all refrained from asserting their strength and crowding back the women and children?"
Lightoller: "They could not have stood quieter if they had been in church."

Buley: "I saw two masthead lights. You could not see the stern lights. You could not see her bow lights. I saw it from the ship. That is what we told the passengers. We said, 'There is a steamer coming to our assistance.' That is what kept them quiet, I think."

Clearly, one of the strangest circumstances surrounding the loading of number 6 was the fact that Captain Smith assisted, while holding the knowledge that the ship was going to sink—and sink relatively soon.

Smith: "From what you saw of the captain, was he alert and watchful?"

Captain Smith standing on the port side of the boat deck in the area of lifeboats 6 and 8.

Mr. Peuchen: "He was doing everything in his power to get women in these boats, and to see that they were lowered properly. I thought he was doing his duty in regard to the lowering of the boats, sir."

How Captain Smith allowed so many empty seats to go away with number 6 and 8 boats is a mystery. He was aware of the ratio of passengers to the number of lifeboats, yet he stood by at number 6 while a prevailing atmosphere of calm inhibited women from climbing aboard.

Smith: "How many were put into this second boat?"
Mr. Peuchen: "I did not know at the time of the lowering, but as I happened to be a passenger later on, they were counted and there were exactly 20 women, 1 quartermaster, 1 sailor, and 1 stowaway that made his appearance after we had been out about an hour."
Smith: "Twenty-three altogether?"
Mr. Peuchen: "Twenty-three altogether."

Perhaps Smith was still intent on the nearby ship making a difference. As he stood by, he and Lightoller directed the boat to go over to it and come back.

Fleet (6): "It was a light, all right, because Mr. Lightoller, when I got into the boat, made us pull straight for it."
Burton: "What did you think it was?"
Fleet: "It might have been a fisher sail, or

something. It was only just one bright light. I could not say what it was."

Hichens (6): "He told us to go away and make for the light. We had them orders before we went down below."

The lack of manpower continued to nag at Lightoller's evacuation attempts. As a result of the darkness on deck and the crowds standing about, the man working one side of the davits could not see the other. Lightoller was either distracted, or could not see. As he yelled out the command to lower away, there was only one man at the ropes and while he released his side, no one released the other. The lifeboat went down by only one end and quickly looked like it was going to dump its passengers into the water.

Lightoller: "As a matter of fact, I ordered two seamen into that boat, as far as I remember, and then, when I turned around to lower away, when I asked if everything was all right, I got an answer from the after fall, but I got no reply from the forward fall. Then I turned around and asked for a seaman, but apparently no seaman was there. While I was asking for a seaman someone sang out, 'Aye, aye' and then I gave the order to lower away."

Mrs. Smith (6): "As the boat was lowered he yelled from the deck, 'Keep your hands in your pockets. It is very cold weather.' That was the last I saw of him and now I remember the many husbands that turned their backs as that small boat was lowered, the women blissfully innocent of their husbands' peril, and said good-bye with the expectation of seeing them within the next hour or two. By that time our interest was centered on the lowering of the lifeboat, which occurred to me—although I know very little about it—to be a very poor way to lower one. The end I was in was almost straight up, while the lower end came near touching the water."

The angle of the lifeboat was corrected from the boat deck, but now a new problem arose.

Hichens (6): ". . . we was willing to pull away for this light but when we got down we told him we had to have one more man in the boat. We wanted two or three more men if we could get them."

Lightoller's manpower problem continued to haunt him and unravel his attempts to get his boats away in an orderly manner. On the heels of almost dumping its passengers into the water, lifeboat 6 dangled along the side of the ship with someone yelling up to him. One has to wonder, with all the stress he was under if Lightoller was thinking to himself, "Now what?"

Lightoller: " When the boat was halfway down some of the women sang out that they had only one man in the boat. This was owing to the fact that this seaman stepped out of the boat, unknown to me, going to the fall. He knew I was short of a man to lower away the fall, and therefore he left his station in the boat to go to the fall."

Mr. Peuchen: "After that the boat was lowered down some distance, I should imagine probably parallel with C deck, when the quartermaster called up to the officer and said, 'I cannot manage this boat with only one seaman.' So he made this call for assistance, and the second officer leaned over and saw he was quite right in his statement, that he had only one man in the boat, so they said, 'We will have to have some more seamen here,' and I did not think they were just at hand, or they may have been getting the next boat ready. However, I was standing by the officer, and I said, 'Can I be of any assistance? I am a yachtsman, and can handle a boat with an average man.' He said, 'Why yes, I will order you to the boat in preference to a sailor.' The captain was standing still *by him at that time, and I think, although the officer ordered me to the boat, the captain said, 'You had better go down below and break a window and get in through a window, into the boat.' That was his suggestion. And I said I did not think it was feasible, and I said I could get in the boat if I could get hold of a rope. However, we got hold of a loose rope in some way that was hanging from the davit near the block anyway, and by getting hold of this I swung myself off the ship, and lowered myself into the boat. The danger was jumping off from the boat. It was not after I got a straight line. It was very easy lowering. But I imagine it was opposite the C deck at the time."*

Lightoller: "The boat was half way down when the women called out and said that there was only one man in the boat. I had only two seamen and could not part with them, and was in rather a fix to know what to do, when a passenger called out and said, 'If you like, I will go.' I said, 'Are you a seaman?', and he said, 'I am a yachtsman.' I said, 'If you are sailor enough to get out on that fall'—that is a difficult thing to get to, over the ship's side, eight feet away, and means a long swing on a dark night—'if you are sailor enough to get out there, you can go down.' And he proved he was, by going down. And he afterwards proved himself a

This would have been the approximate view from lifeboat 6 as it dangled alongside the ship waiting for Major Peuchen to descend the ropes into it.

brave man, too."
Smith: "How old a man was he?"
Lightoller: "Forty five or fifty."
Smith: "When you called Major [Peuchen] *you had no seamen?"*
Lightoller: "Not that I could see, and I couldn't waste time looking for them."

Mr. Peuchen (6): "On getting into the boat I went aft in the lifeboat and said to the quartermaster, 'What do you want me to do?' He said, 'Get down and put that plug in,' and I

made a dive down for the plug and the ladies were all sitting pretty well aft, and I could not see at all. It was dark down there. I felt with my hands, and I said it would be better for him to do it and me do his work, and I said, 'Now you get down and put in the plug, and I will undo the shackles,' that is, take the blocks off. So he dropped the blocks, and he got down and he came rushing back to assist me, and he said, 'Hurry up.' He said, 'This boat is going to founder.' I thought he meant our lifeboat was going to founder. I thought he had some difficulty in finding the plug, or he had not gotten it in properly. But he meant the large boat was going to founder, and that we were to hurry up and get away from it. So we got the rudder in, and he told me to go forward and take an oar. I went forward and got an oar on the port side of the lifeboat. The sailor was on my left, on the starboard side. But we were just opposite each other in rowing."

Fleet (6): "We had a stowaway. Where he came from I do not know. He was underneath the seat. We saw him as soon as we got clear. He had a bad arm. He had a bandage around it, and he said he could not pull. So he put his oar in."

As lifeboat number 6 descended onto the water just before 1:00 a.m., Lowe was loading lifeboat number 1 and Murdoch was positioning a crew for loading number 11. Before heading aft on the port side to boats 10, 12, 14, and 16, Lightoller may have checked on the progress of clearing access to lifeboat 4, dangling along the windows of the promenade deck. A number of passengers considered themselves assigned to this boat and waited near the entranceway to the Grand Staircase on the boat deck until it was ready.

Mrs. Ryerson: "My husband joked with some of the women he knew, and I heard him say, 'Don't you hear the band playing?' I begged him to let me stay with him, but he said, 'You must obey orders. When they say 'Women and children to the boats, you must go when your turn comes. I'll stay with John Thayer. We will be all right. You take the boat to New York.' This referred to the belief that there was a circle of ships around waiting. The Olympic, the Baltic, were some of the names I heard. All this time we could hear the rockets going up – signals of distress."

It would make sense that those passengers standing on the port side of the deck near lifeboat number 6 would have a better chance of picking up some tidbits of information regarding the wireless transmissions.

The entrance to the wireless room was only a few feet away and Smith likely passed along information he received from the operators to some of the other passengers he had become acquainted with over the years.

The *Titanic* proceeded all this time to settle by the head. There were five lifeboats in the water now, rowing away from the dying vessel.

Mr. Peuchen (6): "The quartermaster who was in charge of our boat told us to row as hard as we could to get away from this suction, and just as we got a short distance away this stowaway made his appearance. He was an Italian by birth, I should think, who had a broken wrist or arm, and he was of no use to us to row. He got an oar out, but he could not do much, so we got him to take the oar in."

The *Titanic* continued to fire rockets with a hint of increasing desperation. But the ship in the distance would not respond. Earlier, it looked like it was approaching, but as the hour came up on 1:00 a.m., the vessel seemed to turn away to the west.

Boxhall: ". . . but my attention until the time I left the ship was mostly taken up with firing off distress rockets and trying to signal a steamer that was almost ahead of us. I saw

his masthead lights and I saw his side light."

With lifeboat 9 safely in the water, Murdoch returned to the boat deck to round up men for the loading of the next boat aft, number 11.

Ray: "I saw that [boat 9] lowered away. Then I went along to number 11 boat, and saw that loaded with women and children."

Wheelton (11): "I walked along when number 9 went, and Mr. Murdoch, the first officer, turned around. He sent the assistant second steward down to A deck, and he said to me, 'You go, too.' He got hold of me by the left arm and he said, 'You go, too." We went down to A deck. All the women and children were sent down because a steward brought them down."

Brice (11): "I helped to lower the boat from the boat deck to A deck."

On the forward end of starboard boat deck, Lowe started loading number 1 from the rail. It was dark and shadowy near the bridge where this lifeboat was located. This craft was also known as an emergency boat because it was always kept ready for lowering in the event the crew needed to get down to the water in a hurry.

The *Titanic* fires another rocket into the night air as her bow slowly settles into the water.

The scene around lifeboat 1 must have been odd for Lowe. There was virtually nobody there except for a handful of passengers and some crew. Off in the distance toward the stern, he could see more people on deck. Why they were not shepherded down the deck to Lowe's boat is unknown. Lowe was not about to take the time to go and round them up. The loading began.

Perkins: "Then were you assigned to any particular boat?"
Symons: "My name was put in for number 1."

Crowe: "When I got outside of the companionway, I saw them working on boat number 1."

Lowe: "I went to the emergency boat. She is supposed to carry 40–that is, floating. I think there were about five women. I suppose there would be, about as near as I can judge, 22 men. There was not any officer. I think there was a quartermaster, unless I am mistaken."

Passengers and crew standing on the forward boat deck suddenly saw a blinking light above the *Titanic*'s bridge wing. Some took an interest and moved closer. Combined with the rockets, passengers and crew alike were probably able to figure out that the *Titanic* was trying to communicate

After lowering lifeboats 6 and 8, Lightoller walked aft to boats 10, 12, 14, and 16 where he was joined by Chief Officer Wilde and Sixth Officer Moody.

with another ship. In fact, seeing the Morse lamp in action must have been an encouraging sight since it meant someone was near enough to signal about the *Titanic*'s plight. Help would no doubt be on the way soon.

Boxhall: " She got close enough, as I thought to read our electric morse signal, and I signaled to her. I told her to come at once; we were sinking. I told the captain about this ship, and he was with me most of the time when we were signaling. He said, 'Tell him to come at once, we are sinking.' I cannot say I saw any reply. Some people say she replied to our rockets and our signals, but I did not see them."
Smith: "In referring to 'some people', whom do you mean?"
Boxhall: "People who were around the bridge."
Smith: "Passengers?"
Boxhall: "No. I should say not passengers."
Smith: "Officers?"
Boxhall: "I think it was stewards. And people waiting in the boats, or something"

As the midnight hour came to a close, the *Titanic* was exactly halfway through her swan song. It had been one hour and twenty minutes since the collision and in that time the crew managed to get five lifeboats into the water out of twenty on board. Ambivalence, confidence, worry, disorder, and caution circulated around the ship in equal measure.

The next hour and twenty minutes would be very different from the first, as the evacuation of the *Titanic* approached full stride. No one on board knew exactly how much time was left, and most had no idea of how things were going to end. As 12:59 passed into the next hour, the passengers and crew were simply following directions.

Triangle of Tragedy - The Third Ship

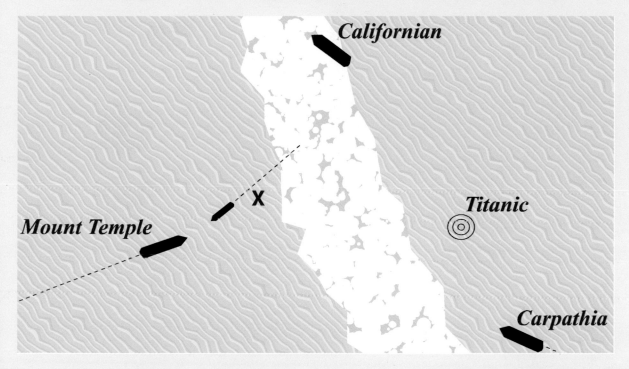

The *Mount Temple,* under the command of Captain Moore, was heading west over 50 miles away from the scene of the accident at the time of the *Titanic*'s distress call. Moore turned his vessel around at 12:30 a.m. and steamed toward the *Titanic*'s reported position. Several hours later, prior to sunrise, the *Mount Temple* came upon an unidentified vessel, heading from the general scene of the accident. Approximately 20 minutes later, the *Mount Temple* came upon the same ice field that the *Titanic* and *Californian* had run into several hours earlier. In the book, *Titanic At Two*, the visual relationship between the *Californian* and the *Titanic* was examined with the conclusion that both ships were within view of each other. But as the *Titanic* and the *Californian* studied each other from afar, is it possible there was a third ship which passed between –or nearby–the two ships? Could the presence of this craft have created conflicting and confusing observations? The following are a few fragments of key accounts.

Moore: "At 3:25 by our time we stopped. I simply stopped the engines and let the way run off the ship and then proceeded slowly. Before that I want to say that I met a schooner or some small craft, and I had to get out of the way of that vessel, and the light of that vessel seemed to go out. It was just shortly after 3 o'clock I saw the schooner. When this light was on my bow, a green light, I starboarded my helm. I should say this light could not have been more than a mile or a mile and a half away, because I immediately put my helm hard astarboard, because I saw the light, and after I got the light on the starboard bow then the light seemed to suddenly go out."

Boxhall: "Yes, I saw it for a little while and then lost it."

Osman: "I thought it was a sailing vessel from the banks."
Burton: "What do you think about it? Did it sail away?"
Osman: "Yes, sir. She sailed right away."

Moore: "She was a little off our bow, and I immediately starboarded the helm and got the two lights green to green. I should say

With Binoculars

Was this the view of the *Titanic* from the *Californian*?

the schooner, from the position of the *Titanic*, would be perhaps 12½ to 13 miles. I dare say she would be making a couple of knots an hour."

Lord: "When this man was coming along he was showing his green light on our starboard side, before midnight. He was stopped until 1 o'clock and then he started going ahead again; and the second officer reported he changed from south-southeast to west-southwest, 6 ½ points; and if he was 4 miles off, the distance he traveled I estimated to be 7 or 7½ miles in that hour."

Fletcher: "Apparently that ship came within

4 or 5 miles of the *Titanic*, and then turned and went away in what direction, westward or southward?"
Boxhall: "I do not know whether it was southwestward. I should say it was westerly."

Lord: "I said, 'This is not the *Titanic*. There is no doubt about it. She came and lay at half past 11, alongside of us until, I suppose, a quarter past 1, within 4 miles of us. We could see everything on her quite distinctly; see her lights. We signaled her at half past 11, with the Morse lamp. She did not take the slightest notice of it."

Fletcher: "Was he evidently coming from

the direction in which the *Titanic* lay?"
Moore: "Somewhere from there, sir."

To highlight just how close this third vessel was to the scene of the accident, Captain Moore mentions the mysterious boat and another steamer (almost certainly the *Californian*) in the same sentence.

Smith: "What I am trying to get at is this: One or two of the ship's officers of the *Titanic* say that . . . they saw lights ahead, or saw lights, that could not have been over 5 miles from the *Titanic*. What I am seeking to develop is the question as to what light that was they saw."
Moore: "Well, it may have been the light of the tramp steamer that was ahead of us, because when I turned [from schooner's path] there was a steamer on my port bow."

At 3:00 a.m. Captain Moore could see both the schooner and the *Californian*. The small vessel was traveling away from the *Californian* and where the *Titanic* had gone down. If the *Californian* and this small craft were within view of each other at 3:00 a.m., one must wonder how they appeared to each other—and the *Titanic*—a whole three hours earlier, when it seems that the small craft would have been much closer to the scene of the accident.

One O'Clock

It was now one o'clock in the morning and 2,000 passengers and crew stood on the deck of the *Titanic* not quite knowing what to make of the current state of affairs. The disturbing list to starboard had faded and the ship was on an even keel.

Although the *Titanic* was obviously down by the bow, it was generally thought that this lifeboat business was still a matter of precaution. The *Titanic* was probably going to limp into New York under tow. Perhaps she would even be pumped out and get under way on her own again. They might even have to be transferred to another ship, perhaps to the one approaching from the north. In any event, it seemed that the White Star Line was being cautious and putting

passengers into the lifeboats until they sorted the whole mess out. When viewed in this light, it seemed a lot smarter to wait things out with the conveniences of a luxury liner, rather than the hardships of a lifeboat.

But the emotional tide was also turning at this hour. While confidence in the *Titanic* certainly influenced the behavior of many, a sense of caution was gradually increasing as the upper decks grew more and more crowded. As the tilt toward the bow slowly increased and the number of lifeboats on deck decreased, a percentage of passengers and crew changed their minds and decided to take a more conservative approach. Despite their confidence in the ship, women and children began to step forward for the boats at an increasing rate.

From the lifeboats already away from the ship, water could be seen just a foot or two below the bow lights of D deck. Watching the downward movement of the E and F deck portholes amidship was like watching the minute hand on a clock.

Ward (9): "She went very gradually for a while. We could just see the ports as she dipped. We could see the lights in the ports, and the water seemed to come very slowly up to them. She did not appear to be going fast, and I was of the opinion then that she would not go. I thought we were only out there as a matter of precaution and would certainly go back to the ship. I was still of the opinion she would float."

Mr. Harper (3): "The water was smooth as a lake, not a piece of ice anywhere except the big iceberg that had wrecked us, far astern. And at every stroke of the oars great glares of greenish-yellow phosphorescent light would swirl aft from the blades and drip in globules like fire from the oars as they swung forward. The phosphorescence was so brilliant that it almost dazzled us at first. I have never seen it so fine. As we drew away from the Titanic she was brightly lighted as ever and not a sound came from her."

Having finished with lifeboats 6 and 8, Lightoller walked up the mild slant of the deck on the port side toward the aft group of four lifeboats. As he arrived at number 10, a gate that divided the second class from the engineer's space stood right where passengers had to assemble for loading. Although only a minor obstruction, this complication seemed enough of one to drive Lightoller onward to number 12, as his third and next boat for lowering. He still had no intention of filling them to capacity while they dangled some 75 feet above the water.

Smith: "You must have been painfully aware

Sometime around 1:00 a.m., the Turkish Baths began to flood. *(Olympic)*

of the fact that there were not enough boats there to care for that large passenger list, were you not?"
Lightoller: "Yes, sir."

The forward section of the boat deck was constructed with a natural incline, that during normal times resulted in a slight upward slant. While Lightoller had been lowering boats 6 and 8, this incline minimized his perception of the *Titanic*'s tilt toward the bow. But when he left this area and walked aft to where there was no such incline, the contrast was striking and made an impact on Lightoller's memory of things.

Smith: "How many did the third boat contain?"

Lightoller: "By the time I came to the third boat I was aware that it was getting serious, and then I started to take chances."
Smith: "How many did you have?"
Lightoller: "Thirty five, I should say, sir."

Unfortunately, Lightoller's idea of taking chances was to increase the number of passengers from 25 to 35–for a boat designed to hold 65.

Hemming arrived back on deck from his errand with an armful of lamps. He pressed through the growing number of people standing about the stern boats and distributed them while Lightoller, Lowe, and Moody were busy with loading activities.

Hemming: "Then I lit the lamps and brought them up, four at a time, two in each hand. The boats that were already lowered, I put them on the deck, and asked them to pass them down on the end of the boat fall. As to the boats that were not lowered, I gave them into the boats myself."
Smith: "How many had been lowered before you got there with the lamps?"
Hemming: "Quite three or four."
Smith: "That was the port side?"
Hemming: "They were on the port side, sir."

Unlike the passengers, a higher percentage of crew had earlier witnessed the inflow of water below deck. For those men whose instincts were telling them to get off the ship, word was getting around that Murdoch was allowing more crewmen into the starboard boats than Lightoller was allowing on the port side.

Newlands: "On the port side they put in, on an average, in each boat only about two men of the crew, and sometimes less. How do you account for the fact that there were so few?"
Taylor: "I could not tell you, sir. I never went on that side of the ship."
Newlands: "On the other side were there a large number of the ship's crew?"
Taylor: "Yes, sir."

Lightoller's strict discipline on restricting the number of crewmen in each boat resulted in an inadvertent backlash, as the ship's resources migrated over to the starboard side where opportunities for a crewman were better.

Mr. Peuchen: "We heard afterwards that the officers on the starboard side were more generous in allowing the men in than on the port side. That is what I heard afterwards, that some of the officers on the starboard side had allowed some of the men into the boats."

Smith: "You put two men in each?"
Lightoller: "I think I was getting short of men, if I remember rightly. I started to putting one seaman and a steward in."

This shortage of crew also made it difficult to keep an eye on everything and created opportunities.

Clench (12): "There was only one male passenger in our boat, and that was a Frenchman who jumped in, and we could not find him, sir."
Bourne: "Where was he?"
Clench: "Under the thwart, mixed with the women."
Bourne: "How do you think he was able to do that?"
Clench: "I could not say that, sir. We were, of course, attending to the falls and looking out to see that they went down clear."

Lightoller never knew why his area was suffering a shortage of men. When asked, the only explanation he could think of was that he had sent some of them away on an errand.

Smith: "How do you account for your inability to get hold of more than nine seamen to man those lifeboats on the port side?"

Lightoller: "Earlier, and before I realized that there was any danger, I told off the boatswain to take some men—I didn't say how many, leaving the man to use his own judgment, to go down below and open the gangway doors in order that the boats could come alongside and be filled to their utmost capacity. He complied with the order, and so far as I know, went down below, and I did not see him afterwards. That took away a number of men, and we detailed two men for each boat and two men for lowering down."
Smith: "How many of the ship's crew survived?"
Lightoller: "43 seamen, 96 stewards and stewardesses, and 71 firemen."
Smith: "So you lost 28 seamen?"
Lightoller: "Yes."

Under Lightoller's supervision and the circumstances described, women and children were again called forward. Although two forward boats had already been lowered on the port side, this was the official start of the process for second class passengers who had remained in their own area. By this time, they had been standing around on the boat deck on the average of a half an hour or more. Some found themselves emotionally unprepared when the time came to get in.

Miss Lehmann: "I went and when I came

The aft port side of the ship with lifeboats 10, 12, 14 and 16 visible. As the boats descended by the promenade deck, passengers crowding the rail looked for an opportunity to jump in. The A la Carte Restaurant windows (groups of three) are on B deck. The discharge of water can be seen below lifeboats 12 and 14.

Miss Lehmann (12): "The lifeboats had been lowered to the deck level. I was taken out there and then, as I stepped into the lifeboat, it was dark and, of course, the inside of the boat was lower than the deck, I fell. I thought for a moment that I was going to fall right into the water, but I hit the bottom of the boat. I don't remember if I was hurt or not. I guess I forgot about it in the excitement. I was not frightened or excited at first at all. I suppose the only reason I wasn't was that I did not realize what had happened. When the boat had been partly filled I saw two men jump from the deck into the lifeboat and hide behind their wives' skirts. One of them was found but the other one got away."

In the meantime, Lowe continued loading lifeboat number 1 near the starboard bridge while Boxhall continued sending up pleas for help nearby.

Boxhall: "I saw someone filling the starboard emergency boat at the time that I went and was firing off rockets. I fired them just close to the bows of this emergency boat . . . these distress rockets are dangerous things if they explode and I had to keep people away clear while I fired the rockets."

After Lightoller had gone aft toward

back he put a life belt on me and took me to another deck. He said to a couple of officers that here was another lady. As I was standing there waiting my turn to get in the lifeboat I could see and hear women crying and hanging on the arms of loved ones. There were some ladies there that did not want to go because their husbands could not go."

It was dark near the boats and the deck house lights cast shadows everywhere that made it difficult to see. The task of stepping into a dangling boat was not as easy as it might have seemed. While women stepped forward, some of the married couples plotted on ways to get their husbands into Lightoller's boat.

lifeboat 12, Smith returned to the bridge, where he could be found by all of his officers and crew. The aft lifeboats on the port side were too far away from the bridge for the captain to follow. On the bridge, Smith and Boxhall focused their attention on the light on the northern horizon. So far the news from the wireless office was not good regarding ships coming to their rescue, and it was becoming increasingly clear that the ship within view was their only chance.

Perkins: "Where was the captain at this time?"
Symons: "The last I saw of him he was on the bridge, sir. That was just before I went away in boat number 1."

Rowe and Bright assisted Boxhall and Smith in their ongoing attempt to make contact with the distant ship. They were still not having any luck. But in between the rockets, Rowe and Boxhall kept at their efforts with the lamp. This form of communication used the same language that the wireless office used, except it was transmitted by blinking a powerful light on and off.

Rowe: "When I was on the bridge firing rockets. I saw it [the ship on the horizon] myself, and I worked the Morse lamp at the port side of the ship to draw her attention."

The starboard wing of the bridge. The close proximity of the emergency boat on the right worried Boxhall while he fired distress rockets from the rail. One of the morse lamps can be seen on the roof. (*Olympic*)

Henry Stengel had been loitering near the forward end of the boat deck ever since he saw his wife off in lifeboat number 5. Eyeing the activity going on with the emergency boat, he walked down the slope of the deck and approached Lowe.

Mr. Stengel: "I do not know what led me there, but there was a small boat that they called an emergency boat, in which there were three people, Sir Duff Gordon and his wife and Miss Francatelli. I asked the officer—I could not see them it was so dark, and

I presume I was agitated somewhat – I asked him if I could not get into that boat. There was no one else around, not a person I could see except the people working at the boats, and he said, 'Jump in.' The railing was rather high – it was an emergency boat and was always swung over toward the water – I jumped onto the railing and rolled into it. The officer then said, 'That is the funniest sight I have seen tonight,' and he laughed quite heartily. That rather gave me some encouragement. I thought perhaps it was not so dangerous as I imagined."

The neighborhood around the bridge was relatively quiet for the time being as most activity was aft on both A and boat decks. While lifeboat number 1 loaded in a relaxed and almost deserted atmosphere, passengers climbed into number 11 under very different circumstances.

By 1:10 a.m. the aft portion of the starboard promenade deck was a bee hive of activity. The area was very crowded with first and second class passengers, and now, even third class women. Lifeboat 11, which had begun loading a little before 1 a.m., was almost ready to go. Murdoch left the passengers on the promenade deck in the care of the stewards, and returned to the boat deck. From the edge he could see straight down into the lifeboat.

Wheelton (11): " Number 11 boat was hanging in the davits. We got into the boat. Mr. Murdoch shouted, 'Women and children first.' He was on the top deck there, standing by the taffrail."

Ismay was down on the promenade deck amidst the crowd around number 11. Throughout the night women and children would approach the vicinity of a lifeboat, but the crowd surrounding it would be too intimidating. For many, it would be improper for them to push their way through. A number of women mentioned attempts to get into a boat unsuccessfully before finally succeeding several boats later. Ismay took note of this problem.

Wheelton: "He helped the women and children into the boat, sir, and told the men to make way. They were all standing round in a circle and a lady would come on deck, and he meant to make a gap so that she could come through."

Passengers had to awkwardly climb over the rail through the promenade opening and carefully place their feet on the other side in the lifeboat. Some found the task too stressful to deal with.

Wheelton (11): "We loaded the boat with

women and children, and took in a few of the crew. The only trouble we had was with one lady who would not get into the boat. We attempted twice to get her in, and the last time I said to my friend helping me, 'Pull her in' and we pulled her in."

If there was ever an opportunity for men in the crowd to gain access to the lifeboats, it was during the loading of boats 9 through 15 on the starboard side. As stewards assisted on A deck with this boat, many of them took advantage of their positions and climbed in. Once enough women and children were in, Murdoch did not care if men filled it out before it was sent away.

Brice (11): "The boat was filled from A deck. There was an officer said, 'Is there a sailor in the boat?' Which officer it was I could not say, amongst the crowd. There was no answer. I jumped out and went down the fall into the bow of the boat. There was nobody in the stern of the boat. I went aft and shipped the rudder, and in that time the boat had been filled with women and children. About 60."
Bourne: "Fifty-two passengers, 6 stewards, yourself, and your mate?"
Brice: "And one fireman, sir."

Wheelton (11): "I think there were about –

well, there were eight or nine men in the boat, all together. That was including our crew. I think there were one or two passengers, but I really could not say. I shouted to Mr. Murdoch, 'The boat is full, sir.' He said, 'All right.' He said, 'Have you got your sailors in?' I said, 'No, sir.' He told two sailors to jump into the boat. We lowered away."

Estimates of numbers and times fluctuated from person to person with respect to many observations of the evening, and lifeboat number 11 was no different.

Brice (11): "Well, about 45 women and about 4 or 5 children in arms."

Wheelton (11): "I should say there were about 58, all told sir."

Whereas Murdoch had until now assigned an officer or crewman to take charge of each of the boats he supervised, he apparently forgot to put someone in charge of number 11.

Bourne: "Who had charge of the boat?"
Brice (11): "Mr. Humphreys. He was an able seaman."
Bourne: "Who designated him to take charge of the boat? The officer?"

Brice: "No, sir. He took charge himself."

Ismay returned from the promenade deck to the boat deck once number 11 was filled. After seeing what almost happened with lifeboat 5, he and Murdoch were attentive to coordinating the pace each rope was let out on both davits to avoid tipping.

Newlands: "What was Mr. Ismay doing?"
Wheelton (11): "He was standing aft, sir. Mr. Murdoch was standing forward, and he was going like this [indicating], 'Lower, lower, lower,' lowering the boats."
Newlands: "Who was?"
Wheelton: "Mr. Ismay, sir. He stood right by the davit with one hand on the davit and one hand in motion to the officer lowering."

Brice (11): "They lowered the boat. We had a bit of difficulty in keeping the boat clear of the outlet, a big body of water coming from the ship's side. The after block got jammed, but I think that must have been on account of the trip not being pushed right down to disconnect the block from the boat. We managed to keep the boat clear from this body of water coming from the ship's side. It was the pump discharge."

Lifeboat 11 was able to manage around this exhaust from the *Titanic*. The placement of lifeboats above this stream of water coming out of the side of the ship was clearly a mistake in the ship's design and it is fortunate that starboard boats 11 and 13, and port boats 12 and 14 did not get swamped by this rush of water.

Wheelton (11): "Everything went very nice, very smoothly until we touched the water. We pushed away from the ship's side and had just a slight difficulty in hoisting the after block. We were not there a minute. The sailor got at the block and loosened the tackle. We pulled away from the ship. I looked around into the boat. I saw the boat was pretty well crowded, because I had some little difficulty in rowing, because the passengers were so close together and I kept hitting my hands against the passengers."
Newlands: "When you left the ship, where were the bulk of the remaining passengers located?"
Wheelton (11): "There was no bulk at all, sir. They were scattered all around the deck."

Under Murdoch's command of the starboard side, five boats were now away and lifeboat 1 was just about to be lowered. In all, six lifeboats would be in the water under Murdoch's supervision before Lightoller could get his third one away.

Titanic's starboard side aft. Lifeboats 15, 13, 11 and 9 sit on deck. The exhausts of water which menaced lifeboats 11 and 13 can be clearly seen.

and sent the boats away half empty. Two different command styles on opposite sides of the ship yielded two different results.

Wheelton (11): "I would like to say something about the bravery exhibited by the first officer, Mr. Murdoch. He was perfectly cool and very calm."

With number 11 safely in the water, Murdoch left the area. As he headed toward the bow and the rest of the crowd moved aft to number 13, lifeboat 11 pulled away on their own initiative, acclimating themselves to their new environment.

Brice (11): "We pulled away from the ship. I suppose about a quarter of a mile from the ship. Under our own direction. We had nobody to give us any orders at all."
Bourne: "Were there other boats pulling away about the same time?"
Brice: "There was one boat ahead of us that we could see."
Bourne: "Did you have a light on your boat?"
Brice: "No, sir. No lantern, sir. I searched for the lantern. I cut the lashing from the oil bottle and cut rope and made torches."
Bourne: "Any provisions and water in the boat at all?"
Brice: "I could not say that, sir, because we never bothered to look."

This success in efficiency seems to stem from two approaches. First, either Wilde or Murdoch had delegated some of the responsibilities of lifeboat 9 to Purser McElroy and lifeboat 1 to Lowe, both proving themselves to be very capable of getting things done. On top of that, he implemented a policy of loading the boats with available women and children in the immediate area and then allowed men to climb in and fill the boat out. This comparably more lenient attitude, using a policy of women and children *first*, versus women and children *only*, resulted in a rapid lowering of boats. Lightoller, by comparison, seemed intent on holding the boats until he could fill them with enough women and children. On average, he could only muster about 30 or so for each boat,

Meanwhile, lifeboat 1 was hanging lethargically along the side of the ship when Murdoch came down the deck to see how things were going and to perhaps duck into the officers' quarters for a few minutes. Seeing the lack of passengers in the area and the crew standing on deck, he issued some common sense commands, but apparently did not stay in the area.

Symons: "There were seven men ordered in –two seamen and five firemen. They were ordered in by Mr. Murdoch."

With no one else around, Lowe or Murdoch ordered number 1 away. Since this boat was always swung out along the side of the ship in case of an emergency, it was secured against the ship by two ropes so that it did not bounce around while the *Titanic* was at sea. These two ropes were attached on the far side of the lifeboat, wrapped around its underside, and attached against the *Titanic* just above the promenade deck. Nobody realized that the lifeboat was still secured, and when the boat started to descend, the ropes pulled on the far side and began to roll it over. Frank Evans was one of the crewmen releasing the ropes, and had no idea of what was going on.

Smith: "And then it was lowered?"

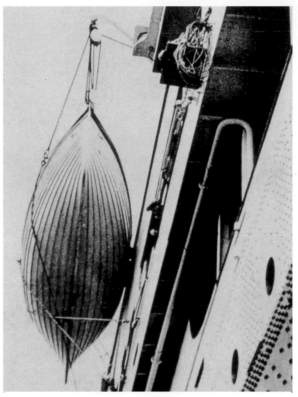

Emergency lifeboat 1. The ropes securing it to the ship almost tipped the boat during its descent.

Evans: "Then it was lowered to the next deck."
Smith: "To A deck?"
Evans: "Yes."
Smith: "And at A deck, what happened?"
Evans: "I could not tell you, because I could not see."
Smith: "Whether anybody got in there or not

you do not know?"
Evans: "I could not say."

Mr. Stengel (1): "After getting down part of the way there was a painter on the boat, and we were beginning to tip, and somebody hollered to stop lowering. Somebody cut that line and we went on down."

The sound of the commotion brought the captain out of the bridge to investigate. He probably knew right away what the trouble was and instructed Lowe and the crew on how to resolve it.

Smith: "Did you see the captain that night?"
Evans: "Yes. He came to the starboard action boat that I was lowering, sir."
Smith: "What did he say, if anything?"
Evans: "He passed some remark to a tall military gentleman there with white spats on, but what it was I could not say, as I was attending to the fall. It was a tall military-looking gentleman who was giving orders as to lowering away forward or aft or both together. As soon as we lowered the starboard action boat to the next deck the gripes of the boat caught and we had to cut them with an axe. It caught up underneath, or else it had not been untied. I could not look at it, because it was holding it in. It was

179

lowered, then, to the water's edge."

Once the emergency boat reached the water, a preoccupied Lowe found himself wondering who he had just assigned to it. He decided to find out.

Lowe: "I remember asking, I remember I hollered down from the boat deck to the water and said, 'Who is that in the emergency boat?' And I could not quite hear what he said. I knew that there was a quartermaster in it but I did not know his name."
Smith: "How long did it take to lower a lifeboat, or an emergency boat, and clear her away–lower her into the water?"
Lowe: "I could not tell you how long it would take, because it varied."
Smith: "Did it take 20 minutes; or approximately how long?"
Lowe: "Yes, I should say from the start to finish of putting a boat over, until you get her into the water, it will take you somewhere about 20 minutes."

It was now sometime around 1:15 a.m. Collapsible C lay flat on the deck near Lowe's feet as he yelled down to lifeboat 1 in the water. It must have been obvious to him that it would take some time to set the collapsible up and get it into the davits. Without further consideration, he left the

A ladder connecting A deck to the boat deck can be seen behind this lady's shoulder.

area. Lowe headed aft, leaving a string of empty lifeboat davits in his path.

Smith: "Where did you next go?"
Lowe: "I next went across the deck."

Archer: "Then an officer came along–I could not mention his name–and he sang out that they wanted some seamen on the other side, on the port side, to assist over there."

Lawrence Beesley stood quietly aft on the starboard boat deck in second class. The remaining lifeboats were just out of sight below the edge of the deck, hanging along the promenade rail. When the officer yelled for men to go over to the port side, many male passengers mistook this command that they too were to go. Although this misunderstanding would soon enough create problems on the port side, it created an opportunity for some on the starboard.

Mr. Beesley: ". . . a report went round among men on the top deck, the starboard side, that men were to be taken off on the port side. How it originated, I am quite unable to say, but can only suppose that as the port boats, numbers 10 to 16 were not lowered from the top deck quite so soon as the starboard boats (they could still be seen on deck), it might be assumed that women were being taken off on one side and men on the other. But in whatever way the report started, it was acted on at once by almost all the men, who crowded across to the port side and watched the preparation for lowering the boats, leaving the starboard side almost deserted. Two or three men remained, however; not for any reasons that we were consciously aware of. I can personally think of no decision arising from the reasoned thought that induced me to remain rather than to cross over. But while there was no process of conscious reasons at work, I am convinced that what was my salvation was a recognition of the necessity of being quiet and waiting in patience for some opportunity of safety to present itself."

Third class women were permitted to come up from the stern and were starting to appear on the promenade deck. It was not a simple task, getting to first class.

Mr. Abelseth: "A while later these girls were standing there, and one of the officers came and hollered for all of the ladies to come up on the boat deck. The gate was opened and these two girls went up."

Miss Mulvihill: "At the top of the passage I met a sailor with whom I had become acquainted on my passage across. I later learned his name was Robert Hickens of Southampton, England. I asked him what the matter was. 'There is no danger little girl,' he replied to me. 'We have hit an iceberg.' 'We're lost! We're lost!' I cried, but he took me by the arm and told me to follow him. My sailor friend told me to follow him

The view from the poop deck in third class. When third class women were allowed up to the higher decks, the routes they chose varied. For those who did not use the second class stairs, the way to the boat deck required that several ladders be climbed. A steward can be seen climbing one of those ladders from B deck to A deck in the lower left. (*Olympic*)

181

This was an area of much chaos when hundreds of passengers and stewards crowded the starboard promenade deck. Lifeboats 9, 11, 13 and 15 were loaded in rapid sequence from this location. (*Olympic*)

Barrett: "The women were coming up from aft. I don't know where they were coming from."

The new arrivals and the stress of the crowd began to fuel emotions as the pace of the evacuation heated up. The starboard A deck crowd moved on to lifeboats 13 and 15 now, which were being loaded together. Number 13 had a slight head start.

Miss Sjoblom: "When I was pulled on the deck of the ship by an officer, I rushed to the lifeboats. There seemed hundreds of people right around me. Some were screaming and crying, some were praying, oh, a great many of them were down on their knees praying. I saw a lot of people, Catholics, make the sign of the cross. I had to step on many of these people to reach the side of the deck."

Newlands: "Was it crowded?"
Taylor: "Oh, there was a crowd, a big crowd around the boats."
Newlands: "Was the order and discipline good, or was there disorder?"
Taylor: "The order was good, sir."

As mentioned earlier, there was not always an easy path to the boats, and many women found it impossible to gain access through the crowds during their first couple attempts at a seat.

and he would try to get me into a lifeboat. We climbed up bolts and cleats until we got to the next deck. Nearly every woman had left the ship then, I guess, and only two boats remained."

The women who chose to go had to work their way through the scores of steerage passengers crowded on the well deck, then walk up the deck stairs to B deck, then climb a narrow ladder up to A deck, and finally climb over a railing. An alternative was the second class staircase. The first route led to boats 13 and 15. The second led to boats 10 through 16. It was around this time that Barrett arrived from the boiler rooms and walked out onto the starboard side of the promenade deck.

Miss Sjoblom: "I tried to get into one boat and I was pushed back. The boats kept filling up and going over the side, and it seemed as though I would go down with the ship. I remember watching a little boy about 13 years old, whose parent had gone off in one of the lifeboats. He slipped into a boat and was thrown back on deck by a sailor. He crept into another boat, and again they threw him back to the deck. The third time he slid down in the bottom of a boat and was saved."

The upper decks of the *Titanic* were a blur of activity at 1:15 a.m. as the sixth distress rocket burst into the sky. Wilde was supervising boats 12, 14, and 16. Lightoller was at boat number 12. Murdoch was down at the bridge for the moment with Smith and Boxhall. Moody was at boat 16. Ismay and McElroy were at 13. Lowe was on his way over to rear of the port side boat deck.

And the passengers—they were everywhere. Some of the first class passengers were near the Grand Staircase entrance, waiting for action on lifeboat 4. Hundreds of first and second class passengers were aft on the boat deck, and on the starboard side of A deck. Third class women were climbing the ladders from B deck to the promenade deck, while others were taking the second class stairs. And hundreds of men and families in third class remained on the stern

well deck, poop deck, and in the third class lounges just under the poop deck.

Lowe: "I next went across the deck. To the other side, that is, the port side, and I met the sixth officer, Moody, and asked Moody, 'What are you doing?' He said, 'I am getting these boats away.' So we filled both 14 and 16 with women and children."
Smith: "Which one did you fill first?"
Lowe: "Number 14. I did not fill 16. Moody filled 16."

The group of first class passengers standing about the port side entranceway to the Grand Staircase had watched boats 6 and 8 loaded and lowered and then watched the crew move aft into the second class area of the boat deck. At a quarter past the hour, the ship's band was playing on deck nearby, and this elite group listened to ragtime music wondering what to do next. While they made small talk, Chief Officer Wilde came along and herded some of them away.

Miss Minahan: "An officer came and commanded all women to follow, and he led us to the boat deck on the starboard side. He told us there was no danger, but to get into a lifeboat as a precaution only. After making three attempts to get into boats, we succeeded in getting into lifeboat number 14."

In observing Minahan's comments, it should be noted that passengers were not being loaded into the boats on the starboard side from the boat deck; instead they were loading from A deck. Also, boat number 14 was not on the starboard side, but was instead on the port side. For this reason, it is likely that Daisy Minahan was actually led from the area where boats 6 and 8 had been, up the deck on the port side where boats 10, 12, 14, and 16 were loading from the boat deck.

Wilde supervised an operation whereby three boats—12, 14, and 16—were being loaded at the same time. Lifeboat 12 had a head start from Lightoller and it was the first of the three boats to be lowered.

Clench in the meantime wandered from boat to boat on the port side assisting with the mechanics of each while three were loaded simultaneously. Eventually, he returned to lifeboat 12.

Clench: "After we finished number 16 boat, I goes out and looks at the falls again to see that they are all ready for going down clear. I got three boats out, and we lowered them down level with the boat deck. Then I assisted Mr. Lightoller . . ."
Bourne: "The second officer?"
Clench: "The second officer. Him and me stood on the gunwale of the boat helping

load the women and children in. The chief officer was passing them along to us, and we filled the three boats like that."
Bourne: "You filled number 16 first?"
Clench: "No; filled 12 first."
Bourne: "How many people did you put in number 12?"
Clench: "I could not tell you exactly, but I should say from 40 to 50 people."

Evans: "We then lowered the starboard boats. After they had been lowered I went over to the port side and seen my own boat with the women and children being passed into it. Number 12 was my proper boat, on the port side."

Even though lifeboat 12 was the first of the three boats to begin loading, Clench actually managed to help with all three boats and still return to 12 before it departed.

Clench (12): "When I got back to number 12 again, the chief officer happened to come along and he said, 'How many men have you in this boat?' There was one man in the boat, one sailor, and I said, 'Only one, sir.' He looked up, and me being the sailor there, he said, 'Jump into that boat,' he said, 'and make the complement,'—that was two seamen. I goes into the boat and then, of course, we had to wait for orders to lower away."

Lifeboat 12 is third from the stern. The seven-deck descent was a long way down for the small boat.

Back on the starboard side, lifeboat 13 was loading.

Newlands: "Who was directing the passengers there?"
Taylor: "A lot of stewards were around directing the passengers, and there was an officer up on the boat deck then, sir."
Newlands: "But he could not see these peo-

ple down on deck A, could he?"
Taylor: "He was looking over to see who was getting into the boats."

The officer that Taylor makes mention of was either Murdoch, or Purser McElroy. Since Taylor was a fireman, he should have recognized his ship's officers, although this would not be a certainty since this was a first voyage and the crew were getting to know each other. More than likely, it was McElroy that he saw supervising things from the boat deck. This would explain why stewards were loading the passengers one deck below, since they reported to the purser in the chain of command.

When Murdoch had gone down the deck to see lifeboat 1 away, he likely checked in with the captain on the bridge to get an assessment of things and to give Smith a status on the starboard boats. So far, boats 1, 3, 5, 7, 9, and 11 were lowered on the starboard side. The captain may have informed Murdoch that only boats 6 and 8 had been launched on the port side under Wilde and Lightoller.

By this time Hardy reached the forward starboard side after getting his passengers all up on deck, he realized he was too late for his assigned boat. Looking for ways to be useful, he bumped into Murdoch heading toward the aft lifeboats.

Hardy: "I got them all up on the outer decks, and . . . I went to my station at the boat, which was boat 1, on the starboard side. I saw that lowered before I myself got there. By that time all the starboard boats had gone . . ."

With all the forward starboard boats away, including his assigned boat number 1, Hardy walked toward the remaining aft boats with Murdoch.

Hardy: "He was walking toward the after part of the deck. That was before all the boats had gone. Of course I had great respect and great regard for Chief Officer Murdoch, and I was walking along the deck forward with him and he said, 'I believe she is gone, Hardy,' and that is the only time I thought she might sink, when he said that."

One can only guess what was going through Murdoch's mind at this point. His encounter with Smith might have been sobering, leading him to make the candid comment that he did to Hardy. The loading of lifeboats 13 and 15 were already under way when Murdoch returned. With only these two lifeboats left and loading already in progress, Murdoch decided the starboard side, with six unlaunched lifeboats, was in greater need of his attention.

Separations

Many tearful separations were witnessed as husbands said good-bye to their wives and children next to a lifeboat. As a small consolation, some survivors were at least able to say some final words to their men—even if they thought they would see them later on another boat. But in the midst of the crowds, some separations occurred unexpectedly.

Mr. Thayer: "We proceeded to the deck below. Father, Mother, and the maid went ahead of Long and myself. The lounge on B deck was filled with a milling crowd and as we went through the doorway out onto the deck, people pushed between my Father and Mother, and Long and me. Long and I could not catch up, and were entirely separated from them. I never saw my Father again."

Mr. Karun: "What became of my brother-in-law? I do not know. He went on top too, but I lost sight of him. You could not see much there. He went down with the ship."

Mrs. Futrelle: "Again I saw a boat lowered away and once again I turned back not wishing to leave Jack. I could not find him this time."

Mr. Beesley: "An officer—I think First Officer Murdoch—came striding along the deck, clad in a long coat, from his manner and face evidently in great agitation, but determined and resolute. He looked over the side and shouted to the boats being lowered, 'Lower away. And when afloat, row around to the gangway and wait for orders.' 'Aye, aye sir,' was the reply and the officer passed by and went across the ship to the port side."

Hardy went over with him.

Hardy: "and I went over to the port side and assisted the ladies and children in getting into the boats . . ."

This left the loading boats 13 and 15 in the hands of stewards on A deck, and unknown supervision on the boat deck. It is possible that Ismay and McElroy remained for a while since they supervised 9 and 11.

Fletcher: *"Was there any one officer who seemed to have charge of it* [boat 13]*?"*
Ray: *"If he had charge of it—if he had charge when number 13 was lowered—he must have been on the boat deck. I did not see any officer on the A deck when it was lowered."*

Steward Ray saw boats 9 and 11 off from the promenade deck and was helping out with 13. Again, the area was very crowded and the stewards were doing an excellent job in loading the increasingly frightened passengers into the boats. Passengers had to be hoisted up over a three foot wall so that they could step out and down into a lifeboat dangling 70 feet above the water. The task required skill and passenger diplomacy. There was no presence of a strong, authoritative officer supervising things at this time, and many men took advantage of the situation to gain a seat, particularly in boats 13 and 15. People literally piled into them, turning them into two of the most efficiently loaded boats of the evening.

Ray (13): *"Then I went to number 13 boat. I saw that about half filled with women and children. They said, 'A few of you men get in here.' There were about nine to a dozen men there, passengers and crew. I saw Mr. Washington Dodge there, asking where his wife and child were. He said they had gone away in one of the boats. He was standing well back from the boat, and I said, 'You had better get in here, then.' I got behind him and pushed him and I followed. After I got in there was a rather big woman came along and we helped her in the boat. She was crying all the time and saying, 'Don't put me in the boat. I don't want to go in the boat. I have never been in an open boat in my life. Don't let me stay in.' I said, 'You have got to go, and you may as well keep quiet.' After that there was a small child rolled in a blanket thrown into the boat to me, and I caught it. The woman that brought it along got into the boat afterwards. We left about three or four men on the deck, at the rail, and they went along to number 15 boat."*

Miss Sjoblom (13): *"The boat that I got into finally was the next to the last boat launched. There must have been 50 people in it. The lifeboat was so crowded that I sat on a man's knee and had a woman on my lap. Several others did the same. There wasn't room for another person in the boat."*

Miss Turja (13): *"I did not want to get in the life boat. I wanted to wait for the big boat which would come to get us. It was the hus-band of the young woman in our room and an old Finnish lady who insisted on my getting in the life boat. I can't remember their names, but if it had not been for them, I would not be here, for I did want to stay right on the Titanic. I did not know the ship was sinking, but when we dropped over the side of the steamer, I could see that she was going down. Our boat was next to last to be put in the water."*

When Murdoch went over to the port side, he first had to press his way through a thick crowd before seeing Moody working at boat 16, Lowe at 14, and Wilde and Lightoller at number 12, seeing it lowered to the water. Beyond them was lifeboat number 10, inactive while the other boats were loaded.

Clench (12): *" We had instructions when we went down that we were to keep our eye on number 14 boat, where Mr. Lowe, the fifth officer, was, and keep all together as much as we could, so that we would not get drifted away from one another. We started lowering away and get down to the water. I goes and gets the tumbler and drops clear into the water, and drops clear of the blocks."*
Bourne: *"The tumbler being the loosener from the fall?"*

Clench: "Yes, sir; pulls the hook back so we dropped clear of the falls. Then we had orders to pull away from the ship."
Bourne: "Who gave you the orders?"
Clench: "They were shouted from the deck."
Bourne: "By what officer? Do you know?"
Clench: "I could not say what officer, now. He was too high up and it was so dark I could not see."

Evans: "I should say, on a rough average, there was about 50. There was one seaman standing in the stern sheets of it. After we got them into that, I sung out to the seaman, 'How many have you got in that boat?' I said, 'Ginger, how many have you got?' He said, 'There is only me here.' I lowered that boat and she went away from the ship."

Clench (12): "I could not say about number 14 boat. We had gone ahead of them."

With lifeboat 12 in the water, there would have been four officers in addition to Murdoch already on the aft port deck to see the remaining three boats off. While Murdoch surveyed this situation, lifeboat 13 was ready to go on the starboard.

Mr. Beesley: ". . . I heard a cry from below of, 'Any more ladies?' and looking over the edge of the deck, saw boat 13 swinging level

The starboard boat deck aft. Many men lingered here in the glare and shadows of the deck lights. Lifeboat 13 can be seen on the far right and it was from this location that Beesley jumped down into the boat while it hung alongside the promenade deck.

with the rail of B deck, with the crew, some stokers, a few men passengers and the rest ladies—the latter being about half the total number. The boat was almost full and just about to be lowered. The call for ladies was repeated twice again, but apparently there were none to be found. Just then one of the crew looked up and saw me looking over.

'Any ladies on your deck?' He said. 'No,' I replied. 'Then you had better jump.' I sat on the edge of the deck with my feet over, threw the dressing gown (which I had carried on my arm all of the time) into the boat, dropped and fell in the boat near the stern. As I picked myself up, I heard a shout, 'Wait a moment. Here are two more ladies,' and

they were pushed hurriedly over the side and tumbled into the boat, one into the middle and one next to me in the stern. As they tumbled in, the crew shouted, 'Lower away,' but before the order was obeyed, a man with his wife and a baby came quickly to the side. The baby was handed to the lady in the stern, the mother got in near the middle and the father at the last moment dropped in as the boat began its journey down to the sea many feet below."

Miss Sjoblom (13): "While the boat was being lowered, a man jumped into it from the deck above. He came down feet first on my head, and nearly broke my neck. He sprawled over the people in the lifeboat and nearly fell overboard. I was in intense pain for hours after he had jumped on me."

Mrs. Cook: "I knew there was little or no chance of us getting off, for lots of the women with babies would not get in and those that wouldn't they took the babies and threw them in and they were obliged to follow."

It is important to note Beesley's observation that "the crew" from the lifeboat told him to get in the boat, and "the crew" shouted out to lower away. This appears to confirm that there was no officer present providing direction during the low-ering of boat 13. Murdoch was temporarily over on the port side and it is not clear what happened to McElroy. He may have been there, but as purser, he also might have decided there were other things requiring his attention. Ismay apparently left the scene as well and walked to the bridge.

Smith: "Did you have any conversation with Mr. Ismay that night?"
Boxhall: "Yes, sir."
Smith: "Where?"
Boxhall: "On board of the ship."
Smith: "When?"
Boxhall: "On the bridge, probably about ten minutes or a quarter of an hour before I came away in the boat."
Smith: "What did he say to you?"
Boxhall: "He asked me why I did not get the people in the boat and get away?"
Smith: "What did you say to him?"
Boxhall: "I told him the boat's crew were ready, and the boat was ready to be put away when the captain's order was given."
Smith: "Did he say anything about himself?"
Boxhall: "No, sir. He passed on then."
Smith: "Who was with him then?"
Boxhall: "He was standing alone at that time."

And so, with little supervision, a very crowded lifeboat 13 was haphazardly lowered some 70 feet to the water at approximately 1:25 p.m.

Ray (13): " There were people waiting to get into the boat, and when the boat was filled and ready to be lowered away, we left about four men on the deck and they went along to number 15 and got in there quite easily. The boat was lowered away until we got nearly to the water when two or three of us noticed a very large discharge of water coming from the ship's side, which I thought was the pumps working. The hole was about 2 feet wide and about a foot deep, a solid mass of water coming out from the hole. I realized that if the boat was lowered down straight away the boat would be swamped and we shall all be thrown into the water. We shout-ed for the boat to be stopped from being lowered, and they responded promptly and stopped lowering the boat. We got oars and pushed it off from the side of the ship. It seemed impossible to lower the boat without being swamped. We pushed it out from the side of the ship and the next I knew we were in the water free from the discharge.

To escape the discharge, the occu-pants of boat 13 drifted sideways along the ship's side, away from the force of the water, until resting directly underneath boat 15. Number 13 was still attached by ropes to the davits far above and the occupants began to look for a way to disconnect themselves from the ship. About this time, Murdoch returned from his short visit to the port side boats and found 13 already lowered and 15 wanting for women and children. With his ongoing no-nonsense approach, he announced that men could fill the balance of boat 15. This announcement must have created a distraction as a number of men began climbing aboard. Murdoch and the other crew did not seem to be taking any note of boat 13's predicament.

Rule (15): "At this time the vessel had a slight list to port. We sent scouts around both to the starboard and port sides. They came back and said there were no more women and children. There was a bit of a rush after Mr. Murdoch said we could fill the boat up with men standing by."

Taylor (15): "They shoved out number 15 boat and I was ordered into it. The boat was pretty full."
Newlands: "Did you help load any other boats?"
Taylor: "There was too much of a crowd on. There was a crowd around them at the time. This boat was the only boat that was in the blocks when I went on the deck."
Newlands: "Did you get into the boat from

Unaware that lifeboat 13 drifted aft, the remaining crew on deck continue to hurriedly lower 15.

the boat deck?"
Taylor: "Yes."
Newlands: "Then did the other members of the crew get on there?"
Taylor: "At the boat deck."
Newlands: "And then it was lowered down to deck A?"
Taylor: "That is correct, sir."

Newlands: "Then the passengers got on?"
Taylor: "Yes, sir."
Newlands: Were there any male passengers in the boat?"
Taylor: "Yes, sir."

Below, boiler room 4 remained dry while water collected on the decks directly above it. The ship began to lose its balance and list to port. This would cause problems for lifeboat 15 and eventually collapsible C.

Taylor (15): "I could not see because we kept the boat off the ship, to keep from rubbing down her side."
Newlands: "You realized then that she was sinking?"
Taylor: "After we got clear of her we could see her going down by the bow."
Newlands: "But you did not realize that at the time you got into the lifeboat?"
Taylor: "No, sir. I only thought we were getting in in case there was an emergency."

Down in the water, the occupants of number 13 still grappled with the boat's gear to get free. Murdoch ordered boat 15 lowered. For some reason, he apparently left the scene again before the boat was in the water, as evidenced by the lack of intervention from above as it descended on 13.

Ray (13): "I do not think there were any sailors or quartermasters in the boat, because they apparently did not know how to get free from the tackle. They called for knives to cut the boat loose and somebody gave them a knife and they cut the boat loose. In the meantime, we were drifting a little aft and boat number 15 was being low-

The discharge at the end of boat 13's descent.

ered immediately upon us, about 2 feet over our heads and we all shouted again, and they again replied very promptly and stopped lowering boat number 15."

Steward Ray's note that the crew responded to the pleas to stop lowering number 15 conflicts with Beesley's, who indicates 13 would have been crushed had they not cleared out of the area just in time.

Mr. Beesley (13): "Looking up we saw her already coming down rapidly from B deck; she must have filled almost immediately after ours. We shouted up, 'Stop lowering 14,' and the crew and passengers in the boat above, hearing us shout and seeing our position immediately below them, shouted the same to the sailors on the boat deck."

Mr. Harper (3): "We were lying off perhaps a quarter of a mile from here when I heard several bursts of cheering. I suppose that was when the people on board received the news by wireless that other ships were hurrying to the rescue."

Mr. Beesley (13): "But apparently they did not hear, for she dropped down foot by foot - twenty feet, fifteen, ten - and a stoker and I in the bows reached up and touched her bottom swinging above our heads, trying to push away our boat from under her. It seemed now as if nothing could prevent her dropping on us, but at this moment another stoker sprang with his knife to the ropes that still held us and I heard him shout, 'One! Two!' as he cut them through. The next moment we had swung away from underneath 15 and were clear of her as she dropped into the water in the space we had just before occupied."

Regardless of whether lifeboat 15 had paused or not in its descent, the event was a dramatic one for passengers. Finally, the boat was cleared and the occupants headed out of the area.

Ray (13): "We pushed out from the side of the ship. Nobody seemed to take command of the boat, so we elected a fireman to take

Several occupants of lifeboat 13 frantically work at the ropes to free themselves from their precarious position.

charge. *He ordered us to put out the oars and pull straight away from the ship.*

It was coming up on 1:30. With the exception of collapsible C still lying flat on the deck, every lifeboat on the starboard side was gone. Many passengers were frequently on the move, migrating from one location to another in order to see if opportunities existed somewhere else on this enormous boat deck. Archibald Gracie at one time was aft on the promenade deck.

Mr. Gracie: ". . . I passed through the A deck, going from the stern toward the bow. I saw four gentlemen all alone in the smoking room, whom I recognized as Mr. Millet, Mr. Moore, and Mr. Butt, and a fourth gentleman was there with them whom I did not know, but who I afterwards ascertained to have been Mr. Ryerson. They seemed to be absolutely intent upon what they were doing, and disregarding anything about what was going on on the decks outside."

Arthur Ryerson, like many other men, had become separated from his wife and family when the officers ordered the women and children to the port side of the promenade deck almost an hour earlier. Ryerson probably thought his family was away in a lifeboat, and decided to pass the

time with a game of cards. Shortly after Gracie's sighting, however, Ryerson somehow became aware that his family was still on board. The group threw down their cards and hurried to the port side of the forward boat deck.

Murdoch returned to the port side of the ship to help with the aft lifeboats.

Boxhall: "I never saw Mr. Lightoller on the starboard side. Whenever I did see him it was on the port side. I saw Mr. Murdoch on the port side at times."

Lowe continued filling lifeboat 14. After 12 was lowered to the sea, Wilde and Lightoller went to number 14 to help Lowe, but Wilde quickly departed to attend to boat number 2, the forward most boat on deck.

Clench: "But at any rate, we had to go to boat 14 and do the same there. Me and Mr. Lightoller and the chief officer passed them in as we stood on the gunwale in all three of the boats, that was."

Smith: "You filled 14?"
Lowe: "Yes."
Smith: "Was Lightoller, the second officer, there?"
Lowe: "He was there a part of the time, and he went away somewhere else. He must

have gone to the second boat forward."
Smith: "Who had charge of the loading of lifeboat number 14?"
Lowe: "I had."

When Wilde and Lightoller left the area, the ratio of officers to passengers was cut in half. Some of the passengers took note of this development and upon their departure started to make attempts for a seat on boats 14 and 16. As the number of available boats dwindled, the number of passengers congregating around the remaining ones increased. Added to this, steerage women were continuously trickling up from the third class area, providing a steady inflow of people to a swelling crowd.

Daisy Minahan was standing in the crowd waiting for a chance to move up to the edge of one of the lifeboats. Walking the decks could be a tricky matter that night. There were ropes all around in preparation of lowering. There were sails and masts lying about that had been removed from the boats. And, oddly enough, there was the bread to contend with.

Miss Minahan (14): "After making three attempts to get into boats, we succeeded in getting into lifeboat number 14. The crowd surging around the boats was getting unruly. Officers were yelling and cursing at men to stand back and let the women get into the boats. In going from one lifeboat to another we stumbled over huge piles of bread lying on the deck."

Andrews: "With that I walked up on deck and stood by my boat. There were lots of people around, and I saw stores brought to the boat, and bread. I did not see the stores put in the boat."

Wilde, Murdoch, Lightoller, Lowe, and Moody were all on the move at 1:30 a.m., making it difficult to keep track exactly which officer was where, and when. When reviewing all of the survivor observations, it appears that Wilde headed toward the bow to work on boat 2 after seeing number 12 away. After finishing with number 12, Lightoller went to 14 for a short while, before departing to work on 4. Murdoch arrived on the port side after barely seeing 15 away on the starboard, then took command of numbers 14 and 16. Moody, who had been handling 16, was put in charge of keeping men from rushing the boats.

Bourne: "How many occupants were there in boat number 14?"
Crowe: "Fifty-seven women and children and about 6 men, including 1 officer. And I may have been 7. I am not quite sure about that."

Passengers are loaded into lifeboats 14 and 16 in the shadowy glare of the deck lights.

Even during the stress of the loading, the officers frequently managed a courteous overture toward the women and children as they approached the boat.

Mrs. Cook (14): "Well, we got along to number 14, the last one that was lowered in safety and I asked the officer if there was room for two and he said yes, for you two and a good many more. So with that we got in as we promised one another we would stick together through it all."

Miss Minahan (14): "When the lifeboat was filled there were no seamen to man it. The officer in command of number 14 called for volunteers in the crowd who could row. Six men offered to go."

As the boat filled to near-capacity, Murdoch or Lowe needed seamen for rowing. A full lifeboat would be a challenge to maneuver through the water.

Crowe: ". . . I went to boat number 14, the boat allotted to me–that is, in the case of fire or boat drill–and I stood by according to the proceedings of the drill. I assisted in handing the women and children into the boat, and was asked if I could take an oar, and I said, 'Yes', and was told to man the boat. I am not sure whether it was the first officer or the chief officer, but I believe the man's name was Murdoch."

Smith: "And how many people did you put into it?"
Lowe: "Fifty-eight."
Smith: "How many women? Do you know?"
Lowe: "They were all women and children, bar one passenger, who was an Italian, and he sneaked in, and he was dressed like a woman."
Smith: "Had woman's clothing on?"
Lowe: "He had a shawl over his head, and everything else; and I only found out at the last moment. And there was another passenger that I took for rowing."
Smith: "Who was that?"
Lowe: "That was a chap by the name of C. Williams."

Smith: "Was he one of the men whose names you have on that paper?"
Lowe: "I have his name, that is, his home address, but not his New York address."
Smith: " I would like his home address."
Lowe: "(referring to book) 'C. Williams, racket champion of the world,' he has here, 'Number 2 Drury Road, Harrow on the Hill, Middlesex, England.'"

As the loading continued, the crowds grew desperate. Suddenly, some men broke through and rushed the boats.

Mr. Daly: ""We afterwards went to the second cabin deck and the two girls and myself got into a boat. An officer called on me to go back, but I would not stir. They then got hold of me and pulled me out."

Crowe (14): "There were various men passengers . . . who attempted to rush the boats. The officers threatened to shoot any man who put his foot into the boat. He fired the revolver, but either downward or upward, not shooting at any of the passengers at all and not injuring anybody."
Bourne: "Did that stop the rush?"
Crowe: "Yes, sir."
Bourne: "There was no disorder after that?"
Crowe: "No disorder. Well, one woman was crying, but that was all."

Scarrott (14): "The men stood back to allow the women to pass, except in one or two cases where men tried to rush, but they were very soon stopped. This occurred at the boat I was in charge of, number 14. About half a dozen foreigners tried to jump in before I had my complement of women and children, but I drove them back with the boat's tiller. Shortly afterwards the fifth officer, Mr. Lowe, came and took charge of the boat. I told him what had happened. He drew his revolver and fired two shots between the boat and ship's side into the water as a warning to any further attempts of that sort."

Smith: "Did you hear any pistol shots?"
Lowe: "Yes."
Smith: "And by whom were they fired Sunday night?"
Lowe: "I heard them, and I fired them."

Clench (14): "Mr. Lowe was in number 14 boat and he sings out, 'Anybody attempting to get into these boats while we are lowering them, I will shoot them,' and he shot three shots. He shot straight down in the water. Just shot to frighten the people."

Mrs. Brown (14): "He led us to boat 14. The men were all standing back from the boat. I heard an officer threaten to shoot them if they came near. The boat was crowded mostly with women. I afterward found there were sixty persons in it. We stood or sat wherever we could in a thick crowd. They began to lower the boat over the side. It seemed a terrible distance. I looked back for my husband. I saw him turning away. We never said good bye."

With such a threatening crowd pushing toward Lowe, the fifth officer was hard pressed to get the lifeboat lowered and away from this dangerous scene. Each second they remained dangling alongside the deck presented a new opportunity for trouble and Lowe's temper began to flare during the final moments on deck.

Mrs. Collyer (14): "The boat was practically full and no more women were anywhere near it when Fifth Officer Lowe jumped in and ordered it lowered. The sailors on deck had started to obey him when a very sad thing happened. A young lad hardly more than a schoolboy, a pink cheeked lad, almost small enough to be counted as a child, was standing close to the rail. He had made no attempt to force his way into the boat though his eyes had been fixed piteously on the Officer. Now, when he realized that he was really to be left behind, his courage failed him. With a cry he climbed upon the rail and leapt down into the boat. He fell among us women and crawled under a seat. I and another woman covered him up with our skirts. We wanted to give the poor lad a chance, but the officer dragged him to his feet and ordered him back onto the ship. We begged for his life. I remember him saying that he would not take up too much room, but the officer drew his revolver and thrust it into his face. 'I give you just ten seconds to get back onto that ship before I blow your brains out,' he shouted. The lad only begged the harder and I thought I should see him shot where he stood. But the officer suddenly changed his tone. He lowered his revolver and looked the boy squarely in the eyes. 'For God's sake be a man,' he said gently. 'We have got women and children.' The little lad turned round eyed and climbed back over the rail without a word. He was not saved. All the women about me were sobbing and I saw my little Marjorie take the officer's hand. 'Oh, Mr. Man, don't shoot. Please don't shoot the poor man!' she was saying, and he spared the time to shake his head and smile."

Without wasting another second, Lowe got going again, but not in time to avoid yet another incident to the troubled boat.

Mrs. Collyer (14): "He screamed another order for the boat to be lowered, but just as we were getting away, a steerage passenger, and Italian I think, came running the whole length of the deck and hurled himself into the boat. He fell upon a young child and injured her internally. The officer seized him by the collar and by sheer brute strength, pushed him back onto the Titanic. As we shot down towards the sea I caught a last glimpse of this coward. He was in the hands of about a dozen men of the second cabin. They were driving their fists into his face and he was bleeding from the nose and mouth."

Brown (14): "Ours was the second boat off. As it lay in the water alongside the Titanic a foreign steerage passenger suddenly dived from way up on the boat deck right into our boat. We were afraid somebody would be struck and killed. The man did not seem to be hurt. Some of the men in the boat threatened to kill anybody else who tried that. We pushed off."

Minahan (14): "At times when we were being lowered we were at an angle of 45 degrees and expected to be thrown into the sea. As we reached the level of each deck men jumped into the boat until the officer threatened to shoot the next man who jumped. We landed in the sea and rowed to a safe distance from the sinking ship."

The port boat deck aft. Lifeboat 16 can barely be seen in the foreground, followed by 14, 12 and then 10. Emotions boiled over in this area, forcing Lowe to fire his gun to control a rush on the boats.

There was simply too much taking place on the vast deck spaces of the *Titanic* for any one person to take it all in. As an example of how local many events were, Woolner, who was somewhere up on deck, took no notice of Officer Lowe's gun fire.

Smith: "Mr. Lowe says he fired three shots as his lifeboat was being lowered."
Mr. Woolner: "I do not remember them."

The descent was a stressful one for Lowe and the occupants of 14. The boat was packed and the prior rush left him worried on the way down that someone could still come flying into it from above.

Lowe: "As I was going down the decks I knew, or I expected every moment that my boat would double up under my feet. I was quite scared of it, although of course it would not do for me to mention the fact to anybody else. I had overcrowded her, but I knew that I had to take a certain amount of risk. So I thought, 'Well, I shall have to see that nobody else gets into the boat or else it will be a case . . ."
Smith: "That was as it was being lowered?"
Lowe: "Yes. I thought if one additional body was to fall into that boat, that slight jerk of the additional weight might part the hooks or carry away something, no one would know what. There were a hundred and one things to carry away. Then I thought, well, I will keep an eye open. So, as we were coming down the decks, coming down past the open decks, I saw a lot of Italians, Latin people, all along the ship's rails—understand , it was open—and they were all glaring, more or less like wild beasts, ready to spring. That is why I yelled out to look out, and let go, bang, right along the ship's side."
Smith: "How far from the ship's side was the lifeboat you were in?"
Lowe: "I really do not know. I should say, oh, 3 or 4 feet."

Mrs. Cook (14): "Then as several Italians

were making for jumping into our boat, our officer said he would shoot any man who dared jump into the boat. With that he fired but only down the side of the boat. He then gave the men orders to lower the boat. We had 58 in ours."

Bertha Lehmann was nearby in boat 12 listening to the drama surrounding the descent of number 14.

Miss Lehmann (12): "We were not very far from the boat and could still hear people crying and yelling to one another. All at once there were three loud reports, they sounded something like a very loud crash of thunder when it strikes very close to you."

On deck, lifeboat 16 immediately became the center of attention once 14 had departed. It was loaded with passengers at the same time as 14, but was still hanging in the davits, taking on more passengers and crew. These few aft boats on the port side took away a number of people much closer to their capacity.

Archer: "I went over there and assisted in getting numbers 12, 14, and [16] out. I assisted in getting the falls and everything ready, and the passengers into number 14 boat. Then I went to number 16."

Smith: Do you wish to be understood as saying that a large lifeboat like number 14 or number 12 or number 10 could be filled to its full capacity and lowered to the water with safety?"
Evans: "Yes, because we did it then, sir."
Smith: "That is a pretty good answer."

While Murdoch finished with boat 16 on deck, 14 was nearing the water. It seemed that this particular boat was destined to experience one dramatic event after another before getting away from the ship.

Crowe (14): "After getting the women and children in we lowered down within 4 or 5 feet of the water and found the block and tackle had gotten twisted in some way, causing us to have to cut the ropes to allow the boat to get into the water.
Bourne: "Who called to you to do that?"
Crowe: "The fifth officer, sir."
Bourne: "He was in the boat with you?"
Crowe: "Yes, sir. I stood by the lever. The lever releases the blocks from the hooks in the boat and he told me to wait, to get away and cut the line to raise the lever, thereby causing the hooks to open and allow the boat to drop in the water."

And drop it did. The sensation was an unpleasant one for the occupants as it slammed down onto the surface.

Mrs. Cook (14): " Then they started to lower and when we got so far down the ropes would not act so they gave orders to cut them and we dropped almost on another boat. One or two of us shrieked but was soon told to shut up."

As if the latest drama of dropping four feet onto the water was not enough, when boat 14 came down, part of it landed in front of the exhaust–the same exhaust that had caused 13 so much trouble fifteen minutes earlier on the other side of the ship.

Mrs. Collyer (14): "The bottom of our boat slapped the ocean as we came down with a force that I thought must shock us all overboard. We were drenched with ice cold spray but we hung on and the men at the oars rowed us rapidly away from the wreck."

The lifeboat was apparently damaged now from the drop, although it is possible that the water was from the exhaust that sprayed into the boat. Whatever its source, it only added to the misery and the stress of the occupants of lifeboat 14.

Crowe (14): " I might state in between there

the boat had sprung a leak and taken in water, probably 8 inches of water. That is, when the boat was released and fell, I think she must have sprung a leak. . . . I should imagine when we transferred our people was when we discovered the amount of water that was in the boat."

Mr. Buckley: "There was a girl from my place and just when she got down into the lifeboat she thought that the boat was sinking into the water. Her name was Bridget Bradley. She climbed one of the ropes as far as she could and tried to get back into the Titanic again, as she thought she would be safer in it than in the lifeboat. She was just getting up when one of the sailors went out to her and pulled her down again."

Mrs. Brown (14): "The men in the boat seemed to be mostly members of the crew. It was terribly cold. Most of the women seemed too lightly clad or half clad. I stood almost knee deep in water which had gotten into the bottom of the boat. We pulled a short way from the wreck."

Mrs. Cook (14): "Then the officer rowed us out from the sinking boat and got all the boats that were only 100 yards from the Titanic and we begged him to take us further away in case we should be sucked under but

he assured us we were quite all right. I was all this time watching the vessel and she looked a splendid sight and the forepart of the ship was gradually sinking deeper into the water."

By now, Wilde arrived at the bridge and ordered the crew to prepare for loading collapsible C and lifeboat 2, each on opposite sides of the bridge. Lifeboat 2 was another emergency boat, and Captain Smith may have reminded the crew to cut the stay-ropes to avoid a repeat of boat 1.

It was after 1:30. Murdoch was at number 16. Moody was still in charge of crowd control. There was not a minute to spare.

Bourne: "What officer was in charge of number 16?"
Andrews: "I could not tell you what officer, sir."
Bourne: "Was it an officer, or one of the petty officers?"
Andrews: "An officer, sir."

Mr. Gracie: "Moody was his name. He said, 'No man beyond this line.' Then the women went beyond that line. I saw that these four ladies with whose safety I considered myself intrusted, went beyond that line to get amidships on this deck, which was A deck."

Archer (16): "Then when I got to number 16 boat the officer told me to get into the boat and see that the plug was in. So I got in the boat. I seen that the plug was in tight. They then started to put passenger in, and I assisted to get them in. I never saw any men get in. Only my mate."

As the *Titanic's* condition worsened, many crewmen looked for opportunities to man one of the few remaining boats. Collins was one such example as he approached lifeboat 16 with hopes of rendering assistance.

Collins: "So I went up to number 16 boat, and I seen both firemen and sailors with their bags ready for number 16 boat. I said to myself, 'There is no chance there.'"

The process of keeping a dangling lifeboat steady while helping passengers climb aboard was a tall task. As swarms of passengers and crew surrounded the boat, those who were supervising had little time to make detailed mental notes of events. Lifeboat 16 had a larger percentage of children than others, many of them being from third class and recently brought up on deck.

Archer (16): "I was busy with the children. I did not know who was speaking."

Andrews: "I assisted in helping the ladies and children into the boat. After the boat was full the officer called out for able seamen, or any individuals then, to man the boat."

It is disturbing that so many children were still on board by the time the last of the lifeboats were being filled. Of the 109 children on board, half would go down with the ship—all but one from third class. When women and children were offered access to the upper decks late in the night, the men had to remain behind in steerage. Many families were not willing to split up under those circumstances, particularly since they did not speak English and in some cases, would have required a mother to take charge of all of her children and work them through crowds on several decks. And why should they? First and second class families were allowed up to the boat deck. Since third class men were kept back at the stern, family decisions were made to wait until they could go up together. The result was disastrous. While 52 children waited in steerage with their parents, first and second class adults were encouraged to board the boats.

As the number of available boats decreased and the night wore on, many first class women who had been offered opportunities earlier to board a lifeboat were still on the ship. Even at this late hour, they were not convinced of the need to leave and could not be bothered with the amount of effort it took to get through the crowds and into a boat. It was very common for families to become separated from each other amidst the crowds on deck.

Mrs. Futrelle (16): "For the second time I was on the promenade deck. There was real alarm shown on the faces of the officers now and the boats were being filled hurriedly. Again I saw a boat lowered away and once again I turned back not wishing to leave Jack. I could not find him this time. I ran through the cabin. With my heart full of fear, not with the fear of death but with the fear of leaving my husband, filled with the agony which the separation brought. Finally I encountered him at one side standing with an officer. When he saw me he said, 'This will never do. You must get into a boat.' He took me on the starboard side and put me in boat number 16. I thought my heart would break at the thought of leaving him. He told me that I was only endangering his chances by staying for he could get along himself in the water with a life belt but he could not hold me up with him. He told me he would cling on to one of the boats and be picked up. I would never have left him, even then, but he whispered to me, 'Remember the children.' Just as I got placed in the boat Mrs. Hoyt got out. She brushed by the officers and I heard her say, 'Oh, I can't go without my husband. Please let him come with me, please do.' The officers refused, but in kindly tones, telling her that it was impossible. The absolute rule was that only women and children were to be put in the boats."

Miss Mulvihill: "Beside me there was a family named Rice, consisting of the father and mother and six children. The father was not permitted to leave the ship, but the mother and her six children could leave if they wished. The mother was crying and weeping. She wouldn't go into the lifeboat and leave her husband to perish. 'I can't go and leave my husband,' she cried to the officers. 'Let him come with me, oh, please let him come with me,' she pleaded, 'I don't want to live if he can't come. There will be nobody to earn bread for my little children,' she wailed. But the officers wouldn't let the father go. 'I'll stay with my husband, then,' the woman cried. I saw her clinging to her husband and children just before I left the vessel. That was the last I ever saw of her. The whole family went down together."

The scene described by Futrelle where Jane Hoyt was resisting and making a fuss must have been exasperating for officers working against the clock. The Hoyts walked forward, perhaps with the intent of talking to the captain about their situation.

Many women were still on board when lifeboat 16 was loaded. As a result, Murdoch was no longer accommodating men. His approach had always allowed men into the boats when women and children were no longer available, but this was definitely not the case now on the port side. While seated in 16 during the loading, May Futrelle had watched the dramatic events take place at the next boat over, lifeboat 14. She saw the crowd rush Lowe's boat and she watched him fire a gun to keep them back.

Mrs. Futrelle (16): "Our boat was lowered away without being half filled. As it swung down the high sides, I saw in the gleam of the lights the men from the steerage who had rushed to the deck and were being held back by the officers with loaded revolvers. There were only four first cabin women in my boat, three besides myself. Mrs. Harris was with me as well as Miss Thaw. There were some women from the steerage and some men. I was absolutely stunned. The horror of it all just seemed to paralyze me."

Bourne: "There were 50 people in the boat?"
Archer: "Yes, sir."

Archer (16): "I heard him give orders to lower the boat. The last order I received after I heard that was from the officer, to allow nobody in the boat, and there was no one else to get into the boat. That was just prior to starting the lowering. We lowered the boat, and my mate pulled at the releasing bar for both falls, and that cleared the boat, and we started to pull away. The master-at-arms came down after us. He was the coxswain. Came down the fall. I presume he was sent by an officer. He said he was sent down to be the coxswain of the boat. He took charge."

Andrews (16): "Five had got into the boat, and I was the sixth. The master-at-arms, there was two master-at-arms, and one was in charge of our boat. After they were all in the boat the officer looked around at me and asked me if I could take an oar, and I said I could. At that he told me to get into the boat. After I got in the boat I assisted by putting the rowlocks in. We lowered the boat to the water and rowed away from the ship."

The events witnessed on deck, combined with the shocking appearance of the *Titanic* viewed from the water, resulted in a surge of fear in lifeboat 16. Some were overwhelmed, and feelings of panic set in when they could not detach the ropes from the falls. They were stuck to the sinking ship if they could not get them separated.

Mrs. Futrelle (16): "I was startled from my dazed condition by the cries of a man in my lifeboat. They could not unfasten the lashings. 'For God's sake,' I heard one ask, 'has no one a knife?' Not a man in the boat carried a knife. The men were in a frenzy of fear. The women sat like statues, arms outstretched and eyes turned towards the Titanic. All around were heard cries of 'Quick, now, let's get away as far as possible. When the Titanic sinks she will suck us down if we don't.' One great hulking fellow in the boat, frantic with fear, managed with almost superhuman strength to break the lashings. The men seized the oars, but they were perfectly helpless to handle them. Their clumsiness verged on the grotesque. It was perfectly obvious to me that the crew was unfamiliar with the handling of a boat. They were not seamen. They were cooks and stewards. I asked one man why he was in the boat if he couldn't row. He replied in a tense, strained voice, 'I want to save my life just as much as you do yours.' But I didn't care whether the lifeboat made any progress or not. As a matter of fact, it didn't. We could plainly see a group of men gathered on the stern. Rockets were still shooting into the sky. We heard noises that sounded like pistol shots."

May Futrelle likely saw the last rocket go up shortly after her lifeboat reached the water. Up near the bridge, Wilde was ready to begin loading number 2 boat, but needed a crewman by his side.

Rowe (2): "I assisted the officer to fire them, and was firing the distress signals until about five and twenty minutes past one. At that time they were getting out the starboard collapsible boats. The chief officer, Wilde, wanted a sailor. I asked Captain Smith if I should fire anymore and he said, 'No. Get into that boat.' I went to the boat. Women and children were being passed in."

It was 1:40 a.m. The port side evacuation was finally operating with an efficiency it should have had an hour earlier. Three boats were being loaded at one time. Wilde was at boat 2. Lightoller was at boat 4 alongside the promenade deck and Murdoch had just arrived at boat 10.

Buley: "Number 12 was the last boat before me to be lowered and Evans was one of the men that lowered that boat, and after he lowered that away I called him and told him Chief Officer Murdoch gave me orders to find a seaman and tell him to come in the boat with me, and he jumped in my boat."

The list to port was growing downright serious. It was so bad now that passengers had to leap into the port side boats.

Evans (10): "I then went next to number 10 to that boat, and the chief officer, Mr. Murdoch, was standing there and I lowered the boat with the assistance of a steward. The chief officer said, 'What are you, Evans?' I said, 'A seaman, sir.' He said, 'Alright, get into that boat with the other seamen.' He said, 'Get into that boat,' and I got into the bows of this boat, and a young ship's baker was getting the children and chucking them into the boat, and the women were jumping. Mr. Murdoch made them jump across into the boat. It was about two feet and a half. He was making the women jump across and the children he was chucking across along with this baker. He throwed them onto the women and he was catching the children by their dresses and chucking them in."

Time was running out and Murdoch could not afford the luxury of allowing each woman and child to cross the divide between the deck and boat on their own terms. As the boat neared capacity, it looked like this hurried loading would be pulled off without a hitch. But it was too rushed.

Evans (10): "One woman slipped and fell. She seemed a bit nervous. She did not like to jump, at first, and then when she did jump, she did not go far enough, and the consequence was she went between the ship and the boat. Her heel must have caught on the rail of the deck and she fell down and someone on the deck below caught her and pulled her onto the next deck. She was a woman in a black dress. She came up onto the boat deck again, and then jumped again, and she came into the boat that time alright."

Burke (10): "I might say that about the last woman that was about to be passed in slipped and was about to fall between the ship and the boat when I caught her. I just saved her from falling. Her head passed toward the next deck below. A passenger caught her by the shoulders and forced me to leave go. It was my intention to pull her back in the boat. He would not let go of the woman, but pulled her right on the ship."

The situation on the *Titanic* appeared much more threatening than it had just half an hour earlier. Few people still pinned their hopes on the integrity of the ship, particularly with the ominous list to port. Even more

The port side of the promenade deck. A woman who fell between the boat deck and lifeboat 10 was pulled back onto the ship here. Lifeboat 4 was loaded from this deck, in the far distance.

disconcerting was the number of empty lifeboat davits. Earlier, a passenger had the luxury of thinking they could get off on a boat if it became serious enough to justify later on. But it was now "later" and the option of getting off the *Titanic* was fading fast. Human nature frequently leaves a person with a desire for something off limits, and with so few boats left on deck–combined with the worsening slant of the ship, many passengers were becoming desperate for one of the remaining seats.

Miss Mulvihill (10): "Only two boats remained. One of these pushed off. I stood directly over the other. 'Jump,' said the sailor. I jumped and landed in the boat."

Burke (10): "As I got to number 10 boat, the chief officer was there. I just heard him say, 'How many seamen are in that boat?' The answer came back, 'Two, sir.' He turned to some man standing there and said, 'Is there any man here can pull an oar?' Nobody answered, but a man who seemed to me like a foreigner got close to him and I didn't hear what he said, but he simply pushed him aside and he said, 'You are of no use to me.' I went to him and told him I could pull an oar but was not anxious to go unless he wanted me to go. He said, 'Get in there,' and he pushed me toward the boat and I simply stepped in the boat and got in."

Buley (10): "There was number 10 boat and there was no one there, and the chief officer asked what I was, and I told him, and he said, 'Jump in and see if you can find another seaman to give you a hand.' I found Evans and we both got in the boat, and Chief Officer Murdoch and Baker also was there. I think we were the last lifeboat to be lowered."

Fletcher: "How many people were in that boat?"

Buley: "From 60 to 70. Women and children. There were the steward and one fireman. And myself and Evans, the able seaman. All the others were ladies and children."

At some point Murdoch was joined by Moody as they worked on getting the last lifeboat aft loaded.

Burke (10): " After I arrived in the boat the chief officer seemed to be joined by another officer, and they were shouting for women on the decks, and as they came along they made room, cleared the men away, and passed the women along. Each one, as they were passed along was put in the boat. I remained where I landed in the boat and helped to pass them in. There were also about three children passed in at the same time. When there were no more women to be had around the deck, the chief officer gave the order for the boat to be lowered."

Evans (10): "There were about 60 persons, women and children."
Smith: "How many women?"
Evans: "I should say about 57, sir. There were only me and another seaman and a steward, and two men besides."

Buley (10): "Ours was the last boat up there, and they went around and called to see if there were any, and they threw them in the boat at the finish, because they didn't like the idea of coming in. They threw them in. One young lady slipped and they caught her by the foot on the deck below and she came up then and jumped in."

Evans (10): "The chief officer, Murdoch, had cleared all the women and children from that side of the ship and he asked if there was any more, and there was no reply came and the boat was packed, and as this boat was being lowered this foreigner must have jumped from A deck into the boat."

Miss Mulvihill (10): "Then a big Italian jumped and landed on me, knocking the wind out of me."

Mr. Karun (10): "There was a lifeboat lowered and I think that it was the last one put down. They put my little girl down first, letting her down with a rope. Then they let me down. I do not know why they did this, perhaps it was because it was the last boat and there was still room for somebody. When I got into the boat I found that I was the only man there. All the rest were women and children. Of course the sailors were in the boat to pull it. I think that I was the last man to get off the ship. There were fifty-two people in the boat. There were seven babies in the company."

Smith: "And how many children?"
Evans (10): "Seven or 8 children, sir."
Bourne: "Who caught the children as they were thrown into the boat?"
Evans: "The first child was passed over, sir, and I caught it by the dress. It was dangling. I had to swing it, and a woman caught it. The remainder of the children—there was a fireman there and with the assistance of a young woman they caught the children as they were dropped into the boat There was none of the children hurt."

How strange the boat deck must have appeared once lifeboat 10 descended. For the last forty five minutes or so, the port side aft was buzzing with activity as four lifeboats were sent away with over 200 people. There had been screaming, panic, and gunshots, but now the boats were gone and a grim reality set in on those still standing on the deck. The empty davits made a sobering image with their arms stretched out over the sea, as though they had just offered the world the latest round of chosen survivors. The *Titanic* would keep most of the rest.

It was 1:45 and the forward well deck was just inches above the waterline. If anyone had made the effort to look over the rail, they would have seen how close the bow was to disappearing beneath the surface. Things were getting very serious.

Fletcher: "How long after you were lowered and put in the water was it before she went down?"
Buley (10): "I should say about 25 minutes to half an hour."

Fletcher: "How much of the bow was under water when you left?"
Evans (10): "She was about 10 feet from the

port bow light, sir."

Smith: "When you got to the water, what did you do?"

Evans: "We unhooked the falls, sir. It was impossible to get to the tripper on account of the women being packed so tightly. It was impossible to get to the tripper underneath the thwart."

Smith: "What was done then?"

Evans (10): "We had to lift the fall up off the hook to release the spring, to get the block and fall away from it. We unhooked it by hand. We pushed off from the ship and rowed away. About 200 yards"

Burke (10): "The boat was lowered then into the water. One of the sailors took an oar and I took an oar and the only other member of the crew, a fireman got an oar. The sailor steered the boat and we rowed away from the ship. We got probably a quarter of a mile away and remained there."

Time was running out. Wilde hurried passengers and crew into lifeboat 2. There were fewer people here compared to the crowds aft, but he was not about to hold the boat until he could find enough to fill it.

Lightoller: "In the meantime the forward emergency boat had been put out by one of the other officers."

Boxhall: "I talked to Mr. Ismay a little while before I left the ship. I had just fired a distress signal and was going to the chart room to put the lanyard back in the chart room and go out again, and Mr. Ismay was standing by the wheelhouse door. He just came to the door on the bridge, as nearly as I can tell. Walked up as far as the door. He was not there when I went to stow the lanyard, at least not when I went to fire the distress signal a moment before. He asked me why I was not getting the boat away. I said the crew were ready and people were getting in the boat. I went on with my work."

Boxhall's observation provides a glimmer of the real Bruce Ismay, a man accustomed to orchestrating events directly and indirectly by way of his position.

Some of the first class couples and families had been congregating around the forward port boat deck since coming on deck over an hour ago. Among them were some of the elite such as the Astors, Thayers, Ryersons, Douglases, Wideners, Carters, and Stephensons. These were socially prominent families of the upper class and this inner circle of wealth was clearly sticking together despite the shifting masses of people on deck. With the crew periodically restricting men from certain areas of the deck, this was not always easy.

Passengers who were biding their time around the entrance to the Grand Staircase eventually saw Chief Officer Wilde march down the deck sometime around 1:30 a.m. and begin preparations for boat number 2 near the bridge. This deck area was behind a gate that separated first class from the bridge, but passengers were called over once Wilde was ready to load.

Mrs. Douglas: "Finally, as we stood by a collapsible boat lying on the deck and an emergency boat swinging from the davits was being filled, it was decided I should go."

It appears that Wilde was juggling preparations for lifeboat 2 and collapsible C on opposite sides of the bridge at the same time, and would disappear from boat 2 every so often. As a result, when the emergency boat was ready to be loaded, it got off to a rocky start. A number of crew decided to take advantage of the situation and climb into the lifeboat in Wilde's absence. But their actions were noticed by Captain Smith on the bridge. He would have none of this behavior and came out toward the boat.

Mrs. Douglas: "Just before we got into the boat the captain called, 'How many of the crew are in that boat? Get out of there, every man of you,' and I can see a solid row of men from bow to stern, crawl over onto the deck."

Imagine the scene of these men climbing out of the boat at the terse direction of the captain, and the expressions that must have been on their faces. Wilde returned to the area and the loading began.

Boxhall (2): "I was assisting to get people along there, but I was not standing at the side of the boat, lifting them in, actually."
Smith: "Did you see Mr. Lightoller at that time—when you got in, I mean?"
Boxhall: "No sir. I saw Mr. Wilde."
Smith: "Did you see Mr. Murdoch at that time?"
Boxhall: "No. Only Mr. Wilde and the captain."
Smith: "Where was the captain?"
Boxhall: "The captain was standing by this emergency boat."
Smith: "How far from it?"
Boxhall: "He was standing by the wheelhouse door, just abreast of this boat."
Smith: "What was he doing?"
Boxhall: "Supervising the boats being loaded, I think."

Although Boxhall notes Captain Smith's presence, he makes a point that it was Wilde who was in charge of the details.

Smith: "The captain was there also?"

Captain Smith standing on the bridge of the *Titanic* near the wheelhouse door.

Boxhall: "Yes; but Mr. Wilde superintended the loading of the boats.

The loading went into motion in the shadowy darkness of the area around the bridge. Just about this time, Arthur Ryerson met up with his family again, accompanied by his companions from the smoking lounge.

Mrs. Douglas (2): " We women then got in. I asked Mr. Douglas to come with me but he replied, 'No. I must be a gentleman,' turning away. I said, 'Try and get off with Mr. Moore and Major Butt. They will surely make it.' Major Butt and Clarence Moore were standing together near us, also Mr. Meyer, and I remember seeing Mr. Ryerson's face in the crowd. There were many people about. I got into the boat and sat under the seats on the bottom, just under the tiller."

Sometime around this point, George Dodd, at Lightoller's direction, came along and rounded up part of the crowd around the emergency boat and directed them to the crew staircase nearby.

Mrs. Stephenson: "... the order came from the head dining room steward to go down to A deck, when Mrs. Thayer remarked, 'Tell us where to go and we will follow. You ordered us up here and now you are taking us back,' and he said, 'Follow me.'"

Mrs. Ryerson: "Again, we were ordered down to A deck, which was partly inclosed. We saw people getting into boats, but waited our turn."

One has to wonder if Mrs. Douglas watched from her seat in boat 2 with envy as the elite of upper society, with whom she and her husband had stayed close most of

the night, left for the promenade deck. But Wilde and Smith thought nothing of such frivolous matters while continuing with their efforts.

Oddly enough, one male passenger was allowed into the boat within full view of Wilde. The man was with his wife and children, but this never seemed to make any difference on the port side before. Perhaps Wilde was aware of how many steerage passengers were still on the ship, and this was his way of easing his conscience–by allowing this man to go with his family.

Osman (2): "One steerage passenger, a man, and his wife and two children were in my boat. All belonged to the one family."

Smith: "There were four men in that boat?"
Boxhall: "And one passenger."
Smith: "A sailor man, a steward, a cook, yourself, and one male passenger?"
Boxhall: "One male passenger."
Smith: "Who was that passenger?"
Boxhall: "He was a saloon passenger who did not speak English. He had a black beard."
Smith: "How old a man, apparently?"
Boxhall: "A middle-aged man."
Smith: "Did he seem to have any family there?"
Boxhall: "I think he had his wife there, and some children."

When the boat appeared to be filled sufficiently with women and children, the captain turned to Boxhall and gave him his life.

Boxhall (2): "He told me I had to get into that boat and go away. The boat was already loaded. I did not see the passengers being put in. The order was given to lower the boats away when I was sent to her. I think they were either just starting to lower or I had heard them sing out, 'Lower away,' when the captain told me to get in the boat."

Boxhall worked his way through the crowd of men standing around and climbed over the rail and into the boat. Once in, he had a better view and immediately noticed a lifeboat in the water.

Smith: "The boat was full?"
Boxhall: "Yes, it seemed to me to be pretty full. The order was given to lower the boats away when I was sent to her."
Smith: "How long was this before the ship sank?"
Boxhall: "As near as I can judge it seems to me about 20 minutes to half an hour."

Mrs. Douglas (2): "Mr. Boxhall was trying to get the boat off, and called to the captain on the bridge, 'There's a boat coming up *over there.'   The captain said, 'I want a megaphone.'"*

Unfortunately, Douglas does not elaborate on what the Captain yelled to the lifeboat in the water but one would guess that he told it to come alongside for more passengers. No lifeboat, once it got away from the *Titanic*, ever returned to the side of the ship. But it probably does not matter. Even number 2 went away without being loaded to capacity, and they did not take on any more passengers once in the water.

The emergency boat was ready for lowering. Wilde and others released the ropes and the boat descended. It must have made an impression on Captain Smith. The emergency boats on both sides of the bridge were a mainstay to the scenery. As the small descending craft disappeared behind the rail, it left a deck empty of boats—on a slanting ship.

Osman (2): "After that we loaded all the boats there were, and I went away in number 2 boat, the fourth from the last to leave the ship. There was one able seaman, a cook, and a steward, and an officer. That was all the men there was in the boat out of the crew. There was one man, a third class passenger, and the remainder were women and children. I could not say exactly how many there were, but there were between 25

Chief Officer Wilde

and 30 all told. Including the crew. This was one of the emergency boats."

On the way down, Boxhall and the other occupants could see the last of the passengers crawling through the promenade deck windows into lifeboat number 4. They could see Lightoller standing there assisting the passengers. Someone like Mrs. Douglas may have taken interest in seeing J.J. Astor standing in A deck along with Harry Widener and others.

Boxhall (2): "When I was lowered away I

was the last boat but one on the port side. There was one of the lifeboats lowered away after I left, a few minutes after I left, and then there were no more boats hanging in the davits on the port side."

When the boat reached the surface, there was the same sigh of relief expressed over a dozen times already that night in previous boats. And, as happened many times that night, lifeboat 2 could not get free of the ropes easily.

Mrs. Douglas (2): "Mr. Boxhall had difficulty about getting the boat loose and called for a knife. We finally were launched. Mrs. Appleton and a man from the steerage faced me. Mrs. Appleton's sister's back was to me and on the seat with her, the officer. Mr. Boxhall tried to have us count in order to find the number in the boat, but he did not succeed in getting any higher than 10, as so many did not speak English. I think there were 18 or 20. There was one other member of the crew. The rowing was very difficult for no one knew how. I tried to steer, under Mr. Boxhall's orders, and he put the lantern—an old one with very little light in it—on a pole which I held up for some time. Mr. Boxhall got away from the ship and we stopped for a time. In an incredibly short space of time, it seemed to me, the boat sank."

Wilde sent lifeboat 2 down at 1:50 a.m. Watching from the bridge was the last gathering of an organization that had known each other for years: Captain Smith, Bruce Ismay, Purser McElroy, and Doctor O'Loughlin. These men were responsible for the well being of the passengers, and they were painfully aware now that the *Titanic* was about to dump the majority of them into the icy cold Atlantic in the middle of the night. No one knows what they spoke about as the water swirled over the well deck below the bridge.

Smith: "Did he [Captain Smith] have a personal waiter or steward of his own?"
Ray: "Yes, sir. A man named Phainten. He was last seen on the bridge, standing by the captain."

Ismay was keeping his eyes on collapsible C. As he watched lifeboat 2 go down with only 18 to 20 people, he may have been thinking about his upcoming options.

While lifeboat 2 had been loading, passengers were awkwardly passing through the promenade windows into number 4 under Lightoller's supervision.

Lightoller: "I might say that previous to putting this Berton boat (collapsible D) out we had lowered a boat from A deck one deck down below. That was through my fault. It was the first boat I had lowered. I was intending to put the passengers in from A deck. On lowering it down I found the windows were closed. So I sent someone down to open the windows and carried on with the other boats, but decided it was not worth while lowering them down, that I could manage just as well from the boat deck. When I came forward from the other boats, I loaded that boat from A deck by getting the women out through the windows. My idea in filling the boats there was because there was a wire hawser running along the side of the ship for coaling purposes, and it was handy to tie the boat in to, to hold it so that nobody could drop between the side of the boat and the ship."

Passengers who had been herded down from the boat deck walked down the narrow and steep steps of the crew's staircase to A deck. They stepped through a steel doorway out onto the open forward deck area, turned to their left, and proceeded in through the door to the enclosed promenade deck. There, about 20 feet ahead of them, they saw Lightoller helping passengers through the windows into the darkness outside. Archibald Gracie and Clinch Smith were on the perimeter of the crowd, trying to help. The scene could not have been a welcoming one for these new arrivals.

Mrs. Ryerson (4): "We saw people getting into boats, but waited our turn. There was a rough sort of steps constructed to get up to the window. My boy, Jack, was with me. An officer at the window said, 'That boy can't go.' My husband stepped forward and said, 'Of course that boy goes with his mother. He is only 13.' So they let him pass. They also said, 'No more boys.' I turned and kissed my husband and as we left he and the other men I knew—Mr. Thayer, Mr. Widener, and others—were all standing there together very quietly. The decks were lighted and as you went through the window it was as if you stepped out into the dark. We were flung into the boats. There were two men—an officer inside and a sailor outside—to help us. I fell on top of the women who were already in the boat, and scrambled to the bow with my eldest daughter. Miss Bowen and my boy were in the stern and my second daughter was in the middle of the boat with my maid. Mrs. Thayer, Mrs. Widener, Mrs. Astor, and Miss Eustis were the only others I knew on our boats."

Mrs. Stephenson (4): "On reaching the A deck we could see, for the decks were lighted by electricity, that a boat was lowered parallel to the windows. These were opened and a steamer chair put under the rail for us to step on. The ship had listed badly by that time and the boat hung far out from the side, so that some of the men said, 'No woman could step across that space.' A call was made for a ladder on one of the lower decks, but before it ever got there we were all in the boat."

Mr. Gracie: "Then I found my friend Smith, and on deck A, on the bow side, we worked together under the second officer in loading and helping the women and babies and children aboard the different boats. The only incident I remember in particular at this point is when Mrs. Astor was put in the boat. She was lifted up through the window and her husband helped her on the other side, and when she got in her husband was on one side of this window and I was on the other side at the next window. I heard Mr. Astor ask the second officer whether he would not be allowed to go aboard this boat to protect his wife. I think it was on account of the condition of his wife. He said, 'No, sir. No man is allowed on this boat or any of the boats until the ladies are off.' Mr. Astor then said, 'Well tell me what is the number of this boat so I may find her afterwards,' or words to that effect. The answer came back, '4.'"

Mrs. Stephenson (4): "I remember seeing

Colonel Astor, who called, 'Good bye,' and said he would follow in another boat, asking the number of our boat, which they said was number 4. In going through the window I was obliged to throw back the steamer rug, for, with my fur coat and huge cork life preserver, I was very clumsy."

When lifeboat 2 reached the water at 1:45 a.m., Wilde walked over to the next set of davits and leaned over the edge of the deck to peer down onto lifeboat 4. He still needed to get collapsible C in the water on the starboard side and did not have time to individually count the heads below.

Mrs. Ryerson: "Presently an officer called out from the upper deck, 'How many women are there in that boat?' Someone answered, "Twenty four.' 'That's enough. Lower away.'"

Wilde assisted with letting out the ropes while Lightoller walked forward down the promenade deck and climbed the crew staircase. Gracie and Clinch Smith followed along.

Mr. Gracie: "Then we went to the boat deck, which was the deck above."

The ship felt very strange with its list

to port. As he arrived up on deck, lifeboat 4 was on its way down to the water. Once again, one of the lifeboats angled to such an extent during its descent that passengers worried they would be dumped into the water below.

Mrs. Ryerson (4): "The ropes seemed to stick at one end and the boat tipped. Someone called for a knife, but it was not needed until we got into the water, as it was but a short distance and I then realized for the first time how far the ship had sunk."

When number 4 reached the water, Wilde finished with the ropes and issued an order before heading for collapsible C.

Lightoller: "When the ship was taking a heavy list—not a heavy list, but she was taking a list over to port, the order was called, I think, by the chief officer, 'Everyone on the starboard side to straighten her up,' which I repeated."

It was 1:50 a.m. Lightoller worked at preparing collapsible D and Wilde went over to load collapsible C. Following him were hundreds of passengers. A number of them must have chosen the door to the officers' quarters and wireless cabin as a shortcut to the other side.

Bride: *"The officers' quarters were situated together with the Marconi cabin, the officers room and other places, and the people were running around through these cabins. We had a woman in our cabin who had fainted. And we were giving her a glass of water there and a chair. We set her down on a chair, which she wanted badly, and then her husband took her away again."*

In the middle of all of this, Phillips was sending a message which would ultimately be the last one heard by the *Carpathia*. The power feeding the transmitter was weakening and the reach of her radio signal gradually faded. Cottam concentrated to hear the signal.

Cottam: *"The last one was, 'Come quick. Our engine room is filling up to the boilers.'"*
Smith: *"That was the last communication you received?"*
Cottam: *"Yes, sir."*
Smith: *"Did you make any reply to it?"*
Cottam: *"I acknowledged the message and reported it to the captain."*

Cottam rushed to the captain with the latest dramatic news. It must have been a heavy burden for Captain Rostron to be racing through dangerous waters in the middle of the night for a ship that might not hold on. Rostron instructed Cottam to send a reply of encouragement.

Smith: *"I thought I understood the captain to say that one of the last messages told the sinking ship that they were within a certain distance and coming hard, or coming fast."*
Cottam: *"I called him with that message, but I got no acknowledgment."*
Smith: *"We would like to know about that. Just tell what it was."*
Cottam: *"The captain told me to tell the Titanic that all our boats were ready and we were coming as hard as we could come, with a double watch on in the engine room, and to be prepared, when we got there, with the lifeboats. I got no acknowledgment of that message."*

The *Titanic* continued to settle and water climbed across the well deck, first on the port side, then washing over the wooden deck planking toward starboard. In the water, the lifeboats watched as they rowed away. Most were heading for the ship on the horizon at the time.

Osman (2): *"We saw a light but the other boats were making for it and the officer was not sure whether it was a light or whether it was not . . ."*
Burton: *"Did you see the light?"*

Osman: *"Yes, sir. I thought it was a sailing vessel from the banks."*
Burton: *"What do you think about it? Did it sail away?"*
Osman: *"Yes, sir. She sailed right away."*

Mr. Stengel (1): *"I think between Sir Duff Gordon and myself we decided which way to go. We followed a light that was to the bow of the boat, which looked like in the winter, in the dead of winter, when the windows are frosted with a light coming through them. It was in a haze. Most of the boats rowed toward that light, and after the green lights began to burn I suggested it was better to turn around and go toward the green lights, because I presumed there was an officer of the ship in that boat and he evidently knew his business."*

Mrs. Warren (5): *"We were pulled quite a distance away and then rested, watching the rockets in terrible anxiety and realizing that the vessel was rapidly sinking, bow first."*

Mr. Harder (5): *"At any rate, we were afraid of the suction. So the passengers said, 'Let us row out a little farther. So they rowed out farther, perhaps about a half a mile. It may have been three quarters of a mile. There we waited.."*

Mr. McGough (7): *"But after realizing that*

the Titanic was really sinking, we rowed away for about half a mile, being afraid that the suction would draw us down."

Smith: "You then pulled for that light, and finally discovered you were making no progress toward it?"
Hichens (6): "Yes, sir."
Smith: "And you stopped?"
Hichens: "We stopped then. Yes, sir."
Smith: "And at that time you were a mile away from the Titanic?"
Hichens: "Yes, sir. A mile or more, sir."
Smith: "And was the Titanic still afloat?"
Hichens: "The Titanic was still afloat, sir, and her lights all showing."

Clench (12): "We got the boat out, I suppose, a quarter of a mile away from the ship. Then we laid on our oars and stood by, and all stopped together. Then we rested on our oars. According to orders."

Archer (16): "We rowed, I should say, a quarter of a mile away from the ship and we remained there. We stood by the ship. We would not go right away from it. To tell you the truth, I did not think the ship would go down. I thought we might go back to her again afterwards."

Mrs. Futrelle (16): "Lower and lower the Titanic sunk into the sea. We prayed during those few minutes when the boat was settling. We could see the last of the two collapsibles putting away from the steamer. The water by this time was so close to the upper deck that it was hardly necessary to lower the boat. I tried to shut my eyes but I could not. There was a horrible fascination about it. The ocean was aflame with the gleaming phosphorus which looked like a million little spirits of light dancing their way to the horizon.

Meanwhile, lifeboat 4 languished by the side of the Titanic as they worked at cutting the ropes to free themselves from the ship.

Mrs. Ryerson (4): "The deck we left was only about 20 feet from the sea. I could see all the portholes open and water washing in, and the decks still lighted. Then they called out, 'How many seamen have you,' and they answered, 'One.' 'That is not enough,' said the officer. 'I will send you another,' and he sent a sailor down the rope."

Perkis (4): "I lowered number 4 into the water, and left that boat and walked aft. And I came back and a man that was in the boat, one of the seamen that was in the boat at the time, sung out to me, 'We need another hand down here.' So I slid down the life line there from the davit into the boat."

Mrs. Stephenson (4): "When we reached the sea we found the ship badly listed, her nose well in so that there was water on the D deck, which we could plainly see as the boat was lighted and the ports on D deck were square instead of round. No lights could be found in our boat and the men had great difficulty in casting off the blocks as they did not know how they worked. My fear here was great, as she seemed to be going faster and faster and I dreaded lest we should be drawn in before we could cast off."

At 1:50 a.m. the remaining officers on board the Titanic took up new positions toward both sides of the forward boat deck for their last duties. Wilde arrived at collapsible C just about the same time that Murdoch and Moody arrived from the aft section of the boat deck, having recently sent away lifeboat number 10. Lightoller was at collapsible D. Captain Smith was walking back and forth to both sides.

Lifeboat C was originally stored under the emergency boat. After number 1 was lowered, the davits were reused to hook up C. At 1:50 a.m., Wilde started loading.

When lifeboat 10 shoved off from the side of the Titanic, it left behind a deck barren of lifeboats. The passengers migrated down the slope of the decks towards the last two boats near the bridge. Back at the stern well deck, third class men were still waiting. As the tilt grew, the crew there finally reconsidered. Perhaps Murdoch had a word with them once he finished with boat 10. Either way, the *Titanic* was about to be overrun by hundreds of passengers who had been kept toward the back of the ship.

By 1:55 a.m. collapsible C was filling with passengers and D was almost ready for loading. At first, it was relatively calm in the area. The officers were having trouble finding enough women and children to fill the boats. Within minutes, however, the crowds that had been congregating near the port boats 10 through 16 came down the deck. Hugh Woolner was near collapsible C at the time.

Mr. Woolner: "Then they eventually lowered all the wooden lifeboats on the port side, and then they got out a collapsible and hitched her onto the most forward davits."

As the hour came to a close, steerage women were climbing into C. Ismay and a friend of his, William Carter, stood nearby one of the davits, assisting. Ismay no doubt had his eye on this boat and probably felt apprehensive each time another seat was

Bruce Ismay. While helping with collapsible C, he kept a mindful eye on the empty seats still remaining.

taken. No matter, he continued to assist. Little did he know that hundreds of third class passengers had been released from the stern area and a rush for the boat was about to occur. Boxhall made an observation of the occupants he saw the following morning in collapsible C.

Smith: "Were there any women or children in the boat?"
Boxhall: "Yes, it was full of them."

Getting the collapsible boats set up in the davits required a lot of muscle power and time. While collapsible C was loading on the starboard side, the men were working on collapsible D. First, the tackle had to be hooked back up to the craft. Then, the boat had to be lifted over a mid wall that stood along the side of the deck.

Hemming: "After I had finished with the lamps, when I made my last journey they were turning out the port collapsible boat. I went and assisted Mr. Lightoller to get it out."

Hardy: ". . . and finally, I was working on deck until the last collapsible boat was launched. We launched the boat parallel with the ship's side, and Mr. Lightoller and myself, two sailors, and two firemen—the two sailors were rigging the poles and getting them in working order . . ."

Mr. Gracie: "It seemed to me it was rather a little bit more difficult than it should have been to launch the boats alongside the ship. I do not know the cause of that. I do not know whether it was on account of the newness of it all, the painting, or something of that sort. I know I had to use my muscle as best I could in trying to push those boats so as to get them over the gunwale. I refer to it in a general way, as to there being difficulty at that point in that way, in trying to lift them and push them over the gunwale. The crew seemed to resent my working with them, but they were very glad when I worked with them later on. Every opportunity I got to help, I helped."

Bright: "After we had finished firing the distress signals there were two boats left. I went and assisted to get out the starboard one, that is, the starboard collapsible boat. I was on the opposite of the deck to what that was. On the port side, right forward, close to the bridge. We got that one out and filled it up with passengers."

Sometime around 1:55 a.m., Lightoller started loading passengers into collapsible D. There was a recurring problem for Lightoller, though, and that was the lack of women and children to fill the boat.

Lightoller: "In the case of the last boat I got out, I had the utmost difficulty in finding women. It was the very last boat of all, after all the other boats were put out and we came forward to put out the collapsible boats . . . so we rounded up the tackles and got the collapsible boat to put that over. Then I called for women and could not get hold of any. Somebody said, 'There are no women.'"

Mr. Gracie: "We had now loaded all the women who were in sight at that quarter of the ship, and I ran along the deck with Clinch Smith on the port side some distance aft shouting, 'Are there any more women? Are there any more women?' On my return, there was a very palpable list to port as if the ship was about to topple over."

Lightoller was beginning to feel the crush of male passengers pressing forward toward the last boat on the port side. The fact that he was having trouble locating women beyond the crowd, combined with the serious list to port, prompted Lightoller to repeat a command that had already been issued by Smith and then Wilde five minutes earlier.

Mr. Gracie: "The deck was on a corresponding slant. 'All passengers to the starboard side,' was Lightoller's loud command, heard by all of us."

Wilde and Murdoch were in for a surprise when hundreds of passengers crossed over the raised deck area midship, and came marching down the starboard side toward collapsible C. They had been supervising the loading of C under relatively calm circumstances. But now, within a few minutes, the area swelled with desperate passengers and crew. To worsen matters, the crowd was about to increase on account of a surge of arriving steerage passengers, desparate for a seat in the last boat.

As the hour closed, third class passengers were advised that everyone, including men, could go up to the boat deck. The gate was opened and men poured through. Families who would not separate from each other also went up. Hundreds rushed for the boats, climbing the deck ladders or heading for the second class stairs. Others ventured further into the ship, entering first class.

Mr. Abelseth: "We stayed a little while longer, and then they said, 'Everybody.' I do not know who that was, but I think it was some of the officers that said it. I could not say that but it was somebody that said, 'Everybody.' We went up."

The Titanic was going through a metamorphosis of sorts in the eyes of those in the lifeboats. When the last row of C deck lights in the bow approached the surface, the Titanic did not look good. But now, when those same lights actually dipped beneath the surface, extinguishing almost 200 feet of the Titanic within moments, the liner suddenly looked much worse—like she was going to sink. As the occupants of the lifeboats gazed upon the eerie sight, some must have wondered to themselves if this whole thing could really happening.

Captain Smith

Despite the fact that he was ultimately responsible for the safety of the *Titanic* on her maiden passage, Captain Edward J. Smith was held up as a hero shortly after the tragedy. As the man who went down with his ship, he was seen as someone who took responsibility for his own actions, serving as a symbol of cool, calculating courage. In firm command to the end, one account has him shouting to people on the plunging deck, "Be British!"

In recent times, Smith has come under increasing scrutiny. Failing to tell most of his officers that the ship was actually sinking, then needing to be prodded into issuing the order to lower the lifeboats, Smith has sometimes been portrayed as lapsing into a dazed state, incapable of making decisions or providing real leadership.

There are a number of credible eyewitness accounts of his behavior in the early hours of April 15 that provide ample light on the state of his mind and his leadership. Although referenced in other places in this book, they are strung together here to provide a focus on the man who shouldered the largest responsibility that night. Which was the real Captain Smith? You decide.

Bride (12:10): "He said, 'You had better get assistance.' When Mr. Phillips heard him he came out and asked him if he wanted to use a distress call. He said, 'Yes; at once.'"

Mrs. Bishop (12:10): "After being there about five or ten minutes one of the men we were with ran up and spoke to the captain who was just then coming down the stairs. The captain told him something in an undertone."

Mrs. White (12:10): "Nothing had been said about the lifeboats in any way, when suddenly Captain Smith came down the stairway and ordered us all to put on our life preservers, which we did."

Ismay (12:15): "I heard Captain Smith give the order when I was on the bridge. I know I heard him give the order to lower the boats. I think that is all he said. I think he simply turned around and gave the order."

Pitman (12:15): "So I went to the bridge and saw Captain Smith, and I told him that I thought it was Mr. Ismay that wished me to get the boat away with women and children in it. So he said, 'Go ahead. Carry on.'"

Boxhall (12:15): ". . . then went in and worked the position out. I submitted her position to the captain. He said, 'Take it to the Marconi room.'"

Bride (12:25): "Mr Phillips told me. He told me to go to the captain and report the Frankfurt. He was on the boat deck. Being the decks where the boats are. He wanted to know where she was. [Her latitude] and longitude. I told him we would get that as soon as we could."

Mr. Woolner (12:35): "He said, 'I want all

the passengers to go down on A deck, because I intend they shall go into the boats from A deck.' I remembered noticing as I came up that all those glass windows were raised to the very top and I went up to the captain and saluted him and said, 'Haven't you forgotten sir, that all those glass windows are closed?' He said, 'By God, you are right. Call those people back.'"

Mrs. Stephenson (12:35): "Miss Eustis and I took each other's hands not to be separated in the crowd, and all went on deck, we following close to Mrs. Thayer and her maid and going up narrow iron stairs to the forward boat deck, which on the Titanic was the captain's bridge. At the top of the stairs, we found Captain Smith looking much worried and anxiously waiting to get down after we got up."

Lightoller (12:35): "When I asked him, 'Shall I put the women and children in the boats?' he replied, 'Yes; and lower away.'"

Crawford (12:50): After that Captain Smith came to the boat and asked how many men were in the boat. He gave me orders to ship the rowlocks and to pull for a light. Captain Smith could see the light quite plain, as he pointed in the direction that we were to make for. Captain Smith and the steward

lowered the forward falls of the boat I was in."

Mr. Peuchen (12:55): "He was doing everything in his power to get women in these boats, and to see that they were lowered properly. I thought he was doing his duty in regard to the lowering of the boats."

Mr. Woolner (1:00): "It was not filled, but a great many people got into it, and finally it was quietly and orderly lowered away. The captain was close by at that time. He sort of ordered the people in. He said, 'Come along, madam,' and that sort of thing."

Mrs. Smith (1:00): "In the meantime Captain Smith was standing with a megaphone on deck. I approached him and told him I was alone and asked if my husband might be allowed to go in the boat with me. He ignored me personally, but shouted again through his megaphone, 'Women and children first.'"

Mr. Peuchen (1:00): "After that the boat was lowered down some distance, I should imagine probably parallel with C deck, when the quartermaster called up to the officer and said, 'I cannot manage this boat with only one seaman. The captain was standing still by him at that time, and I think,

although the officer ordered me to the boat, the captain said, 'You had better go down below and break a window and get in through a window into the boat.' That was his suggestion and I said I did not think it was feasible, and I said I could get in the boat if I could get hold of a rope."

Bride (1:05): "She [Carpathia] turned around and was steaming full speed, or words to that effect. It was taken to the captain. He was in the wheelhouse. He came back with me to the cabin. He asked Mr. Phillips what other ships he was in communication with. He interrupted Mr. Phillips when Mr. Phillips was establishing communication with the Olympic, so he was told the Olympic was there. He worked out the difference between the Carpathia's position and ours. He roughly estimated it. He went out of the cabin then . . ."

Boxhall (1:10): "I told the captain about the ship and he was with me most of the time when we were signaling. I went over and started the Morse signal. He said, 'Tell him to come at once, we are sinking.'"

Evans (1:15): "He came to the starboard action boat that I was lowering. He passed some remark to a tall military gentleman there with white spats on, but what it was I *could not say, as I was attending to the fall."*

Symons (1:15): "The last I saw of him he was on the bridge. That was just before I went away in boat number 1."

Hardy (1:30): "He was superintending the rockets, calling out to the quartermaster about the rockets."

Mrs. Douglas (1:35): "Just before we got into the boat the captain called, 'How many of the crew are in that boat? Get out of there, every man of you,' and I can see a solid row of men from bow to stern, crawl over onto the deck."

Boxhall (1:40): "The captain was standing by this emergency boat. He was standing by the wheelhouse door, just abreast of this boat; supervising the boats being loaded, I think. Supervising passengers being put into the boat. He told me I had to get into that boat and go away.

Rowe (1:40): "I asked Captain Smith if I should fire anymore and he said, 'No. Get into that boat.'"

Mrs. Douglas (1:45): "Mr. Boxhall was trying to get the boat off, and called to the captain on the bridge, 'There's a boat coming up over there.' The captain said, 'I want a megaphone.'

Hardy (2:00): "He walked on the deck, watching the filling of the boats. That is the last thing I saw of him."

Bride (2:05): "He came along in a very short period afterwards and told us we had better look out for ourselves. He came around to the cabin to tell us."

Hemming (2:10): "The last time I saw the captain was just as I was coming down off the house. The captain was there, and he sung out, 'Everyone over to the starboard side to keep the ship up as long as possible.' He was by himself when I saw him last."

Lightoller (2:10): "I think the bridge was the last place I saw him. I am not sure. I think he was crossing the bridge. I merely recognized a glimpse. Just walking straight across, as if he had some object that he was walking toward; from starboard to port."

Bride (2:15): "He jumped overboard from the bridge when we were launching the collapsible lifeboat. It would be about five minutes before the boat sank."

Once the accident occurred, the deci-

sions facing Captain Smith were difficult, but were grounded in some logic. Right or wrong, his decision to downplay the extent of the danger on board during the evacuation was a calculation to avoid a panic. Having to be prodded by Lightoller and Pitman to begin loading the boats seems to be a minor offense considering that he was busy on the bridge at the time and issued a decisive response to their inquiries. His decision to remain near the bridge even as the crowds moved aft during the lowering of the lifeboats also seems logical. If the captain was needed by anyone, they knew where they could find him. From the bridge, he maintained a level of control over the unfolding chaos in an age where cellular phones or other portable communication devices did not exist. In addition, Captain Smith appears to have properly prioritized things by devoting most of his time to Boxhall's attempts to gain the attention of the ship on the horizon. It was, after all, his only remaining chance at saving everyone on board.

Mistakes were made during that voyage which are now easy to see in hindsight. But through all the errors and the consequences they produced, there is little evidence to suggest that Edward J. Smith ever lost his edge during an awful situation where few would fare better.

Two O'Clock

From the bridge, the bow of a ship is a significant part of the view, reaching forward with its vast expanse of deck, masts, cargo holds, cables and cranes. It is a symbol of strength and purpose, pointing the way through seemingly endless miles of ocean to the ship's ultimate destination. At 2:00 a.m., the bow of the *Titanic* quietly slipped beneath the water with barely a ripple, under the fretful eyes of Captain Smith. Hours ago, the bow of the *Titanic* was pointing toward New York. Now it was pointing to the bottom of the Atlantic.

Once the bow disappeared, the *Titanic*'s tilt shifted dramatically. Before, the two hundred feet of bow area provided a significant buoyancy at the forward end. But now, that same area was submerged, and instead of helping to keep the ship afloat, it was dead weight. The *Titanic* underwent a shift in her center of balance. Standing on the starboard side, forward, Jack Thayer and Milton Long detected the change.

Mr. Thayer: "Long and I debated whether or not we should fight our way into one of the last two boats. We could almost see the ship slowly going down by the head."

The routine on the *Titanic* changed. Previously, the officers were focused on the hard work of loading one lifeboat after another. For the last hour and a half, when they finished with one boat, there was always another after it. Now, Lightoller and Wilde found themselves supervising the last boat on their respective sides of the deck.

Captain Smith, Purser McElroy, and Doctor O'Loughlin were still on the bridge. With 1,500 people in their care and the bow of the *Titanic* under water, they were concerned about the latest news from the wireless room. McElroy probably questioned the captain about what to do with the contents of the safes, apparently electing not to place them in the remaining two boats.

Lightoller: "It was obvious to me that everything with regard to their duty had been done by the mere fact that shortly before the vessel sank I met a purser, Mr. McElroy, Mr. Barker, Dr. O'Loughlin and Dr. Simpson, and the four assistants. They were just coming from the direction of the bridge."

Most of the passengers crowding around collapsible D moved to the starboard side in response to orders. Upon their departure, Lightoller stationed crew near the raised deck amidship to prevent men from crossing back over to port. Hugh Woolner was one of the passengers who followed orders and crossed over to collapsible C.

Mr. Woolner: "... and they filled that up [collapsible D], *mostly with steerage women and children and one seaman, and a steward, and I think one other man—but I am not quite certain about that—and when that boat seemed to be quite full, and was ready to be swung over the side and was to be lowered away, I said to Steffanson, 'There is nothing more for us to do here.' We went across there because we heard a certain kind of shouting going on . . ."*

The scene on the starboard side near the bridge turned dramatic. The area had quickly taken on the characteristics of the earlier loading of boat number 14—but in an even worse way. Hundreds pressed forward there for a seat in the last lifeboat. Wilde, Murdoch, Ismay, and Moody were besieged just as they were getting ready to lower away.

Along with the onslaught of men came steerage women as well. Wilde held collapsible C a little longer in order to get the new arrivals safely aboard. Murdoch stood inside the collapsible and helped them into it. But it was not easy. The crowd was becoming dangerous. Men were lunging into the boat as it hung from the davits. Some of the women were stuck toward the back of the crowd with little hope of getting through the claustrophobic mob. Something

Sometime around 2:00 a.m. the gate at the top of the stairs, seen here in the center, was opened and all steerage passengers were allowed up. A swarm of people rushed for the only two remaining boats in the davits —collapsibles C and D. (*Olympic*)

drastic had to be done to get the situation under control. Murdoch had seen the effectiveness of a gun in controlling the unruly mobs at lifeboat 14. Standing in the collapsible as it hung level with the rail, elevated above the surging crowd, he raised his gun into the air and fired.

Mr. Woolner: "There was a sort of scramble on the starboard side, and I looked around and I saw two flashes of a pistol in the air. We went across there because we heard a certain kind of shouting going on, and just as we got around the corner I saw these two flashes of the pistol, and Steffanson and I went up to help to clear that boat of the men who were climbing in, because there was a bunch of women—I think Italians and foreigners—who were standing on the outside of the crowd, unable to make their way toward the side of the boat. So we helped the officer to pull these men out, by their legs and anything we could get hold of. But they were really flying before Mr. Murdoch from inside of the boat at the time. I think they were probably third class passengers. It was awfully difficult to notice very carefully. I got hold of them by their feet and legs. Then they cleared out, practically all the men, out of that boat, and then we lifted in these Italian women, hoisted them up on each side and put them into the boat. They were very limp. They had not much spring in them at all. Then that boat was finally filled up and swung out . . ."

In the rush and confusion, several men managed to scramble underneath the seats of the boat and hide in the shadows from sight.

Rowe (C): "39 all told. When daylight broke we found four men, Chinamen, I think they were, or Filipinos. They came up between the seats."

The stowaways that could be seen were pulled out. It is possible the officers decided not to bother with the rest hiding under the seats. It was probably not worth the amount of time it would take to pull each and every one of them out while they clung to the planks of the boat.

Archer (16): "I heard a couple of explosions. I should say they would be about 20 minutes between each explosion. From the time I heard the first one until I heard the second one it would be about 20 minutes, sir."

Brice (11): "I heard two rumbling noises. She was well down."
Bourne: "How far apart in time, probably, were the two explosions?"
Brice: "From eight to 10 minutes."
Bourne: "When the first explosion occurred, were the lights out?"
Brice: "The lights were still on in the after end of the ship after the first and second explosions."

Ismay must have been in a panic himself. Earlier, when this area of the deck was just about deserted, he realized he could probably get away in boat C, and informed a nearby acquaintance, William Carter. But things changed. He did not anticipate the appearance of such a desperate crowd. Despite the scores of steerage men pressing forward in hopes of a seat, Ismay listened to his instincts. As Wilde ordered the boat lowered, Ismay, with Carter in tow, followed through with his escape plan anyway.

Smith: "Who, if anyone, told you to enter that lifeboat?"
Ismay (C): "No one, sir."
Smith: "Why did you enter it?"
Ismay: "Because there is room in the boat. She was being lowered away. I felt the ship was going down, and I got into the boat."

Rowe (C): "I assisted six—three women and three children. The order was then given to lower the boat. The chief officer wanted to know if there were more women and children. There were none in the vicinity. Two gentlemen passengers got in. The boat was then lowered. When Chief Officer Wilde asked if there was any more women and children there was no reply. So Mr. Ismay came aboard the boat."

As Ismay descended into infamy, the *Titanic*'s lean to port presented collapsible C with a serious logistical problem.

Rowe (C): "She did not list, so far as I know, until the time when my boat was lowered. Then she listed to port. She listed about five or 6 degrees. All the time my boat was being lowered the rubbing strake kept on catching on the rivets down the ship's side, and it was as much as we could do to keep her off. When we left the ship the fore well deck was awash, that is when we pushed off from the ship. When the boat was in the water, the well deck was submerged. It took us a good five minutes to lower the boat on account of this rubbing going down. When we reached the water we steered for a light in sight, roughly five miles. We pulled away for about three quarters of a mile, when the ship sank."

Ismay (C): "The ship had quite a list to port. Consequently this canvas boat, this collapsible boat, was getting hung up on the outside of the ship, and she had to rub right along her, and we had to try to shove her out, and we had to get the women to help to shove to get her clear of the ship."

On the port side, lifeboat 4 freed themselves at last and were ready to pull away from the ship when an order came down from above.

Mrs. Stephenson (4): "When we were finally ready to move, the order was called from the deck to go to the stern hatch and take off some men."

Mrs. Ryerson (4): "In a few minutes after, several other men, not sailors, came down the ropes over the davits and dropped into our boat. The order was given to pull away."

By now there were seventeen boats drifting on the water. Some remained pretty close to the ship while others were so worried about the suction at the end that they rowed as far away as they could get. Many boats rowed for the light on the horizon.

Miss Mulvihill (10): "The Titanic was going down slowly, yet surely. I had marked in my mind's eye two portholes on the vessel. I watched the water come to them, pass them and swallow them up from sight. I was fascinated."

Hichens (6): "We were all together. We were looking at each other's lights. We all had lights and were showing them to one another . . . but before the Titanic sank we were all pulling for a light which we thought was to be a cod banker. We all made for this light."

Boxhall (2): "I pulled around the ship's stern and was intending to go alongside, and tried to see if I could get alongside of the ship again. I reckoned I could take about three more people off the boat with safety. I did it of my own accord. I was in charge of the boat. I kept a little distance off the ship . . . probably a hundred yards or so . . . when I got so close as that I thought it was wiser not to go any closer . . . because there was only one man who understood my orders as to how to handle a boat. I think there was a little suction. The boat seemed to be drawn closer to the ship. I think, myself, that there was more suction while the ship was settling bodily. I think there was more suction then than there was when she actually went down, because I pulled some distance off then."

Jones (8): "I pulled for the light, and I found that I could not get near the light, and I stood by for a little while. I wanted to return to the ship, but the ladies were frightened, and I had to carry out the captain's orders and pull for that light. So I did so."

Crawford (8): "He [Captain Smith] told us to row for the light and to land the people there and come back to the ship. We pulled until daybreak and we could not catch the ship. There were two lights. I should say it

was not farther than 10 miles. They were stationary masthead lights, one on the fore and one on the main. Everybody saw them –all the ladies in the boat. They asked if we were drawing nearer to the steamer, but we could not seem to make any headway . . ."

Newlands: "How far could you see on the water that night? How far off could you see another boat?"
Taylor (15): "About 50 yards. We could see the boats."
Newlands: "In which direction was that light?"
Taylor: "I could not tell you the directions."
Newlands: "But all the boats were rowing for it?"
Taylor: "Yes, sir."

Mrs. White (8): "Oh, it was 10 miles away, but we could see it distinctly. There was no doubt but that it was a boat. But we rowed and rowed and rowed and then we all suggested that it was simply impossible for us to get to it."

Buley (10): ". . . and we all started for the same light, and that is what kept the boats together."

Lifeboat 14 was an exception. After Lowe managed to get away from the ship, he apparently felt the worst was over. It was

Lowe who laughed as Henry Stengel stumbled into lifeboat 1 an hour earlier and now that lifeboat 14 was safely lowered, his spirits picked up again. For the time being, he kept lifeboat 14 stationary and isolated from the other boats in the water. If Daisy Minahan's observation is accurate, he clearly did not realize the fate that awaited the *Titanic* and the 1,500 souls still on her.

Miss Minahan (14): "The officer, whose name I learned afterwards to be Lowe, was continually making remarks such as, 'A good song to sing would be 'Throw Out the Life Line,' and 'I think the best thing for you women to do is to take a nap.' The Titanic was fast sinking."

Some of the passengers with excellent night vision began to see shadowy shapes of ice off in the distance once they were away in the lifeboats.

Mrs. Collyer (14): "It was then that I saw for the first time the iceberg that had done such terrible damage. It loomed up in the clear starlight, a bluish white mountain, quite near to us. Two other icebergs lay quite close together, like twin peaks. Later I thought I saw three or four more, but I cannot be sure. Loose ice was floating in the water. It was very cold. We had gone per-

haps half a mile when the officer ordered the men to cease rowing."

Miss Mulvihill (10): "We pushed off among the ice cakes. It was a beautiful starry night. You could see the poor Titanic sinking. She was surely going down. The women in the boats were screaming. They cried for their husbands. Every once in a while a cake of ice would crash into our boat."

Moore (3): "All the people in the boat wanted to get clear of the ship. They did not want to go near her. They kept urging me to keep away, to pull away from her. In fact, they wanted to get farther away. We started to pull away in the boat. There was one bright light away on the starboard bow, 2 or 3 miles away, I should judge."
Newlands: "And you rowed for that light?"
Moore: "Yes, sir. While we were rowing, we came on small ice. You could see small ice in the distance."
Newlands: "That night? Before dawn?"
Moore: "Yes. We got away from it."
Newlands: "When you looked out that night after you struck, did you see any iceberg?"
Moore: "I never saw any ice at all until after we got away in the boat."
Newlands: "Did you see very much then?"
Moore: "No, sir. It did not look like much."
Newlands: "Was it high?"

Moore: "No, sir. It was low."

Fletcher: "Did you keep about the same distance from her until she went down?"
Ward (9): "Yes, sir, until Haines thought she was going down. He was rather afraid of suction and he gave orders to pull away, which we did. We pulled as hard as we could and we increased our distance to about a quarter of a mile."

Crowe (14): "After getting into the water we pushed out to the other boats. Fifth Officer Lowe suggested standing by in case of any necessity for us to do so. His idea was to stand by in case of an emergency, that is, anybody coming over the sides, with the idea of picking them up. We did not keep time or anything like that, but I should imagine when we transferred our people was when we discovered the amount of water that was in the boat, because just prior to getting to the other boat a lady stated that there was some water coming over her ankles and two men and this lady—I believe the lady—assisted in bailing it out with bails that were kept in the boat for that purpose."

Andrews (16) "On our way out we came in contact with another boat and stood by. The remark was passed by someone in the boat to go back but as the two boats were full, we stood at a distance away."

Bourne: *"Who passed the remark to go back?"*

Andrews: *"One of the passengers, sir. The boats were full, sir."*

Ray (13): *"We had got about three quarters of a mile, I suppose, to a mile, so far as I could judge."*

All of the lifeboats managed to get free of the davit ropes in one manner or another within several minutes of reaching the water; all, that is, except for boat 4. They had been lowered sometime around 1:50 a.m. and it was shortly after 2 a.m. that they finally freed themselves.

Mrs. Ryerson (4): *"Then they rowed off – the sailors, the women, anyone – but made little progress. There was a confusion of orders. We rowed toward the stern. Someone shouted something about a gangway and no one seemed to know what to do. Barrels and chairs were being thrown overboard."*

Joughin: *"I went down to my room and had a drop of liquor, and after speaking to the old doctor I went up again on deck and saw that all the boats had gone. I went down to B deck and threw some deck chairs overboard. I was looking out for something to cling to. I threw about 50 overboard."*

Captain Smith now stood on deck for the last few minutes of his command.

Hardy: *"He walked on the deck, watching the filling of the boats. That is the last thing I saw of him."*

Hemming: *"After the boat [D] was out I went on top of the officers' house and helped to clear away the port collapsible boat on that house. The last time I saw the captain was just as I was coming down off the house. The captain was there, and he sung out, 'Everyone over to the starboard side to keep the ship up as long as possible.' He was by himself when I saw him last."*

Jane Hoyt was one of the occupants of collapsible D. Her husband, Frederick spoke with the captain about his options.

Mr. Hoyt: *"I knew Captain Smith for over fifteen years. Our conversation that night amounted to little or nothing. I simply sympathized with him on the accident; but at that time, as I then never expected to be saved, I did not want to bother him with questions, as I knew he had all he wanted to think of. He did suggest that I go down to A deck and see if there were not a boat alongside."*

It was approximately 2:05 a.m. and

the water was lapping against the B deck windows directly beneath collapsible D. Even with the water so close, Lightoller still refused to allow any of the men into the numerous empty seats, and held out for any late arrivals of women and children.

Lightoller: *"On the port side on deck, I can say, as far as my own observations went, from my own endeavor and that of others to obtain women, there were none."*

While he waited, scores of steerage passengers arrived from the stern. These passengers had obeyed earlier orders from the crew and waited on the aft well and poop decks during most of the night. Now that they were up on the boat deck, all they saw were a string of empty lifeboat davits. They were gone – all of them except this last boat near the bridge.

Mr. Gracie: *"When we were loading the last boat, just a short time before it was fully loaded, a palpable list toward the port side began, and the officer called out, 'All passengers to the starboard side,' and Smith and myself went to the starboard side, still at the bow of the ship. Then we went to the starboard side. On the starboard side, to my surprise, I found there were ladies still there, and Mrs. Browne and Miss Evans* particularly, the ones whom I supposed had been loaded into a boat from A deck below, about three quarters of an hour before."

Smith: "Were there many people on the boat deck at the time?"
Hemming: "I could not tell you. A good many."

While Gracie spoke with Caroline Browne and Edith Evans, the scene was getting ugly on the port side where he had just left. The steerage passengers pressed for a seat in the last boat. Some broke through the crowds and forced their way into them. Just like a few minutes earlier at collapsible C, Lightoller was beginning to lose control of the situation. And there was certainly no time left for this type of a struggle.

Mr. Abelseth: "We went over to the port side of the ship . . . We were standing there looking at them lowering this boat. We could see them, some of the crew helping take the ladies in their arms and throwing them into the lifeboats."

Lightoller: "I filled it with 15 or 20 eventually mustered up. It took longer to fill that boat than it did any other boat, notwithstanding that the others had more in them. On two occasions the men thought there were no more women and commenced to get in and then found one or two more and then got out again."

Since arriving from the forward well deck a little after midnight, Daniel Buckley had watched one lifeboat after another go away from the ship. Like many, he saw the last one and decided it was his last chance.

Mr. Buckley (D): "I was holding the ropes all the time, helping to let down the five lifeboats that went down first, as well as I could. When the sixth lifeboat was prepared, there was a big crowd of men standing on the deck. And they all jumped in. So I said I would take my chance with them. When they jumped, I said I would go too. I went into the boat. Then two officers came along and said all of the men could come out. And they brought a lot of steerage passengers with them. And they were mixed, every way, ladies and gentlemen. And they said all the men could get out and let the ladies in. But six men were left in the boat. I think they were firemen and sailors. I was crying. There was a woman in the boat, and she had thrown her shawl over me, and she told me to stay in there. The men that were in the boat at first fought and would not get out, but the officers drew their revolvers and fired shots over our heads and then the men got out."

Mr. Gracie: "As to what happened on the other side during our departure, the information I was given by the second officer was that some of the steerage passengers tried to rush the boat, and he fired off a pistol to make them get out, and they did get out."

Mrs. White (8): "I heard four distinct explosions, which we supposed were the boilers. Of course, we did not know anything about it. They were tremendous."

Mr. Gracie: "When I arrived on the other side, as I have said, there were these women and all of sudden I heard the cry that there was room for more women on the port side. So I grabbed by the arm these two ladies, Miss Evans and Mrs. Browne, and conducted them to the port side. But I did not get but half way, that is, directly at the bow, when the crew made what you might call a dead line, and said, 'No men are allowed beyond this line.' So I let the ladies go beyond and then about six ladies followed after the two that I had particular charge of."

Wilde returned to the scene now that he had just finished lowering collapsible C.

Hardy (D): ". . . and Mr. Lightoller and myself loaded the boat. When the boat was full, Mr. Lightoller was in the boat with me.

And the chief officer came along and asked if the boat was full, and he said yes. He said he would step out himself and make room for somebody else, and he stepped back on board the ship and asked if I could row. I told him I could and I went away in that boat. We lowered away and got to the water, and the ship was then at a heavy list to port by the time we commenced to lower away."

Mr. Buckley (D): "When the boat was ready, we were lowered down into the water and rowed away out from the steamer. We were only about 15 minutes out when she sank."

It was sometime between 2:05 and 2:10 when collapsible D lowered away. As it disappeared behind the rail, passengers were left with an empty boat deck. From the perspective of the officers working near the bridge, they succeeded in getting all the women off the ship. Some may have hoped that the men left on deck would be able to fend for themselves in the water until help arrived. But the hundred or so men standing on the forward boat deck was misleading. There were actually over 1,500 men, women, and even children still on board.

Lightoller: "He [Hemming] went from the port side to the starboard side of the deck, as I did, and after that, when she went under water forward, instead of taking to the water he walked aft the whole length of the boat deck previous to sliding down the aft fall on the port side, and in the whole length of the deck and in crossing the bridge he saw two women. They were standing amidships on the bridge perfectly still. They did not seem to be endeavoring to get to one side or the other to see if there were any boats or not. The whole length of the boat deck, so far as he went, he did not see any women."

Fletcher: "Where were all the passengers, these 1,600 people?"
Hardy (D): "They must have been between decks or on the deck below or on the other side of the ship. I cannot conceive where they were."

They had been held back at the stern. And even though they were finally told they could go up to the higher decks, that would take time – too much time for most steerage passengers. Meanwhile, boat D descended.

Mr. Woolner: "Then that boat [C] was finally filled up and swung out and then I said to Steffanson, 'There is nothing more for us to do. Let us go down onto A deck again.' And we went down again, but there was nobody there that time at all. It was perfectly empty the whole length. It was absolutely desert-

ed, and the electric lights along the ceiling of A deck were beginning to turn red, just a glow, a red sort of glow. So I said to Steffanson, 'This is getting rather a tight corner. I do not like being inside these closed windows. Let us go out through the door at the end.' And as we went out through the door the sea came in onto the deck at our feet."

Lightoller: "I lowered the last boat 10 feet and it was in the water."

A number of men saw the last two collapsibles go with empty seats and those with enough initiative decided there was one last chance. Woolner and Steffanson went down to the promenade deck directly along the path of collapsible D's descent.

Mr. Woolner (D): "Then we hopped up onto the gunwale preparing to jump out into the sea because if we had waited a minute longer we should have been boxed in against the ceiling. And as we looked out we saw this collapsible, the last boat on the port side, being lowered right in front of our faces. It was full up to the bow and I said to Steffanson, 'There is nobody in the bows. Let us make a jump for it. You go first,' and he jumped out and tumbled in head over heels into the bow, and I jumped too, and hit the gunwale with my chest which had on this life preserver, of course, and I sort of bounced off the gunwale and caught the gunwale with my fingers and slipped off backwards. As my legs dropped down I felt that they were in the sea."

Next, Frederick Hoyt jumped. But he did not jump into the boat. He jumped into the water before it was all the way down, and waited nearby to be picked up.

Mr. Hoyt (D): ". . . and it occurred to me that if I swam out and waited for her to shove off they would pick me up, which was what happened."

Hardy (D): "We picked up the husband of a wife that we had taken off in the load in the boat. The gentleman took to the water and climbed in the boat after we had lowered it."

Emilio Portalupi watched these two separate efforts from the port side of the boat deck with great interest. He watched as collapsible D pulled Hoyt into the boat and started to row away. It looked easy in one way, but it required a leap from the deck into the icy black water. It took some time to work up his courage.

Mr. Portalupi: "I finally made up my mind

that the ship was going down. I jumped into the water, hoping to make one of the lifeboats which were being lowered from the upper deck."

But in the moments it took Portalupi to decide whether he should swim after a boat, collapsible D had added distance between itself and the *Titanic*.

Mr. Woolner: "We got out three oars first and shoved off from the side of the ship. Then we got her head more or less straight-away, and then we pulled as hard as we could until, I should think, we were 150 yards away . . . "

Portalupi jumped into the ocean and the water stole his breath. By the time he got his wits and began to swim for the boat, it was too late. His plan had been foiled.

Mr. Portalupi: "The boat which I was making for was rowed rapidly away. I could not overhaul it."

Portalupi remained in the water in hopes of finding another boat. Back by the stern of the ship, lifeboat 4 had just given up its search for an open gangway door and headed away from the *Titanic* on the same side collapsible D was rowing.

At 2:10 a.m. the water climbed over the forward promenade deck and was just a few feet below the bridge. Attention was fixed on the two collapsible boats stored on the roof of the officers' quarters. On the starboard side, Murdoch and Moody set to work getting collapsible A down. It was slow going and the pressure on the officers must have been unbearable.

Mr. Abelseth: "We saw them lower this boat, and there were no more boats on the port side. So we walked over to the starboard side of the ship and just as we were standing there, one of the officers came up and he said just as he walked by, 'Are there any sailors here?' I did not say anything. I have been a fishing man for six years and, of course, this officer walked right by me and asked. I would have gone but my brother-in-law and my cousin said, in the Norwegian language, as we were speaking Norwegian, 'Let us stay here together.' I do not know, but I think the officer wanted some help to get some of these collapsible boats out. Then we stayed there, and we were just standing still there. We did not talk very much. Just a little ways from us I saw there was an old couple standing there on the deck and I heard this man say to the lady, 'Go into the lifeboat and get saved.' He put his hand on her shoulder and I think he said,

'Please get into the lifeboat and get saved.' She replied, 'No, let me stay with you.' I could not say who it was, but I saw that he was an old man. I did not pay much attention to him because I did no know him."

Mr. Gracie: "Meanwhile the crew were trying to launch a boat, a collapsible canvas boat as they call it, that was on the hurricane deck, or the bridge deck. This was let down from the bridge deck, and we tried to slide it along those oars that they put in there for that purpose. I may say that before this happened one of the men on the deck, when loosening this boat from the hurricane deck, called out, 'Is there any passenger who has a knife?' I said I had my penknife, if that would do, and I passed that up. There was no other boat at that time being lowered from the deck davits. Finally this boat came down on the deck. I do not know whether it was injured or not by the fall, but we were afraid that it had been injured. I had not noticed in the meantime that we were gradually sinking. I was engaged all the time in working, as I say at those davits, trying to work on the falls to let this boat down."

Time was just about up for the Titanic, and just about everyone on board realized it, especially those on the forward boat deck.

Bride: "When we had finished with the Frankfurt and we had thoroughly informed the Carpathia of our position, Mr. Phillips again went out to look and see how things were going outside. I tried to establish a communication with the Baltic, and it was not very satisfactory and I judged myself, from the strength of her signals, that she was too far away to do any good and it was not worth taking any trouble, and I told her we were sinking fast and there was no hope of saving the ship."

Phillips came back from his brief tour on deck with a cryptic observation.

Bride: "Mr. Phillips told me that things looked very queer outside. Beyond that I knew nothing."
Smith: "What did you do then, Mr. Bride?"
Bride: "Mr. Phillips sat down again at the telephones and gave a general call of CQD, but I think that our lamps were running down. We did not get a spark. We could not tell, because the spark of our wireless was in an enclosed room. We could not hear at any time whether it was sparking."

Power to the equipment was ebbing. The voice of the Titanic was fading fast.

Bride: "The motor and alternator that was working our wireless set were running when we left the cabin, 10 minutes before the ship went down."

Phillips and Bride were ready to get out of the wireless office, but waited for the captain to relieve them. While they waited, Phillips figured he would make the most of the time and continued sending signals.

Bride: "On Mr. Phillips' request I started to gather up his spare money and put on another coat, and made general preparations for leaving the ship."
Smith: "How did you expect to leave the ship?"
Bride: "We had to wait until the captain told us first."
Smith: "You had to wait until the captain told you?"
Bride: "Yes, sir. He came along in a very short period afterwards and told us we had better look out for ourselves."

After Lightoller saw collapsible D off, he started to head for the roof of the officers' quarters when he came across the pursers and doctors.

Lightoller: "They [the pursers and doctors] were evidently just keeping out of everybody's way. They were keeping away from the crowd so as not to interfere with the loading of the boats. McElroy, if I remember, was walking along with his hands in his pockets. The purser's assistant was coming behind with the ship's bag, showing that all detail work had been attended to. I think one of them had a roll of papers under his arm, showing that they had been attending to their detail work. That is why I draw the conclusion. They were perfectly quiet. They came up to me and just shook hands and said, 'Good-bye, old man.' We said good bye to each other, and that is all there was to it."

Richard Norris Williams, otherwise known as Dick, wandered about the decks with his father biding his time and waiting for events to play themselves out.

Mr. Williams: "It was a very peculiar feeling wandering around with the knowledge that all means of escape seemed cut off. Everything was still, although I would say very cheerful under the circumstances."

Meanwhile, everything was *not* still near collapsible A. The lifeboat was down from the roof of the officers' quarters and had been dragged across the deck to the same davits that held lifeboat C fifteen minutes earlier. But Wilde, Murdoch, and Moody were up against an impossible situa-

tion. The crowds swarming around the boat were making it very difficult to get it prepared for launching, and the water was now only a few feet from the deck. First they had raced to get the boat set up, but at some point changed their minds and decided it would be launched from the deck.

Hemming: ". . . I went over to the starboard side. The starboard collapsible boat had just been lowered. She was away from the ship. I rendered up the foremast fall, got the block on board and held onto the block while a man equalized the parts of the fall. He said, 'There is a futterfoot in the fall,' which fouls the fall and the block. I says, 'I have got it,' and took it out. I passed the block up to the officers' house and Mr. Moody, the sixth officer said, 'We don't want the block. We will leave the boat on deck.' I put the fall on the deck, stayed there a moment, and there was no chance of the boat being cleared away, and I went to the bridge and looked over and saw the water climbing upon the bridge."

With water so close to the starboard deck, some decided to put distance between themselves and the collapsible A crowds.

Mr. Gracie: "Mr. Smith and myself thought then that there was no more chance for us

there, there were so many people at that particular point, so we decided to go toward the stern, still on the starboard side, and as we were going toward the stern, to our surprise and consternation, up came from the decks below a mass of humanity, men and women, and we had thought that all the women were already loaded into the boats."

Sadly, at 2:15 a.m. some third class passengers were only just now arriving up on deck in search of a lifeboat. Some of the stewards were still helping them find their way up top.

Collins: ". . . I ran back to the deck, ran to the port side on the saloon deck with another steward and a woman and two children, and the steward had one of the children in his arms and the woman was crying. I took the child off of the woman and made for one of the boats [collapsible B]."

Others in third class never even tried to save themselves. They were waiting for their fates in the third class general room as if waiting for the arrival of a train.

Mr. Wennerstrom: "One of our friends, a man by the name of Johan Lundahl who had been home to the old country on a visit and was going back to the United States said to us, 'Good-bye friends; I'm too old to fight the Atlantic.' He went to the smoking room and there, on a chair, was waiting his last call. So did an English lady; she sat down by the piano and with her child on her knee, she played the piano until the Atlantic grave called them both."

With the list to port, the water came up the crew's emergency staircase on the port side and spilled down the deck toward the bridge–an unwelcome visitor.

Fletcher: "Do you know if any of the logs were saved?"
Pitman: "None, sir. We had something else to think of besides log books, sir."

With the bridge only moments from going under, Captain Smith decided there was nothing further the officers and crew could do. It was time to abandon ship.

Bride: "The last I saw of the captain he went overboard from the bridge. He jumped overboard from the bridge when we were launching the collapsible lifeboat . . . it would be just about five minutes before the boat sank."

Senior: "I had seen the captain on the bridge. He was walking up and down, and giving orders. When he shouted his last command the ship was sinking fast. While we were preparing to lower these [collapsibles] we heard the captain shout, 'Every man for himself.'"

Bride: "I now assisted in pushing off a collapsible lifeboat, which was on the port side of the forward funnel, onto the boat deck. Just as the boat fell, I noticed Captain Smith dive from the bridge into the sea."

As the boat deck began to dip under, recollections of what was being played by the band on deck vary.

Mrs. Futrelle (16): "She sank to the requiem, 'Nearer, My God to Thee,' played by the band."

Miss Turja (13): "I didn't hear it [Nearer My God To Thee]. I only remember the crying and the groaning and the screaming."

Mrs. Brown (14): "I did not at any time hear the band play, but we may have been on the other side and consequently shut off from hearing them."

Miss Mulvihill (10): "The men on the Titanic were all gathered about the rail. They were singing. It sounded like, 'Nearer My God, To Thee.'"

Bride: "From aft came the tunes of the band. It was a ragtime tune. I don't know what. Then there was 'Autumn.'"

Since Bride had been cooped up inside the wireless office, his senses would have been heightened as he stepped out onto the boat deck. The band was playing only a few feet aft of where he came out. For this reason, Bride's account of hearing the tune Autumn bears a significant amount of weight over other conflicting opinions on what–if anything–was being played by the band at the end.

But music was the least of anyone's priorities on board the Titanic at that moment. With water on the port side of the boat deck, the ship was really sinking now in the eyes of the passengers and crew. Some began to make their move to save themselves. Most had no idea what to do.

Hemming: "I went over to the port side and saw a boat off the port quarter and I went along the port side and got up the after boat davits and slid down the fall and swam to the boat and got it."
Smith: "How far was it from the side of the Titanic?"
Hemming: "About 200 yards."
Smith: "Did you have a life belt on?"
Hemming: "No, sir."

Collins: "Then the word came around from the starboard side there was a collapsible boat getting launched on the starboard side and that all women and children were to make for it. So me and another steward and the two children and the woman came around on that side, the starboard side, and when we got around there we saw then that it was forward. We saw the collapsible boat taken off the saloon deck, and then the sailors and the firemen that were forward seen the ship's bow in the water and seen that she was intending to sink her bow, and they shouted out for all they were worth we were to go aft . . . "

Bride: "Then followed a general scramble down on the boat deck, but no sooner had we got there than the sea washed over. I managed to catch hold of the boat we had previously fixed up and was swept overboard with her."

The reality of the situation was crashing in on everyone, both on the ship and in the lifeboats. Passengers and crew still on the *Titanic* backed away from the water washing onto the deck and headed for the stern.

Mrs. Brown (14): "We could see the Titanic quite plainly. As she began to sink at the bow we could see the men climb and run toward the upper parts of her. There they stood in groups quite silent. Some seemed to have their arms folded."

Just as the bridge started to go under, one of the officers fired a gun. It was heard by a number of survivors and the origin of the shots remains a matter of dispute.

Miss Turja (13): "One Finnish man who had been in the water for six hours was picked up by one of the life boats. He told us when we got aboard the Carpathia that there had been some shooting, and that he had just escaped being shot for trying to get in a life boat when there was plenty of room for him and others."

Mr. Daly: "At the first cabin when a boat was being lowered an officer pointed a revolver and said if any man tried to get in, he would shoot him on the spot. I saw the officer shoot two men dead because they tried to get in the boat."

Mr. Rhiems: "While the last boat was leaving, I saw an officer with a revolver fire a shot and kill a man who was trying to climb into it."

Crawford (8): "I heard an explosion when we were lying to in the water, in the boat, sir. Sort of a sharp, like as if there were things being blown up."

Smith: "Did you hear any explosion?"
Lowe (14): "I heard explosions. Yes. I should say about four. That was after I left the ship. About, I should say, a quarter of an hour or 20 minutes."

Rowe (C): "I heard one, sir, after we left the ship. It was not an explosion; a sort of a rumbling. It was not an ordinary explosion, you understand. More like distant thunder."

Ward (9): "She gave a kind of sudden lurch forward, and I heard a couple of reports, reports more like a volley of musketry than anything else. You would not exactly call them a heavy explosion. It did not seem to me like an explosion at all."

Mr. Stengel (1): ". . . and all of a sudden there were four sharp explosions about that far apart, just like this [snapping his fingers], and then she dipped and the stern stood up in the air and then the cries began for help."

Two survivors who were standing around collapsible A later wrote that they saw an officer shoot himself. A third reported only hearing the shot.

Mr. Rheims: "As there remained nothing more for him to do, the officer told us, 'Gentlemen, each man for himself. Good bye.' He gave a military salute and then fired a bullet into his head. That's what I call a man!"

Mr. Daly: "Afterwards, there was another shot, and I saw the officer himself lying on the deck. They told me he shot himself, but I did not see him. I was up to my knees in water at the time. Everyone was rushing around and there were no more boats."

Mr. Williams: "I heard the crack of a revolver shot from the direction where I had left Captain Smith. I did not look around."

Down at the forward end of the boat deck, numerous men made the decision they would not retreat to the stern, but rather stand their ground and face the inevitable. Many were still hoping to get a seat in the last collapsible on deck, even though it was just about to float off with the rising water. Collapsible A was damaged when it was pushed off the roof of the officers' quarters and the last desperate efforts to fix the sides of the boat were abruptly cut off. The *Titanic* took a sudden, noticeable plunge at the bow and a wave came rushing over the forward boat deck.

Gracie and his friend stood in the corner behind the winch as the wave approached. One of several gates can be seen to the left, which bottlenecked scores of people during their retreat from the water. (*Olympic*)

Weikman: "The men were trying to pull up the sides when the rush of water came ..."

Collins: "... we were just turning around and making for the stern end when the wave washed us off the deck—washed us clear of it—and the child was washed out of my arms."

Mr. Gracie: "Soon after that the water came up on the boat deck. We saw it and heard it. The water was then right by us, and we tried to jump, Mr. Smith and myself did. We were

in a sort of cul-de-sac which was formed by the cabin and the bridge, the structure that is right on the boat deck. We were right in this cul-de-sac. Mr. Smith jumped to try and reach the deck. I jumped also. We were unsuccessful. Then the wave came and struck us, the water came and struck us and then I rose as I would rise in bathing in the surf and I gave a jump with the water which took me right on the hurricane deck, and around that was an iron railing and I grabbed the iron railing and held tight to it. And I looked around me. I turned to the right and to the left and looked. Mr. Smith was not there, and I could not see any of this vast mass of humanity. They had all disappeared."

Bourne: "And the waves broke over the deck and washed you off?"
Collins: "Washed the decks clear."
Bourne: "How many were around you at that time that were washed off?"
Collins: "There were hundreds on the starboard side."
Bourne: "And you think every one of the hundreds were washed in the water?"
Collins: "Yes, sir. They were washed off into the water."

Miss Gibson (5): "Suddenly there was a wild coming together of voices from the *direction of the ship and we noticed an unusual commotion among the people huddled about the railing. Then the awful thing happened, the thing that will remain in my memory until the day I die. The Titanic seemed to lurch slightly more to the side and then the fore."*

The result was mayhem on the boat deck. Scores of people were engulfed by the rush of water. Some were thrown against the walls and decks, while others were sucked down with the vessel.

Lightoller: "As I say, I was on top of the officers' quarters, and there was nothing more to be done. The ship then took a dive, and I turned face forward and also took a dive."

Mr. Williams: "The ship seemed to give a slight lurch. I turned towards the bow. I saw nothing but water with just a mast sticking out of it. I don't remember the shock of the cold water, I only remember thinking, 'suction,' and my efforts to swim in the direction of the starboard rail to get away from the ship."

Lifeboat 4 had barely managed to get away from the ship before she started to take her plunge.

Mrs. Ryerson (4): "Then suddenly, when we still seemed very near, we saw the ship was sinking rapidly. I was in the bow of the boat with my daughter and turned to see the great ship take a plunge toward the bow . . ."

Olaus Abelseth was standing with some of his family near the empty davits where lifeboat 15 had hung 45 minutes earlier. They watched the passengers rush by in their desperate attempt to get to the highest part of the ship—the stern.

Mr. Abelseth: "I was standing there, and I asked my brother-in-law if he could swim and he said no. I asked my cousin if he could swim and he said no. So we could see the water coming up, the bow of the ship was going down, and there was a kind of an explosion."

The crow's nest stood ahead of the sinking boat deck, almost level with the surface but steadily descending toward the water. It was last occupied at 12:25 a.m. when the lookouts abandoned their post. For a moment, it looked like an inviting haven from the madness.

Lightoller: "Ahead of me the lookout cage on the foremast was visible just above the water—in normal times it would be a hun-dred feet above. I struck out blindly for this, but only for a short while, till I got hold of myself again and realized the futility of seeking safety on anything connected with the ship."

Lightoller was floundering in the frigid water just above the submerged bridge. It proved to be a dangerous location.

Lightoller: " . . . a little to the starboard side, where I had got to, and I was driven back against a blower which is a large thing that shape [indicating] which faces forward to the wind and which then goes down to the stokehole. But there is a grating there, and it was against this grating that I was sucked by the water and held there."
Smith: "Was your head above water?"
Lightoller: "No, sir."
Smith: "You were under water?"
Lightoller: "Yes, sir. And then this explosion, or whatever it was took place. Certainly, I think it was the boilers exploded. There was a terrific blast of air and water, and I was blown out clear."
Smith: "And how far from the sinking ship did it throw you?"
Lightoller: "Barely threw me away at all, because I went down again against these fiddley gratings immediately abreast of the funnel over the stokehole."

The bridge dips beneath the waves as the *Titanic* begins her final plunge.

Smith: "Was anybody else sucked down at the time?"
Lightoller: "Colonel Gracie, I believe was sucked down in identically the same manner. He was sucked down on the fiddley gratings."
Smith: "There must have been considerable suction?"
Lightoller: "That was the water rushing down below as she was going down."
Smith: "Going down into the ship?"
Lightoller: "Exactly."
Smith: "How did you get released from that?"

Lightoller: "Oh, I don't know, sir. I think it was the boilers again, but I do not distinctly remember. I do not know."
Smith: "Where did you find yourself next?"
Lightoller: "Alongside of that raft."
Smith: "Where?"
Lightoller: "Alongside of that upturned boat that had been launched on the other side."
Smith: "Where had you gone at that time? Had you gone around the ship?"
Lightoller: "No, sir. The boat had come around."
Smith: "Was there anyone on it?"

Lightoller: "I don't think so. I think they were around it."

Cunningham: "I waited on the ship until all the boats had gone and then I took to the water. I swam clear of the ship. I should say about three quarters of a mile. I was afraid of the suction. I had a mate with me. We both left the ship together."

Mrs. Brown (14): "As the Titanic went down by the head there was an explosion. Then we heard screams and saw people jumping."

Several of the men who jumped immediately struck out for the lifeboats. They had kept an eye on them from the ship as they rowed away into the darkness. Now that these men were in the water, they swam in the same direction.

Smith: "When you reached the boat [4], what did you find?"
Hemming: "I tried to get hold of the grub line on the bows, and it was too high for me, so I swam along and got hold of one of the grab lines amidships. I pulled my head above the gunwale and I said, 'Give us a hand in, Jack.' Foley was in the boat. I saw him standing up in the boat. He said, 'Is that you, Sam?' I said, 'Yes,' and him and the women and children pulled me in the boat.'"

Smith: *"Did you suffer from the cold?"*

Hemming (4): *"Yes, sir. It made my feet and hands sore, sir."*

Smith: *"What was done after you got into the boat?"*

Hemming: *"They had been backing her away, to get out of the zone from the ship before the ship sank."*

Behind Hemming and lifeboat 4, an enormous human struggle was set in motion as the slant of the *Titanic* proceeded to dump hundreds of people into the icy Atlantic.

Weikman: *"After I was washed overboard I started to swim, when there was a pile of ropes fell upon me and I managed to get clear of these and started to swim for some dark object in the water."*

Williams was no match for the rush of water swirling about, and while attempting to swim away from the ship, he was literally washed back onto the deck.

Mr. Williams: *"Before I had swam more than ten feet I felt the deck come up under me and I found we were high and dry. My father was not more than 12 or 15 feet from me."*

Collapsible B floated out ahead of the sinking ship. Its white bottom in the darkness of the ocean drew attention and men began to swim for it.

Collins: *"And the wreckage and the people that was around me—they kept me down for at least two or three minutes under the water."*

Bourne: *"Two or three minutes?"*

Collins: *"Yes. I am sure."*

Bourne: *"You cannot stay under water two or three minutes, can you?"*

Collins: *"Well, it seemed that to me. I could not exactly state how long, but it seemed that to me. When I came to the surface I saw this boat that had been taken off. I saw a man on it. They had been working on it taking it off the saloon deck, and when the waves washed it off the deck they clung to that. Then I made for it when I came to the surface and saw it, and I swam over to it."*

Bourne: *"How many were on the collapsible boat?"*

Collins: *"Well, sir, I could not exactly say, but I am sure there was more than 15 or 16."*

Bourne: *"Did those who were on help you get on?"*

Collins: *"No, sir. They were all watching the ship. I had not much to do. All I had to do was to give a spring and I got onto it."*

Just then, the cables holding the first funnel broke loose and the smokestack unexpectedly fell forward into the water right where dozens were swiming away. Lightoller and others holding onto collapsible B were very lucky.

Lightoller (B): *"We were thrown off a couple of times. It was cleared. It was a flat, collapsible boat. When I came to it, it was bottom up, and there was no one on it. And it was on the other side of the ship. Immediately after finding that overturned lifeboat, and when I came up alongside of it, there were quite a lot of us in the water around it preparatory to getting up on it. Then the forward funnel fell down . . . it fell alongside of the lifeboat, about four inches clear of it. It fell on all the people there were alongside of the boat, if there were any there."*

There is evidence to suggest that only moments after the first funnel fell into the water, the second one followed. The chaos of both funnels toppling over presented the illusion that the ship was breaking apart in that area.

Mr. Thayer: *"Suddenly the whole superstructure of the ship appeared to split, well forward to midship, and blow or buckle upwards. The second funnel, large enough for two automobiles to pass through abreast, seemed to be lifted off, emitting a cloud of sparks. It looked as if it would fall on top of me."*

After Williams and his father found themselves washed back onto the deck, Dick was planning to jump from the starboard side and called to his father about ten feet away to jump with him. But at that moment, the second funnel came between them.

Mr. Williams: "He started towards me just as I saw one of the four great funnels come crashing down on top of him. Just for one instant I stood there transfixed–not because it had only missed me by a few feet . . . curiously enough not because it had killed my father for whom I had a far more than normal feeling of love and attachment; but there I was transfixed wondering at the enormous size of this funnel, still belching smoke."

Gracie was lying along the roof of the officers' quarters when it slid beneath the water. The collapse of the second funnel created an enormous suction as water poured into the bowels of the ship through the empty casing. He was very lucky the ship did not swallow him whole, which may have been due to the fact that he was at the time holding onto an iron railing.

Mr. Gracie: "I was taken down with the ship and hanging onto the railing, but I soon let go. I felt myself whirled around, swam under water, fearful that the hot water that came up from the boilers might boil me up. Down, down, I went; it seemed a great distance. There was a very noticeable pressure upon my ears, though there must have been plenty of air that the ship carried down with it. When under water I retained, as it appears, a sense of general direction, and as soon as I could do so, swam away from the starboard side of the ship, as I knew that my life depended upon it. I held my breath for what seemed an interminable time until I could scarcely stand it any longer, but I congratulated myself then and there that not one drop of sea water was allowed to enter my mouth. I swam with all my strength and I seemed endowed with an extra supply for the occasion. Swam, it seemed to me with unusual strength, and succeeded finally in reaching the surface and in getting a good distance away from the ship. When I came up to the surface there was no ship there. The ship would then have been behind me, and all around me was wreckage. I saw what seemed to be bodies all around."

Those close to the *Titanic* in her final moments were witness to a ghastly scene. In more detail than most would ever want to see, they watched hundreds of desperate people cling to the ship in an attempt to escape the inescapable. The final actions of many, as they faced their impending deaths, are undocumented, including those of Thomas Andrews, Chief Officer Bell, Chief Officer Wilde, Sixth Officer Moody, Doctor O'Loughlin, Archibald Butt, Hugo Ross, Isador and Ida Straus, Purser McElroy, Jacques Futrelle, Arthur Ryerson, Annie Funk, Francis Millet, the band, the engineers, and most of all, the steerage passengers.

Osman: "The steerage passengers were all down below, and after she got a certain distance it seemed to me all the passengers climbed up her. She was white around there [indicating] and it looked like a big crowd of people."

Etches (5): "I saw, when the ship rose–her stern rose–a thick mass of people on the after end. I could not discern the faces, of course."

Not only could they see the struggle of the masses, they could hear them panic as the decks grew to a terrifying angle. Families, friends, acquaintances, and single people left on board found themselves in an impossible situation as the stern lifted several hundred feet into the air.

Collins (B): "I could see when I got onto the raft. I saw the stern of the boat, and I saw a mass of people and wreckage and heard cries."

Miss Sjoblom (13): "I watched the big steamer every second of the last few minutes she was afloat. The reports are wrong when they say the boilers exploded. The ship just gradually sank in front. The bow went down out of sight, the lights, the low ones first and then the higher around the side of the hull, blinked out, one after the other. Then the steamer, without a sound, except for the shrieks of the people still on board, stood right up on end."

The *Titanic* was rearing up now and the angle of the decks made it increasingly difficult for the terrified victims to stand. Amazingly, the lights continued to shine, creating a hypnotic scene for those in the lifeboats and water.

Mr. Peuchen (6): "While the lights were burning I saw her bow pointing down and the stern up, not in a perpendicular position, but considerable. I should think an angle of not as much as 45 degrees."

Abelseth was still on board, clinging to the ship. He and his companions watched the water's ominous approach.

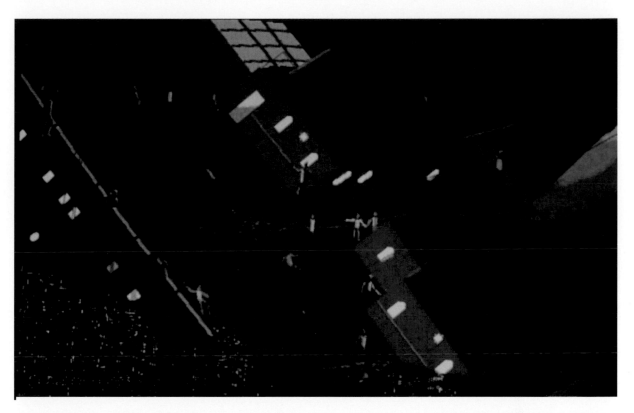

As everything moveable within the ship crashes forward, passengers near the third smokestack struggle with the almost impossible tilt. Within moments of this scene the *Titanic* will break apart, casting the ship into darkness.

Mr. Abelseth: "We could hear the popping and cracking and the deck raised up and got so steep that the people could not stand on their feet on the deck. So they fell down and slid on the deck into the water right on the ship. Then we hung onto a rope in one of the davits. We were pretty far back at the top deck. My brother-in-law said to me, 'We had better jump off or the suction will take us down.' I said, 'No. We won't jump yet. We ain't got much show anyhow, so we might as well stay as long as we can.' So he stated again, 'We must jump off.' But I said, 'No. Not yet.'"

The view of the *Titanic* from distant lifeboats becomes an unbelievable one, as the giant liner almost stands straight on end. Seconds after this scene, the lights will go out as the ship breaks apart.

The boats with more of a distance between themselves and the *Titanic* were too far away to see the awful struggle by the last of *Titanic*'s passengers, but many could still hear them before the ship went down.

Mr. Stengel (1): "I could not see any of the people, but I could hear them. I have never been familiar with bulkheads giving way, but they were quite hard explosions. She dipped then, forward, and all you could see was the stern sticking up. When I heard the cries I turned my back. I said, 'I cannot look any longer.'"

Charles Joughin was in the pantry on the promenade deck looking for something to eat. As one of the bakers, he was in his element when the ship's end approached.

Joughin: "I went to the deck pantry and heard a noise as if something was buckling and some people running along. I went up on deck again and found people running and clambering onto the poop. The buckling seemed like the cracking of iron. I kept out of the crush of people getting towards the well of the ship."

Miss Sjoblom (13): "The sounds as the ship sank were the most awful sounds I ever heard. I never expect to hear worse. When the boat first began to sink, the people on board began to shriek and wail, and moan. As it went down farther and farther, the shrieks arose louder and louder and more awful. Then, as the boat began to tip on end, the sound of cries was like something terribly weird. I can't describe it. I can't say how it was. It was just terrible. I can still hear it."

Mrs. Crosby (5): "I heard the terrible cries of the people that were on board when the boat went down, and heard repeated explosions, as though the boilers had exploded and we then knew that the steamer had gone down, as her lights were out and the cries of the people and the explosions were terrible."

Lowe (14): "She went down bow first and inclined at an angle, that is, when she took her final plunge she was inclined at an angle of about 75."

Just about everyone from a distance watched the incredible scene with a stunned silence. While their eyes were transfixed, the lights of the *Titanic* finally and suddenly went out. To the farthest lifeboats, that was the end of it.

Boxhall (2): "I suppose I was about a half a mile away. Resting on the oars."

Smith: "Did you see the Titanic sink?"
Boxhall: "No. I cannot say that I saw her sink. I saw the lights go out, and I looked two or three minutes afterwards and it was 25 minutes past two. So I took it that when she sank would be about 20 minutes after two. I would say we were then about three-fourths of a mile from her."

Mrs. Douglas (2): "I heard no explosion. I watched the boat go down, and the last picture to my mind is the immense mass of black against the starlit sky, and then—nothingness."

Hichens (6): "About 1 mile. We could not see her at all. When I seen the lights disappear, that was all I could see, because it was very dark."

Mr. Peuchen (6): "I saw it when the lights went out. You could not tell very much after the lights went out. I could only see the outline of the boat, you might say."

Clench (12): "About a quarter of a mile away."
Bourne: "Did she break in two?"
Clench: "That I could not say."
Bourne: "Did you hear any explosion?"
Clench: "I heard two explosions, sir."
Bourne: "How far were you from the Titanic at the time?"

Andrews (16): "I should say about a half a mile, sir."
Bourne: "Did you hear any explosion or noise?"
Andrews: "I heard just a small sound, sir. It was not very loud, but just a small sound."
Bourne: "Did you think that the ship broke in two?"
Andrews: "That I do not know, sir. When we got away in the boat at the last, everything seemed to go to a black mist. All the lights seemed to go out and everything went black."

Hardy (D): "There were two reports or explosions. What it was, I do not know. I was not able to say."

But for those closer to the *Titanic*, it was not the end. The lights went out when the ship tore itself apart. The huge liner could not deal with the full weight of its stern being lifted into the air and it broke off from the rest of the plunging ship.

Burton: "How far were you away from the boat when she sank?
Osman (2): "Sixty to 100 yards. After she got to a certain angle she exploded, broke in halves, and it seemed to me as if all the engines and everything that was in the after part slid out into the forward part . . . but

you could see the explosions by the smoke coming right up the funnels. It was all black; looked like as if it was lumps of coal and all that, through the funnels; just after the explosion."

Burton: "And there were lumps of coal, etc., coming up?"

Osman: "Yes. Pretty big lumps. I do not know what it was."

Burton: "Did any water come up?"

Osman: "I never seen no water; only the steam and very black smoke."

Mrs. Ryerson (4): "... the two forward funnels seemed to lean and then she seemed to break in half as if cut with a knife and as the bow went under the lights went out."

Mrs. Cook (14): "The lights were still burning. She then made a sudden plunge and disappeared. The noise was dreadful, worse than any thunder and all around was thick smoke. It seemed terrible to think that the ship had gone down with all those poor souls. The cries were too terrible for words."

Collins (B): "She exploded once in the water, and her stern end was up out of the water and with the explosion out of the water it blew her stern up."

Bourne: "You saw while it was up?"

Collins: "Yes, sir. Saw her stern up."

Bourne: "How long?"

Collins: "I am sure it floated for at least a minute."

Bourne: "If it was dark, how could you see?"

Collins: "We were not too far off. I saw the white of the funnel. Then she turned over again, and down she went."

Miss Lehmann (12): "All at once there were three loud reports, they sounded something like a very loud crash of thunder when it strikes very close to you. We all looked at the Titanic. It had broken apart! The front part of the boat went under first. The helm of the front half sank and then the middle. The last part of the boat was still above the water. The broken part of the last half of the boat sank slowly into the water and then the stern. That was the last of the ship that could not sink. The work of many men destroyed and along with that the lives of 1,600 men, women, and children."

At the waterline, the breakup of the ship created another wave that moved outwards from the wreck and pushed Weikman and others away from an extremely dangerous area.

Weikman: "I was about 15 feet away from the ship when I heard a second explosion. I think the boilers blew up about in the middle of the ship. The explosion blew me along with a wall of water toward the dark object I was swimming to, which proved to be a bundle of deck chairs which I managed to climb on. While on the chairs I heard the terrible groans and cries coming from people in the water. There was a great number of people killed by the explosion and there was a great number that managed to get far enough away that the explosion did not injure them, and these are the people that I think could have been saved had the lifeboats been closer. I was afloat on some chairs about 100 feet away, looking toward the ship. I seen her sink."

Once the ship broke apart, the stern settled back into the water, still carrying horrified passengers and crew who were clinging to what was left of the darkened decks, not knowing what to expect next.

For Abelseth and many like him, the unavoidable moment arrived. The Atlantic crept up the deck and plucked its victims from the flailing liner one by one. When the water reached them, there was no time left to put off the inevitable.

Mr. Abelseth: "So then, it was only about 5 feet down to the water when we jumped off.

It was not much of a jump. Before that we could see the people were jumping over. There was water coming onto the deck, and they were jumping over then out in the water. My brother-in-law took my hand just as we jumped off and my cousin jumped at the same time. When we came into the water, I think it was from the suction, or anyway we went under, and I swallowed some water. I got a rope tangled around me and I let loose of my brother-in-law's hand to get away from the rope. I thought then, 'I am a goner.' That is what I thought when I got tangled up in this rope."

Joughin: "The ship then gave a great lurch and a great crowd of people were thrown in a heap—many hundreds of people. The ship never recovered from the lurch. I eventually got to the starboard side of the poop on the side of the ship. I clung to the rail on the outside of the ship."

The stern of the *Titanic* rolled over on its side before going up on end for a second time. Hundreds of passengers were suddenly dumped into the water, one on top of another, first sliding down the deck, colliding with railings, cranes and other obstacles. Eventually they all landed in the frigid 28 degree fahrenheit water as the *Titanic* started to go down for the final time.

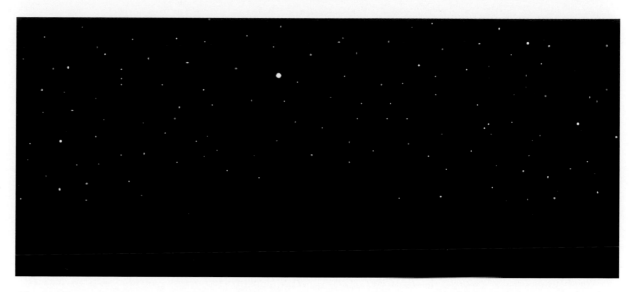

The broken stern piece of the *Titanic* settles back and floats upright in the dark. Many survivors mistakenly believed for a few moments that it was going to stay afloat.

Miss Mulvihill (10): "The big vessel quivered and seemed to settle. Then she leaned over on the other side a little and slowly sank to her grave."

Newlands: "How far were you from the ship when it sank?"
Taylor (3): "I should say just over a quarter of a mile, sir. I saw the forward part of her go down, and it appeared to me as if she broke in half, and then the after part went. I can remember two explosions."

Bright (D): "I heard something, but I would not call it an explosion. It was like a rattling of chain more than anything else."*

Buley (10): "We were lying to there. The people in the boat were very frightened that there would be some suction. If there had been any suction we should have been lost. We were close to her. We couldn't get away fast enough. There was nobody to pull away. We were about 200 yards."

Mrs. Ryerson (4): "The stern stood up for several minutes, black against the stars, and then that, too, plunged down and there was no sound for what seemed like hours . . ."

Buley (10): "She went down as far as the after funnel, and then there was a little roar, as though the engines had rushed forward, and she snapped in two, and the bow part went down and the after part came up and stayed up five minutes before it went down."
Fletcher: "How do you know that?"
Buley: "Because we could see the after part afloat, and there was no forepart to it. You could hear the rush of the machinery, and she parted in two, and the after part settled down again, and we thought the after part would float altogether."
Fletcher: "The after part kind of righted up horizontally?"
Buley: "She up righted herself for about five minutes, and then tipped over and disappeared."

Etches (5): "She seemed to raise once as though she was going to take a violent dive, but sort of checked, as though she had scooped the water up and had leveled herself. She then seemed to settle very, very quiet until the last, when she rose up, and she seemed to stand 20 seconds, stern in that position, and then she went down with an awful grating, like a small boat running off a shingly beach."

Mr. Woolner(D): "A sort of rumbling roar, it

sounded to me, as she slid under."
Bourne: "Were you sufficiently near so that you could see the ship itself when you were about a quarter of a mile away?"
Archer (16): "Yes, sir; quite distinguish it."
Bourne: "Do you think the ship broke in two?"
Archer: "Well, I could not say that, sir."
Bourne: "There was nothing that gave you such an impression?"
Archer: "No, sir."

Mrs. Futrelle (16): "All of a sudden the lights snapped out. There was a terrible creaking noise. The Titanic seemed to break in two. There was a tremendous explosion. For a fraction of a second she rose in the air and was plainly visible in the light caused from the blowing up of the boilers."

Osman (2): ". . . and the after part came up right again, as soon as it came up right, down it went again."

Evans (10): "She parted between the third and fourth funnels. The foremost part was gone, and it seemed as if the engines were all gone out. I should say about 200 feet was afloat, that is, of the stern part. About four or five minutes, I should judge. You could see that in the outline. Then she made a sudden plunge and the stern went right up."

Smith: "As you were looking at her when she went down, do you think she broke in two?"
Mr. Woolner (D): "I did not think so. You could not really see a thing when the lights went out. It was all brilliantly lighted at the stern end, and suddenly the lights went out, and your eyes were so unaccustomed to the darkness, you could see nothing, and you could only hear sounds."

Olliver (5): "... to my idea she broke forward, and the after part righted itself and made another plunge and went down. I fancied I saw her black form. It was dark, and I fancied I saw her black form going that way."

Crowe (14): "She sank around half past two, from statements made by a man that was supposed to have jumped from the poop of the ship—that is, the quarter deck—into the water. He had a watch on, and as his watch stopped at 20 minutes past two, he said she was in a sinking condition then and her stern on end—a man named Burnett, a storekeeper aboard ship."
Bourne: "Did you, yourself hear the explosions?"
Crowe: "Yes, sir. There were several explosions, a kind of muffled explosion. It seemed to be an explosion at a very great distance,

although we were not very far away."

Burton: *"How far from the ship were you when she went down?"*
Rowe (C): *"About three quarters of a mile, sir."*
Burton: *"Did you see her go down?"*
Rowe: *"I saw her stern disappear at the finish, sir."*

Mr. Peuchen (6): *"We heard a sort of a rumbling sound and the lights were still on at the rumbling sound, as far as my memory serves me. Then a sort of an explosion, then another. It seemed to be one, two, or three rumbling sounds, then the lights went out. Then the dreadful calls and cries."*

Joughin stood on the painted white band alongside the starboard side of the poop deck as the enormous stern slid under.

Joughin: *"I clung to the rail on the outside of the ship. I was wondering what next to do, and was changing some things from one pocket to another when she went. I don't think I went under at all. My head might have been wet."*

As Joughin stepped off the ship, the stern of the *Titanic* had one last look at its buoyant world—a black sky sparkling with a diamond-like glitter in farewell.

When the stern angled up one last time, hundreds fell into the icy water. (Image rotated for effect.)

Ismay (C): *"I did not see her go down. I do not know how far we were away. I was sitting with my back to the ship. I was rowing all the time I was in the boat. We were pulling away. I did not wish to see her go down. I am glad I did not."*

Over Ismay's shoulder, the creation that was to make the International Mercantile Marine Company and White Star Line the envy of the industry and the talk of society slipped beneath the surface. The *Titanic*—the newest, the largest and the most

luxurious ship in the world—was gone.

The survivors did not have long to contemplate the significance of what they had just watched. A chorus of anguished cries rose from the wreck site that traumatized most of the lifeboat occupants for the rest of their lives.

Mrs. Ryerson (4): *". . . and then began the cries for help of people drowning all around us, which seemed to go on forever. Someone called out, 'Pull for your lives or you'll be sucked under,' and everyone that could rowed like mad. I could see my younger daughter and Mrs. Thayer and Mrs. Astor rowing, but there seemed to be no suction."*

Miss Turja (13): *"The thing that haunts me most is the sound I still hear in my ears . . . the cries, screams, and pleadings of the people who were struggling in icy water, begging for help, then the silence."*

Mrs. Futrelle (16): *"It seemed to me that I would die when the end came. It was an inferno, the wail of the dying, the crying of the women and children, the appeals for help from those who still lived and the bobbing corpses of men who had died from the exposure, or who were torn and bleeding from the effects of the explosion. It was a vision of hell. A little French woman in the boat with me wailed and writhed in hysteria. I was calm. I couldn't cry. I didn't want to. I felt that I was dead."*

Scarrott (14): "The cries from the poor souls struggling in the water sounded terrible in the stillness of the night. It seemed to go through you like a knife."

Miss Lehmann (12): "All was silent for a while and then the people that was taken under from the suction of the boat came up again. And, of course, those that had life belts on stayed up. We could hear them yelling and screaming for help. As we rowed farther and farther away the cries were lost in the distance between us and the boat."

Miss Minahan (14): "After she went down the cries were horrible. This was at 2:20 a.m. by a man's watch who stood next to me."

Mr. Peuchen (6): "We could not distinguish the exact cry for assistance; moaning and crying; frightful. It affected all the women in our boat whose husbands were among these, and this went on for some time, gradually getting fainter, fainter. At first it was horrible to listen to."

Smith: "Did you hear any cries of distress?"
Pitman (5): "Oh yes; crying, shouting,

moaning. From the water, after the ship disappeared. No noises before."

When the *Titanic* went down, 1,500 people were left in the icy cold water. Because seawater has a lower freezing temperature, it was actually 28 degrees fahrenheit. Most expected a struggle in the water, but few could have expected this. A person submerged in water this temperature could easily go crazy from the shock.

Mr. Abelseth: "But I came on top again, and I was trying to swim and there was a man —lots of them were floating around—and he got me on the neck like that [illustrating] and pressed me under, trying to get on top of me. I said to him, 'Let go.' Of course, he did not pay any attention to that, but I got away from him. Then there was another man and he hung onto me for a while, but he let go. Then I swam."

Fletcher: "Have you any idea as to how long a person could live in water like that?"
Mr. Peuchen (6): "It depends on his constitution, but I should imagine that if a person could stay in the water a half an hour he would be doing very well."

There were only a few boats nearby. Most others purposely rowed far away from

the *Titanic* before it went under.

Smith: "Why did you not row toward the scene of the Titanic?"
Hichens (6): "The suction of the ship would draw the boat, with all her occupants under water, I thought, sir."

The closest boats were numbers 4 and 14. As Lowe stood in lifeboat 14, he listened and watched.

Lowe (14): "I was just on the margin. If anybody had struggled out of the mass, I was there to pick them up. But it was useless for me to go into the mass."

No one in the water approached Lowe and his boat. For the most part, the hundreds of people in the black water were too disoriented in the dark and had no idea where to swim. Some probably set off from the wreckage only to never come in contact with a boat. But there were a couple of passengers and crew who made it. A clock was ticking for those in the frigid Atlantic. If they did not get out of that water within minutes, there would be little hope of survival. The intense cold of a 28 degree immersion quickly sapped away their strength.

Mr. Peuchen (6): "I feel quite sure that a

person could not live in that water very long. Those who had been in the water had their feet frozen; that is, those who were standing up in a boat in the water. I happened to have the cabin with three of them who were rescued, and they said they sustained their life by punching each other during the two or three hours they stood up. The minute anyone got tired and sat down in the water, or at least very shortly thereafter, he floated off the raft, dead, I believe."

Moore (3): "...we were about a quarter of a mile away and the cries did not last long. I do not think anybody could live much more than 10 minutes in that cold water."

Boxhall (2): "I heard the water rumbling or breaking on the ice. Then I knew that there was a lot of ice about."

With the icy hands of the Atlantic pulling at him, Cunningham swam for all he was worth to a place he thought a boat should be. He met up with lifeboat 4.

Smith: "Who had charge of that boat?"
Hemming (4): "Perkis."

Perkis (4): "We picked up eight. I should say about the length of the ship away. And two died afterwards, in the boat."

Perkins: "Were they passengers or men of the crew?"
Perkis: "One was a fireman and one was a steward."
Perkins: "The others were all passengers?"
Perkis: "Yes, sir."

Mrs. Ryerson (4): "Then we turned to pick up some of those in the water. Some of the women protested, but others persisted and we dragged in six or seven men. The men we rescued were principally stokers, stewards, sailors, etc. and were so chilled and frozen already they could hardly move."

Cunningham: "We saw the ship go down then. Then we struck out to look for a boat. I heard one and I called to it. I went toward it."

With panicky relief, Cunningham reached the side of boat 4 and was awkwardly pulled up out of the water over the side of the leaning lifeboat. As his drenched body rolled into the boat, passengers probably flinched by instinct so as not to get wet. Perkis ordered the boat to head back to the scene of the wreckage.

Hemming (4): "After the ship had gone we pulled back and picked up seven. Stewards, firemen, seamen, and one or two men passengers. I could not say exactly which they were. Anyway, I know there were seven altogether."
Smith: "Did they swim to the boat, or did the boat go to the men?"
Hemming: "Both. They swam toward the boat, and we went back toward them."

After collapsible D got away from Emilio Portalupi, he floundered about in the water from the intense cold while the *Titanic* reared up for her final plunge. He had been in the water for almost twenty minutes without success in finding any lifeboats. Just as his strength was fading and it started to look hopeless, Perkis came by with lifeboat 4.

Mr. Portalupi (4): "I remained in the water, swimming about for a long time. I swam over 500 yards from the place where the ship was going down. One of the boats which had left the ship crossed right in front of me. I called for help. Someone reached over the boat, grabbed me by the collar of my clothes, and pulled me into the boat. Three others were pulled in later, all of whom are now among the survivors. A fourth was pulled in but he died soon afterwards."

Mrs. Ryerson (4): "Two of them died in the stern later and many were raving and moaning and delirious most of the time."

Smith: "Do you know who these passengers were?"
Hemming (4): "I know one was a third class passenger."
Smith: "What was his name?"
Hemming: "I do not know, sir."
Smith: "Where was he from?"
Hemming: "That I could not tell you, sir. I spoke to him, and I do not think he was an Englishman."
Smith: "Do you think he was an American?"
Hemming: "He spoke very good English, but I have an idea that he was a foreigner of some sort."

Cunningham (4): "There was a quartermaster in charge—Perkins or Perkis. It was number 4 boat. They picked us up. There was also a lamp trimmer in it named Hemmings and another sailor called Foley, and a fireman. The rest were ladies. Two of my own passengers happened to be there. Then there was a fireman there as well. A fellow called Smith—F. Smith. Of course, we picked up another man after I was picked up. Prentiss, the storekeeper."

While Cunningham sat drenched and shivering in lifeboat 4 trying to regain his strength, Florence Cummings recognized him as her steward from on board.

Seemingly oblivious to Cunningham's ordeal, she sent him on an errand within the small boat.

Cunningham (4): "The reason I know the names of any of them is that Mrs. Cummings, one of my passengers, sent me around to find out who was in the boat. Otherwise, I would not know their names. I think there was another fireman in the bottom of the boat and besides that there was my mate, who died just after he was pulled in. A man called Sidney Seibert."

Even though these men got themselves out of the water into lifeboat 4, for two of them it was too late. Already mortally cooled, hypothermia set in on Lyons and Seibert. They were unable to recover.

Smith: "How many died?"
Hemming (4): "Two. Lyons and—I do not know whether it was a steward or a fireman—one man besides Lyons."

Hardly any of the survivors happened to notice that the mast head light of the *Carpathia* was already appearing on the southern horizon. In short order, the rescue ship apparently disappeared behind one of the numerous icebergs as she approached the scene of the disaster.

Rostron: "At 2:40 I saw a flare, about half a point on the port bow, and immediately took it for granted that it was the Titanic itself and I remarked that she must be still afloat, as I knew we were a long way off, and it seemed so high. However, soon after seeing the flare I made out an iceberg about a point on the port bow, to which I had to port to keep well clear of."

Andrews (16): "We saw a light that seemed over the Titanic—back of the Titanic. The coxswain of the boat, the master-at-arms thought it was another ship coming up to give assistance, but after a while the light disappeared."

The cries for help continued. They were so horrible that some in the lifeboats were perhaps not honest with themselves with respect to what they heard, or were so guilt ridden after the tragedy, that they created an implausible explanation.

Mr. Harder (5): "After it went down we heard a lot of these cries and yells. You could not hear any shouts for help or anything like that. It was a sort of continuous yelling or moaning. You could not distinguish any sounds. It was more like, what I thought it was, the steerage on rafts, and that they were all hysterical. That is the way it sounded in the distance."

Evans (10): "We heard these cries, but we took them to be the boats that went away from the starboard side of the ship, that they were cheering one another."

Mrs. Smith (6): "We were some distance away when the Titanic went down. We watched with sorrow, and heard the many cries for help and pitied the captain because we knew he would have to stay with his ship. The cries we heard I thought were seamen or possibly steerage who had overslept, it not occurring to me for a moment that my husband and my friends were not saved."

Some of the victims in the water were badly hurt from their recent ordeal on the ship and could only float in a stationary position. Others tried various things to survive. Some struck out in search of the boats. Some could do nothing in the cold but scream for help. And some made it a priority to try and get themselves out of the water one way or another.

Mr. Gracie: "I did not notice any coldness of the water at that time. I was too much preoccupied in getting away. There was a sort of gulp, as if something had occurred, behind me, and I suppose that was where the water was closing up, where the ship had gone down. But the surface of the water was

Fifteen hundred people found themselves in the dark icy Atlantic, desperate for help. Some struck out in search of a lifeboat or something to climb on. Others were hurt from the ordeal or too weak to move.

perfectly still, and there were, I say, this wreckage and these bodies, and there were the horrible sounds of drowning people and people gasping for breath. While collecting the wreckage together I got on a big wooden crate, some sort of wooden crate, or wood of that sort."

Abelseth was separated from his cousin and brother-in-law and instinctually swam in search of something that would help him. For a while, he had no luck.

Mr. Abelseth: "Then I swam. I could not say, but it must have been about 15 or 20 minutes. It could not have been over that."

Gracie, in the meantime, had a slightly better view now that he was up on some crates and wreckage. While biding his time, he could see collapsible B in the distance under several men and decided to pin his hopes for survival on it.

Mr. Gracie (B): "I saw an upturned boat and I struck out for that boat and there I saw what I supposed were members of the crew on this upset boat. I grabbed the arm of one of them and pulled myself up on this boat. I was among the first. I suppose the boat was then about half full. Our concern now was to get out of the wreckage and to get away from the swimmers in the water before they tried to get on the boat, and all of us would be lost. You do not want the details of that, nor the horrors of it."

In a ruthless necessity for survival, some of the freezing victims who came upon the boat were turned away by a forceful whack, or by simple words.

Collins (B): "If a gentleman had got on we would all have been turned over. We were all on the boat. If this man had caught hold of her he would have tumbled the whole lot of us off. We were all telling him not to get on. He said, 'That is all right, boys, keep cool,' he said, 'God bless you,' and he bid us good-bye and he swam along for about two minutes and we seen him, but did not see him moving off. We saw his head, but we
did not see him moving his hands. Then we were washed out of his road. There were others that tried to get on, but we would not let them on. A big foreigner came up. I think he was a Dutchman. He came up to the stern and he hung on to me all the time."
Bourne: "Was he saved?"
Collins: "He was, sir."

Daniels (B): "So I swam to that and it was the upturned lifeboat with the crowd out there. It was the lifeboat out there that they'd tried to cut adrift. So I climbed on that and the other fella apparently followed me and he tried to climb on too, but he was too exhausted to get fully on there. I managed to sit up on the keel of the lifeboat, but he just laid across there. He eventually died of exposure."

While dozens approached collapsible B for a chance to get out of the water, collapsible A, which was upright but swamped, drifted about with only a few aware of its existence. Because Abelseth chose to continuously swim, he had improved his odds of finding a means to survive.

Mr. Abelseth: "Then I saw something dark ahead of me. I did not know what it was, but I swam toward that, and it was one of those
collapsible boats. When I got on this raft or collapsible boat, they did not try to push me off, and they did not do anything for me to get on. All they said when I got on there was, 'Don't capsize the boat.' So I hung onto the raft for a little while before I got on."

Mr. Williams (A): "There were about 15 of us on her including three women, one of them whom survived . . . Our drift away from the crowded waters continued and during the next ten minutes only about five more joined our party. I estimate roughly that at this time, which was the peak of our load, we numbered about 20 to 22 people."

The screams and cries for help were so disturbing to the occupants of the lifeboats that they produced an opposite reaction than one would expect under these extreme circumstances. Instead of using their half empty boats to assist the struggling mass of people–in many cases their own husbands and fathers–the occupants instead froze from fear while the victims froze to death.

Pitman (5): "As soon as she disappeared I said, 'Now men, we will pull toward the wreck.' Everyone in my boat said it was a mad idea, because we had far better save what few we had in my boat than go back to the scene of the wreck and be swamped by the crowds that were there."

Smith: "You were in command. They ought to have obeyed your orders?"

Pitman: "So they did."

Smith: "They did not, if you told them to pull toward the ship."

Pitman: "They commenced pulling toward the ship and the passengers in my boat said it was a mad idea on my part to pull back to the ship, because if I did we should be swamped with the crowd that was in the water and it would add another 40 to the list of the drowned, and I decided I would not pull back."

Mr. Harder (5): "It is true this officer did want to go back to the ship, but all the passengers held out and said, 'Do not do that. Do not do that. It would only be foolish if we went back there. There will be so many around. They will only swamp the boat.' And, at the time I do not think those people appreciated that there were not sufficient lifeboats to go around. I never paid any attention to how many lifeboats there were. I did not know."

Miss Gibson (5): "After the vessel had disappeared, the officer in command of our boat wanted to return, saying that there was room for several more passengers and pointing out the possibility of being able to rescue some of those who might be swimming. But immediately behind us was another lifeboat carrying forty people and as no one could be seen in the water, some of the passengers in the other boat were transferred to ours."

Burton: "Did you hear Pitman give an order to go back to the ship?"

Olliver (5): "Yes, sir."

Burton: "What happened?"

Olliver: "The women passengers implored him not to go, because they reckoned it was not safe."

Burton: "How far were you away from the ship then?"

Olliver: "I should say about 300 yards."

Smith: "Officer, you really turned this number 5 boat around to go in the direction from which these cries came?"

Pitman (5): "I did."

Smith: "And were dissuaded from your purpose by your crew and by the passengers in your boat?"

Pitman: "Certainly."

Smith: "Then did you turn the boat toward the sea again?"

Pitman: "No. Just simply took our oars in and lay quiet."

Smith: "You mean you drifted?"

Pitman: "We may have gone a little bit."

Smith: "Drifted on your oars?"

Pitman: "We may have drifted along. We just simply lay there doing nothing."

Smith: "How many of these cries were there? Was it a chorus, or was it -"

Pitman: "I would rather you did not speak of it."

Smith: "I would like to know how you were impressed by it."

Pitman: "Well, I cannot very well describe it. I would rather you would not speak of it."

Smith: "I realize that it is not a pleasant theme, and yet I would like to know whether these cries were general and in chorus, or desultory and occasional."

Pitman: "There was a continual moan for about an hour."

Lifeboat 5 was not the only boat that discussed the matter of returning to the wreckage.

Smith: "While these cries of distress were going on, did anyone in the boat urge the quartermaster to return?"

Mr. Peuchen (6): "Yes. Some of the women did. But as I said before, I had had a row with him [Hichens], and I said to the women, 'It is no use you arguing with that man at all. It is best not to discuss matters with him.' He said it was no use going back

247

Lifeboat 6 with Margaret ("Molly") Brown, Helen Candee, Mary Smith and others. Hichens can be seen at the stern, wrapped in a blanket. Frederick Fleet is at the bow, with Major Peuchen to the right of him.

spoke to me."

Mrs. Dyer-Edwards (8): "Signora de Satode Penasco began to scream for her husband. It was too horrible. I left the tiller to my cousin and slipped down beside her to be of what comfort I could. Poor woman! Her sobs tore our hearts and her moans were unspeakable in their sadness. Several of us –and Tom Jones–wanted to row back and see if there was not some chance of rescuing any one that had possibly survived, but the majority in the boat ruled, that we had no right to risk their lives on the bare chance of finding any one alive after the final plunge. They also said that the captain's own orders had been 'to row for those ship lights over there,' and that we who wished to try for others who might be drowning had no business to interfere with his orders. Of course that settled the matter, and we rowed on."

there, there was only a lot of stiffs there, later on, which was very unkind, and the women resented it very much. I do not think he was qualified to be a quartermaster."

Hogg (7): "As soon as she went down, I

went to try to assist them in picking up anybody if I could. I met another boat on my way, and they said to pull away. They said, 'We have done all in our power and we cannot do any more.' I cannot remember the number of the boat or who the man was who

Haines (9): "I called the sailors aft, and I passed the remark to them, 'There is people in the water.' I said, 'Do you think it advisable?' I said, 'We can't do nothing with this crowd we have in the boat,' because we had no room to row let alone do anything else, and it was no good of our going back. By the time we got back there, we could not have done anything. We could not move in the boat, let alone row. I thought it unsafe to go back there, having so many in the boat."

Smith: "Did the women urge you to go back toward the boat?"

Haines: "No, sir. The women did not, sir. I was in charge of the boat and if I had thought it possible I would have gone back."

Miss Minahan (14): "At this time three other boats and ours kept together by being tied to each other. The cries continued to come over the water. Some of the women implored Officer Lowe of number 14 to divide his passengers among the three other boats and go back to rescue. His first answer to these requests was, 'You ought to be damn glad you are here and have got your own life.'"

Miss Turja (13): "I did not seem to be a bit afraid, through it all, but the worst part of the thing was the moaning and calling for help as we floated around the water in our boat. This continued for two or three hours from the place where the Titanic sank. It was terrible to hear, but I was told we could not help because we had about forty in our own boat."

Archer (16): "It was spoken by one of the lady passengers to go back and see if there was anyone in the water we could pick up, but I never heard anymore of it after that.

Walter Perkis
An Unsung Hero

Much has been made—rightfully so—of Fifth Officer Lowe's return to the wreckage after the ship went down to pick up survivors from the water. Although it became obvious in hindsight that he had waited too long to return, his act still managed to save three people who would have otherwise frozen to death. But Lowe was not the only one who acted heroically in this manner.

Few people realize that another crewman, Quartermaster Walter Perkis, also returned to the site of the wreck—with much better results. Perkis helped lower lifeboat 4 from the boat deck. While the occupants tried to free themselves from the ropes, he had time to head aft on the boat deck. Finding nothing there that needed his services, he returned to the same area of deck only to find the lifeboat he helped lower still along the side of the ship. He went down one of the ropes and took command of lifeboat 4 on his own initiative.

After the *Titanic* went down, Perkis returned to the outer perimeter of the wreckage almost immediately and picked up eight men out of the water. He continued the rescue until the cries subsided. Two died in the boat shortly thereafter, but six men owed their lives to Perkis for his decisive and heroic deed.

The master-at-arms had charge of the boat."
Bourne: "What did he say?"
Archer: "I did not hear. I was in the forepart of the boat."

By 2:55 a.m. collapsibles A and B had all the occupants they would see for the rest of the night. The slow, grim wait began. On both of these ruined lifeboats, it was critical to avoid contact with the water as much as possible. In the case of collapsible A, that meant standing, drenched in soaking wet clothing, in 28 degree water up to their shins until daybreak. For collapsible B, it meant staying alert enough so as not to tip the overturned boat. The time passed in an extremely slow and gruesome manner for these two boats, as the hand of death periodically reached up from the dark waters to take another victim.

Mr. Williams (A): ". . . two women, evidently mother and daughter, were back of me so I had not noticed them during the night. A slight stirring made me look around. The daughter had gone first but the mother clutched her body to her and held her. The strain was too much. Clutched in each other's arms, they floated away."

Mr. Wennertrom (A): "All the feeling had left us. If we wanted to know if we still had legs (or any other part) left, we had to feel down in the water with our hand. The only exercise we got was when someone gave up hope and died, whom we immediately threw overboard to give the live ones a little more space and at the same time lighten the weight of the boat."

Mr. Abelseth (A): "I got up on this raft or collapsible boat and raised up and then I was continually moving my arms and swinging them around to keep warm. Some of them were trying to get up on their feet. They were sitting down or lying down on the raft. Some of them fell into the water again. Some of them were frozen. And there were two dead that they threw overboard. There was one lady aboard this raft and she got saved. I do not know her name. I saw her on board the Carpathia, but I forgot to ask her name. There were also two Swedes, and a first class passenger – I believe that is what he said – and he had just his underwear on. I asked him if he was married and he said he had a wife and child. There was also a fireman named Thompson on the same raft. He had burned one of his hands. Also there was a young boy, with a name that sounded like Volunteer. He was at St. Vincent's Hospital afterwards. Thompson was there, too."

Mr. Gracie (B): "There was one man who was in front, with an oar, and another man in the stern with what I think was a piece of a board, propelling the boat along. We did not stand on it until just before the sun came up. We were taken through the wreckage and away from the screams of the drowning people, and we were on the lookout then in every direction for lights and ships to come to our rescue, hallooing all the time, 'Boat ahoy,' or 'Ship ahoy.'"

As the hour came to a close, many in the water were already unconscious from the intense cold. Others were just barely hanging on. Gracie's ears were exposed not only to the cold air, but to the detailed sounds of events in the water during the aftermath that few ever verbalized.

Mr. Gracie (B): "Though I did not see, I could not avoid hearing what took place at this most tragic crisis in all my life. The men with the paddles, forward and aft, so steered the boat as to avoid contact with the unfortunate swimmers pointed out struggling in the water. I heard the constant explanation made as we passed men swimming in the wreckage, 'Hold on to what you have, old boy. One more of you aboard would sink us all.'"

Estimates vary as to how long the cries and screams for help continued across the water, but as the hour came to an end, the lives of over 1,500 people were slowly fading away. The intense cold robbed them of their energy, gradually freezing their limbs, and then finally extinguishing their inner thoughts. The crowded surface where the *Titanic* sank finally went quiet.

Abelseth (A): "We were standing on the deck. In this little boat the canvas was not raised up. We tried to raise the canvas up but we could not get it up. We stood all night in about 12 or 14 inches of water on this thing and our feet were in the water all the time."

Daniels (B): "Well, we sat there, about twenty of us, right through the night. Nothing to do; just living in hopes. Well, someone started to curse and swear further down on the ship but someone said, 'This is no time for swearing, it's time to say your prayers.' Which we did. So we all said our prayers there, the Lord's Prayer. But I said to this fella, sitting with his back to me, I said, 'I'm tired. I'm going to sleep.' He said, 'For God's sake, son, don't go to sleep.' 'Course I didn't. Had I gone to sleep I'd never of woke up again, it being so cold."

Three O'Clock

As 3:00 a.m. arrived, an unsettling quiet gradually, but finally descended upon the water. The *Titanic* was gone and the remaining survivors found themselves bobbing about in lifeboats in the dark under a brilliant starlit night. It was cold and many were not properly dressed. Some of the lifeboats were leaking because the plug at the bottom had not been properly installed, and water sloshed about the occupants' feet, between periodic bailings. On a human note, some probably needed a bathroom. Many were very uncomfortable sitting on a plank with no place to rest one's back. Others had babies to care for. Only a few hours ago, they were in their staterooms asleep. Now the entire ship was gone, as though it never existed, and they were left in the middle of the ocean, in the dark, with just a small boat to protect them.

Mr. Williams (A): "*. . . everything was quiet, the ocean calm—a deathly stillness.*"

While they drifted about, each lifeboat took on a personality of its own.

Mr. Woolner (D): "A sailor offered some biscuits which I was using for feeding a small child who had waked up and was crying. It was one of those little children for whose parents everybody was looking—the larger one of those two."
Smith: "It's mother was not on this boat?"
Woolner: "No."
Smith: "How old was that child?"

Woolner: *"I should think it [a child] was about 5, as nearly as I can judge. It looked like a French child, but it kept shouting for its doll, and I could not make out what it said before that. It kept saying it over and over again. This is the only one I had anything to do with. There were several other children in the boat."*

Miss Graham (3): *"I counted our fellow passengers. We were 34, including 2 sailors, 2 ship's boys, and a half a dozen or more other men. The men didn't say a word. The women quarreled a little because some of them didn't have room to sit down."*

Mrs. Ryerson (4): *"We had no lights or compass. There were several babies in the boat but there was no milk or water. I believe these were all stowed away somewhere, but no one knew where, and as the bottom of the boat was full of water and the boat full of people it was very difficult to find anything."*

Miss Gibson (5): *"It was a sense of desolation never to be forgotten. To make matters worse, the weather became bitterly cold and many of the women in the boat were clad in the lightest of evening gowns and some more scantily. The men behaved like heroes, except for one chap, who calmly stretched himself in the forepart of the lifeboat and promptly fell asleep regardless of what might happen. There was a young Englishman who managed to wear his monocle throughout the excitement and proved himself a much better man than he looked. He divested himself of what clothing he could spare for the shelter of the women and cheered us with his drawling dialect and his words of hope."*

Mrs. Smith (6): *"Our seaman was Hichens, who refused to row, but sat on the end of the boat wrapped in a blanket that one of the women had given him. I am not of the opinion that he was intoxicated, but a lazy, uncouth man, who had no respect for the ladies and who was a thorough coward."*

Mr. McGough (7): *"Although there were several of us wanted drinking water, it was unknown to us that there was a tank of water and also some crackers in our boat, having no light on our boat, and we did not discover this fact—that is as to the tank of water—until after reaching the Carpathia."*

Mrs. White (8): *"As I said before, the men in our boat were anything but seamen, with the exception of one man. The women all rowed, every one of them. Miss Young rowed every minute. The men could not row. They did not know the first thing about it. Miss Swift, from Brooklyn, rowed every minute from the steamer to the Carpathia. Miss Young rowed every minute, also, except when she was throwing up, which she did six or seven times. Countess Rothe stood at the tiller. Where would we have been if it had not been for our women, with such men as that put in charge of the boat? Our head seaman would give an order and those men who knew nothing about the handling of a boat would say, 'If you don't stop talking through that hole in your face there will be one less in the boat.' We were in the hands of men of that kind. I settled two or three fights between them, and quieted them down. Imagine getting right out there and taking out a pipe and filling it and standing there smoking, with the women rowing, which was most dangerous."*

Mr. Karun (10): *"Then for four and a half hours we were in the boat. The sea was smooth but it was full of chunks of ice, some small and some large. It was cold like Christmas and we shivered from it. My little girl was in the same boat and was very brave. I tried to keep her warm."*

Ray (13): *"We pulled all night with short intervals for rest. I inquired if the ladies were all warm and they said they were quite warm and they had a blanket to spare. There seemed to be very little excitement in the boat. They were all quite calm and collected. I should imagine there were two thirds women and one third men. As far as I can remember there were about four or five firemen, one baker, and three stewards. The remainder were second and first class passengers and third class passengers. There was one Japanese."*

Mrs. Cook (14): "As we were tossing about, we could see the iceberg we had struck which looked like a mountain and we were obliged to stop for some time for the wreckage was awful around us. All this time we were almost frozen with the cold and it was heartbreaking to see the poor things with only their night attire. We were all mixed up together, first, second, and third class passengers. The poor women were crying and the children were also seasick. And then there was a little hole at the bottom of our collapsible boat and we had to keep bailing the water out for nearly 7½ hours."

Mrs. Futrelle (16): "Had there been a heavy sea our lifeboat would surely have been swamped, since the crew knew nothing whatsoever about the handling of oars. They admitted to me later that they were stewards. There was no compass on the

boat and no water. In shipping an oar one of the men struck me on the head and for a few minutes I was senseless. When I revived we were a long distance from where the Titanic went down. The men in the boat were laughing and talking. Some of them were smoking. The little French woman sobbed hysterically."

Without the *Titanic* to rally around, the survivors took an interest in the whereabouts of other lifeboats. At first, they were following their own agendas. Some headed for the light on the horizon while others simply drifted about. Some remained relatively close to the *Titanic* while others had, by their own estimates, rowed a mile away.

Mr. Peuchen (6): "We could see those different lifeboats that had lights. They were all over. They were not all staying together at all. Some of them were going east, west, north, and south, it seemed to me, but there was one boat that had a sort of an electric light, and one a sort of bluish light, as well, which we thought at first was a steamer or something."

Haines (9): "I had a lamp there, a little pocket lamp."

Lifeboats 1, 2, 5, 6, 8 and collapsi-

bles C and D were following Captain Smith's orders—probably not realizing that he was now dead—and rowing for the light. Some lifeboats, like D and 5, gave up and turned around sooner than others.

Mr. Stengel (1): "We rowed for it at first, and then it vanished like."

Mrs. Douglas (2): "Mrs. Appleton and some of the other women had been rowing and did row all of the time."

Etches (5): "We pulled away and a light we thought was a mast headlight of a ship was across where the port bow of the Titanic would have been at the time. We saw a light that there was quite an argument over. Some said it was a star. Others said it was a ship. But we pulled toward it, and we did not seem to approach it an inch nearer. It had every appearance of a masthead light of a ship, but rather a faint light."

Mr. Peuchen(6): "I did not say anything. I knew I was perfectly powerless. He [Hichens] was at the rudder. He was a very talkative man. He had been swearing a good deal, and was very disagreeable. I had had one row with him. I asked him to come and row, to assist us in rowing, and let some woman steer the boat, as it was a perfectly calm night. It did not require any skill for steering. The stars were out. He refused to do it, and he told me he was in command of that boat, and I was to row."

Fleet (6): "We kept on pulling. We thought we could get up to this light, but we could not. It seemed to be getting away from us all the time."

Hichens (6): "When the lights were gone out we were still heading for this cod banker, all of us. I pulled for that light—this imaginary light. We were pulling for it all the time."

Jones (8): "I pulled for about two hours, and then it started to get daybreak, and we lost the light. And then all of a sudden we saw the Carpathia coming, and we turned right back and made for the Carpathia."

Rowe (C): "I saw the light; that was the light we were pulling for when we left the ship. A white light. We did not seem to get nearer to it. We kept on pulling for it, because it was the only stationary light. I think there was a ship there. Indeed, I am sure of it and that she was a sailer. Toward daylight the wind sprung up and she sort of hauled off from us."

Bright (D): "There was a light sighted away, I should say, possibly 4 or 5 miles away, off the port bow of the ship. It looked to me like a sailing ship—like a fishing boat. There were no lights to be seen about the hull of the ship, if it was a ship. We pulled toward that for a time."

Mr. Woolner (D): "We rowed on and on for some time. For quite a considerable time we simply rowed out into the sea. I should say a quarter of an hour. We heard other boats around us, and when the eyes got accustomed to the darkness one could see a certain amount. There was a lantern but there was no oil in it."

Buley (10): "She was stationary there for about three hours, I think, . . . and when we were in the boat we all made for her, and she went by us. The northern lights are just like a searchlight, but she disappeared."

The darkness seemed eternal to the survivors. Light—any light—was valued and sought to nourish their shattered spirits.

Mr. Beesley (13): "It is not easy at this time to call to mind who were in the boat, because in the night it was not possible to see more than a few feet away . . . "

Miss Turja (13): "After we left our ship, it was so dark that the men and women had to burn their hats, coats, or anything else they could spare so that the other boats could see and keep together."

While lifeboats 1, 2, 6, and 8 rowed for the distant light, numbers 5 and 7 came together sometime around 3:00 a.m.

Mr. Harder (5): "...and after waiting around for a while there was this other boat that came alongside, that Pitman hailed alongside . . . in which Mr. and Mrs. Bishop were. We tied alongside of that, and they had 29 people in their boat and we counted the number of people in our boat, and at that time we only counted, I think it was, 36. So we gave them four or five of our people in order to make it even, as we were kind of crowded. They say those boats hold 60 people, but we had only the number of people I have mentioned and believe me, we did not have room to spare."

Mr. McGough (7): "Our boat was launched with 28 people. We, however, transferred 5 from one of the other boats after we were out in the ocean, which was sometime after the ship went down."

Lifeboats 3, 9, 11, 13, 15, 16 continued to drift with no plan of action.

This photograph shows how crowded some of the lifeboats were that night, making rowing and other activities difficult. Some of the boats were flooded at the bottom with up to a foot of water and had to be periodically bailed out. Most did not have a working lamp, and drifted about in darkness.

Fletcher: "Did you assemble with any of the other boats after that?"
Ward (9): "No, sir. We never got near to another boat again."

Bourne: "Did any other boat come in your vicinity?"
Brice (11): "No, sir. There was one ahead of us and one directly astern of us."

Mr. Beesley (13): "We were then in touch with three other boats. One was 15, on our starboard quarter, and the others I have always supposed were 9 and 11, but I do not know definitely. We never got into close touch with each other, but called occasionally across the darkness and saw them looming near and then drawing away again. We called to ask if any officer were aboard the other three, but did not find one. So in the absence of any plan of action, we rowed slowly forward—or what we thought was forward, for it was in the direction the Titanic's bows were pointing before she sank. I see now that we must have been pointing northwest, for we presently saw the Northern Lights on the starboard . . . "

The surface was still flat—unusually so. It was as if the Atlantic had prepared a dance floor for these lifeboats while they rowed in some kind of waltz of the macabre.

Hogg (7): "It was bitter cold. Not a ripple on the water. It was as smooth as glass."

Mrs. Cook (14): "The water was as calm as a table top when we first got on . . ."

Lowe and lifeboat 14 were on their own at first, but sometime after 3:00 a.m. he sprang to action and took direction of the other lifeboats in the area. He thought they would have a better chance at being sighted as a larger image on the surface, so he decided to tie the boats together. Not having made a decision yet about going back to the wreckage, he herded together the port boats 4, 10, 12, and collapsible D alongside his own lifeboat, number 14.

Hardy (D): " We got clear of the ship and rowed out some little distance from her, and finally we all got together, about seven boats of us, and I remember quite distinctly Boatswain Lowe telling us to tie up to each other, as we would be better seen and could keep better together. Then Officer Lowe, having a full complement of passengers in his boat, distributed among us what he had, our boat taking 10. We had 25 already, and that number made 35."

Bright (D): "... after we got away there was Mr. Lowe, the fourth officer, came alongside

of us in another boat, and told us to stick together and then he asked the number in the boat, and there was a steward by the name of Hardy counted them and told him, and then they put ten or a dozen men into our boat because it was not filled up. There were five boats all close up together, and where boats were overloaded he was taking the people out and putting them into the boats that had room to carry them."

Mr. Woolner (D): "Then some officer came along and said, 'I want all these boats tied up by their painters, head and tail, so as to make a more conspicuous mark,' and we did that, and there was no call to row much after that because we were simply drifting about."

Mrs. Ryerson (4): "After the Titanic sank we saw no lights and no one seemed to know what direction to take. Lowe, the officer in charge of the boat, had called out earlier for all to tie together, so we now heard his whistle and as soon as we could make out the other boats in the dark, five of us were tied together and we drifted about without rowing as the sea was calm, waiting for the dawn."

Evans (10): "We stopped there about an hour, I think it was, when number 14 came over with one officer."

Clench (12): "We was rowing up there, and up come the officer, after the ship was gone down, come up with us with his boat, and transferred some of his people he had in his boat into two boats of ours."

And then there was the matter of deciding wether to go back to the site of the sinking. At some point when Lowe was distributing passengers more evenly among the boats, he decided return. In his mind, he reasoned that the mass of humanity back at the wreckage had become less threatening to any lifeboat that returned to offer assistance.

Lowe (14): "Then I had 10, I had 12, and I had another collapsible, and one other boat the number of which I do not know. I herded them together and roped them–made them all tie up–and of course I had to wait until the yells and shrieks had subsided–for the people to thin out–and then I deemed it safe for me to go amongst the wreckage."

Buley (10): "We got away from the ship and about an hour afterwards Officer Lowe came alongside and he had his boat filled up and he distributed them among the other boats, and he said to all the seamen in the boat to jump in his boat until he went back among the wreckage to see if there were any people that had lived."

Evans (10): "The fifth officer, I think it was. He came over in number 14 boat and he says, 'Are there any seamen there?' We said, 'Yes, sir.' He said, 'Alright. You will have to distribute these passengers among these boats. Tie them all together and come into my boat,' he said, 'to go over into the wreckage and pick up anyone that is alive there.'"

Lowe was feeling the stress of the situation by now. He had just watched the vessel, for which he was an officer, sink beneath the water. He listened, along with the other survivors, to the screams and cries of hundreds of people. Some of the passengers had pleaded with him to return to the site but their requests went against his instincts. As the cries died down, he decided to act. The cocky and somewhat cavalier attitude he displayed earlier was gone as he realized what a complete horror the night had become. The strain on the 28-year old officer showed through his temper as he orchestrated a reshuffling of passengers to free up space in preparation for the return.

Miss Minahan (14): "After some time he was persuaded to do as he was asked. As I came up to him to be transferred to the other boat he said, 'Jump, God damn you, jump.' I had showed no hesitancy and was waiting

Fifth Officer Harold Lowe

only my turn. He had been so blasphemous during the two hours we were in his boat that the women at my end of the boat all thought he was under the influence of liquor."

One by one he cleared the sixty or so passengers out of his boat into lifeboat 4 and collapsible D–both monuments to lost opportunities to save more people. When he cleared his boat, he selected a group of men that looked physically capable of pulling

waterlogged passengers out of the water.

Miss Minahan (4): "Then he took all of the men who had rowed number 14, together with the men from the other boats, and went back to the scene of the wreck."

Lowe (14): "So I transferred all my passengers–somewhere about 53 passengers– from my boat, and I equally distributed them between my other four boats. Then I asked for volunteers to go with me to the wreck, and it was at this time that I found this Italian. He came aft, and he had a shawl over his head and I suppose he had skirts. Anyhow, I pulled this shawl off his face and saw he was a man. He was in a great hurry to get into the other boat, and I caught hold of him and pitched him in."

Since collapsible D was one of the lifeboats tied up with Lowe, it could have been Buckley that he noticed wearing a shawl. But if Buckley had removed it earlier, then Lowe's observation would establish that more than one person used this device to gain a seat in a lifeboat. Buckley was Irish. Lowe mentions an Italian.

After collapsible D was rearranged, number 10 was next to produce some surprises.

Burke (10): "After the two seamen left that

This photograph of collapsible B, taken a week after the disaster, shows how lifeboats 12 and 4 would have pulled up to the overturned collapsible to take off the survivors.

ly they were unprepared for what they were going to find. Returning with the intent of filling the boat with waterlogged, but appreciative passengers and crew, Lowe and his group were instead heading into a floating morgue. It was after 3:30 a.m. and the victims had been submerged in the water for well over an hour.

Evans (14): "So we got into his boat and went straight over toward the wreckage."
Smith: "When you went over toward the wreckage, how many people were in your boat?"
Evans: "Eight or 9, sir."

Fletcher: "You were then with Lowe in his boat and went back to where the Titanic sank?"
Buley (14): "Yes, sir, and picked up the remaining live bodies. There were not very many there. We got four of them. All the others were dead."
Fletcher: "Were there many dead?"
Buley: "Yes, sir. There were a good few dead, sir. Of course you could not discern them exactly on account of the wreckage. But we turned over several of them to see if they were alive. It looked as though none of them were drowned. They looked as though they were frozen. The life belts they had on were that much out of the water and their

boat some of the women in the forward end said to me, "There are two men down here in the bottom of the boat.' I said, 'Are there so?' I made down in the bottom of the boat and got hold of those two men and pulled one out. I found he was apparently a Japanese and could not speak any English. I explained to him and put him on an oar. The other man appeared to me to be an

Italian, about 18 stone. I tried to speak to him in Italian and he said, 'Armenian.' That was all he could say. I also put him on an oar."

Lowe drew his crew from the boats. He took Evans and Buley from boat 10, leaving Burke. He already had Crowe and Scarrott originally. When he felt he was ready, Lowe set off in lifeboat 14. It is like-

heads laid back, with their faces on the water, several of them."

Fletcher: "How soon after the Titanic went down was it before you got back there with Lowe to help rescue people?"

Buley: "From an hour to an hour and a half."

Lowe (14): "Then I went off and I rowed off to the wreckage and around the wreckage and I picked up four people." Four alive. I do not know who these three live persons were. They never came near me afterwards, with to say this, that, or the other. But one died and that was a Mr. Hoyt of New York, and it took all the boat's crew to pull this gentleman into the boat, because he was an enormous man and I suppose he had been soaked fairly well with water and when we picked him up he was bleeding from the mouth and from the nose. So we did get him on board and I propped him up at the stern of the boat, and we let go his collar, took his collar off, and loosened his shirt so as to give him every chance to breathe. But unfortunately, he died. I suppose he was too far gone when we picked him up. But the other three survived."

William Hoyt's body weight was a contributor to preventing him from freezing. Unfortunately, he suffered from internal injuries during the awful ordeal he likely went through when the Titanic upended and broke apart.

Crowe (14): "Returning to the wreckage we heard various cries, and endeavored to get among them, and we were successful in doing so and in picking one body up that was floating around in the water. When we got him into the boat, after great difficulty, he being such a heavy man, he expired shortly afterwards. Going farther into the wreckage we came across a steward or one of the crew, and we got him into the boat and he was very cold and his hands were kind of stiff, but we got him in and he recovered by the time we got back to the Carpathia. Also, a Japanese or Chinese young fellow that we picked up on top of some of the wreckage – it might have been a sideboard or table – that was floating around."

Evans (14): "One died. He died in the boat. He was a very stout man. A large, fleshy man. We had great trouble in getting him into the boat."

Smith: "Who were these three other persons?"

Evans: "I did not recognize two of them, sir."

Smith: "Did you recognize one?"

Evans: "Yes, sir. The steward, young Stewart."

Scarrott (14): "When we got to it the sight we saw was awful. We were amongst hundreds of dead bodies floating in life belts. We could only see four alive. The first one we picked up was a male passenger. He died shortly after we got him in the boat. After a hard struggle we managed to get the other three. One of these we saw kneeling as if in prayer upon what appeared to be a part of a staircase. He was only about twenty yards away from us but it took us half an hour to push our boat through the wreckage and bodies to get to him. Even then we could not get very close so we put out an oar for him to get hold of and so pulled him to the boat. All of the bodies we saw seemed as if they had perished with the cold as their limbs were all cramped up. As we left that awful scene we gave way to tears. It was enough to break the stoutest heart."

Evans (14): "We picked up four persons alive. One died on the way back. There were plenty of dead bodies about us. You couldn't hardly count them. I was afraid to look over the sides because it might break my nerves down. We had great difficulty in getting through them to get to the wreck."

Sometime after 3:30 Officer Boxhall ignited a second green flare which immediately drew the attention of all boats.

Mrs. Douglas (2): "Mr. Boxhall had charge of the signal lights on the Titanic, and he had put in the emergency boat a tin box of green lights, like rockets. These he commenced to send off at intervals and very quickly we saw the lights of the Carpathia, the captain of which stated he saw our green lights 10 miles away, and of course, steered directly to us so we were the first boat to arrive at the Carpathia."

Mr. Woolner (D): "But there was a green light that appeared, not all the time, but most of the time, down to the south. I could not tell, but I should think about half a mile or a mile."
Smith: "That was probably the green light that was on Officer Boxhall's boat."

Collins (B): "We were drifting about there. We drifted, I am sure, a mile and a half from the Titanic, from where she sank, and there was some lifeboat that had a green light on it, and we thought it was a boat after the Titanic sunk. We thought this green light was some boat, and we commenced to shout. All we saw was the green light. We were drifting about for two hours . . ."

Mr. Stengel (1): "Most of the boats rowed toward that light and after the green lights began to burn I suggested it was better to turn around and go toward the green lights, because I presumed there was an officer of the ship in that boat and he evidently knew his business. We did not reach its side."

While Lowe and his grim crew searched the wreckage, the four boats that he left behind eventually disbanded. It was around 3:40 a.m. when the drifting currents brought the upside down collapsible B within their sight and boats 4 and 12 broke away and organized a rescue.

Clench (12): "And while Mr. Lowe was gone I heard shouts. Of course, I looked around and I saw a boat in the way that appeared to be like a funnel. We started to back away then. We thought it was the top of the funnel. I put my head over the gunwale and looked along the water's edge and saw some men on a raft."

Mrs. Ryerson (4): "It was very cold and soon a breeze sprang up, and it was hard to keep our heavy boat bow on, but as the cries died down we could see dimly what seemed to be a raft with about 20 men standing on it, back to back. It was the overturned boat and as the sailors on our boat said we could still carry 8 or 10 more people, we called for another boat to volunteer and go to rescue them. So we two cut loose our painters and between us got all the men off. They were nearly gone and could not have held out much longer."

Hemming (4): "Then we heard some hollering going on and we saw some men standing on what we thought was ice. Half a mile as nearly as I can judge. I guess about 20, I should say, stood up on the boat. On the bottom of this upturned boat. Mr. Lightoller was on the upturned boat. Two boats cast off, us and another boat cast off, and pulled to them, and took them in our two boats."

Collins (B): "Then came daylight and we saw our own lifeboats, and we were very close to them. We were about from this window here to over there, almost opposite them, but in the dark we could not see them. When it became daylight we spied them and shouted to them, and they came over to us and there was two of our lifeboats that lifted the whole lot that were on the collapsible boats."

Mr. Thayer (B): "It took them ages to cover the three or four hundred yards between us. As they approached, we could see that so few men were in them that some of the oars were being pulled by women. In neither of them was much room for extra passengers, for they were two of the very few boats to be loaded to near capacity."

Miss Lehmann (12): "That night was the longest one I ever put in in my life. It seemed that it would never be dawn. Sometime during the night we met a capsized lifeboat with three men on the bottom of it. They were wet and cold. We picked them up and that made us even more crowded. We still rowed on and on. Would morning ever come?"

Clench (12): "Then I heard two whistles blown. I sang out, 'Aye, aye. I am coming over,' and we pulled over and found it was a raft—not a raft, exactly, but an overturned boat—and Mr. Lightoller was there on that boat, and I believe—I do not know whether I am right or not, but I think the wireless operator was on there, too. We took them on board the boat and we shared the amount of the room that was there."
Bourne: "How many were there on this boat that was there?"
Clench: "I should say about 20, sir."
Bourne: "They were all standing on the bottom?"
Clench: "On the bottom of the boat, sir, and Mr. Lightoller, he came aboard of us. They were all wet through, apparently. They had been in the water."

Other lifeboats heard the whistle but continued to avoid any connection with the wreckage site.

Mr. Peuchen (6): "As we rowed, pulled away from the Titanic, there was an officer's call of some kind. We stopped rowing. A sort of whistle. Anyway, the quartermaster told us to stop rowing so he could hear it, and this was a call to come back to the boat. So we all thought we ought to go back, to the boat. It was a call. But the quartermaster said, 'No, we are not going back to the boat." He said, "It is our lives now, not theirs,' and he insisted upon our rowing farther away."

Survivors from the overturned collapsible carefully climbed aboard boats 4 and 12. They had been in that deadly water once already and made certain, even in their exhausted states, not to tip themselves back into it. As an indication of the state of mind the survivors were in, a mother and son were too dazed to even take note of each other while only several feet apart in the same lifeboat.

Mr. Thayer (4): "The first took half of us. My mother was in this boat, having rowed most of the night. She says she thought she recognized me. I did not see her. The other boat took aboard the rest of us. We had to lift Harold Bride. He was in a bad way, and I think, would have slipped off the bottom of our overturned boat if several of us had not

held onto him for the last half hour."

Mr. Gracie (4): "Just before the bows of the two boats reached us, Lightoller ordered us not to scramble, but each to take his turn so that the transfer might be made in safety. When my turn came, in order not to endanger the lives of the others, or plunge them into the sea, I went carefully, hands first, into the rescuing lifeboat. Lightoller remained to the last, lifting a lifeless body into the boat beside me."

Lightoller (4): "I know a great number were taken out of the water. I made it my special business to inquire, and as far as I can gather, for every six people picked out of the water five of them would be firemen or stewards. On our boat, as I have said before, there was Colonel Gracie and young Thayer. I think those were the only two passengers."
Smith: "There were no women on the boat?"
Lightoller: "No. I am speaking of the overturned boat."
Smith: "I refer to that. There were no women on your boat?"
Lightoller: "No, sir. These were all taken out of the water and they were firemen and others of the crew."
Smith: "How many were there on that boat?"

Lightoller: "Roughly, about 30."
Bourne: "Did they all survive, that you rescued?"

Clench (12): "Yes, sir. Although, we thought it was a case with the wireless operator, who was very bad. We said we thought he was going to croak."

About the same time that Lightoller climbed aboard lifeboat 4, many of the boats were taking an interest in a light to the north. It was lifeboat 8, turning around from their failed attempt to reach the distant ship.

Mrs. White (8): "Then we turned and went back, and lingered around there for a long time, trying to locate the other boats, but we could not locate them except by hearing them. The only way they could locate us was by my electric light. The lamp on the boat was absolutely worth nothing. They tinkered with it all along, but they could not get it in shape. I had an electric cane—a cane with an electric light in it—and that was the only light we had. We sat there for a long time . . . I stood up all night long because I could not get up onto the seats, which were very high, on account of my foot being bound up. I had no strength in my foot, and I stood all night long."

Miss Young (8): "In those hours spent face to face with the solemn thoughts of trials still to undergo, before possible rescue, it was inspiring to see that these twentieth century women were, in mentality and physique, worthy descendants of their ancestors, who had faced other dire perils in Colonial and Revolutionary periods. Women rowed all night, others in the bow waved the lantern light in air as a signal to the ship, toward whose light our boat crept slowly till dawn, with only a young girl at the tiller to keep the boat headed straight in spite of the jerky, uneven rowing. Treasured above all else was the electric light in the handle of a cane belonging to Mrs. J. Stuart White, who waved it regularly while counting strokes for the haphazard crew."

Mr. Stengel (1): "There was a lady had a cane, I believe, with an electric light, and she was flashing this light, and they were going to that boat, and we were going toward that boat, and there were two other boats around, so the two or three of us kept together. That is, all the boats besides our own kept together."

Hemming (4): "We made for a light. We pulled toward them and got together, and we picked up another boat and kept in her company."

Others were in the area. Boats 1, 4, and 8 were together, although every so often they would drift or row away again. Most boats were rowing simply to stay warm. In the darkness of the night, they passed by each other and then slowly faded from sight, like some strange survivor ritual.

Mrs. Smith (6): "It was bitterly cold, but I did not seem to mind it particularly. I was trying to locate my husband in all the boats that were near us. The night was beautiful. Everything seemed to be with us in that respect and a very calm sea."

Miss Gibson (5): ". . . we had been wondering whether the operator of the wireless on the Titanic had been able to send out his signal of distress. This thought bothers us greatly. To drift about aimlessly in the open sea with the assurance that the wireless had communicated with a vessel, no matter how far distant would be a consolation, but to drift in the hope that we might encounter a vessel accidentally was different."

It had been an hour since the *Titanic* went down and most people by now were exhausted and dazed. With everything that had happened during the night, the survivors were becoming a bit stoical. Events that would earlier have aroused them, now made little impression upon their senses.

Mr. Woolner (D): "Somebody fired, I think, 4 shots in rapid succession, and we in our boats were wondering what it was, and somebody in our boat said, 'I suppose it is meant for a signal.' It did not excite anybody. Nobody took any notice of it. They did not know what it meant, and they did not take any notice of it."

But Boxhall's green flares grabbed their attention—and more than just those in the lifeboats. At this time a sense of tremendous relief swept through the crowds on the lifeboats. The *Carpathia* emerged from the obscurity of a distant iceberg, and it was then that the survivors noticed a light on the southern horizon brighter than the surrounding stars. Everyone studied it. Many were probably wary of believing that a ship was coming, on the heels of their disappointment with the other light to the north. But eventually, the light proved itself to be better than a star. It was coming closer.

Rostron: "Between 2:45 and 4 o'clock, the time I stopped my engines, we were passing icebergs on every side and making them ahead and having to alter our course several times to clear the bergs."

Boxhall (2): "I saw rockets on the Carpathia. It was in the morning. It was quite dark."

Mr. Stengel (1): "It was toward morning that we turned, and by that time another man and myself thought we saw rockets—one rocket, that is, a rocket explode. And I said, 'I think I saw a rocket,' and another one said, 'I think I saw a rocket,' and one of the stokers, I think it was, said, 'I see two lights. I believe that is a vessel.' Then after that, when another green light was burned, there was a flash light from a boat, and I said, 'Now I am pretty positive that is a boat because that is an answer to the green signal,' and one of the stokers said, 'The green light is the company's color,' I understood him to say. Whether he was right or not, I do not know. When we saw the flashlight it was like powder was set off. I said, 'Now let us give it to her and let us steer in between the green light where we saw the green light, and that boat, and that being a very light boat, we left the other boats quite a way behind."

Collins (12): "Then the Carpathia came into sight. We saw her masthead lights first and saw her starboard and port side lights. When she came near us, we saw her, and we did not know what boat it was."

Ward (9): "We saw her at a distance. She was headed our way."

Miss Mulvihill (10): "Dawn was just breaking when I saw a light way off in the distance. I spoke to the nearest sailor about it and asked if it possibly could be a vessel coming to help us. He said it must be a ship's light, but someone spoke up and said it was probably a boat's light. Then two big green lights broke through the mist above it, and we knew it was a ship coming to rescue us. We cheered and cheered and cheered. Some cried. I just sat still and offered up a little prayer."

Mr. Abelseth (A): "There was one man from New Jersey that I came in company with from London. I do not know what his name was. I tried to keep this man alive, but I could not make it. It was just at the break of day, and he was lying down and he seemed to be kind of unconscious. He was not really dead and I took him by the shoulder and raised him up so that he was sitting up on deck. I said to him, 'We can see a ship now. Brace up.' And I took one of his hands and raised it up like that [illustrating] and I took him by the shoulder and shook him and he said, 'Who are you?' He said, 'Let me be. Who are you?' I held him up like that for a while, but I got tired and cold and I took a little piece of a small board, a lot of which were floating around there, and laid it under his head on the edge of the boat to keep his head from the water, but it was not more than about half an hour or so when he died."

The first hint of dawn began a little before 4:00 a.m. Lowe was circling the wreckage sight for one last time. The results were crushing.

Lowe (14): "I then left the wreck. I went right around and, strange to say, I did not see a single female body, not one, around the wreckage.
Smith: "Did you have a light in your boat?"
Lowe (14): "No, sir. I left my crowd of boats somewhere, I should say, about between half past 3 and 4 in the morning, and after I had been around it was just breaking day, and I am quite satisfied that I had a real good look around, and that there was nothing left."

While they stared into the darkness for any sign of life, a faint blue light from the first sign of dawn began to illuminate objects in the distance with a ghostly hue.

Buley (14): "We were right in amongst the wreckage and we thought it was a sailing ship, until the light came on and we saw it was an iceberg."

Evans (14): "I had a thorough good look around everywhere in the wreckage. To see if I could see any live ones—any live bodies."

Smith: "Was it daylight at this time?"
Evans: "Just breaking daylight."
Smith: "When you found there were no live persons whom you could rescue, why did you not take some of the dead ones aboard? You had lots of room."
Evans: "That lay with the officer."
Smith: "And what did he say about it?"
Evans: "He did not pass any remark about at all, sir. He said, 'Have a good look around, and see if you can see anybody alive at all.'"
Smith: "And when you didn't find anybody alive, what did the officer say?"
Evans: "The officer said, 'Hoist the sail forward.' I did so and made sail."

Bourne: "Did any of the ladies in the boat ask to help row or take a trick at the oar?"
Archer (16): "There was one, a stewardess. She tried to assist. She did so. I told her it was not necessary for her to do it, but she said she would like to do it to keep herself warm. And we fancied we saw a light, and we started to pull toward the light for a time, and then, after we had been pulling for it half an hour, we saw the Carpathia's side lights. We did not know what became of that. When we saw the Carpathia, we turned to go back."
Bourne: "Were any of the people transferred from your boat after you lowered her, or

taken from the water by you?"
Archer: "Yes, sir. One fireman. There was one fireman found in the boat after we got clear. I do not know how he come there. He was transferred from another boat, I think it was number 9, after we were pulling toward the Carpathia . . . to help row the other. I believe there was only one other able seaman in it."

Hogg (7): "I saw the lights of the Carpathia. I said, 'It is alright now ladies. Do not grieve. We are picked up. Now, gentlemen, see what you can do in pulling these oars for this light.' It was practically daylight then."

The *Carpathia* came closer . . . and closer, aiming for Boxhall's green flares. When Captain Rostron felt he was close enough, he brought the ship to a standstill, with the engines still running. The last thing he wanted was for the *Carpathia* to accidentally run over one of the lifeboats drifting about in the dark.

The lifeboats studied the ship with intense interest, trying to determine its next move. It would take some time for each lifeboat to realize that the *Carpathia* was coming to a stop and would remain in the distance. It was 3:59 a.m. and a faint blue light illuminated the scene, slowly increasing in intensity with the arrival of dawn.

Four O'Clock

The *Titanic* was gone, replaced by a much smaller and less glamorous vessel called the *Carpathia*. But its size and appearance did not matter to the survivors. It was a knight in shining armor on all accounts. In the darkness of the morning, most of the boats started rowing for her.

Rostron: "At 4 o'clock I stopped."

Bisset: "The light of the green flare toward which we were steering had burned out. Captain Rostron ordered the engines to be stopped. It was 4:00 a.m. We had arrived in three and a half hours. Powerful is the force of routine. As eight bells sounded for the change of the watch, the lookout man in the crow's nest sang out in the long-drawn wailing cry, 'A-a-all's well and lights burning brightly . . .'"

But a few boats were too busy with nearby matters to set off just yet for the ship. The dim light of the impending morning increased just enough to make out images around them.

Collapsible D with Hugh Woolner, Frederick Hoyt, Daisy Minahan and others. Some of the occupants had climbed aboard from collapsible A, including Rosa Abbott and Olaus Abelseth. John Hardy is likely at the tiller.

Miss Minahan (D): "We were left with a steward and a stoker to row our boat, which was crowded. The steward did his best, but the stoker refused at first to row, but finally helped two women, who were the only ones pulling on that side."

Mr. Woolner (D): "She [Carpathia] seemed to come up very slowly and then she stopped. Then we looked out and we saw that there was a boat alongside her, and then we realized that she was waiting for us to come up to her instead of her coming to us, as we hoped. Then, just at that time, when we began to row toward the Carpathia, Mr. Lowe came down with his boat under sail again, and hailed us and said, 'Are you a collapsible?' We answered, 'Yes.' He said, 'How are you?' I said, 'We have about all we want.' He said, 'Would you like a tow?' We answered, 'Yes, we would.' So he took our painter and towed us away from the Carpathia and then we looked and saw that there was another little group of people standing up in the sea who had to be rescued."

The rescue mission was over for lifeboat 14–or so they thought. A breeze began to kick up and Lowe decided to set up the sail that was lying in a drenched condition at the bottom of the boat. He set his men to work, mounting the mast and then attaching the dripping wet canvas to it. Sometime around 4:10 a.m., he set sail for the lights of the ship. Lowe quickly noticed the ghostly shape of a lifeboat in the distance and decided to sail over and check on it. As he got closer, it seemed to be floundering about. It was collapsible D and as the occupants were all staring at the rescue ship, they probably did not even notice lifeboat 14 approach.

Lowe (14): "I could see her coming up, and I thought, 'Well, I am the fastest boat of the lot,' as I was sailing, you see. I was going through the water very nicely, going at about, well, I should say, four knots, five knots, maybe, it may have been a little more, it may have been six, but anyhow, I was bowling along very nicely. In the direction of the Carpathia. And I thought, 'I am the fastest boat, and I think if I go toward her, for fear of her leaving us to our doom'—that is what I was scared about, and you will understand that day was dawning more and more as the time came on. And by and by, I noticed a collapsible boat, and it looked rather sorry, so I thought, 'Well, I will go down and pick her up and make sure of her.' So I went about and sailed down to this collapsible and took her in tow."

Buley (14): "We set sail and went over to them, and in a brief time picked up another one. Another boat filled with women and children, with no one to pull the oars, and we took her in tow."

Crowe (14): "We took in tow a collapsible boat containing fully 60 people—women, children, and men."

While lifeboat 14 tied up with collapsible D, they were being studied from afar in the murky light by the desperate and dazed occupants of collapsible A. With the boats in view, they rallied enough energy to gain their attention.

Mr. Abelseth (A): "The next morning we

could see some of the lifeboats. One of the boats had a sail up, and he came pretty close and then we said, 'One, two, three.' We said that quite often. We did not talk very much except that we would say, 'One, two, three,' and scream together for help."

Lowe (14): "I had taken this first collapsible in tow, and I noticed that there was another collapsible in a worse plight than this one that I had in tow. I was just thinking and wondering whether it would be better for me to cut this one adrift and let her go, and for me to travel faster to the sinking one, but I thought, 'No, I think I can manage it.' So I cracked on a bit, and I got down there just in time and took off, I suppose, about 20 men and 1 lady out of this sinking collapsible."
Smith: "Did you leave any bodies on there?"
Lowe: "I left three bodies on it."

Evans (14): ". . . and we altered the course into the direction of this collapsible boat which had been swamped. On the way down we picked up another collapsible that had some women and children in it, and took her in tow and then we sailed to this sinking boat. It was a boat that was swamped."

Buley (14): "In the morning, after we picked up all that was alive, there was a collapsible boat we saw with a lot of people and she was

An unidentified lifeboat – possibly number 4. It is not clear what the situation is at the stern. Either the image has been partially obliterated, or it is filled with blanketed survivors and/or bodies.

swamped and they were up to their knees in water. There were several in the broken boat that could not walk. Their legs and feet were all cramped. They had to stand up in the water in that boat."

Evans (14): "Then we went over to this other collapsible that was swamped. There was one woman in it, and I should say there were about 10 or a dozen men, and 3 dead bodies were lying across the thwarts in the stern sheets. She was up out of the water, but she was swamped."

Lowe (14): "As to the 3 people that I left on her–of course, I may have been a bit hard-hearted, I cannot say–but I thought to myself, 'I am not here to worry about bodies. I am here for life, to save life, and not to bother about bodies,' and I left them."

Smith: "Were they dead when you left them?"

Lowe: "They were dead. Yes, sir. The people on the raft told me they had been dead some time. I said, 'Are you sure they are dead?' They said, 'Absolutely sure.' I made certain they were dead, and questioned them one and all before I left this collapsible."

Mrs. Cook (D): "We sighted a raft with about 9 men and 1 woman. We then rowed to them and only rescued them just as it was sinking and one poor man on it had only his pants and his white star shirt on and he was blue with cold. All this while I had been hugging my rug so seeing him I asked Mr. Hardy to throw it to him but he asked me if I minded a woman having it [probably Rosa Abbott]. With that he threw it to her and I got it back the day we landed."

Crowe (14): "A second-class passenger named Williams, the champion racket play of England returned with us."

The lighting was improving by the minute. The *Carpathia* had stopped so as not to run over any of the lifeboats. All of the survivors saw the rescue ship by now. Some waited a while to see if the boat was going to come to them. But over the course of approximately an hour, it became apparent that the *Carpathia* was stopped and the lifeboats would have to row to the ship.

Miss Mulvihill (10): "Slowly the mist cleared and the big boat pushed toward us. From then we drifted about, waiting for the Carpathia to pick us up. It was bitter cold, and the only thing I can remember very distinctly about those hours is a white cake of ice, which bumped and bumped and bumped against the boat near me. I watched it and once I remember I laughed when another cake of ice pushed between it and the boat. I think I must have been ill then."

Bourne: "Then what did you do?"

Clench (12): "Mr. Lightoller took charge of us and sighted the Carpathia's lights. Then we started heading for that. We had to row a tidy distance to the Carpathia because there was boats ahead of us, you see, and we had a boat in tow with us, besides all the people we had aboard."

Miss Turja (13): "As it was, when the other big boat came, she had to wait for some of the life boats, which were a great distance away from her."

Mrs. Futrelle (16): "It seemed that we rowed for hours after the Titanic sank. With our extra wraps we helped the poor, wild-eyed steerage women to keep their babies warm. Many of the poor little things were almost naked. For the most part the women were dry eyed and silent. The men talked only of being rescued. We didn't care, for our hearts were near breaking when we thought of our men at the bottom of the sea."

Thanks to Boxhall's flare, lifeboat 2 had the good fortune of having the *Carpathia* pull up right next to it. The rest of the boats would not have it so easy.

Rostron: "At 4:10 I got the first boat alongside."

Boxhall (2): "I think it was a little after 4 o'clock sometime when I got on board the Carpathia. It might have been three quarters of an hour before."

Mrs. Douglas (2): "When we pulled alongside Mr. Boxhall called out, 'Shut down your engines and take us aboard. I have only one sailor.' At this point I called out, 'The Titanic has gone down with everyone on board,' and Mr. Boxhall told me to shut up."

Bisset: "If the boat had been well manned, she could have passed under our stern to the leeward side, but as she drifted down toward us, the officer sang out, 'I can't handle her very well. We have women and children and only one seaman.'"

Lifeboat 2 pulled up alongside the *Carpathia*, under an open gangway door. The first of the *Titanic*'s survivors were taken aboard the *Carpathia* one-by-one.

Bisset: "Many of the women and children castaways were seasick from the sudden choppy motion of the boat caused by the dawn breeze. All were numbed with cold, as most of them were lightly clad. Some were quietly weeping. As they were in no fit condition to climb safely up the short Jacob's ladder to the side door, bosun's chairs were lowered, also canvas bags into which we placed the children, and, one at a time, they were all hauled to safety."

One can imagine the suspense of the moment, as the fourth officer climbed on board and was escorted to Captain Rostron's bridge. It must have been a strange sensation to be walking the passageways of a different ship early that Monday morning.

Rostron: "I asked that this officer should

With collapsible D in tow, boat 14 drops its sail as it approaches the *Carpathia*. Lowe is standing at the stern.

come to me as soon as he was on board and to him I put that heartrending enquiry, knowing with a terrible certainty what his answer was to be. 'The Titanic has gone down?' 'Yes,' he said; one word that meant so much–so much that the man's voice broke on it. 'She went down at about 2:30.' An hour and a half ago! Alas, that we had not been nearer."

Bisset: "I followed him up . . . The officer was a young man, Joseph Boxhall, Fourth

Several lifeboats pull up alongside the *Carpathia* in the early light of Monday morning.

Officer of the Titanic. I took him up to the bridge, to report to our captain. Without preliminaries, Rostron burst out excitedly, 'Where is the Titanic?' 'Gone!' said Boxhall. 'She sank at 2:20 a.m.' In the moment of stunned silence that followed, every man on the bridge of the Carpathia could envisage the appalling reality, but not yet to its fullest extent. It was now 4:20 a.m."

Meanwhile, the rest of the boats continued to row for the *Carpathia*. Some were fairly close by chance, while others were miles away.

Mr. Stengel (1): "I felt somewhat enthused to see the boat, and I began to jolly them along to pull. I said, 'Keep pulling.' We kept pulling and I thought we were the first boat aboard, but I found that the boat that had the green lights burning was ahead of us. We were the second boat aboard."

Ward (9): " She stopped and slued around a little, and we surmised that she was then picking up a boat. It was hardly light enough to see at the time. It was just breaking day at that time, but we could see her lights. Then, of course we started to pull toward her. I think we were about the fourth or fifth boat to be picked up."

Collapsible D was very fortunate to receive a tow by Officer Lowe to the *Carpathia*. By comparison, lifeboat 4, which was relatively nearby the collapsible when D was tied to number 14, arrived at the rescue ship considerably later.

Miss Minahan (4): "It was just 4 o'clock when we sighted the Carpathia, and we were three hours getting to her."

As daylight came upon the area, the view was a fascinating on−sunrise over the middle of an iceberg-laden ocean.

Mr. Williams (14): "As my eyes swept the horizon I had my first sight of icebergs. Five or six were visible, and the irony of it was that with the morning sun shining on their gleaming and sparkling whiteness, they made a beautiful never-to-be-forgotten picture."

The crew on the *Carpathia* had their work cut out for them as the lifeboats arrived one after another.

Bisset: "Our immediate task was only too clear−to search for the people in boats or rafts, and any other survivors. The increasing daylight revealed dozens of icebergs within our horizon. Among them were four of five big bergs, towering up to two hundred feet above water level. One of these was the one that the Titanic had struck. Dozens of smaller calves or growlers drifted sluggishly on the choppy seas. To the northwards was a field of pack ice extending westwards for many miles. On all sides we could see lifeboats making laboriously toward us, some dangerously overcrowded, some half empty. A mile away was the wreckage, like an island, marking the spot where the Titanic had gone down."

The sun rose and cast a strong orange light across the faces of the survivors. The nightmare of the past five hours was behind them and their blurred thoughts had been reduced to those of the physical needs. They were tired and cold—burned out. Their long wait in the lifeboats had been an extremely uncomfortable one and the slow, cumbersome trip to the *Carpathia* seemed, for some who were further away, to be an endless trip. Williams, one of the first to arrive, watched from the railing.

Mr. Williams: "Finally the sun came up. It was a beautiful sparkling morning looking down on a group of widely scattered small life boats with their cargo of heart-broken bedraggled humanity–all that was left of the greatest ocean steamer ever built."

Mrs. Ryerson (4): "Then, when the sun rose we saw the Carpathia standing up about 5 miles away, and for the first time we saw the icebergs all around us. The Carpathia steamed toward us until it was full daylight. Then she stopped and began picking up boats and we got on board about 8 o'clock. Very soon after we got on board they took a complete list of the names of all survivors."

Over the course of three and a half hours, the *Carpathia* plucked the remaining survivors from the surface of the Atlantic. They were greeted on deck and escorted to the dining saloon, where blankets and coffee were offered to the dazed group. Once their physical needs were attended to, they slowly emerged from their shock. Warmed by blankets and coffee, the women turned their attention to finding their husbands–and in some cases–their children.

Boat number 12, carrying Lightoller among others, was the last one to arrive along side the *Carpathia*. By now, women were lining the railings in an increasingly alarmed state, realizing that their husbands were not yet on board. The grim reality of the disaster was emerging. There were no more lifeboats rowing toward the ship. For hundreds of women, the awful realization set in that their husbands and sons were missing. The women searched the same waters that Murdoch had searched for ice several hours earlier. Looking out over the railing on that brilliantly sunny morning, they only saw death staring back at them.

With the last lifeboat aboard, Captain Rostron circled the area in search of any other survivors. The *Californian* had meanwhile come along and asked the *Carpathia*, "What's the matter?" Strangely, when the *Carpathia* passed through the wreckage, there were no bodies to be found. They had separated from what was left of the *Titanic* and drifted apart. It seemed obvious to the crew that no one could still be alive in these waters. By mid morning, the decision was made to set off for New York.

The *Carpathia* left the scene of the disaster that morning with a sense of mission. The *Titanic* would never keep her appointment with New York City, but Captain Rostron was determined that her remaining passengers would. Some of them would never be able to talk about their ordeal, forbidding their families to discuss it with them. Others would tell the world about the night they had just lived through in bits and pieces, creating what would forever remain a partially completed puzzle-like insight to what happened. The world would be held captivated each time they spoke about it.

Eventually, the survivors healed and moved on with their lives, growing older with time and facing life's continuous hurdles, challenges, and joys. There was World War I. The roaring twenties. The Great Depression of the thirties. World War II. The Cold War of the fifties. And for some, even man walking on the moon.

But throughout the rest of their lives they always had the distinction of something special, whether they wanted that distinction or not. They were survivors. They were *Titanic* survivors.

Sources of Quotations and Brief Biographies

Abelseth, Olaus: *U.S. Senate Hearings.* He was returning to North Dakota from a visit to Norway. 25 years old. Traveling in third class with his brother-in-law and cousin. He survived by climbing aboard collapsible A.

Andrews, Charles: *U.S. Senate Hearings.* Second class steward. 20 years old. Escaped in lifeboat 16.

Archer, Ernest: *U.S. Senate Hearings.* Able seaman. 36 years old. Escaped in lifeboat 16.

Barrett, Frederick: *British Enquiry.* Fireman who was in boiler room 6 when the iceberg opened the side of the compartment. He escaped in lifeboat 13.

Beesley, Lawrence: *Loss of the SS. Titanic.* Beesley was a college teacher traveling in second class on vacation. He was 34 years old and escaped in lifeboat 13.

Bishop, Dickinson and Helen: *U.S. Senate Hearings.* They were 25 and were returning from a honeymoon in Europe and Africa. They escaped in lifeboat 7.

Bisset, James: *Tramps and Ladies.* Second Officer of the Carpathia during the rescue of the Titanic survivors.

Boxhall, Joseph: *U.S. Senate Hearings.* Fourth Officer. 28 years old. Escaped in lifeboat 2.

Bourne, Jonathan: *U.S. Senate Hearings.* U.S. Senator who assisted with survivor interviews during the hearings.

Bride, Harold: *U.S. Senate Hearings.* Junior wireless operator. 21 years old. Escaped by climbing on top of overturned collapsible B.

Brice, Walter: *U.S. Senate Hearings.* Able seaman. 42 years old. Escaped in lifeboat 11.

Brown, Elizabeth: *Seattle Post Intelligencer, April 27, 1912.* Second class passenger travelling with her husband and daughter. Her husband went down with the ship. She and her daughter, Edith escaped in lifeboat 14. [Acknowledgment: Titanic Historical Society]

Buckley, Daniel: *U.S. Senate Hearings.* Emigrating from Ireland and chose the *Titanic* "because she was a new steamer." 21 years old. Although not completely clear, he likely escaped in collapsible D.

Buley, Edward: *U.S. Senate Hearings.* Able seaman who had just left 13 years in the merchant service of the British Navy and the *Titanic* was his first trip. 27 years old, he escaped in lifeboat 10.

Burke, William: *U.S. Senate Hearings.* First class dining room steward. 30 years old. Escaped in lifeboat 10.

Burton, Theodore: *U.S. Senate Hearings.* U.S. senator who assisted with survivor interviews during the hearings.

Butt, Archibald: *Archibald Butt Letters.* Military aide and friend to President Taft and his predecessor, "Teddy" Roosevelt. 45 years old, he went down with the *Titanic.*

Chambers, Norman: *U.S. Senate Hearings.* Mechanical engineer traveling first class with his wife, Bertha. They both escaped in lifeboat 7.

Clench, Frederick: *U.S. Senate Hearings.* Able seaman who escaped in lifeboat 12.

Collins, John: *U.S. Senate Hearings.* Assistant cook for first class, he was 17 years old. He was washed off the boat deck and survived by climbing onto overturned collapsible B.

Collyer, Charlotte: *American Semi Monthly, May 1912.* Traveling from Europe with her husband and daughter in second class. 31 years old. Her husband went down with the ship but she and her daughter escaped in lifeboat 14.

Cook, Selena: *Titanic Commutator, February–April 1997.* Second class passenger. 22 years old. She escaped in lifeboat 14.

Cottam, Harold: *U.S. Senate Hearings.* Wireless operator for the Carpathia. 21 years old. He heard the call for help from Titanic and communicated with it during the sinking.

Crawford, Alfred: *U.S. Senate Hearings.* Bedroom steward for first class. 41 years old. He escaped in lifeboat 8.

Crosby, Catherine: *U.S. Senate Hearings.* Returning to Milwaukee from vacation in Europe with husband and daughter. 69 years old. She and her daughter escaped in lifeboat 3.

Crowe, George: *U.S. Senate Hearings.* Dining room steward. 30 years old. He escaped in lifeboat 14.

Cunningham, Andrew: *U.S. Senate Hearings.* Bedroom steward for first class. 38 years old. He went down with the ship and swam to lifeboat 4 where he was picked out of the water.

Daly, Eugene: *Daily Sketch, May 4, 1912.* Traveling from Ireland. 29 years old. He climbed aboard the swamped lifeboat A as the ship went down.

Daniels, Sidney: *Voices.* Third class steward. Climbed aboard overturned collapsible B.

Douglas, Mahala: *U.S. Senate Hearings.* Returning to Minnesota with her husband. 48 years old, she escaped in lifeboat 2. Her husband went down with the ship.

Dodge, Washington: *Address Before the Commonwealth Club.* Returning from a vacation in Paris with his wife and baby. His wife and child escaped in boat 5. He escaped in lifeboat 13.

Dorking, Edward: *Buda Plain Dealer, May 17, 1912.* Traveling from England. Third class passenger. 19 years old. He survived by climbing onto overturned collapsible B. [Acknowledgment: Encyclopedia Titanica]

Dyer-Edwards, Lucy: *New York Herald, April 22, 1912.* Also known as the Countess of Rothes. 27 years old. She was traveling first class with her maid and cousin, Gladys Cherry. All were saved in boat 8.

Etches, Henry: *U.S. Senate Hearings.* Bedroom steward in first class, including Thomas Andrews' room. He was 40 years old and escaped in lifeboat 5.

Evans, Cyril: *U.S. Senate Hearings.* Wireless operator on the Californian. He attempted to warn the Titanic that the Californian was stopped in ice and was told to "Shut up." He was 20 years old.

Evans, Frank: *U.S. Senate Hearings.* Able seaman. 27 years old. He escaped in lifeboat 10.

Fleet, Frederick: *U.S. Senate Hearings.* He was the lookout who spotted the iceberg. He was 24 years old and escaped in lifeboat 6.

Fletcher, Duncan: *U.S. Senate Hearings.* U.S. Senator who assisted with survivor interviews at the hearings.

Futrelle, Lily May: *Boston Sunday Post, April 21, 1912.* First class passenger traveling with her author husband, Jacques, who went down with the ship. 35 years old. She escaped in boat 16.

Gibson, Dorothy: *New York Morning Telegraph, April 21, 1912.* Moving pictures actress, she was traveling first class with her mother. 22 years old. She and her mother escaped in lifeboat 5. [Acknowledgment: Titanic Historical Society]

Gill, Ernest: *U.S. Senate Hearings.* Seaman on the Californian, he saw the Titanic come up on the horizon and watched her fire rockets. He was 29 years old.

Gracie, Archibald: *U.S. Senate Hearings* and *The Truth About the Titanic.* Returning from a vacation in Europe in first class. He survived by climbing onto overturned collapsible B, but died in December 1912. He authored an account of the disaster which was published in 1913.

Graham, Margaret: *New York Times, April 20, 1912.* Traveling first class with her mother while returning to Greenwich from vacation. 19 years old.

Escaped in lifeboat 3.

Haines, Albert: *U.S. Senate Hearings.* Boatswain, in charge of keeping the decks clean and the paint fresh. 31 years old. He escaped in boat 9.

Harder, George: *U.S. Senate Hearings.* A manufacturer traveling first class with his wife. 25 years old. He and his wife escaped in lifeboat 5.

Hardy, John: *U.S. Senate Hearings.* Chief steward of second class. He was 36 years old and escaped in collapsible D.

Harper, Henry: *Harper's Weekly, April 27, 1912.* First class passenger traveling with his wife and pet Pekinese dog. All escaped in lifeboat 3.

Hemming, Samuel: *U.S. Senate Hearings.* Able seaman. 43 years old. He jumped as the Titanic was going down and swam to lifeboat 4.

Hichens, Robert: *U.S. Senate Hearings.* Quartermaster. He was at the wheel when the ship struck the iceberg. 30 years old. He escaped in lifeboat 6.

Hogg, George: *U.S. Senate Hearings.* Lookout. He escaped in lifeboat 7.

Hoyt, Frederick: *The Truth About the Titanic.* First class passenger returning from Europe with his wife, Jane. 38 years old. His wife escaped in collapsible D and he jumped into the water right near the boat and was pulled into it.

Ismay, Bruce: *U.S. Senate Hearings.* Managing director of the White Star Line and Chairman of the International Mercantile Marine Company. He was 49 years old and escaped in collapsible C.

Jones, Thomas: *U.S. Senate Hearings.* Able seaman. He escaped in lifeboat 8.

Joughin, Charles: *British Enquiry.* Chief baker. He climbed onto the starboard side of the stern as it heeled over for the final plunge, and was perhaps the last man to leave the Titanic.

Karun, Frank: *Galesburg Register, April 23, 1912.* Traveling second class with his daughter, he jumped into lifeboat 10 as it was being lowered with his

daughter already in it. 39 years old.

Lehmann, Bertha: *Brainerd Daily Dispatch.* Traveling second class from Switzerland. 17 years old. She escaped in lifeboat 12. [Acknowledgment: Titanic Historical Society]

Lightoller, Charles: *U.S. Senate Hearings* and *Titanic and Other Ships.* Second officer who strictly imposed the women-and-children only rule while supervising the port side boats. He was 38 years old. Jumped from the roof of the bridge and climbed aboard overturned collapsible B.

Lord, Stanley: *U.S. Senate Hearings.* Captain of the *Californian,* the ship stopped in ice nearby the *Titanic.* 35 years old.

Lowe, Harold: *U.S. Senate Hearings.* Fifth officer. 28 years old. He escaped in lifeboat 14.

Marconi, Guglielmo: *U.S. Senate Hearings.* Inventor of the Marconi wireless radio.

McGough, James: *U.S. Senate Hearings.* 36 years old. First class passenger Escaped in lifeboat 7.

Minahan, Daisy: *U.S. Senate Hearings.* First class passenger who escaped in lifeboat 14.

Moore, James: Captain of the *Mount Temple,* the second ship to arrive at the scene of the disaster the following morning.

Moore, George: *U.S. Senate Hearings.* Able seaman. 51 years old. Escaped in lifeboat 3.

Mulvihill, Bertha: *Providence Daily Journal, April 20, 1912.* Returning to live with her sister in America after an extended stay with parents in Ireland. On a whim, she purchased her third class ticket the day before the Titanic stopped at Queenstown. 24 years old. She escaped in lifeboat 10.

Newlands, Senator: *U.S. Senate Hearings.* Assisted with the survivor interviews.

Olliver, Alfred: *U.S. Senate Hearings.* Quartermaster; he was on the bridge at the time of the collision. 27 years old. He escaped in lifeboat 5.

Osman, Frank: *U.S. Senate Hearings.* Able seaman.

38 years old. He escaped in lifeboat 2.

Perkins, Senator: *U.S. Senate Hearings.* Assisted with the survivor interviews.

Perkis, Walter: *U.S. Senate Hearings.* Quartermaster.. He lowered lifeboat 4 to the water and then climbed down the ropes. Brought boat 4 back to the scene of the disaster and picked up 8 people out of the water.

Peuchen, Arthur: *U.S. Senate Hearings.* First class passenger. 53 years old, he slid down a rope about 10 feet at the direction of Captain Smith and Lightoller, into lifeboat 6.

Pickard, Berk: *U.S. Senate Hearings.* A Russian immigrant to the U.S. and a leather and bag maker by trade. He was 32 years old and traveling in third class. He escaped in lifeboat 9.

Pitman, Herbert: *U.S. Senate Hearings.* Third officer. He was 34 years old. He escaped in lifeboat 5.

Portalupi, Emilio: *Nashua Telegraph, April 20, 1912.* Sculptor and Drawing Instructor. Returning from a visit to his former home town in Italy, he traveled in second class. He jumped from the sinking liner and was picked up by lifeboat 4 after the ship sank.

Ray, Frederick Dent: *U.S. Senate Hearings.* First class dining room steward. 33 years old. He escaped in lifeboat 13.

Rhiems, George: *The Night Lives On.* First class passenger traveling from Paris. He survived by climbing into collapsible A as the ship went down.

Robinson, Annie: *British Enquiry.* First class stewardess. 40 years old. She escaped in lifeboat 11.

Rostron, Arthur: *Home From the Sea.* Captain of the *Carpathia* who rushed to the scene of the disaster only to arrive too late. He went on to become a hero for rescuing the remaining survivors from the Atlantic.

Rowe, George: *U.S. Senate Hearings.* Quarter-master who was on the aft bridge and saw the iceberg glide by within feet of the stern. He was 32 years old. He escaped in collapsible C.

Rule, Samuel: *British Enquiry.* Bathroom steward.

He escaped in lifeboat 15.

Ryerson, Emily: *U.S. Senate Hearings.* First class passenger, 48 years old. She was returning with her family to Haverford on sudden notice to attend to the death of her son in a car accident. She escaped in lifeboat 4.

Scarrott, Joseph: *British Enquiry.* Able seaman. 34 years old. He escaped in lifeboat 14.

Senior, Harry: *Daily Sketch, April 29, 1912.* Fireman. 31 years old. He escaped by climbing aboard the overturned collapsible B.

Shelley, Imanita: *U.S. Senate Hearings.* Returning from vacation to Kentucky via second class. It is not clear which boat Mrs. Imanita escaped in, but it was likely number 14.

Sjoblom, Anna: *Tacoma Daily News, April 30, 1912.* Third class passenger from Finland. She turned 18 on the fateful Sunday of the collision. She escaped in lifeboat 13. [Acknowledgment: Titanic Historical Society]

Smith, Senator: *U.S. Senate Hearings.* Led the Senate inquiry into the sinking of the Titanic.

Smith, Mary Eloise: *U.S. Senate Hearings.* Returning with her husband, Lucien from a honeymoon in Egypt, they were booked in first class. She was 18 years old and escaped in lifeboat 6.

Stengel, Charles Henry: *U.S. Senate Hearings.* A first class passenger traveling with his wife, Annie. He was 54 years old and escaped in lifeboat 1 after seeing his wife off in number 5.

Stephenson, Martha: *The Truth About the Titanic.* First class passenger returning from vacation to Haverford. 52 years old. She escaped in lifeboat 4.

Symons, George: *U.S. Senate Hearings.* He was a lookout on watch from 8:00 to 10:00 p.m. the night of the collision. 24 years old and escaped in lifeboat 1.

Taylor, William: *U.S. Senate Hearings.* Fireman. 28 years old. Escaped in lifeboat 15.

Thayer, John: *The Sinking of the S.S. Titanic.* Returning to Haverford from a vacation with his

father and mother. His mother escaped in lifeboat 4 and his father went down with the ship. 17 years old. He escaped by climbing onto overturned collapsible B.

Turja, Anna: *Ashtabula Star Beacon, April 1912.* Traveling in third class, from Finland. 18 years old. She escaped in lifeboat 13. [Acknowledgment: John Rudolph]

Ward, William: *U.S. Senate Hearings.* Second class saloon steward. Escaped in lifeboat 9.

Warren, Anna: *Portland Oregonian, April 1912.* Returning from a vacation in Europe with her husband, Frank, who went down with the ship. 60 years old. She escaped in lifeboat 5. [Acknowledgment: Titanic Historical Society]

Weikman, Augustus: *U.S. Senate Hearings.* Barber. Escaped by climbing into collapsible A after the ship went down.

Wennerstrom, August: *Titanic, End of a Dream.* Third class passenger from Sweden. 27 years old. He escaped by climbing aboard collapsible A while the ship was going down.

Wheelton, Edward: *U.S. Senate Hearings.* First class steward. 28 years old. Escaped in lifeboat 11.

White, Ella: *U.S. Senate Hearings.* First class passenger. 55 years old. Escaped in lifeboat 8.

Widgery, James: *U.S. Senate Hearings.* Second class bathroom steward. Escaped in lifeboat 9.

Williams, Richard: *Main Line Life, December 18, 1997.* Returning to Radnor from Switzerland in first class with his father. 21 years old. His father went down with the ship, but Dick survived by climbing aboard collapsible A.

Woolner, Hugh: *U.S. Senate Hearings.* Business director of various companies, he traveled in first class. He escaped by jumping into collapsible D on its descent to the water.

Young, Marie: *National Magazine, October 1912.* Musician who had previously instructed President Roosevelt's daughter on the piano. 36 years old. First class passenger. She escaped in lifeboat 8.

Glossary
This book features the unique language of the sea.

Aft: toward the rear, in the direction of the stern.

Boat Deck: the top deck of the ship that contained all of the lifeboats.

Boiler Rooms: four stories high containing furnaces, or "boilers" to burn coal creating heat to generate steam to drive the engines. There were six boiler rooms centered in the bottom of the ship.

Bow: the front of the ship.

Bridge: area at the very front of the boat deck where the ship was navigated. Although the room in the center is the main part of the bridge, the open deck immediately on both sides is also considered part of the bridge.

Bulkhead: wall.

Cabin: room.

Classes: the Titanic had three; first, second, and third class. First class was the most comfortable way to travel, second was standard, and third was economy. During routine travel, third class was not allowed into the second class areas, and second and third class were not allowed into first class.

Collapsible: a lifeboat with canvas sides which would lift up into place. There were four on the ship and two were successfully launched. The other two floated off the ship as it went under.

Davits: The steel "arms" that held the ropes and lifeboats over the side of the ship while it was being lowered.

Decks: floors. On the Titanic, the boat deck was the highest, followed by A, B, C, D, E, and F decks. There were four more decks below F deck at the bow and the stern. The boiler rooms in the middle were four decks high.

Docking Bridge: The small enclosed area on opposite sides of the bridge at the forward corners of the boat deck.

Falls: the mechanisms and ropes used to lower each lifeboat. There were two per lifeboat, the forward falls and the afterfalls.

Forecastle Deck: the open deck at the very front of the ship.

Founder: to sink.

Funnel: smokestack. The Titanic had four, the fourth being a dummy and used only for ventilation and steam exhaust.

Gangway Doors: doors located on the sides of the ship at various locations on different decks.

Grand Staircase: an elaborate staircase that ran all the way from boat deck down to E deck in the first class area. It was one of the showpieces of the Titanic.

Gunwale: the upper edge of a ship's side.

Knots: a measurement of distance. One knot equals 1.15 mile. The Titanic's approximate speed of 22 knots would equate to 25 miles per hour.

Lifebelt: same as life preserver and life vest. They were made of white canvas with cork slabs sewn inside them and were fastened around the upper sides of a person.

List: a lean to one side of the ship.

Masts: poles. The Titanic had two; one was a foremast near the bow and the other a stern mast.

Passageways: corridors and/or entranceways on a ship.

Poop Deck: the open deck at the very back of the ship.

Port: when standing on the ship facing forward, the left side.

Promenade Deck: one deck below the boat deck, it was another name for A deck because it had a promenade walkway the full length of the deck on both sides of the ship.

Running Lights: located on the outside of the ship on both sides, they were an indication to a distant ship of which direction a vessel was pointing. A green light was on the starboard side, and a red on the port.

Service Speed: the standard and economical speed at which a ship would routinely travel while in service.

Scotland Road: another name for the E deck corridor on the port side of that deck that ran the entire length of the ship from bow to stern.

Sidelights: same as running lights.

Starboard: the right side of the ship.

Steerage Passengers: third class passengers.

Stern: the back of the ship.

Watertight Compartments: divisions created by watertight bulkheads throughout the bottom of the ship. Unfortunately for the Titanic, they were not sealed off at the top, being open by stairs.

Well Deck: there were two of them. They were the open deck areas just forward of the poop deck at the stern, and just behind the forecastle deck at the bow.

Wireless: the early use of radio. Voice could not be transmitted, but instead a series of short signals representing letters of the alphabet would be transmitted to send messages.

Bibliography

Anderson, Roy. *White Star.* Prescot: Stephenson, 1964.

Beesley, Lawrence. *The Loss of the SS. Titanic.* New York: Houghton Mifflin, 1912.

Behe, George. *Titanic, Safety Speed and Sacrifice.* Polo: Transportation Trails, 1997.

Bisset, James. *Tramps and Ladies.* New York: Criterion, 1959.

Brands, H.W. *TR, The Last Romantic.* New York: Basic Books, 1997.

Bryceson, Dave. *The Titanic Disaster.* New York: Norton, 1997.

Cooper, John Milton Jr. *Pivotal Decades.* New York: Norton, 1990.

Eaton, John P. and Haas, Charles A. *Titanic, Triumph and Tragedy.* New York: Norton, 1986.

Forsyth, Alastair, Hyslop, Donald, and Jemima, Sheila. *Titanic Voices.* New York: St. Martin's Press, 1994.

Gracie, Archibald. *The Truth About the Titanic.* New York: Mitchell Kennerley, 1913.

Great Britain Parliament. *Report on the Loss of the S.S. Titanic.* London, 1912

Hachey, Thomas E., Hernon, Joseph M., and McCaffrey, Lawrence J. *The Irish Experience.* London: M.E. Sharpe, 1996.

Judd, Denis. *Empire, The British Imperial Experience From 1765 to Present.* New York: Basic Books, 1996.

Lightoller, Charles H. *Titanic and Other Ships.* London: Ivor Nicholson and Watson, 1935.

Lord, Walter. *The Night Lives On.* New York: Morrow, 1986.

Lynch, Donald. *Titanic, An Illustrated History.* New York: Hyperion, 1992.

MacManus, Seumas. *The Story of the Irish Race.* Old Greenwich: Devin Adair, 1921.

Olympic & Titanic. Mattituck: Amereon, 1995.

Quinn, Paul J. *Titanic At Two A.M.* Hollis: Fantail, 1997.

Rostron, Arthur H. *Home From the Sea.* New York: Macmillan, 1931.

Thayer, John B. *The Sinking of the S.S. Titanic.* Riverside: 7 C's Press, 1974.

Titanic Commutator. Indian Orchard: Titanic Historical Society, Quarterly.

U.S. Senate. *Titanic Disaster Hearings.* Washington: Government Printing Office, 1912.

Viault, Birdsall S. *English History.* London: McGraw Hill, 1992.

Wade, Wyn Craig. *The Titanic, End of a Dream.* New York: Rawson , Wade, 1979.

Illustrations

Some black and white photographs were cropped for subject emphasis.

8 Author's collection
10 (left) Robert Welsh
10 (right) Daily Sketch
11 Author's collection
13 Paul Quinn
15 Kennedy
16 Paul Quinn
19 Paul Quinn
24 Paul Quinn
25 Harris & Ewing
29 White Star Line
30 Shipbuilder
31 (top) Shipbuilder
31 (bottom) Daily Graphic
33 Harland & Wolff
34 Paul Quinn
36 Author's collection
38 Author's collection
40 Harland & Wolff
41 Paul Quinn
43 Author's collection
44 Paul Quinn
45 Harland & Wolff
46 Paul Quinn
47 Paul Quinn
49 Paul Quinn

52 Harland & Wolff
55 Harland & Wolff
56 Harland & Wolff
57 Author's collection
59 Paul Quinn
64 Paul Quinn
66 (left) Paul Thompson
66 (right) Paul Thompson
67 Paul Quinn
68 (left) Francis Browne
68 (right) Francis Browne
72 Francis Browne
73 Robert Welsh
75 Paul Quinn
77 William Ross
79 Author's collection
84 Author's collection
89 Paul Quinn
91 Paul Quinn
92 Daily Sketch
93 Author's collection
95 Paul Quinn
99 Paul Quinn
101 Paul Quinn
108 Author's collection
112 William Ross
118 Author's collection
120 Harland & Wolff
122 Author's collection
123 Author's collection
127 Paul Quinn

129 William Ross
131 Francis Browne
139 Thomas Barker
142 Harland & Wolff
145 Thomas Barker
147 Author's collection
149 Thomas Barker
150 Robert Welsh
151 Thomas Barker
156 Paul Quinn
157 William Ross
158 Francis Browne
159 Daily Sketch
160 Daily Sketch
163 Illustrated London News
165 Francis Browne
167 Paul Quinn
168 Author's collection
169 Paul Quinn
170 Paul Quinn
171 Paul Quinn
172 Harland & Wolff
174 Thomas Barker
175 Robert Welsh
178 Author's collection
179 Francis Browne
180 Francis Browne
181 Author's collection
182 Robert Welsh
184 Thomas Barker
187 Thomas Barker

189 Paul Quinn
190 Author's collection
191 Paul Quinn
193 Paul Quinn
196 Author's collection
202 Author's collection
205 Daily Sketch
207 Paul Thompson
212 Author's collection
214 Author's collection
217 Paul Quinn
218 Author's collection
230 William Ross
232 Paul Quinn
235 Paul Quinn
236 Paul Quinn
239 Paul Quinn
241 Thomas Barker
245 Paul Quinn
248 Louis Ogden
249 Author's collection
251 Paul Quinn
255 Louis Ogden
257 Author's collection
258 Author's collection
265 Paul Quinn
266 Louis Ogden
267 Lewis Skidmore
269 Louis Ogden
270 Louis Ogden